THE FLAWED SPECIES

A. J. BROWN

DEDICATION

This book is dedicated to all rational thinking men and women, past and present – the foundations of positive change. Secondly, I honour the legacy bequeathed by the great story tellers of history, particularly those who complemented their craft with qualities of the former category of men and women cited.

ABOUT THE AUTHOR

Anthony James Brown is an expat Australian domiciled in West Sussex, England. He came to the UK in 1966 after an extensive tour of Southern and East Africa, India, Afghanistan, Iran, and thence overland through Europe. He was a teacher in his youth and soon became a businessman on arriving in England. He retired from this in 2015 and wrote The Flawed Species as a beginning to his writing career. He has studied Philosophy extensively and hence the heavy emphasis on this in The Flawed Species. He is working on a sequel to this novel currently.

PART ONE

CHAPTER ONE

I could hear this sporty engine sound behind me. I turned and saw a cyclist slowly taking the curve in the road and the source of the revving engine not far behind him. This may not end well, I thought. I stood still, watching the scene unfold, from this opposite side of the road.

Next was the sharp screeching of tyres. The predicted moment of disaster was about to occur. The cyclist, no doubt unnerved by the sounds behind him, wobbled a bit. I was willing the driver of the sports car to bring his momentum under control. I failed. The cyclist was soon being propelled through the air to an uncertain landing, on the side of the pavement. His bicycle carried on some yards beyond.

The sports car came to a halt fifty yards on, its driver fearing the worst no doubt. I wasted no time racing across the road to attend to the prone figure lying on the pavement. This guy was unconscious but breathing. Good. I started to check out his head. As I did so other passers-by gathered to the scene. I signalled for them to stand back and be quiet. You don't need a whole bunch of anxious people adding to the confusion.

'Is he alright?' I heard from a panicked voice behind me – the driver.

'Sh..' I signalled with forefinger to mouth. I carried on examining his head – well at least that seems ok. Let's see if his skeleton is ok. Arms and shoulders seem all right. Now the legs. A swollen shin – that seems the likely place of impact. I better keep these spectators back. 'Please stand back would you. Someone call the emergency services.'

The cyclist was coming to. Gradually he started focusing and commensurately starting to feel pain. He raised his head – a good sign. I examined his neck and propped a proffered coat under it.

'Hullo,' I said. 'You have a few abrasions and a suspected broken leg. Just lie back. The ambulance is on its way.'

I explained quietly to 'the crowd' what my diagnosis was. 'Just remain quiet while the ambulance people arrive.'

Next I grabbed hold of the driver. 'He's all right I think. You could take charge of the bicycle. That would help the most right now.'

The police and ambulance staff arrived in quick order. 'I saw the whole event. I've examined the victim all over and he seems to have nothing more serious than a broken leg. The driver of that sports car was ramming it round the corner here and the cyclist freaked a bit and was knocked off the road. The driver is dealing with that bicycle over there. He may need a few sedatives himself.'

As the crowd had started dispersing and I'd debriefed the authorities I made my way towards my destination. At least I'll have a good excuse for being late. A couple of the crowd, walking in my direction, came beside me and one said, 'well handled young man. You've no doubt done a first aid course. We feared it was more serious than that, we'll be honest.' I thanked them and continued on.

I arrived at school late, as the obvious was being pointed out to me by the Deputy Head. I explained to him the circumstances and all I got was 'a likely story'. Here we go again – belittlement. No accolades for helping a stricken citizen. He must think we pupils are all out of a mould, bent on devious behaviour, fodder for the adult disapproval machine, not to be reasoned with. Now I suppose I will have to experience a reprise of this when I get to my classroom. Just as well not all adults deal with people this way (and I AM a person, even if young). Maybe a youngster is a sub person in this world.

I opened the classroom door and was 'welcomed to the late show' by my beloved 'teacher' Mr. Jim Casey. I hope he didn't have children of his own. I sat down at my desk near the front of the class. The drawings on the blackboard told me that Geometry was the subject in progress. I think I know more about this than Casey, so I settled into my late morning slumber. I slowly sank down in my chair without sliding off, legs straight out in front of me, elbows on the desk, hands around my jaws and ears. I was miles away in no time, but not for long. My red rag to the bull resulted in Casey charging down the aisle from the back of the classroom to slam a book down on my desk. 'What say you Waterboy?'

I wasn't going to give him the satisfaction of scaring the blazes out of me. I slowly sat up straight and said calmly, 'Sorry sir, I wasn't listening.'

'That's just the point son,' he roared whilst standing over me, hands on hips.

'I was talking Geometry son.' He strode to the front of the class and said, 'I'll give you another chance to embarrass yourself further, son.' The word 'son' was said as a belittlement of course. 'How do you determine the length of the hypotenuse of a right-angle triangle, given the length of the other two sides?' He was hoping for the cue for more invective.

I answered him quickly, not just to score points but simply to show I know my stuff. 'The square on the hypotenuse is equal to the sum of the squares of the other two sides.'

'How do you do it son? Do you learn while you are asleep?'

I couldn't answer that one, not to Casey anyhow. I guess he was left on no score. I looked around and saw a lot of amused faces. It wasn't my intention to embarrass Casey, but the net result was just that. This was a common occurrence.

What the hell am I doing here? I don't need the lessons nor the attempted belittling.

I was on my way home that day, pondering the conundrum further. My home was an end-of-terrace semi in one of the many similar streets packed around the High Street of Finchley, in North London.

Thinking further, I wondered about this state of 'dictatorship' called 'adult'. Are many adults only really provisional? Take that event that just occurred with Casey. He's fully grown (and some) but not fully mature yet. My parents and Grandpa don't behave like that. So the definition of the word 'adult' needs some modification. And by reverse vector, so do the words 'adolescent' and 'teenager', I guess. Maybe if your body isn't fully grown you can't be an adult. Or, if you behave like an idiot you can't be mature. What if you were a youth and had grown a big body? Would that classify as adult in the eyes of normal adults? Probably not. So there must be mature adults and immature adults. Then there could be mature and immature teenagers. Either way, if you aren't twenty one years old you can't have the status of adult so you are a sub-species. I was having fun with this concept, while working out my objection to unfair treatment.

This society, this world I suppose, is a mixed bag. Not everyone has the raw materials and maybe the opportunity for proper maturity. Well, Casey is definitely an example of this. He's missed the boat. What can I do about this situation? I can't go on like this. Do I just wait out my next incubation stage? That would be seven or eight more years!

———————————

At home that night, I'd had my dinner and was doing my family thing – wiping up the dishes. I didn't mind doing these chores but I couldn't pass up the opportunity for a bit of fun with my mum. I think she enjoys our little banters. 'There should be a machine for this,' I suggested. 'Come to think of it, it's one of those many curious things we humans do – get up in the morning, wash the body, cook for it, feed it, clean up, then do something a little more of one's choosing, then feed it again, work to make some money to feed and shelter it some more, and then put it into unconsciousness for eight hours or so to recover from all the above, day after day, forever. Then when it wears out it's dumped in a hole with big ceremony.'

I couldn't help laughing at myself; but food for thought, not so?

'How depressing.' Mum replied, and then, smiling, added, 'I think I should roll over and die right now.'

'That's a dry old way to look at it, I know,' I responded, 'but there's got to be some time-saving here and some interesting challenging things to do instead.'

Mum came in with the most apt reply. 'You go and find something like that now. I'll labour on so you can do just that, son.'

'I don't want you to roll over and die. I'm sure there's more to it than that,' I said, trying to mock console her. 'I'll go and work on this matter right now.' I hung up the tea towel and put the crockery away, and said as I departed, 'I'll keep you posted. Watch this space.'

Yes, she loves my little games I know. She is a tidy, house-proud woman. She's the more forthright of my two parents. As adults go, she's a gem. She doesn't instruct me, disapprove of my universe, control my interests. She just loves me. What else could I want from a parent? My job, as I see it, is to contribute to the family, learn and prepare for the future, whatever that may be, and discharge myself somewhere up the line from my dependence. The sooner the better I reasoned; become the product my parents would be proud of. Nothing stands in my way, at home at least.

I removed myself to my domain. My room is a bed, a desk and chair, one wardrobe and LOTS of books. You could trace my literary life by the latter – nursery rhymes, comics, Boys Own adventure books, a range of encyclopaedia sets, classics and all. I think I must be ahead of a lot of kids, if not adults too. I have always wanted to read and know things.

I lay on my bed thinking. I am thirteen now, officially a teenager, 'that difficult phase of immaturity', that milestone that signalled a forthcoming promotion from boy to man – the bigtime. I wasn't finding it difficult though, except in others finding it so. Should I backtrack and indulge in a hormonal struggle for identity just to fit in with my peers and the 'ruling class'? Or should I.......? I know the answer to that.

There was a knock on the door. Grandpa opened it a little and saw me in contemplation. He came in and sat down on the chair. 'How goes it Brandon?' I sat up and leaned against the wall behind my bed.

'Interesting day,' I said. I related the events of the roadside and at school that day. 'It's got me thinking. I can't go on like I am. I'm not going to go on being a kid or a teenager any longer.'

'I see,' Grandpa said, wondering what was coming next. He sort of expected that this day was coming any day soon. And here we were. While I was thinking, Grandpa was looking around the room. I could hear him thinking – all these books, almost a whole library, and he's read and taken in nearly all of their content, plus God knows how much of the local Library he's digested as well.

I watched Grandpa. He seemed almost to be tracking with me and was about to arrive at the same place. He'd been responsible for this library he was looking at. He'd been my librarian and had decided what I could and should devour. And I HAD devoured it all. He decided what presents I should be given at birthdays and other occasions. I had needed a local Library to deal with the logistics of my needs.

'I can take a certain amount of stick from the Education quarter but I feel I don't deserve it and would rather swap it for some more encouraging and grateful audiences. I got a bit of a buzz from being a first aid man today. In fact I got some recognition from some less dogmatic but appreciative adults at the scene. See what I mean?'

'I do, my man. So what's next?'

'Give me a few hours to process all this and I'll tell you what's next.' Grandpa small-talked for a bit, then left.

My Grandpa is a right good counsellor. He listens, prompts and poses piercing questions. He gives little advice, unless asked for. Even then he gets me to work it out myself, so much so that I have fallen into the habit of being proactive in being my own advisor; very effective. I think I am on the verge of being able to 'fly solo', so to speak, that is, work out the solutions to questions or problems with the more ideal characteristics of our species. What is the point of being disgruntled and asserting one's rightness? I have to be pragmatic.

Take my brother Andrew who is a year or so younger than I. He gets himself all worked up about some point or some injustice or other. No point trying to reason with him until he calms down a bit. Best to try him again later. Take Casey. It's like walking on eggshells with him at the best of times. Quite a few of our race are wired in to being 'push button'. Push the button and off they go; automatic behaviour.

I'm going to work out how best to resolve this 'waiting to grow up' situation I am in. What about a plot for my life? Let's start with the immediate situation of being a bored slob in the classroom. How can I get the best response from my teachers? I think I've been making my own problems there.

I'm going to brighten up and attend, or at least be a good actor. I know, I'll offer the teachers some help with the sluggards in the classroom. The teachers could then set me some advanced Maths or Science to balance it all up.

I'll have to work around the egos of the adults. Hm, isn't this me being the solution for inept adults? How has it come to this? Well, it is what it is. I've been ambling along, interesting myself in lots of things but not much else. Time to do something effective.

I sprung up from my bed and spoke to the ceiling: 'to hell with being a victim kid'. I sat at my desk and started to work out a rough plan for my life. I didn't get very far beyond my prospective Education game at the school. There are more wrongs than this in the world, I am perceiving. For these I don't know enough. I'll start at school right now.

CHAPTER TWO

The next night I was sitting out on the veranda of the house, talking to Grandpa.

'Grandpa I've decided to kiss goodbye to my life up to now,' I expounded.

'Don't do it,' joked my mentor, sipping his tea.

'No, not that. I've got a few plans. Firstly it's this school thing. Might as well waste my time productively, if you see what I mean.'

'Oh yes, do tell.' Grandpa, at the ripe old age of 58, semi-retired, had spent a lot of his time doting on his grandsons, especially me. He'd taken on the role of nurturing we boys, instead of our parents who have enough problems of their own just coping with the material logistics of the family. He was well read and had done a few things in his life.

He and I discussed all sorts of adult subjects ranging from world affairs to teenage hormones and lots in between.

'Well firstly, I'm taking full charge of my own education academically, and in the ways of the world I suppose. I have lots of questions I need answering and I won't get many answers at school, especially as I'm 'studying' subjects I'm no longer interested in. Secondly I can pass all the exams they give me in my sleep.

'You can go so far with Arithmetic and Geometry and stuff. I don't want to be a Scientist or a Mathematician, so what is carrying me through all this? There is no interest or career aspiration. I like to know things but beyond just being curious, which is ok, where does it leave me? I don't affect anything. School doesn't educate you in the ways of life. You learn academic subjects but nothing much about real life. Seems wrong way to, to me.'

Grandpa was just listening and prompting.

'I can always improve my English, my vocabulary, but I get that from my own extracurricular stuff.

'Geography and History are good to a point, I'm not going to be a Historian or whatever an expert in Geography is – a Geographorian?'

'I see,' said my sounding board. 'In that case, what DO you plan for yourself.'

'The way I'm beginning to see it, correct me if I'm wrong, an awful lot of people around me are struggling. Take Mum and Dad; they struggle to make ends meet. The wind blows a bit stronger and they snap, such as we saw recently with Dad being made redundant and then going off to the doc to be given some pills to help him from being depressed. There are a lot of people like that, especially if the newspapers and radio are to be even minimally believed. Then there are the kids and teachers at school – lots of struggle.

'Take my main teacher – and there are lots like him at my school – he can't keep an even humour with his class. He loses it at the drop of a hat. He doesn't know how to teach, and he certainly doesn't know how to deal with us kids.'

'Isn't that all normal life?' Grandpa asked.

'You might say that's normal. Well it may be common or usual, but is it normal? If that's the natural state of human being, then it seems there's a lot to be desired or to learn or to evolve to. That seems more in the realm of Psychology or maybe Religion, or more likely something that hasn't been discovered yet, which, now that I mention it, seems to be the way to go as a career. What is this species I am part of?'

'Wow, you are becoming a Philosopher, and a pioneer! Maybe that's what you should be, a Philosopher. What does a Philosopher do?' Grandpa added, not being patronising.

'Hm, what is a Philosopher anyway? I don't know any and know only a bit about past ones. Seems like they may have dreamed up a few civilising things…..but has it made enough difference to it all?'

Grandpa continued his prompting. 'So, considering all you have come up with, what will you do tomorrow to start your career in this direction?'
'I don't know… I'd like to be able to improve the lot of the strugglers. Having started out on this Education idea, I'll see how that goes. If I can increase the abilities of these 'normal' kids who aren't going anywhere it will give me heart to tackle the bigger problem. If I can create a big enough effect for the school itself, that would be even better.

'I need to see the world. What is this society I've been born into? I've felt a bit like some wound up toy which aimlessly animates itself automatically without any thought about its direction or goal. I only read books or papers and listen to radio occasionally, and listen to you. This week I woke up I think. I'm going to look some more and then decide more exactly what to do, beyond Education.'

'So won't you have to go travelling to see the world? Grandpa asked.

'Yes and no. When I say 'see' I mean more in the way of REALLY facing what I see in front of me with my senses.

―――――――――

I was done with my 'speech'. I watched Grandpa for his next comments. He was smiling at me while in thought. He was always measured in his responses. He seemed a bit astounded at my announcements. He would have his own opinions but wouldn't give them of course.

'You are like a sleeping giant who has been awoken, my boy. Look out world, here you come. I'm totally on your side. I must say there is an awful lot of truth in what you have so artfully articulated.'

I wouldn't have been surprised if he was a bit stunned as the conversation would have stirred up his often-raised concerns about life around him. Whilst he wasn't a doomsday merchant, more of an optimist in fact, I'm sure he was feeling like some 'living in hope' philosophy hadn't been that successful. I could tell he was a little disturbed. 'This would be a great topic for our Debating Society,' he said. Then, blow me down, he fell asleep, 'at the wheel', so to speak. That's interesting, I thought.

I decided I would tempt fate and put a few proposals to my Headmaster. I waited my moment, loitering as inconspicuously as possible in the hallway at the end of the day's proceedings. Everyone else had gathered their stuff and seemed to be making more noise than usual stampeding out of the place.

The HM's door was ajar a fraction. I peeked in. The poor man was sitting at his desk, hands propping up his head as if the day had been too much for him. I gave the door a healthy rap, ran my hands through my thick sandy hair and waited to be asked in.

'Come in,' I heard. I did, and walked to his desk and stood with my hands behind my back, respectfully.

'What's on your mind Waterman?' He was actually quite a young man for a Head, probably about thirty five or forty, pleasant looking, but prematurely balding. He was starting to pack up his things and stuff them into a briefcase as if my presence wouldn't take long.

'Sir, I have a proposal to make about my education, and I suppose all the other students in the school.'

'Ah, a takeover, eh? Unexpected I must say Waterman. Are we not looking after you well enough?' He was amiable rather than sarcastic.

I replied, 'in a way sir, but I'm stagnating. I'm teaching myself really, but I see some of the others are really struggling to stay with the curriculum, and more to the point, the teachers are struggling to get them up to the mark, especially our main teacher, Mr. Casey. He can't really deal with the top and bottom end students all at once. And I can't see how he can as they each have different problems and IQ's. This a problem of class sizes and how to keep us all happy.'

'Well you've hit the nail on the head there Waterman. Would you like to take over my chair?' he asked humorously. His attention was piqued.

'I'd like to help,' I added quickly. 'I have a few ideas. My proposals will take away one of those problems immediately, that is, how to handle and utilise the bright ones. We (and I mean the top ten or fifteen percent) learn easily and by and large are self-motivated. I would like to suggest an extra curriculum for us, incorporating subjects that aren't mainstream, but are practical – for example, Parliamentary Democracy, or The History of Philosophy.'

Brian Hobbs sat down, starting to enjoy this, even if at first to humour me. I had noticed he was quite a serious chap, but now, toward the end of the day, he had softened a bit.

I went on. 'This would have to come within the acceptable bands of Education and ignore revolutionary subjects that the powers-that-be may find improper, even if interesting and current.'

Hobbs raised his eyebrows slightly. I could see a bit of incredulity on his part.
I continued. 'I'd make sure we all kept up our grades but spent some of our time, somewhat competitively, bringing the slowies up to speed with one-on-one attention.'

I embellished a bit more and ended up asking Mr. Hobbs what he thought of the idea.

The HM by this was relaxed back in his swivel chair, hands behind his head, taking all this in. He was looking at me and musing.

'Sir, give it a go for the rest of the term, and if things are better, take the credit for the liberalisation you'd have let into the school.' I wondered if he had noticed the mischievous glint in my eye.

'Waterman, Brandon, I can see you are really earnest about this. If it were all up to me I'd give you your head… . There are corns to avoid treading on

15

here, you understand.'

I thought I'd actually made some, frankly, unexpected progress. 'I appreciate you listening. I'm really excited about this.' The HM rose and I took that to be it for the moment. As I exited I pondered the subject of 'corns'. Is it that other authorities would object? How does that work? It looked like my proposal had touched a somewhat open wound in Hobbs. Perhaps the HM wasn't the master of his school in all respects. Apart from the Department itself, did someone else influence the show?

———————

I thought it had gone rather well, but wondered if Mr Hobbs was being polite, it all being possibly rather too revolutionary for this conservative man. Let's wait and see, I thought. In the meantime I'll start to plan in my mind what exactly I'd like to do with the slow coaches.

Yes, being motivated is half the battle. The kids were just sent there because 'they had to go to school' and somehow, vaguely learn something for the future – what? Times-table, Trigonometry, Poetry, Shakespeare, ad nauseam?

Well I think I would start with 'why be literate?' and 'why be numerate? To learn you have to be able to find out things, by reading, studying, gaining a vocabulary, discussing. Basic Arithmetic, for instance, is good for everyday calculations – percentages, decimals, and measuring, as tedious as it might seem to learn. If my idea was all accompanied by an end result it might be a winner. And let's make it fun.

So, I'll get all the sluggards together. I got a mental picture of some of the dramatis personae and shuddered at the prospect. I guess I'd have to accept some failures from the factually dense or disadvantaged among the class. Or maybe invent some way out of that one (I didn't know what).

Anyway I was excited. School was becoming interesting, or could it be said that teaching was becoming my prospective vocation? I hope the HM will back me. I decided on a pilot project for the next tier down from myself, that is, the reasonably bright but as yet unmotivated band of, say, five suckers, I thought amusedly.

I was walking home that afternoon singing to myself and whistling out loud, feeling really alive for the first time I could remember. When I got home I sought out the oracle and told him what had happened. Grandpa just put his arm around me, his 'protégé', and smiled broadly. 'You don't waste any time do you?'

'Just what is the purpose of all this knowledge stuff?' he asked me as I settled into a cane chair. 'Actually, when I get down to it, what has it done for ME?'

'Well, I reckon it all comes down to this – knowledge is written or spoken by supposedly experienced or learned people, and if you want to know it you have to learn the lingo, that is the words and the grammar. If you want to become good at, say, car mechanics, you have to know the theory expressed in words and diagrams and play with it all until you are good.'

'Then what?' asked Grandpa?

'Well once you master English first you can then choose what you want to learn or do and then find out all about it because you now know how to find out and you WANT to. You should get a choice. Why study Geometry, beyond the very basics, if you want to be a footballer or a musician, or a salesman, as a career?'

'Makes sense to me,' nodded Grandpa. 'Go for it. Nothing bad will come of it. Someone will get helped and maybe a few teachers will wake up.'

So, for the moment I was on fire and who is to say I wouldn't put the cat among the pigeons and cause a whole bushfire. And so began my adulthood. Except I am still a kid. It's all to do with body size and age, isn't it?

Whichever way you looked at it I was about to concertina the usual development period into a small span of time. To some degree I had already done this and had almost come to terms with this being unreal in the eyes of others.

I am pretty normal aren't I? Yes and no, I mused. I don't see around me quite what others see, or think as most others think. If I am normal for a human being then I consider Education, in a broad sense, has a long way to go. Perhaps I am 'a normal' let's say, and others like me are the potential for others to aspire to, as a norm. In this case this society is way behind, which would be validating such phrases as 'man is a frail species' or 'it is human to err' or 'we all have our frailties', 'societies have always had these problems', ad infinitum.

The Head was in the staffroom talking with a few of the teachers in their lunch hour, including the Deputy Head. 'Had an interesting interview with that Brandon Waterman yesterday,' said the Head. 'Bright lad that one. He offered to help we teachers by coaching the slow ones. I wonder what brought that on.'

Casey was there. 'I don't know where he learns his stuff but it's not in class. He sets a bad example to the others by daydreaming or apparently sleeping. When I try and catch him out …'

One of the other teachers butted in here and finished the sentence for him…'yes, I know, he always has the answers. The rest of the class finds this all so amusing. It's best to let him be or you'll be embarrassed. But you know, why not use him to help with the slouches?'

The Deputy interrupted this train of thought. 'That won't work. It makes us look bad. How can we have the students teaching? That kid needs a bit of waking up. He should be setting a good example to the others. If it happens again just send him to me.'

The Head continued. 'Well we'll see what he comes up with. He seems confident but I don't know how he'll do it. We can't stop him doing it in his own time; perhaps not here on the premises.'

The Deputy scowled and walked off.

Well, I was given a somewhat cautious green light by Sir Hobbs, as long as I got the OK from the parents of said slugs. I visited the parents concerned and explained that I was offering a one-on-one (or two) extra-curricular service to help out my 'mates'.

Fact was that it was an altruistic deed on my part with no ulterior motive other than to extend my under-laden attention to something useful. What's ahead? Was I to discover that what I had bitten off was more challenging to chew than I thought?

My first pilot was Johnny Trimble, a mop- haired scrawny kid who wasn't really a dullard but a scatter-brain. But he could articulate his 'learning disposition' to some degree, with emphasis on the 'dis'.

I decided that Johnny's DESIRE to learn would have to be a sort of carrier wave to the rest of the procedure. I mentally discarded at least six of my class from the process, as they had NO desire to learn anything. In fact, they were outright dissidents from dubious families, more bent on causing trouble or, more likely too apathetic to be motivated. I'll stick to the 'next tier down' from myself for starters.

So I dissected Johnny's 'case' and found some interesting things. Firstly, he had a very limited vocabulary and didn't understand most basic words used in his texts, especially the grammar terms. Secondly, I found that the guy didn't have much purpose in learning Maths and English, and Geography and History too – no carrier wave. Which was the cart and which was the horse?

Where is this all going? How come I gobble up texts and information without really trying? How come Johnny is unmotivated?

Am I just brighter? Maybe, but that only means only the bright can learn something. The rest are doomed. Or maybe they could just 'learn' it by rote, somewhat, and regurgitate it as needed in exams.

First I have to motivate Johnny. What did Johnny want to learn proper English construction for? After a long discussion I got to the discovery that Johnny was studying stuff beyond his ability to understand it. That is, he got left behind way back and had no real chance to catch up and so gave up. But he wanted to be like me; on top of it all, literate, and learned.

We were in Johnny's room at his place. 'How do you absorb all the books I see you reading? How do you do it all so effortlessly?' Johnny asked.

That's a good point. How do I do it?

'Firstly, I really want to know things; not for exams, but for curiosity. Mostly I want to be able to find out things about the world, and things around me. What I have to do at school is a small part of what I want to know,' I explained.

'OK, but I do too but it's such a pain to find out. When I sit down and read a newspaper for instance I soon start to switch off, or get drowsy, as if a cloud descends upon me. Sometimes, at home, I just fall asleep. If I wanted to fall asleep easily I could just pick up some text book and I'd be in the land of nod in no time.'

That's interesting, thought Brandon. Why would he be awake one minute and asleep shortly after? Have I ever done this? Can words or concepts send you to sleep? I'm going to test this on myself later.

'OK Johnny, but beware, you might have to tolerate a bit of pain to get a gain. That's a catchy phrase, isn't it? Are you willing to go through with it if in doing so you find you come out the other side on top? You've gone past so many things you haven't understood that study now equals pain, without a gain.

'It's not pain to me because I understand it as I go along.'

'You are just brighter than me, that's all,' Johnny pointed out, with a sort of despair not far away.

'Maybe, but what makes me bright? I'm a natural? Or is it that I didn't give up as I went along when I didn't get something? I do use dictionaries you know. You could say I have more brains than you, in which case you are doomed boy, or that I took more trouble to find out and didn't accumulate lots of failures in learning. The more I think about it the more I think it's more to do with wanting to know and finding a way to avoid getting discouraged, which means finding out how to learn.'

Johnny was slowly nodding in agreement. I went on, 'when you play football and you start getting tired, or the body just hurts – do you give up or go through the pain?' I had tweaked his interest a bit more with this subject.

'I saw you running a cross country race not so long ago. I saw you training for it. You busted a gut to get fit, so much so I saw you bent over, gasping for air at the end of the training session, and then in the race I saw you going through the pain barrier, to win. YOU provided the motivation. You decided you could win. You got fit. Yes, you probably started with a bit of natural talent, but how did you manage to beat Charlie Watts, a long-legged athlete of-a-kid, member of an athletic club?'

'Hmm, I see what you mean. All right, might as well give it a spin, I suppose. What happens if I start losing like before?' God, this is a bit depressing. This condition lowers the emotion.

'I'll help you along by getting you to do the things that I do when I'm learning. It's a bit of self-analysis for me too. But again, I have a big motivation to learn how to help you, you see. It proves my point. You have to want to. The 'want' will carry you through, within reason. This subject of English and Grammar isn't so complex that it's such a big mountain to climb.

'Let's get started, eh? I'm going to start off by finding out what you really know and what you don't. Write down for me all the terms you don't know cold, or, if it's easier, write down what you really DO know. Question yourself.'

And so it went on for about an hour. It turned out that Johnny didn't know much at all, and that some of what he thought he knew, on questioning him, he didn't really know – it was glib. How quickly people try to cover up not understanding someone or something, just to avoid seeming stupid.

That was an interesting discovery for me: you just don't know what these guys DON'T know, even if they SEEM to know it.

So, I introduced Johnny to the dictionary. I soon found out that some dictionaries were just too learned for most, so I ended up with a simple one for this guy, and even then I had to short-circuit an endless dictionary troll by telling him verbally what some words meant. But I tried to instil a habit in Johnny – your dictionary is your best friend; befriend it and learn how it works, derivations, pronunciation, synonyms and all.

 So Johnny didn't go to sleep quite so easily and he started to enjoy the dictionary. I gave him five new words a day to look up; relatively easy words that Johnny couldn't define. And so Johnny started to gradually come out of his induced stupidity.

I noticed it's not just ideas but exact words. Not fully knowing words, even simple words, created 'switch off' symptoms. To complicate it a bit more, many words had other meanings, and there were idioms on top of these.

Johnny gradually had all of the important grammar terms down cold and could see, by instruction and lots of exercises, how sentences were constructed and what all the parts of speech were. There was hope. Johnny soon even enjoyed his lessons. On top of that I introduced a lot of humour into the whole thing. I had Johnny laughing and making up silly sentences to demonstrate words, just for a laugh. I learned it's not just words. You have to be able to see what the words are saying by doing lots of examples until the tune the words are playing sounds sweet.

Then I got him writing little compositions using proper sentences and paragraphs, and good adjectives and adverbs for a bit of colour. Punctuation started to make his whole stories make sense.

In teaching Johnny Grammar I noticed that Grammar books were almost a deterrent to learning as they were not basic enough. I think I'll write my own Grammar book just for 'my boys'. Now this led on to me thinking about becoming a writer, a 'writer for the masses', not the educated. Educators, I was learning, were not that appreciative of their audience when it came to explaining their subject.

So, another string to my bow – one thing at a time; easy before hard. A simple Grammar book first.

Now I could see what problems a teacher had trying to educate a whole class of thirty odd kids all at different levels and IQ's, not to mention backgrounds. And how ever could they pick up all of them when they began to lose their way?

I was discovering that there were inbuilt obstacles to learning and there was no subject called 'how to learn' and hence a limited subject of 'how to teach'. Wow, I could become an Educator. Now I have two subject paths I can follow – Writing and Education. Life was looking up. THIS was getting above the humdrum activities of life, and getting me nearer to a plot for my life.

I did the same exercise on four other kids in my class without any resistance from the parents. My extra curricula life was well filled. I managed to condense it a bit into groups of two as time went on.

I also feared I'd have a bit of a job to sell all this to my 'seniors' without treading on their egos or sensitivities. However, results must be proof of boast, surely.

CHAPTER THREE

With my 'pilot project' well into its third month I ventured to present my findings to Sir Hobbs. Surely he must be impressed.

'I thought you had given up on the whole thing,' the HM pronounced. 'But in any case I told the staff at a staff meeting and they all laughed at the idea. The Deputy Head even went so far as to tell me you should be disciplined for this outrageous idea. I must admit, though I wouldn't agree it was a crime enough for discipline, I thought about it again and decided it just wouldn't fly, me letting students do the educating. What would the inspectors think?'

'But you were all for it sir,' I protested. 'Look I've got all the evidence here …' I was cut off in my gathering outrage by a different HM I had talked to in the first place. It looked like he'd trodden on some corns.

'Look Brandon, don't pester me with this anymore. It's done. It's not going to fly. Go back to your class and do the best to get yourself in good shape for your exams. Let me worry about this problem. I have some ideas of my own and will introduce them soon. Thanks for your trouble'.

'Won't you even look at what I've done? This guy Johnny Trimble now wants to learn and can parse sentences almost as well as the best of us.'

Hobbs was off as he was distracted by his secretary and just dismissed me with a 'not now son'. There's that speaking-down-to word again.

I went home somewhat dejected and somewhat angry. I went out onto the veranda and sat there trying to come to terms with it all. Grandpa came along with his mug of tea and his newspaper and enquired, 'why so glum?'

I had trouble getting my tongue into gear, but eventually started spouting – 'what chance have we got when the educators can't educate and don't even admit it. How can I get by this stuffy old system which is stuck in the mud.

These kids have no chance. I've..'

'Just a moment, slow down. What happened?' butted in Grandpa.

I told him all about it for at least ten minutes. Then there was a silence.

How to kill off initiative and spirit, Grandpa was thinking.

'Hmm, so you've noticed that your parents have only a small grip on life, nations solve big problems by war, and now this – Education is deeply flawed. What does this tell you?'

I thought long about this. 'It's pushing shit up hill. Sorry about the language, but it is. Is the whole world this crazy?'

'Now, before you sink into oblivion, let's see what you can do immediately. I thought your project was admirable and the results really sterling. Why don't you continue it on privately and continue your new-found quest to be an Educator? Learn all there is to the subject. Experiment with all the kids you want and convince each set of parents you are really helping their children...'

I considered this for a while. 'Yes, and then I could get the parents to back me. Grownups have more sway than a mere kid,' I said sarcastically. I was somewhat revived but as soon as I pictured the formidable tranche of school masters I wasn't quite so sure. But I'll give it a go.

And there I learned my next lesson; one that I was trying to pound into Johnny Trimble in fact – do you want it or not? Are you going to give up that easily? I couldn't believe I'd fallen for it so easily. Understandable though. If at first ...

Old habits die hard. Many negative old habits become regular 'solutions'. There's a philosophical point to keep an eye on.

But it was a bit more than that in fact. I'd become a bit black, not just from my rejection by Hobbs but by what I was starting to perceive about the world immediately around me in addition to what I'd already learned historically about the world at large. One IS a microcosm of the other by the looks of it.

'How did it get to this?' I spouted at Grandpa. 'How do you deal with this apparent irrationality machine that even 'educated' people seem to have in their thinking?

'I'm thinking of Johnny Trimble. He is reasonably bright IQ-wise but he'd become stupid on the subject of grammar and words, and maybe maths too if the truth be told.' Then I thought of myself and compared the two. 'I have more IQ than Johnny, probably, but that doesn't explain the difference in results all by itself as Johnny has become brighter lately by learning something properly. So what explains the rest of it?

'What about Adolf Hitler, one of the craziest men ever it seems. But he must have been bright to have got to where he did and have as much success as he did, when he had it. Can you be crazy and bright, or is that a contradiction?

'I'm thinking of the quietest, mousiest, most timid person I know in my class – Neil Davis. He is a bookworm, quite bright at most subjects, but couldn't say boo to a goose. Me versus him? No contest in all respects. He can be overpowered by raising one's eyebrows.'

'I don't think we are all born equally,' offered Grandpa.

'Probably not....' I tailed off and sank into thought.

Grandpa leaned forward looking at me. When I looked up Grandpa asked, 'where are you?'

'So we have a state of mind thing going on here. I wonder how much I could increase Charlie Watts' IQ. He's one of the dissidents. How much could I improve his state of mind? I don't have an answer to that one but there is a clue in Johnny Trimble's case. He'd gotten worse by failure and better by success, so failure is a clue here. The more you fail the worse you get, both in IQ and state of mind. It would take a strong guy to ride out a lot of failures, or major ones. But people do it.'

'Are you thinking of an example here Brandon?' asked Grandpa.

'I heard about an escaped convict who rowed a boat from Sydney to Chile, right across the whole Pacific! This was back in the colonial days. What obstacles and potential failures he must have encountered, apart from the sheer distance. I doubt I could do it. Maybe he was lucky? What extraordinary luck if so. His solution to slavery was to escape across the widest ocean on the planet. Not a terrible solution, even if the odds were against it, but he made it.' I paused for a moment and laughed.

'Do you know what happened when he got there? He ran into a British ship in port and was apprehended. He surely couldn't have expected that – the odds anyway. So, lady luck dealt him a cruel blow. He wasn't even given any marks or reprieve for having tried so valiantly. Luck – how much of life is luck? Another time.'

Grandpa wouldn't interrupt me in full flow.

'Wow, what am I getting into here? If the world is crazy and beyond redemption then as a whole it must have had a lot of failures. The leaders of nations must have failed to deal with pressing problems a lot and gotten more and more desperate as time went by.'

Grandpa nodded, 'makes sense to me.'

'So, I've now got another potential career path – what is it? Philosophy, Psychology, or something else? Whatever you call it, it involves rectifying the thing called Man. What a job. I hope someone comes along and solves this, but it's a mighty intriguing subject.'

The two of us were starting to yawn a lot. Was it getting late, or ….

'Back to my subject – Education. I know I can improve someone's IQ by Education alone. I've done it. I'm going to forget about Hobbs and the nobs he hobs with and I'm going to continue with Johnny on Maths, Geography and anything else he wants to learn. In fact I've noticed that while Johnny is improving and becoming more alert he is becoming a new person – he is funny even, and is originating things he'd like to do and talking more freely on a range of subjects. He's become a friend almost. And the other four kids I've been working on are progressing similarly.

'I'm going to do my thing with Johnny and present it as a fait accompli to the Parents Association and get them to lean on the stuffy shirts who we are all paying good money, via taxation, to educate our next generation.'

'I'm going to slip away now if you don't mind, my man,' Grandpa said as he slowly raised himself out of his comfortable chair.

I sort of said 'good night' but was actually deep in thought as Grandpa sidled off. With all this battle to get my project off the ground for real I had become a lot more serious; not what I had planned. But I was fighting this mood with some determination in order to make my solution work. This was the first time I'd battled the mental elements for real. But this setback had holed me a little. What would I do next if I failed to get enough allies on side and enough traction to pull it off? My optimism was wearing thin and my relative naivety showing as I was entering the arena for real.

I worked on Johnny some more over the following weeks and got him to a point where he could 'fly solo' so to speak; that is, where he didn't need me at his elbow all the way. He could recognise when he probably didn't understand something and could correct it himself. There was the early warning sign – switching off, getting dull and maybe sleepy or disinterested, distracted or just heavy.

I sorted him out on Maths, only to the point where he got what he wanted from the subjects of Arithmetic, Algebra and Geometry. Did he need Trigonometry or Calculus? Not a bit.

Geography was an easy one. A little knowledge of the planet was probably useful – the countries and capitals, main rivers, oceans and seas, latitude and longitude, and not much else. Johnny was now up to speed.

What else did he WANT to know? Surprisingly enough he became more interested in other things, like History, Biology, and Economics. The last one would be a challenge. Even I can't get my head round that one fully as it seems to be all tied up with politics; and that was a minefield too. Maybe some subjects are hard to understand because they are plain faulty. These I assumed would be giving the most trouble in the world around me. What is that list – Economics, Politics, Mental Health, Philosophy perhaps?

Anyway, I know Mrs Gibson, the PTA Chairwoman, through my parents. I went to her and told her what I was doing and why. She was impressed and spoke to Johnny too to verify the results. I was encouraged but cautiously so, due to my rebuff with Sir Hobbs.

I had to tell her I'd fallen the wrong side of Sir Hobbs, and urged her to build that into her approach at the PTA meetings.

'I'll run it all at the other parents first so I can get it to him from all sides. It's not him that we have to convince, you know.'

'No, I know, I think it's the Deputy and the Deputy has the ear of most of the other teachers. Maybe we should pick out some of the teachers who are having the most trouble and would welcome some help and get them on side too.'

'Leave it to me Prof', she said with a wink. 'To tell you the truth I was beginning to wonder what I could do to salvage my little Nigel from this poor excuse for a school.'

I was with the clouds again and hurried off home to tell Grandpa the latest.

————————————

On the veranda after dinner, I let Grandpa sip his tea for a bit then broached the subject. 'I've come out for round two with this Education thing' I've got the help of some 'bigger bodies' from the PTA. We have a plan.' I then told him the whole story.

'Good on you. War is declared then,' added grandpa.

'No not exactly, but an even playing field is more what I've established. After all, it's their kids that are at stake here. Let's hope that the blooming Deputy isn't a complete stopper.

'So is that the end of your school education then?'

'That ended some time ago truthfully,' I admitted. 'If the system isn't giving me new or important knowledge you can say it ended years ago.'

'Well if you put it like that there is no school that caters for YOUR broad interest. Go for it my man!'

I could hear Grandpa talking to Mum and Dad in the living room. 'Our boy is on the point of adulthood you know. He's not just a boy beholden to us adults, and his teachers too.

'In fact he is starting to fill out a bit, as if on cue. He is getting the beginnings of a beard on his youthful face. He's no longer just a slightly awkward skinny kid. There is real beef developing all over.
'In a year or so, he'll be a strapping handsome youth, attracting the opposite sex no doubt. I wonder how he'd handle that one. Somehow I dont think he'll fall in line with his contemporaries and hang around in groups, whistling at girls and acting all macho and telling crude jokes. He may even be looked on as a weirdo for this.

'Maybe he'll find a special soul mate among the less tribal girls. Maybe he'll be so busy he won't have time for all that. But, doesn't the urge tickle all pubescents? Can't wait for the next chapter. Life can be a lion's den. But he's not exactly naïve or gullible, but he hasn't met up with the worst of life's baddies yet.

Mum and Dad were more or less happy to leave it up to Grandpa for any mentoring I needed. Well, not for long I decided. What about girls now? I haven't got time for them. From what I've seen they bring on trouble at least as much as anything else. But I do notice the odd one of that species in a different way to boys. Why should they be trouble? Many questions to ponder. Not now. Time for a change of activity. Maybe a run and then a good sleep.

CHAPTER FOUR

Mrs Ira Gibson had stood up at the PTA meeting and rallied the troops - the somewhat less forthright than she, yet dutiful foot soldiers. She was the fulcrum. She was telling me the whole episode.

'The Headmaster, Sir Hobbs as I call him, and his Deputy were at the meeting. After they'd disposed of the more mundane items on the agenda I decided I'd better perform my rallying cry and go straight to the heart of the matter. I said, as tactfully as I could that I'd like to know how come there are more than a few children lagging in their studies and not making the grade? I had a lot of particulars and was easily able to counteract the feeble explanations given by the Head to 'deal' with my assault.

'The Deputy said nothing until the end when he said, to assuage (patronise) me, that perhaps the school should look closely at the complaints being made and report back next meeting with their proposals.'

I butted in to her gathering venom, 'I suppose this was fuel to the fire, for you, Mrs G.'

'Well yes, you observant little thing. Up to this point I'd not mentioned your experiment. I thought I'd save my best ammunition for the right moment. I had more than a sneaking suspicion that this Deputy was not all he was trying to portray. I was watching him carefully. He'd been trying to dismiss the matter under a cloud of being reasonable, I decided. Was he just protecting the Head from embarrassment? He's a clever bugger you know.

'Well if the Deputy's deeds were to match his words we were on a winner, I thought. But if it's just more smoke screens then I am determined to use my big gun.'

Mrs G continued. 'At the next meeting a few weeks later I raised the subject again. It hadn't escaped me that, but for me, the subject would have been swept under the carpet.

'I asked Mr Hobbs, if he remembered the subject matter of our last meeting and if he would bring us up to date on that. Never mind diplomacy, you understand.

'Well, he replied that he was glad I had asked. He didn't look glad at all. This was going to be BS, I knew, but I wasn't going to let it happen.

'I asked Hobbs to give it to us straight please. I then demanded what mighty plans he had for our future generation. He squirmed awkwardly.'

I awaited Mrs G's coup de grace, hardly containing my mirth.

'At that point the Deputy, Jake Levison, chimed in and started to explain to me, and I quote, 'we've looked over the problem carefully and mulled it over, and though acknowledging that there was indeed a serious situation here, we feel that the school academia had gotten their heads together and decided that they were going to work harder and institute an examination-based program to monitor who was lagging…blah blah blah… and report the results to each PTA meeting.'

'That's all very fine rhetoric, I'd cut in, but how was he going to bring us up to speed exactly, and why didn't he notice the situation and do something about it before I'd raised the subject? Maybe I should be his inspector I said. So I asked him for the plan. Well, 'asked' wasn't the exact term. You follow me?

'Well, he told me to just leave that to them and that I'd made my point and that now I should let them get on with it. All the time he was averting his eyes from the target, that is, me.

'I told him not to patronise me. I had asked a specific question, and we had a right to know – how? What exactly had these brains come up with suddenly out of the blue? Now I was on the warpath. I could see the fly in the ointment here. This was the mouthpiece. This was the slippery one. I'd make mincemeat of him if I had to.'

'Mrs G, it sounds like you were enjoying yourself,' I said

She continued.'You bet I was. He told me to keep this reasonable. He said I had demanded the school listen and do something, and that they were doing so.

'I interrupted him and said he'd told me nothing. What, specifically, were the plans? I asked him how they'd all suddenly become real educators when before they weren't. I didn't really expect an answer to this but told him his answer would dictate what we'd all do next.

'He then accused me of turning this into an inquisition, raising his voice a bit more and losing his carefully contrived demeanour. He could see he wasn't going to get me to back off easily.

'I told him that if asking a pointed question was an inquisition he had serious problems. It's a question, that's all.

'He then snidely asked me if I'd like to take over the school, as I seemed to be trying to do, and that I should try it for a week and see how difficult it is to run this show. He then more or less told me to get back in my box.'

I was rapt at this relay of events.

Mrs G continued. 'I was in like Flynn at this. I told him he could dodge the issue until the cows came home and that his reply had told us what we needed to know. I said he'd better think about that and that he could write all the plans he liked and that this would have to go to a higher authority.'

'Mrs G, they won't let you into the next meeting,' I said.

She then proceeded to tell me that she had reminded him about me and my exploits with the slow students and that I'd been rejected out of hand but had given them a crash course in learning and resurrected them to boot.

My final stroke was to inform them that I was withdrawing my child from this pathetic establishment and that I could do better myself by doing nothing at worst or something along a successful path, already now proven by you Brandon.

'At that point a silent invitation for other parents to follow suit hung in the air. There was silence. Just enough brave souls gradually plucked up the courage to follow my lead and walk out in protest. I also said that there were a few interested parties, not least the Department of Education, and as a balance, perhaps the local newspaper or even one of the big fish.'

'What do you think will happen now?' I asked.

'Well, the Deputy had gone black and was scuppering off to hide somewhere probably, or hatch some devious plan against his newly acquired nemesis. Hobbs was trying to bring the meeting to order, but it was in vain. He had no presence at all and he had nowhere to go. The meeting disbanded as if by natural law.'

Hobbs and his deputy met in the HM's office, immediately afterwards. 'That woman!' moaned the Deputy. 'She's a troublesome bitch. I hope she's all hot air, but somehow I doubt it. What do you plan Brian?'

'Well, let's just see if she does anything first,' the HM said.

'I don't think that will be enough Brian,' shot in the DHM. 'We can't have her spreading bad news about the school. I think we have to try and smear her in some way. Maybe we should go to the newspapers and report this 'highly scandalous meeting' but in a way that makes her look bad and we the victim of an obvious attempt to derail the educative process and undermine all our earnest efforts to improve this place.'

'Maybe,' the HM added, 'but there's a ring of truth in her protestations, you know, and we have been a bit tardy in getting the matter dealt with. In fact we don't have a plan really, it's only a 'promise' of a plan'.

'Leave it to me Brian,' the Deputy said. Brian wondered what he was cooking up but was sort of content-cum-worried to leave it up to him.

'Let's sleep on it and talk some more tomorrow,' Brian offered, hoping it would all go away.

I was hauled into the Deputy's office the next morning and was read the riot act. 'You have started something here Waterman. What do you mean by getting all these housewives to follow your plan? Weren't you told to let we teachers deal with this? You have whipped up a Union to make us look bad, which won't do your cause any good. We are considering suspending you altogether.' It went on.

I was quite stirred up by this dressing down, a new experience for me. This was real malevolence. It hadn't stopped there. Levison had done his best to totally introvert me. I promptly skulked back to my classroom where I got a sarcastic 'welcome' from Casey which was really an attempt to drive the final nail into the coffin, so to speak.

I couldn't get a word in edgeways during my upbraiding. And I did try. After school, having spent most of the day getting myself back together, I went around to Mrs G's place and somewhat dejectedly related my meeting with the Deputy.

'Now listen here Brandon,' she said empathetically but firmly. 'You have nothing to be ashamed or regretful about. Those jumped-up excuses for educators are cowards, every one of them, and picking on you for being courageous enough to be creative and deal with the situation only proves my point.

'Now be prepared for some more rough weather cos we have twenty parents already on side to move our children out and blacken the school's name. Someone has to put up a stand. You should consider it an honour that you are in this position, even if it is adults picking on an adolescent. And, by the way I don't consider you an adolescent really as you have behaved like a responsible adult should. So, hats off to you Brandon.'

Well it wasn't flattery but all this acknowledgement had served to lift me out of my gloom.

'I can see why I copped it this morning then,' I added.

'Well, what do I do now? I think I'll carry on with Johnny, and your son

Nigel if you like, and my other subjects, and consult with my parents as to whether I return to school or not. I'd rather not have to suffer any more abuse, but frankly I'm coming up to being able to be a bit less of a kid and a bit more of a man out of all this.

'What perturbs me is the effect the crushing had on me. I was really dumbstruck and lost for words for the first time in my life, really. Then again I've not really had to get into these kind of things with adults. But on his home turf as it were Levison really made the most of his authority. Actually, now I feel angry.'

'Well you know what is right and who is right, Brandon. Welcome to the real world. It's not as pretty as you might wish for. There's good people and bad people and a lot of frightened ones in the middle. We'll see how far we can go on this. The odds are that we will ruffle some feathers but that they'll bluster and delay and lie carefully and probably get this swept under the carpet. A lot of the other parents will probably backslide and lose their will. The school may have its embarrassing moments and be ticked off by the Department, but won't we have fun. They at least will be less slack and more afraid to slip up with we PTA people again. I will look forward to future meetings.'

I went off to consider the day's events some more. I bowled into the kitchen at home and, with all present at the table, including Grandpa, I announced I was quitting school and that I would more than likely be suspended for my troubles anyway.

I told them the whole story and just as my shocked parents were about to give me a bit of a shame trip Grandpa chimed in and cut it short, 'what do you two want from this? Look at what has happened here. I'm sorry, I won't have you repeat on your own son the scandalous treatment he's been subjected to. Why aren't you two in Mrs G's camp?'

He went on a bit but at the end the parents backed off and considered how they would cope with the ignominy of their son being suspended, and the discomfort of their dressing down by Grandpa.

Out on the veranda, after the evening chores Grandpa beamed at me and put his arm around my shoulder, not as a comfort, but as a recognition of a momentous occasion in my development.

'Well, my man, welcome to the real world. What do you make of it now?' he asked

This was the second time I'd been welcomed to the real world today. 'Well, I'm beginning to see that there's part of the real world that I've got to start seeing front on. I knew that some people were less able than others and that some guys were a bit irresponsible, but I'm starting to look on society as a product of a frail and flawed species. Our family is a microcosm of this, and we're better off than a lot of others. And our broader society around us is likely a snapshot of the world at large. How many are like Levison and the HM? And how many are like Mrs G?

'That woman incidentally has real guts, but even she is a bit wary of what she calls the Establishment. She doesn't really expect much will come from this. What does that say?

'We've discussed war and a few other human conditions, a bit like bystanders, if you see what I mean - over there, or in the past. Who knows what is brewing for the future?'

 I leant forward in my chair and put my hands under my chin. Grandpa was watching and waiting. I was experiencing a new awakening. I wasn't far from the whole nine yards I thought.

'OK, tomorrow I'm going to organise the next step in the education of Johnny Trimble. You should see this guy read and write now. And he's in danger of becoming a book worm too. But you know, real knowledge isn't only in books, at least not that I know of.'

CHAPTER FIVE

Three months slipped by quickly. The school fracas did get swept under the carpet despite Mrs G going to the Department and the local newspaper. There was a little article in the local paper, relegated to the 'filler' articles.

None of the nationals took it up, and as for the slimy Deputy Head, well he shifted and squirmed, I heard, and rode out the storm and let it all subside and die a natural death, promising action and doing nothing to change anything. The parents who withdrew their children backslid and capitulated under threat of losing their children's' places or being prosecuted for allowing truancy.

I was sitting with Mrs G in her kitchen discussing the whole episode. 'There's a system, an immovable object, an Establishment, which is not just conservative but outright protectionist, and, rather more impolitely, crooked,' Mrs G asserted. She smiled mischievously and added, 'I hope I haven't used too many big words there Brandon.'

'I think I get the gist of your point,' I said humorously. 'Is this a typical example of the malaise affecting our society? Is it the same for our politicians down in Westminster, or our legal system, or our health authorities? What happens at the United Nations? It's like being under a dictatorship, except it's not that obvious. Surely there must be some way of righting wrongs or doing something about things, short of revolution.'

Mrs G looked at me and said, 'That's deep Brandon; you are getting into something there. Do you think perhaps the alternative to battling the powers is to withdraw into one's own little world and look after Number One?' She knew my answer to that one.

Mrs G continued. 'Talking about Number One, what do I do about my little sprog who is now not at school. Do I send him back to school to be brain washed, or de-brained, or whatever it is, or do I educate him myself. That would be a big commitment. I have two more younger ones too.'

'As I suggested before, I'll help you,' I offered.

'I now know what to do, using Johnny Trimble and the other boys as a 'template'. You better send him back to school, at least for some of the week, so we don't get into trouble with authorities. You know, we could set up our own private education establishment, under the radar as it were.'

'We?' Mrs G asked. 'Who is WE?'

'Well I can't do it all myself can I? You know, if you can't beat 'em, join 'em,' I said whimsically but also as if she couldn't refuse.

'Call it supplementary education. We could canvass all the parents who aren't happy with their kids' progress, and offer them what they aren't getting. Besides it's become quite a little pet project of mine since my recent efforts with my 'star pupil'.'

Mrs G looked at me in a funny way. 'I feel like I'm dealing with a seasoned professor and you're a mere teenager, barely out of puberty, if that. You're not normal, not abnormal but, well, different, in a special way.

'OK Brandon you can take on my little Nigel, say, after school, or at weekends, or we could have him be 'sick' for one or two days a week. Then again I officially withdrew him from school, so I'm going to stick to that. Let's do it and as we succeed we'll get others into it. Start on Monday.'

I was excited again. 'I need to assess Nigel first. That will take a few hours at the most.'

––––––––––––

Meanwhile it hadn't escaped the Head and his creepy Deputy that I was absent from school and, funnily enough, so was Nigel Gibson, and Johnny Trimble sometimes. It turned out the Head had paid a visit to Mrs G and was practically thrown off the front door step, by all accounts.

He had then tried Mr Trimble I learned, when at Johnny's place one afternoon. Mr Trimble told me he wasn't quite so animated but in a very slightly more controlled manner had told the Head that when and if this much vaunted 'program of reform' was issued, which was three months in not arriving, so far , and if it was practical and addressed his requirements, he'd return his child to school full time.

'I'm not impressed,' he'd said. 'I'm not sending him to fill in some attendance quota. He's supposed to attend school by law, you say, or he'll be deemed a truant, but the law also says he's got to be given an education, in which case you are rather delinquent, it seems. Meanwhile my son is getting educated by my own means, and is progressing exponentially. You turned down the opportunity to witness this, which tells me all I need to know about your disgraceful establishment. Shame on you. You'd rather listen to that snake-in-the-grass Levison. And your school IS failing.'

Hobbs had scuppered off apparently, with his tail between his legs, muttering that this wouldn't be the end of the matter, in a none-too-convincing manner.

While this was happening the Deputy had been assigned to cave in my parents. The guy was unlucky. My parents were out and Grandpa opened the door and when he realised who this was he stood in the doorway uninvitingly and started in on him while Levison remained on the front porch. I was surreptitiously listening to all this, paused on my way down the stairs. Grandpa was getting into full gear. 'I'm glad you are here now, though I wouldn't have invited you. My grandson was given quite a dressing down at your hands and blamed for the fracas at the PTA. '

Levison was back-footed and made to feel as uncomfortable as possible while he tried to get into gear.

'Well, what you dished out to him in the comfort and authority of your mighty office was something I'm sure you wouldn't have been willing to experience yourself. I hope you can take it as well as you dish it out because that's what you're going to get from me.'
Grandpa was about to carry on with his dressing-down. He had barely got

the next sentence out when Levison huffed off muttering something to the effect that he hadn't come round here to listen to this. 'Just as I thought,'Grandpa told me, 'a coward to boot. Why didn't I go up to the school in the first place and speak up then? I don't think I've heard the last of this.'

And, right enough, in the next few days, two more formidable-looking 'suits' showed up at the house, they being from the Truancy Department. I was in the kitchen but could hear the voices. They asked my mum if they could come in to speak about my absence from school. She was about to let them in when Grandpa appeared at her side enquiring about this event, full well knowing what it was about – he'd been on the veranda and was coming to answer the door bell.

'So Levison has called in the cavalry! Do you know he wouldn't listen to me the other night. I gave him a dressing down for having scared Brandon half to death with his overpowering and, incidentally, untrue accusation that this mild-mannered boy had caused a ruckus at the PTA meeting, which he didn't even attend. He'd tried to offer help to a struggling Head and teacher and your 'men' weren't men enough to even consider it because it came from a mere 'kid'.'

'They were put on the spot at the PTA meeting and offered to come up with a plan to deal with the lagging students, which amounted to nothing in the end.

'Hence, since your Department is not offering an education worth the name, Brandon is teaching himself, which frankly he's been doing all along. Your top student, always first in the class, is not being recognised for what he is, a rarity, some might even say a budding genius. Why does he need to go to school and join in the, at best , mediocrity you are dishing up, along with being plastered against the walls for daring to speak up . Easy to pick on a youngster and not the PTA.'

By this I'd wandered into the hallway. The invaders were squirming and trying to get a word in.

One of the two, a very intense sort of a chap, finally managed just that and said, 'there may well be things at the school that need attending to but our point is all parents have a duty, legally, to send their children to school.' He was about to go on when Grandpa cut him dead.

'You are on the wrong doorstep. Don't tell me he's got to come to school. Tell me you have rectified the situation there and that this boy is going to learn something and that the less fortunate students are getting brought up to speed.'

Mum stood there awkwardly agog at this lambasting. The two less formidable-now officers were almost spellbound by Grandpa's performance. One stuck a piece of paper in Grandpa's hand which was tantamount to a summons. Grandpa put it back in the man's top pocket and told them a piece of paper, whatever it is, is meaningless and they could take it back to from whence it came or put it somewhere else....(where waste eventually exits, I'm sure he restrained himself from saying).

'Don't waste your time. Go back to the school and get those self-importanced, pompous, excuses-for-teachers to do their job. Meanwhile, we don't want our boy exposed to this atmosphere any more. If there is any more harassment I'll go to the top and make a full report on your school there and drum up so much havoc you won't know what has hit you. Goodbye gentlemen.'

With that he'd closed the door just firmly enough to punctuate the point. 'How could you be so rude to those chaps,' Mum asked rather meekly. She turned around and saw me standing there. 'Did you hear all that. son?' she asked me.

Grandpa signalled to me clearly enough that I should go upstairs. I did, but stopped on the landing. I wanted to hear everything.

'Didn't you notice I was standing up for your boy, and on behalf of you, Gladys? Don't you know what you have on your hands here? Your son is, to all extents and purposes, a fully responsible adult but without equal rights. He has completed his school education, AND some. He has a career path mapped out and begun. He's more aware of what is going on in the world than we are. He's together. He's not a kid or adolescent anymore. He's ready to tackle life. When he really sheds himself of any inferiority he may feel at the hands of adults he'll really be there.'

This wasn't news to me really, but I was glad I had at least one adult who was fully on my side, in all respects.

Mum was close to tears now.

Grandpa went on. 'And, if it's any consolation, you and Cliff have done a lot right to have turned out a result like this. You let him grow. Andrew his brother is a good kid too, but doesn't have Brandon's drive or dynamic. Brandon was born a winner, a goer, a special kid, and you and Cliff have helped nurture it, and, to some degree, so have I. Let's not spoil it by letting these officials for one moment threaten this boy. They don't know what they are doing?'

As they walked slowly into the kitchen, now going out of earshot, I heard the kettle being put on. Grandpa continued on 'Do you know what Brandon has done?..........'

I expected Grandpa would make mum a cup of tea. Well, I decided, if I am an adult, as Grandpa agrees, then I should be able to be in the conversation. I walked downstairs and into the kitchen.

'Tea Brandon?' asked Grandpa.

'Please,' I answered. I sat down at the table and confessed, 'I heard all of that. Don't worry Mum I know what this is all about. They will probably go back to their office and call the school and have a good old moan about it all. The Deputy will tell them how that bitch Mrs Gibson has been trying to undermine the school and has started a movement of rebellion, all because that kid Waterman can't pay attention in school and has been trying to make the teachers look small by being a smart arse.'

Grandpa served the tea and sat down. Mum dried her eyes a bit. 'Mum, it's just a fact. I AM way ahead of the school curriculum. I HAVE BEEN only trying to help the school out while I 'mature', as they would say. But they just can't have me doing this. If Levison wasn't there I think there would be no problem. So, there's no point me being there. Let me do my thing with my mates at school and we can probably ride out any other nonsense they try to dish up.'

Grandpa chimed in and added, 'something has to be done here Gladys. This school is substandard and is failing, and the parents know it. That's why Ira Gibson is on the warpath at the PTA.'

Now, officially suspended from school, I tore into my project with Trimble and young Gibson. The other boys under my tutelage were now back at school and doing better. God, I thought, what satisfaction – real results. These teachers, mostly well-meaning to enter this profession in the first place, how must they feel going home each day without such satisfaction?

I was sitting in the kitchen, sipping my tea and chewing on my toast and peanut butter, and now enjoying my suspension life. I thought how do you kid yourself that you know when you don't know? How do people dilute their integrity just to be right? I suppose being able to re-appraise or even be wrong is not the forte of many.

I thought again of Hitler. He must have been innately bright. Or was he? He almost ruled the world. He got a whole nation galvanised into the conquering mode and got a whole economic and war machine all going in one direction. If he'd made it across the English Channel and left Russia until later he'd have done it. But his 'genius' was flawed. He had it in his hand and blew it. In amongst all his escapades there was much destruction. He had one motto it seemed – conquer and destroy, now! If he'd been a benign dictator who wanted to create a flourishing society for all, even in other countries, he'd have been man of the millennium. So there was intelligence but ill directed. What was his purpose? So not intelligent really, which begs for a better definition for 'intelligence' and clarity on the subject of 'insanity'.

You could be bright and mad – dangerous.

I looked at my own little project – it was all 'discover and help', with demonstrable results. I am not trying to be right, just helpful. I am up against an Establishment who couldn't be wrong. How do you get around that? I'd seen it first hand, from Casey, through Hobbs, and Levison. It must go all the way up the line.

Great discoveries …. how do they come about? Some person either trips over them, or goes out to find them, deliberately, or does something to solve a situation and finds out it's a discovery, heretofore not known. The latter might be what I'd done myself. Could little old me have made a great discovery? In the area of Education? Damn right I have.

I ransacked the libraries for all data on Study and Education. Of course I came up with nothing that taught 'how to study'.

I consulted the oracle one Saturday morning, after a period in the library. 'What is this? You have all these great halls of learning, ranging from Oxford to Harvard and nothing tells you how to learn what is on the syllabus! Just read it all and remember. Well something must be learnt or else nothing would work, such as cars, bridges, buildings and more. Hmm.

'Well, I can learn, sort of naturally. So there must be a number of bright sparks who can assimilate stuff, or look and reason. But no one has been interested enough in the subject of Education to examine their skills and share it all out.'

Grandpa joined the process. 'I guess we are held together by the upper end of the scale, by basically sensible people who have intelligence to go with the sense. Even then, how often do you hear about this calamity, that dropped ball, the cost to the public purse for a brainless program of reform?'

I continued, 'yes, the assumption is, obviously, that all can digest and understand what is written and spoken and with enough brow-beating and repetition will 'get it'. 'Passing' exams though is often just a memory test.

You could get eighty percent or even fifty one, and pass.
And that is just written exams.

'It is also assumed that the heads of Education and schools know how to educate, because they did a degree or went to University, got the diplomas and got the jobs. This is the Establishment, plus or minus some ideological or political bias on the thing.'

Grandpa said, 'my boy, I find myself more and more wanting and more and more a spectator. Being a listener and a questioner is making him feel a bit phoney, like I've stopped life and am winding down.

'Brandon, you are now my educator. You are coming up with stuff I've not really looked at. I can only be your sounding board and supporter .You must now appraise for yourself what is right or wrong.

'I might have life experience and have a certain amount of my own integrity, but you are looking at things that I was nowhere near in all my early days. I have to say you are waking me up, and I find it uncomfortable, yet exciting.'

I suppose I AM now at the crossroads of maturity/adulthood, but not a normal adulthood for sure. I am almost a pioneer, a real student of society, a lone man on a mission. I am just now turning fourteen years old and meant to be an immature teenager who would be 'mature' AFTER my 'education' and after full body growth.

Grandpa and I were walking home after a visit to the library and the local café and were talking about the dying throes of the British Empire. Off the subject now I came out with what had been occupying my mind. 'Grandpa, I feel overwhelmed with the enormity of what I have been looking at. Man seems to be seriously wanting in true knowledge. In my study of History and a little of Economics and Politics I've learned that problems have mounted up rapidly since the industrial revolution and population explosion and quicker communication and transport systems.

'It would appear that 'leaders' have been marginally active in solving long-standing problems of starvation, poverty, economics, national disagreements, ignorance. It has all been set up for a big loss it seems. Man is definitely a flawed species, even though the leading species. He's hardly advanced in knowledge on the most important things, mainly about himself. War, ignorance and deprivation have been his constant Achilles heel.

'Someone has to come up with a solution to all this, but fast.' Then I thought about what I was saying here –'someone else'? Would I put my house on it, so to speak? It couldn't be me. What do I know?   'Maybe there are other like-minded altruistic citizens who are talking and not doing. Maybe the Psychologists, the closest thing to experts, will find out how we should really tick. But I can't say I've seen much evidence from them, but then again I haven't really looked.' I was beginning to feel sleepy.

Grandpa just prompted and listened.

I went on. 'OK, one thing at a time. The Education system is but a piece in the puzzle. Why not tackle that first. I need a way into the system. I need some support. I already know I need some flanking armour, like Mrs G – like-minded free thinkers.

'Yes, that's it! This looks to be a brain-washed planet. Not a planet of free thinkers. If you can't reason, you make up or swallow all sorts of stuff.'

It was hitting me rapidly. I was beginning to get a glimmer of the big picture and realised I needed to really educate myself and meet people out of my relative bubble; see if all the world was really as lacking as this miniature one seemed to be.

'My boy,' Grandpa cut in, 'I'm with you here. Not to cut you short here, but by way of a shift of attention why don't we get out and about and go down to White Hart Lane and observe the masses there, particularly the players?

My treat.'

'I'll be in that. Nothing like a bit of enjoyable frivolity now and then.

You are right. Let's observe the flawed species from this viewpoint,' I suggested humorously.

And we did. And quite a specimen of society I found there – different.

CHAPTER SIX

I was at my typewriter – yes, I had acquired one of these contraptions – and was about to embark on one of my careers, as a writer (and educator at the same time). Actually, I mused, these are two different lines but one must follow on from the other, surely, as happens when some great seer (code for 'expert') puts down in writing his thoughts and conclusions for propagation.

I initially thought I'd record my techniques of how I educated Johnny Trimble, et al. Maybe this could be of use to the authorities, or to more searching schools of thought on the subject. Then I thought that this might be a dead end, given the weight of opposition I'd copped.

Hmm, well let's start with a record of my discoveries; one thing at a time. Maybe there were really like-minded people around to help my budding evangelism. Let's make this a game of accurate recording and dissemination of this material, both separate actions.

The first stumbling block was that typewriting is slow. Grandpa bought me a book of instruction on how it was done, without one finger at a time.

So, about one month later after much arduous practice I was up to an acceptable speed, now above handwriting speed. In fact I reckon I was approaching fifty words a minute. I was going through ribbons at a rate of knots. I could now concentrate more on my thoughts and not the typewriting.

Out it flowed like molasses from a barrel. In a few further weeks I had what I thought was a publishable edition or manuscript of 'From Dunce to Diploma – a treatise on how to learn and enjoy it.'

I showed it to Grandpa, who commented, 'I am marvelling at the simple erudition of the thing and the amazing solution before my eyes. I am resolving to resurrect my own failed subjects, such as Mechanics.

'Did you enjoy writing that Brandon?'

'Do you know what, I got a great buzz, like I'd never got from Composition at school, and I confirmed to myself that I do want to be a writer – fact OR fiction,' I enthused. 'In fact, just as a side-line I'm going to write a fictional story. I've even decided the rough idea of it – to do with a sporting hero, from rags to riches sort of thing.'

'In that case I am appointing myself your editor and publisher,' said Grandpa.

'Done!' I exclaimed. 'You can have ten percent.'

'Better turn out some good stuff or it'll be ten percent of nothing,' said Grandpa grinning into his cuppa.

'OK editor, look this over and edit it if you can. I doubt you'll have to change a comma. Then, oh publisher, get me an audience.'

I was full of myself and this camaraderie. Nothing succeeds like making a useful contribution or creating something worthwhile. I could get off on this. I was already.

So, the two of us mulled over what to do with this learned tome and decided we needed more experiments, that is, successful cases. This led into discussion about setting up a school, starting loosely with more kids from my now ex-school.

In next to no time we did just that, mostly extra curricula as far as the kids from my old school were concerned. Within six months we had fifteen cases, fourteen of whom were raving successes, the other being an outright antisocial specimen, who soon was the subject of an addendum to my text, along the lines of 'the unteachable class'.

That was another subject; something in the area of the budding subject of Psychology.

'I'll get into that later,' I pronounced to my editor and publisher.

Of course it hadn't escaped the notice of the Headmaster at my school that certain miraculous grades were being achieved in certain grades. Of course Mrs G and others couldn't resist bringing it up at PTA meetings. They played it as a game, making it sound like a mysterious thing, and who in the school was responsible for this?

Squirm they did, and assign the wrong cause of course, until Mrs G deflated their bombastic egos with a 'shame on you' blast. She invited them to interview the kids and their parents, to find out the truth themselves. Did they? Not on your Nelly.

I expanded my text to include Addendum Number Two – 'how Education changes personality for the better, and increases IQ.'

The truth was that all of the kids in the project were alive for learning and new life experiences. Non-communicative or introverted ones were now more outgoing and confident. I could see that it wasn't a cure-all but definitely a boon to the gateway to real life.

Kids were changing their mind about what they thought they could now achieve because they could actually learn. Add to this ability an aptitude at a given skill, such as Art or Sport or Mechanics, then new horizons were opened, not just for the really talented.

Me and mentor now set about the next chapter of our venture. 'Before we go to the publishers let's set up a Private School for Remedial Learning,' Grandpa announced. 'Let's get some actual premises. We'll invite some authorities from the Department or Local Government and the newspapers to come along and witness the whole thing. We need believable allies. The fact that all this emanated from a mere school student will be all the more amazing. You can see the headlines now –'Child Genius Revolutionises Education' or 'Child Prodigy Solves the Riddle of School Dunces'.

We carried on for another ten minutes bouncing around other more and more humorous headlines –' School Closed Down by PTA' and 'Headmaster Retires from Humiliation' and 'Expelled Student Takes over the School', and more.

Grandpa felt entirely revitalised now that he had something meaty to sink his teeth into. 'I can't imagine what I'd been doing with my time before all this,' he was telling me. 'I even get up out of bed earlier now and hardly stop for breaks. What are you doing to me Brandon?'

As for me, well I was a man possessed and I spent most of my time going around to all the parents at the school gathering subjects to enrol. I wrote up curricula for the various bands of abilities so that we could hit the ground running. I got the indomitably-spirited Ira Gibson to really join the project, full time.

Grandpa searched out premises and looked into finance. As far as he was concerned, we needed a largish room and a few smaller rooms within an office area, with desks and chairs and a blackboard, dictionaries, some paper and pens and of course a phone, and sod all else; oh yes, and a teapot and cups. This was at first an extracurricular activity which was going to morph into a proper fulltime day academy.

The matter of finance was solved partly from donations made by the students' parents and partly from the deep but not endless pocket of Grandpa and his own son and daughter-in-law, now contrite that they'd dropped the ball and needed to make up.

As regards legalities, I'd get into that later. Could it be illegal to set up a private Education establishment?

Grandpa visited the local government offices and invited the Education reps to come to the grand opening of the school. I also threw out an inviting bait to the local newspapermen to cover what I termed an opportunity to witness a miracle.

I was talking to Ira. 'Just for fun let's invite the Head of my old school to come along. We'll give him the opportunity to bask in some glory he's enjoying for his school's improving standards, though he's not done anything to merit this. Maybe he'll send some more sluggards to this project.

'What was that story about flying pigs?'

We invited all local dignitaries, including councillors, police chiefs, all teachers in the area, the Press from far and wide, and the parents we knew from the school.

A surprising number of parents turned up, some local press, one or two councillors, and even the Chief of Police, but hardly any teachers and certainly not the Head and Deputy of the school.

'Bit of a mediocre turnout,' Ira remarked later on. 'One journalist printed a nice spread in his paper with an accent on 'Bright Youth Sparks Education Boost for Slow Learners' as the headline. It was on page Five - not the most prominent.'

We big three did an analysis of the event and decided that in order for any notice to be taken of the matter it would need to be more controversial, and condemnatory of the authorities.

'Let's write an article for the local newspaper editors to print,' I suggested, 'or maybe even get the relevant journalists to come and interview the three of us and print what they are given.' We decided on the latter course of action.

Mrs G was particularly keen to lay on as much embarrassment for the authorities as possible, hence she was elected the spokesperson for this.

In the next week a Jim Naylor from the Hampstead Gazette turned up at our rooms by appointment and Mrs G rolled up her metaphoric sleeves and related the sorry tale from beginning to now. As she'd been advised by Grandpa, she told the story as dispassionately as she could, bottling her outrage as best she could, this itself being a work in progress.

I sat there in our small space, amused. 'We are interested parties here,' she told Jim Naylor. 'I had a child at the local school and I wanted him to be educated… There are at least a dozen other cases like this. We are ostensibly running an alternative school here now, not to be competitive or reactionary, but to simply ensure our kids don't end up in a nowhere in this society.

'The point is Brandon is a gifted chap. He thought originally he could assimilate knowledge simply because he was bright. But he discovered that to a marked degree the so-called duller students could be taught how to learn and avoid the pitfalls that are common for a majority of students.

' The proof is my boy Nigel, and Johnny Trimble, who do attend school a few days a week, are near the top of the class and actually enjoy learning. Brandon is like a mechanic who finds out why they 'won't start' and fixes it. It's not a big variety of reasons; a few major ones, common to all.

'Wouldn't you think the authorities would be interested in how all this was achieved? Not a bit of it. They are simply bumbling along as of old and won't be shown by a mere teenager that they can succeed. There's an educational revolution going on here.'

Jim Naylor was taking all this in and thinking how he could pitch this as an article.

Mrs G was enjoying herself. 'Do you know that the truancy people came to Brandon's house and were given such a lecture by Mr Waterman senior here that they went away with their tails between their legs and haven't been heard of again.

'Do you know that if they came to my door I would threaten to sue them for misrepresentation and violation of the Trades Description Act.'

'I suggest you read the Booklet that Brandon has written on the technical side of Education. Here, I'll give you a copy.' She produced one from the shelf in the corner. 'Do you know he sent this to the Department of Education? Heard nothing; not even an acknowledgement.

'What do think of all this Mr Naylor?' she asked.

'There's a story here for sure', he answered. Jim Naylor was not exactly a

Fleet Street shark, but in his way he knew a story when he saw one. He was a bit entranced by the formidable Ira G.

'What would be your story here exactly?' she asked.
'Well, .. um ..I haven't exactly formed it yet. I could go for the big controversy, like 'Boy surpasses teachers' or 'Pupil solves problems of school dunces. Wha…'

Mrs G cut him off just short of abruptly. 'Sir, that's fine but look at the big import of this. Far be it for me to write your copy for you but we want the Department, (otherwise known as the Establishment) to wriggle and squirm or even some other less savoury bodily reaction. We citizens are being ripped off here! I can't send my kid to the average local school and get an education or a start in life.' Jim could only listen.

'Do you have kids? she asked pointedly. .

'Ah, yes, two – seven and twelve.'

'Are they making it, by which I mean can they read at their age-level, spell every word they can speak, do mental arithmetic without using their fingers and toes? Are they hungry for learning? Are they learning stuff they are interested in?'

'I'm not sure. Do you know, I should look at that.'

'Bring them in here to Brandon for an assessment. I promise, you will be dumbfounded,' she enthused. 'How about tomorrow after school? Can we accommodate that Brandon,' she asked over her shoulder? How could I not nod?

'Why not?' Jim agreed. 'Say, four-thirty?'

'You are on.' she said challengingly.

I then chipped in, 'Come yourself as you will be able to witness this and I can explain what I am doing as we go along. It will be very relaxed and lots of fun – not an exam like at school.'

Jim Naylor, the great white hope from the Hampstead Gazette, and his twelve year old son, did show up as appointed and I got down to it with a few jokes, a bit of life history – a warm-up, to relax the lad.

His name was Neville, a rather sporty, well stacked, extrovert sort of lad. I had him read, spell and do standard grammar to get the general picture. Neville got a bit uneasy because he wasn't really that bright and immediately felt he was on the spot and acutely aware of his 'dumbness'.

I tried to relax him further and cited the examples of the other boys I'd mentored. To demonstrate to Jim, the father, I questioned Nev (as he was known) as to his interests and goals. Most of it was sport stuff, but he did have an interest in Geography too. As to the more academic subjects he couldn't see the point. So I demonstrated my favourite party piece which was to make it really real that if you fail at something and go dull you haven't understood it and more and more failures stack up and push you away from it all. But also that lack of interest could also be just that. Who cares about History or Maths, beyond the basics?

'Tell me Nev, is there any point in being able to spell and read and write down things? Just suppose you could read and understand any book, write good stories or reports in good English. Would that make life easier? Whatever you end up choosing to learn or have as a career, if being able to learn was no problem would it be of any use?'

Neville gave it a minute and then replied, 'I suppose so. I can't really understand all the sport stories sometimes, and there are too many big words in Geography. I don't understand all the News programs. Some girls think I'm a bit thick because I'm slow on the uptake.'

'But is it a pain to just sit there and try and understand what's written down or said?' I asked.

'School is a big turn-off for me because I don't get it. I think I'm just a bit of a dunce. I'll stick to sport I think.'

'Would you like to change it?'

'Well, I suppose so, but …' He blew out some air looking at what seemed a daunting task.

'If you do it would take a lot of work but it would bring big rewards in a bit of time because we wouldn't be adding to all the past; rather rubbing it out. You aren't dumb. You have become a bit that way from neglect. But if you are fired up to become bright, just like these other lads, that will carry you through.

'Anything you want to do takes some learning. My idea is that you tackle your ability to learn so you can do more things. And we CAN teach you here so you don't fall down and then can't get up. It's up to you. Personally I see you as quite a lively person, and brighter than you think. You have potential.'

Nev was now thinking.

'What do you really need to know to get by in life? Take Maths for instance. What would you need to know to manage any situation you come across in day to day life?'

Neville said, 'it would be handy to count, add and subtract easily, do percentages and that's about it. I don't need all that xyz stuff.'

'Ok. So if you could do those things quickly and easily, so you didn't get cheated, or whatever, that would do. I agree. But I would be willing to bet that if your arithmetic was good you might even become interested in other aspects of the subject.

'I personally have no interest in or use for Algebra. So I slept in those classes. But I did become interested in Geometry, just for fun. You know, shapes, distances, angles and so on. But I don't really need that stuff, though it IS general knowledge. But that's me. So what might interest you or should you really know?'

'Let's see, ah, Motor Mechanics and all about the body. What's that called?' Nev answered.

'It's called Physiology. So you've come up with a few subjects. Physiology would help in fitness and sport. Would you like to become a Physiotherapist, or a Mechanic?'

Maybe so. I'd like to be able to mend my car when I get one eventually.' He turned and smiled at his father.

I thought it was time to wrap this up. 'Look Nev, if you want to become someone and get places in life, knowledge is power. It's better to be bright, not dull. But to go to school and university doesn't seem to me to be the answer unless they can teach you properly. That's why we have this little school here. It's a remedy for bad education, which is all that's happened to you.'

I then turned to Jim and asked him had he seen anything of value in this meeting. Jim was impressed and wanted his son to get going on the program.

I reiterated to father and son, 'in schools and universities there is no real way to learn, there's no subject which teaches how to learn. That's where we start. If you want to be a carpenter then you learn HOW to 'carpent'. It's a subject. There are rules and skills; same with learning. How come so many people and kids are failing or are limited because they aren't really able to study, including the so-called big brainstorms; the guys with the high IQ's, the clever clogs? I give you my results here to show I know what I am talking about.

'I know I'm only a 'kid'. Well, so what? Maybe I'm brighter than most, but look at my students. They are really becoming bright, and can DO things. We aren't concerned with just stuffing your head with facts. No good learning Mechanics unless you play with engines while you learn, and THEN become a mechanic.

I could feel I was gaining the persona of an executive – that calm but radiant decisiveness that brooked no real argument and also got attention. On this subject at least I am a man to be listened to – not a boast, just a fact.

And 'man' was the operative word.

The 'child' I was addressing was looking up to me as if I was the real expert, which was of course what I am, though not enough 'experts' knew this.

So now I had another candidate, another potential 'genius'. And he was the son of the local journalist. Could this get us a bit further off the ground I wondered?

We were having a 'Board Meeting'. 'I need to clone myself. One-on-one will never get us there. Better still, let's invent a new classroom setup, where the students don't get lost. I'll work on that right away.

'We need to establish the school as a proper College.'

'There goes my other life outside of this,' Mrs G announced. 'Actually it already has gone now that I look at it.'

'Retirement is yesterday's game,' Grandpa added.

'All agreed then. Show of hands please.' I got wide grins instead. 'Grandpa, you are the Administration geek; the General Manager. Ira, you are the technical enforcer and the PR exponent. I am, well, The Founder, the Techniques geezer, and, like it or not, the Big Boss, to be obeyed without question. That ends our first Board meeting. Tea anyone?'

Grandpa and Mrs G looked at each other and then bowed irreverently.

In fact we all mucked in and crossed 'departments' Of course, I was not just the 'MD', but in charge of the techniques and their teaching. I was the main educator.

My vision was to make this all a legal entity, hopefully with Department of Education sanction. Then we could have a network of colleges and 'infiltrate' the system of schools, both private and public, with the end product of reforming the whole learning process. I was on a winner; it works. How could it possibly fail?

Little did I know that this would all lead into the next subject that contained a dearth of knowledge, but was it even more a genuine vested interest than Education?

But I was looking ahead, fired by our successes and my total desire to do something really meaningful in the flawed society I was seeing around me. Only a matter of months ago I was lazing along like all the others.

It's amazing what a purpose does for you; a true purpose. There's a philosophical point. How many people have few, or no, or watered-down goals in life? If you could kindle, or rekindle this, all by itself, wow, what a winner. Well, Education is one way. It's a start, but I suspect there is more to it than that; a lot more.

Driven by lots of thoughtful planning and a total desire to win the game I'd created, me and my team pressed on with expanding – at first, a new branch in Hampstead, not too far from the Finchley Head Office, as it was now called. Another branch in Hendon followed, then Maida Vale. North London was becoming our patch.

Just for fun I decided to give working class Tottenham a go, an adventure I expected to find a different kettle of fish. Probably only fifty percent of prospective candidates would turn out to be suitable. I was learning that anvils wore out hammers, meaning expending proportionately more time on less qualified kids who would wear out the educators would be largely unproductive. So the qualifying standard would have to be raised.

The subject of what happens to the lower end citizens and their problems I ear-marked for another subject, further up the line. It wasn't all about IQ.

Anyhow, Tottenham would get underway under the prospective tutelage of an ex-school teacher who was inspired by the opportunity to make a real difference to the subject of Education. He had to be put through the learning process and have total confidence in the methods being used, like everyone else.

It was becoming a juggernaut and was gaining free advertising by word of mouth. The only advertising that had to be done was for staff. Disenchanted and hence more free-thinking teachers came out of the woodwork; not only teachers but school leavers and career seekers in universities.

I had become a popular speaker at meetings of PTA's and campuses. Radio programs were inviting me to talk of our project and its methods.

CHAPTER SEVEN

The next year was full of development and I was another year older, which, in my case, meant significant physical filling out; a bit more qualification in becoming an adult, in the eyes of the world.

Perhaps it was going too swimmingly. There had been no real barriers to our expansion … until the visit of the Deputy Executive for Educational Standards.

A Mr Peter Simmonds rolled into the Head Office and asked very brusquely to see the Manager. I was the only person in the office at the time. I was not 'above' being a little intimidated by authority, and this chap seemed to exude intimidation.

The Secretary at the desk had hardly time enough to announce him when he more or less brushed her aside and strode into my 'office' (the room I was occupying at that moment) and curtly announced himself without a smile or a how-do-you-do.

Simmonds was a stoutish middle-aged man under a detective-type coat and carried a sizable brief case which he slammed down on a desk. 'Who is in charge of this establishment' he more or less demanded?

I was a bit taken aback to begin with and somewhat laboured my reply. 'Well there are three of us who operate our colleges – partners you might say'.

'Who are you?' he asked. 'You surely aren't one of the three are you? I want to see someone of authority here.'

I collected myself a little and told Simmonds, 'as a matter of fact I am one of the three. May I ask who you are, and what this is about?'

'And what qualifies you to be one of the three? Is this a kindergarten?'

I somehow stuck to my guns and insisted, 'I would like to know who YOU are sir, and what the purpose of your visit is'.

Simmonds kept up his attempts to unnerve me. 'How old are you son? What sort of a place is this that has a mere teenager, probably a school truant, in charge?'

I persisted. This was an interesting exercise here and yet another attempt by an adult to assert his age and self-importance and not much else over an obviously 'immature youth', shades of the HM and his Deputy, and the truant people I'd heard of. I could just put him off and get him to come back and speak to Mrs G or Grandpa. Somewhere along the way I'm going to have to learn to deal with these situations, so why not now?

I summoned up my best posture and mouthful of courage and gave it to him. 'Sir, I don't know who you are. You have tried to put me in my place and here we are talking about nothing that is a way through whatever your purpose is. Can we start again? I may be young but don't be fooled by that.'

'I'm not going to be talked to like that. I'm from the Department of Education and I want to talk to someone else other than you.'

'Up to you,' I said rather diffidently. 'I suggest you call us at another time and arrange an appointment to speak to us all. That way you will get the whole picture.' I rather suspected he had whatever picture he wanted already.

Simmonds stormed out muttering 'how-dare-yous' into his beard and strode off down the street under a cloud. I was somewhat surprised that I'd got up the temerity to stand up to this chap. I wondered what storm he was going to rain on us now.

But, I thought, that was just the point; this chap could only deal in stirring people up and trying to introvert them. I'd noticed that this resulted in more cowardliness than actual threat when stood up to; and I had stood up to him without getting angry. I did shake a bit for a while and then the elation set in.

———————————

Later that afternoon Mrs G and Grandpa arrived at the office and I enjoyed playing with them a bit when relating the event that day. 'This man from the Department of Education, not sure of his exact title, bounded in and demanded to see someone in charge. When I said there were three of us he promptly left in a huff. I can't for the life of me work out why he did that,' I said with a barely discernible smirk on my face.

Grandpa and Mrs G looked at each other quizzically and then slowly rounded on me. Mrs G played the game – 'I wonder what happened between the lines,' she said with her hand on her chin and looking for the answer in the distance. 'I guess he was really scared of our teenage mouse-of-a-director over here.'

'Well I did have a bit of fun with him, but I was very polite.'

'Ok, this is what happened, chapter and verse.' I then gave them the straight dope. They were grinning from start to finish. I did give it to them straight but with just a tad of added drama.

It was Grandpa's turn. 'You scallywag of a director. Anyone would think you had some sort of vested interest in this place. I can see the conversation Simmonds will be having with his colleagues back at his Department. Well handled Brandon. Mrs G and I will plan to be out when next he calls, won't we Ira?' He went on.

'No, I think we will pretend to be Brandon's underlings. He's the Founder of all this after all. We can tell him we are junior directors and all major decisions come from our Senior Director, Mr. Brandon Waterman who is the Founder, Technical Director, Head Teacher, Disciplinarian and, just for fun, Public Relations Director. Brandon you can saunter in from the back office and pretend to be our senior and wonder what is going on. Invite him into your office, offer him tea and biscuits, and encourage him to spill the beans. We'll be listening outside and trying not to laugh. You can make it up from there.'

Grandpa continued, 'My guess is he'll go official and write a pompous letter, re-iterating the illegality of a teenage truant being in charge of an educational establishment, and summoning us to appear before Her Majesty at x time, and that we have seven days to comply,' continued Grandpa.

'We'll write back and tell him we will consider attending his summons if he and all his Department heads study our booklet laying out our history, purpose and statistical results and testimonials.'

I joined in. 'He's a stopper. I doubt he'll even be back.'

Grandpa brought this to a close. 'Enough. Let's go home and fill our heads with our future successes, not today's stir-ups.'

With that Grandpa donned his hat, Mrs G flung her coat over her shoulders and I gathered my paperwork and we all skipped out of the office and turned off the lights and went on our way. 'Let's go and find a café and have us a good meal Brandon,' Grandpa invited after seeing Mrs G onto her bus.

I would rather have gone home and attended to my paperwork but couldn't burst Grandpa's bubble.

We found a restaurant and sat down and ordered a meal and started chatting.

'I was just thinking Grandpa, I've become very interested, as you know, in the science of people, for want of a better expression. I think they call it Psychology, though this sounds like a vague and esoteric term – 'the study of the psyche, or soul. In simple terms it seems to boil down to "what makes people tick."

'I've seen how Education can make people tick better and make them add life to their existence, but there's more to it than this. We can't get down below a certain level or type of person with Education alone.

'You take that chap Simmonds who came in today. I doubt we could turn him around with Education.

'Take the trial pupils we couldn't motivate to learn. They seem to be a lost cause; some wild and out of control and somewhat malevolent, others just dull and stupid but not directly harmful, just drifting along.'

'Either way, taken as a whole they drag the rest of us down and take a lot of watching.'

Grandpa stopped me a minute as we ordered. 'Have you tried this new fried chicken thing here?' pointing to the menu. I signalled a 'go ahead', still in my monologue train.

'There are a lot of people like my parents who are law abiding and somewhat productive, but dependent on society being a bit padded to keep the ship bearable – a tenuous existence.

'Then there is another band that are reasonably 'get up and go' and are a definite asset to us all, and at the top are the thinkers, the creators who run activities – the business people, the leaders, the artists, the adventurers. Not all of them are running on full steam, like you weren't before we got going on all this.

'But look at the apparently really able strata who run our governments and decide international affairs. A majority of them I think have absorbed a lot of education and have high IQ's. We laud them for their cleverness and apparent superiority. But they don't really seem to deal with the myriad of dangerously unsatisfactory situations which exist in the world - basically war, famine, mental illness, depressions, population increase and so on. And, blow me down, Education.'

Grandpa was sipping his tea. I was too busy expounding.

'So you could argue that we don't really have a functioning intelligentsia. We are here on Earth, and though developing in Science and Technology, we aren't exactly a thriving planet. There are rich and poor, the former apparently thriving, with all of the rest of us, the majority, struggling in our masses.'

Grandpa had been listening carefully to all this and asked, 'what is missing do you surmise?'

I continued. 'Well we have Religion, which is basically a set of principles to live by; in essence a social code of behaviour that the majority agree to and live by, thank God. And it is, paradoxically, a belief and trust that a higher authority than man, a superior being, has a plan for us and will save us from ourselves if we offer ourselves into his hands. This I can't see is logical. It's a bit passing the buck, wishful thinking, putting our remedies into this God's hands. At best it's a maybe and at worst it could be viewed as one big brain washing operation.

'But the jury is still a bit out on that although it has been going along for a long time, from stone idols in primitive societies to a god for this and that in Egyptian and Greek times, to medicine men who were the 'oracles' in tribal life in America and African jungles. It goes right up to our modern religions which seemed to have had a war-like history and don't agree who the true God is.'

'Some people find real inspiration and comfort from their faith,' Grandpa offered. 'Some claim to have had epiphanies or real spiritual uplift and have become better people as a result of having 'found God'. How would you explain that?'

'I don't know', I replied. I thought for a moment. 'You know how people can be hypnotised and become what is suggested by the hypnotist? Maybe it's that. Anyway, as I said, the jury is still out on that. I've become a bit cynical haven't I? I must not let that cloud my judgement,' I said, smiling.

Our meal arrived, all in colourful boxes, and we started in on it.

'Well what is it then that will remedy all this? What are we missing?' Grandpa prompted. 'I am beginning to be both fascinated yet depressed here.'

'OK, I'll try and lift you out of your depression. To answer your question, I don't know really. Man's soul, or his mind is at the heart of this. It is faulty.

'This subject called Psychology seems to be in its infancy but is on the right track. I haven't studied it in detail. But I will. If we said that man could conquer his faulty mind like the scientific subjects seem to be conquering the physical world we'd have the answer. How do you study the soul or the mind? What are these things? I've read that the brain may be the thinking apparatus. I guess it is a lot easier to study than a more nebulous mind or soul. Or is it?

'Maybe it's a very simple answer, like so simple it is staring us in the face.'

We finished our 'meal' and paid up. The restaurant was now closing. We strolled along the High Street towards home. 'That chicken was tasty, eh? Fried in Kentucky? How come it wasn't cold?' We had a good laugh.

I yawned widely. 'I'm not tired but I'm yawning, a bit like what happens to our students when they blank out. Yes, there's so much I don't understand. Anyhow, right now is the time to do something different – I'm going for a run and I'm not going to think, I'm just going to look at what's around me and then I think I'll have a good soak in the bath, read my novel (all about a war escapee), and then hit the sack. What about you Grandpa?'

'I've had enough for today. I'm all in. My energy has been sapped by a long day, though I must say I'm PLEASANTLY weary. It was a good day.'

We arrived at the front gate and strode up the steps and 'hit the house', as they say in America.

———————

Whilst we waited for 'the Department' to do its worst I started following up my conversation with Grandpa the other night, amid my normal college duties. If only there was one central bank of all information to go to, I thought. Someone ought to invent such a thing, 'it' being some sort of electronic device that you could ask questions of, and get all sorts of info from.

Short of that I raided the library and after enquiring of the Librarian and after being directed to a little niche at the back of the library, I pulled out the most simple tomes on Psychology and Psychiatry. These were not actually simple. I had hoped for something less 'learned'. Physics and Chemistry were a breeze compared to this lot.

Vaguely hopeful, I thought that maybe the problem had already been solved and all I would have to do is read up on it and use it. Hmm… it doesn't seem to have spread into society's broad scheme yet, at least results-wise. No fanfare yet.

I eased into the subject by starting with Freud. This man had developed a theory and some practice called Psychoanalysis. The bones of this seemed to be, in amongst a lot of padding and new words, that traumatic experiences become repressed, residing in 'the unconscious', later to exhibit their content in errant behaviour, as if hypnotised.

This is not a bad theory, thought I, perking up. The solution to eradicating these repressions is to talk about them. Talk! I like it.

I had noticed that what I was doing with my students was just that, largely. They felt better to 'let it all out' and could then be led into examining their conclusions and thoughts, and then with guidance re-appraise things.

I read on without much more enlightenment. Other books rambled on about the brain and the nervous system. Apparently all thinking and behaviour had a lot to do with the brain. People do talk about the brain as this piece of machinery that IS the mental hub of existence.. Hmm….

One section went on about there being biological and genetic factors accounting for some thirty percent of individual differences in behaviour, political attitudes and ideology. Genetics I thought? How does that work? Hmm.

Then there came the brain theory. The cerebrum plays a major role in thinking. The thalamus is a relay station that passes information to higher brain centres. The hypothalamus takes care of autonomic functions.

Then there is the midbrain which deals with vision and hearing, movement control, regulation of sleep, arousal and wakefulness.

In the hindbrain there is the cerebral cortex which is divided into four lobes.

The front lobes deal with higher thought processes, such as abstract reasoning and motor processing.

And so it went on. I was looking at diagrams of the brain and its parts all in pretty colours, much the same as in an atlas. Even so I was suffering physiologically from lack of explanation of how this all actually worked. (I noted this reaction as a phenomenon of study). Well, it was all a chemical action and a high function of the nervous system, basically. But how? Where were the experiments and proofs and how did all this lead to a handling for neurosis, psychosis or indeed any variety of behaviours? Lots of theories/opinions.

I wondered how they had come to these conclusions. It might be more helpful if I talk to a few of these brain experts.

I left it at that for the day and went back to the college. Grandpa was there. 'Where have you been, my man? All hell has let loose here – the ' helpful' Mr Simmonds arrived with some cavalry in the form of 'suits' and 'briefcases'.

He went on: 'It took all my genius to keep them in check. They wanted to close us down on the spot.

'I tore into them, along with Ira. We practically tipped them out on to the pavement, scowling as they went.'

I asked, 'how did you leave it? Just like that?'

'Somewhat, but I repeated that they must meet with us politely and with you there too. I advised them to gather a less hostile, more reasonable approach and make an appointment (not a raid), and then we'll talk.'

'OK, round three coming up then,' I mused.

'Anyway,' I grinned, 'I've been down at the library, that community centre of learning, to embark on my next project of discovery – human behaviour. Seems like we just had an interesting cameo of this, right here.'

'Oh my God, you're not kidding are you?' Grandpa put in, rolling his eyes mockingly. 'Are we now to set up a school of Psychology?'

I asked him, 'do you know any Psychologists? I want to see what they know.'

'Well', answered Grandpa, 'so happens I do. Well, I know ONE. He has a clinic down near the hospital. He calls himself a Clinical Psychologist but doesn't delve into real 'Mental Illness'.

'I want to speak with him. If you could tell him I'm into Educational Psychology, which I suppose I am really, and that I want to know more about the subject in order to enhance my field. Maybe we could be of use to each other. Don't tell him I'm a teenager; I'll handle that bit; don't want to put him off before I get there.'

With that I went into my office and decided on my strategy with this man. Then I wrote a few letters and returned a few phone calls and moseyed on home, thinking of brains. I thought to myself as I did this thinking, am I using my brain to do this? If so, what a contraption; a physical organ that thinks? Why don't sheep or cattle brains do this? The mind boggles, or should I say 'the brain boggles?'

In short order the College received a phone call from the Department of Education guys, wanting to arrange a visit to discuss things. All Execs would need to be present.

Mrs G took the call and very patronisingly told them, 'certainly gentlemen, we'd be very honoured to meet and hear what you have to say.'

The meeting was set up for the first Friday of the month at three p.m. by which time the students would be into their last lesson period and about to pack up and leave for the weekend. This was Friday week. The Big Three – Me, Grandpa and Ira – decided to have a strategy meeting at the close of play.

The strategy meeting got underway. Mrs G snarled playfully, 'we'll eat 'em up.'

'Yes we could,' said Grandpa, 'but we want to win this thing. Let's not get their backs up from the outset. We'll munch them stealthily, eh?' directing this to Mrs G.

'A bit of diplomacy then?' I asked, but looking at Ira. 'It seems to me they came here all pompous and authoritarian, bent on closing us down on the spot. I guess it's all my fault for being a 'kid'.

'So what is their case?' asked Grandpa. Answering his own question he went on, 'we didn't get any sanction in the first place, we don't have any recognised educators, we took kids out of the school system somewhat, we incited rebellion at the PTA (sort of). What terrible citizens we are. We are somewhat remiss on all scores, even though we are justified.'

'Eggshells then. It is going to be diplomacy,' I re-iterated. 'But there is too much vitriol behind this, witness the heavy-handed attack we experienced. Someone is behind this, with connections in the Department, perhaps. One guess who this might be…'

Mrs G piped up, 'There's a PTA meeting on Monday night and I'm going to raise this with the Head and Deputy. This will be one hell of a conversation. I'll get the straight dope, as far as that slimy toad will let slip his hand. The Head must be there when I do this. I won't do this openly in front of the others, but I'll get them aside in a separate space. How about you come too Sidney?'

Sidney nodded a somewhat reticent agreement, like 'if you insist'.

'OK, we'll see what becomes of that and then we'll work out the rest of our strategy,' I said. 'But, basically, we'll hear them out first, see what they intend. If it's immediate closure, that's one thing. If they're in any way up for hearing us out, that's another.'

'In hindsight I guess we could have tried to get sanction as a private college or something, or at least applied, but we were quite incensed and otherwise concentrated at the time, eh?' I added.

'We're not going to pussyfoot around,' protested Ira.

'You're right, we won't' I replied, 'but, to continue the metaphor, there's more than one way to skin a cat. It's going to be soft cop, hard cop type of thing. I read that in one of my novels.'

'That's next Friday then,' added Grandpa. 'In the meantime I thought we'd make our nicely presented graphs more prominent, to illustrate our progress with the students, and spread out the syllabus we use for them. Maybe we could give them a demo of how we assess the newcomers.'

'By the way,' he went on, 'over in Tottenham I've scoped a space for the new College – it's just off the High Street, near Spurs football ground. It's going for a song and the landlord will let us have it for free for three months if we do it up a bit.

'Ads will appear in the next edition of the local paper, and as you know I've got an ex-teacher lined up to run it. He's just our sort. I thought we'd back it up with the PTAs of the local schools, just like we did here in Finchley. It's called poaching. We need another Ira G for this one. You up for some more PTA's Ira?'

I chimed in, 'Well we better be sure we deal with these Department characters before we go too far.'

I left for the library, almost my extra curricula residence, to continue my research on Psychology. My meeting with Grandpa's friendly Psychologist was tomorrow night.

Sat in the reverence of the public library I discovered there were two subjects here – Psychology and Psychiatry, the latter dealing more with mental illness than everyday human behaviour not classified as 'illness'. They interacted a lot however. It seemed that if Psychology techniques didn't help the average punter then one was referred on to a Psychiatrist who had other tools, such as drugs, ECT and brain operations for the more severe cases, all under incarceration, most often.

Both subjects, at least by definition, involved the soul or spirit. What exactly are these terms? I thought a soul was a non-physical entity, a being, apart from the body, and possibly the motivating force behind the life in the organism. What are ghosts if not bodiless spirits? But it is hard to see how a 'no physical thing' could energise and animate a body. Was this more plausible than the brain theory?

The mind seemed to be the soul or the brain or a thinking device – a bit confusing. So we have a body which has a brain and a nervous system on it. And we have a soul or something which uses this brain or mind to compute, or hold repressions if it goes wrong? Difficult to wrap one's wits around.

What is this process? I wonder how they determined that the brain does mental processes. And if they are treating mental illness with drugs and electricity and surgery, that leaves out the soul, doesn't it? Maybe they don't really have a clear idea of a soul or it doesn't matter.

Well, I had lots of questions for the Psychologist.

While sitting intent on what I was reading, a voice had permeated my space, a female voice. She coughed. 'You look like you are in the middle of a vast conundrum. Do you mind me asking what you are working on?' She had been sitting opposite me for a few minutes and had been obviously observing my concentrated attention.

I snapped out of my own little world and looked up at an extremely sparkling young lady opposite. I was momentarily more captivated by her aesthetic aura than what she was asking.

Having been drawn in now I responded rather flippantly with, 'ah, I'm trying to solve the age-old philosophical dilemmas of the current and past intelligentsia so that we will all be saved from ourselves.'

This actually ravishing specimen of womanhood replied, 'is that all? I thought it must be something serious.' We both laughed.

I went on, 'actually I have been educating myself on the thorny subjects of Psychology and Psychiatry, if you really want to know. I'm an Educator and want to know if these subjects have anything of use for me.'

'Well do they, have you decided?' she asked hinting at some knowledge of her own on the subject.

I smiled and said, again somewhat jocularly, 'too much for the brain. It seems that Mr Freud had a few useful additions to our knowledge but it all went downhill from there at a rate of knots. Put it this way, if you were to go psychotic I would come quickly to your rescue and save you from the clutches of the brain boys.'

'All very serious. But thanks for offering to save my life. When I go nuts I'll call on you. Speaking of that I don't even know who I should call.' She left that hanging, but not for long as I chimed in and introduced myself.

She responded with a warm handshake and said, 'I'm Julia McDonald. Do you come here a lot?' 'Off and on,' I responded, 'more on of late though. What about you? What brings you here?'

'I'm studying Philosophy,' she replied. 'I'm at the beginning of my quest to sort out the best wisdom I can from a plethora of contributors, talking of which I need to go and meet one of them now. It's been great to meet you. I hope to catch you here some time. I do most of my work here anyway, usually at weekends.'

With that she departed and, having been diverted from the brain theories, I left too, after clearing up my table area. I was now thinking about Philosophy, and the strikingly interesting Julia McDonald.

CHAPTER EIGHT

Sidney took me along to the Psychologist's clinic in Hampstead at the appointed hour. This was in a dual shop front in one of the back lanes behind the main street. It was fairly basic, having a lot of second hand furniture and linoleum flooring and magnolia-coloured walls. The Psychologist was there in Reception to meet us.

Sidney shook his hand and then turned to me. 'Brandon, this is Dr Peter Hillingdon. Peter this is my grandson, Brandon Waterman.' We shook hands.

We moved into an inner room which contained a number of chairs and a couch. With introductions over and a bit of small talk, we got down to it. Sidney had previously genned in Doctor Hillingdon on my position and accomplishments.

Peter Hillingdon was probably in his early forties. He dressed in an open-necked shirt and a buttoned up cardigan and casual trousers.

I proceeded. 'Doctor Hillingdon I've done a lot of work in the subject of Education wherein I noticed, what YOU may call, a psychology to it. I get the student talking about his educational difficulties. I listen and prompt and analyse what the problem is, just like in a Psychology session I would think.

'Then I noticed, as in Freudian analysis, they have repressed traumas on the subject of Education, that is, losses and failures. So they have given up and have quite a lot of emotion on the subject.

'I managed to deal with these with some techniques I developed to help them study – sort of unpicking the mess.

'But that's Education. There are a good proportion of kids in school who can't be educated easily, mainly because of social or psychological problems, or home life.

'And the ones that I've helped are definitely brighter now and more able to cope with life but still have demons of other sorts – like being shy, flying off the handle, or being easily introverted in social situations. You no doubt know the list.

'I've come to you to find out what could be done about these things to get these guys up and running better in life. I guess I'm straying into your field here, and maybe should just quit and be happy with the advances gained in the Education. But I'm very curious. I have a number of questions for you about your subject. I've read up a lot in the library. Some made sense and a LOT didn't.'

'Ok then,' Peter replied. 'I'm listening.'

I continued. 'Does this subject, and its offshoot, Psychiatry, profess to have the answers to mental illness and errant behaviour?'

Dr Hillingdon fielded the question by saying 'that's a big first question. The answer is probably 'no'. It has some understanding and it works on some, relatively. It's a constantly developing subject but it's not a cast iron technique. There are various experts on the subject, each having their own theory. I suppose we know the key to current behaviour and reasoning ability resides in the past but how to release the impediments is not so well known.'

I jumped in here. 'What's confusing me is the brain theory. Most of the books I looked at cited the brain as the source of mental processes and human frailty. How does this work?'

Doctor H was less certain of this area, I soon saw. 'Well it is THOUGHT to be the case, however I'm personally not convinced of this, or that it matters much. But the Psychiatrists, who some of us refer severe cases to, definitely use this as their basic principle. As the brain has many chemical processes (it is argued), 'fiddling' with these by drugs is an attempt to alter behaviour. Then electric shock and lobotomies take it further. But personally, I find all this barbaric and can only lead to a worsening of condition and behaviour.'

I pressed on. 'Did someone PROVE that the brain deals with mental processes and emotions?'

Doctor H replied, 'I don't think so. It's a theory. Whatever else is there to go on?'

'Well what is a mind or a soul then? Are they the same thing?' I asked.

'Gee, you've done some thinking here', answered Doctor H. 'These things are inter-changeable and reside in the brain I suppose.'

I was stunned. 'Then it's all really a theory which has a lot of maybes about it.'

I continued. 'You see, I've heard an awful lot about personality problems, social problems, and, on a world-wide basis, lots of insanity - war, crime, human rights violations, sexual deviance. You know this list. Is it that this subject is so much in its infancy that it hasn't been able to create an effect yet, or is it just not the answer? There are an awful lot of tenuous, unscientific principles here.'

Doctor H saw my point. 'Well we are helping people so we may be on the right track, just like you with your Education. It's developing.' He didn't seem all that convinced himself, even a bit defensive.

At no point did he try to patronise me, I having projected myself adequately enough to command respect now.

I went a bit further now. 'So you yourself are a Psychologist, to help people feel better by analysis, per Freud more or less.'

'More or less,' he agreed. 'There is a wide body written on the subject and an ever-burgeoning number of techniques. I use regression, and free association (basically communication) to help my patients. I don't deal with what you would call 'nut cases'.

'So when someone comes to you for help, how does it go? What's the process?'

Peter H looked over at Sidney, sitting quietly in the corner, who gave him a 'can't help you mate' look plus eye and hand gestures.

'Well let's take an example here, my last patient (no names). He came in a week ago because his parents thought he'd become depressed on account of being bullied at school. He was quite down I must say.

'Well we talked about what went on at school and when it all started and how he felt when it occurred. I decided to put him in a group therapy of like-minded kids, and kids who have been through the mill a bit. It is usually monitored by a colleague or myself, and they start to feel better about things and may come up with suggestions on how to deal with it all.'

I let him go on as he was in full flow by this. 'I might then talk about his earlier childhood or his treatment at home by his parents – they are often the culprits here you know. All this helps us to analyse the causes. That's how it goes.'

I piped up at last 'This mirrors my Education experiences – the longer the failures to learn go on the worse it gets. Failure or losses dampen the spirit.'

'Yes, yes, that's a good way to put it,' agreed Peter H.

I took my opportunity. 'You see, I'm having trouble accepting that any of this has anything to do with the brain or chemistry. We are addressing the person here, whatever that is, but not the meat of the brain. Wouldn't you say that the brain is a physical organ, an important one, like the engine of a motor car, and can only be given the 'privilege' of having mental powers by a large stretch of the imagination and surely some real scientific discovery? It's a theory only and seems a substitute, a scapegoat almost, for actual knowledge.'

Peter H had to admit he couldn't honestly say. He was actually a bit stunned at having his foundations shaken, I noticed.

'I apologise for being a bit forward here. I appreciate your time, sir.

'I'd like to sit in on one of your sessions though. I'm anxious to learn more on the communication skills here.' I joked, 'maybe I should go to University itself and do what you've done. I promise I won't ask you to give me the whole course though.'

'All right,' offered Peter H. 'Come and sit in on the group session next Monday pm.'

'You're on. 'And I invite you to come and see one of my Education analysis sessions, with one of my new students.'

'OK then. You have piqued my interest,' agreed Peter H.

I followed on,.'You can then add 'Educational Psychologist' to your bow.' We laughed.

Sidney and I walked along in the cool night toward our humble abode. Grandpa said, 'you shook him up a bit there. He may not thank me for this.'

I decided something. 'I must go into a typical Psychiatric institution and see what all this brain stuff is. Peter H does what he does, without really talking about brains or addressing them. It doesn't seem to matter.'

'I'd like to get a few animal brains and prop them on a table and play about with them as if they were human brains, there being none of those available to compare. Come to think of it, what's the difference between an animal brain and a human brain, in function? They both seem to send action messages along the nervous system. I just can't see a brain as a motivating force, rather it's a physical servo mechanism: it seems to be what it is, a piece of meat, which, when in a live body performs a lot of physical and chemical processes, all set up genetically, but it doesn't work if the body packs up from disease or accident.

'What's a live body then? I suppose it is one with life in it, obviously. What is 'life' then?'

'Well,' said Grandpa, 'Big question.' He changed the subject. 'I guess you are going to have fun with the Psychiatric hospital. I have a feeling they are not audienced, which may tell you something by itself.'

CHAPTER NINE

I was about to have my sixteenth birthday. To mark the occasion I'd reached six feet tall. People around me were easily seeing me, I'd say, as at least a late teenager. Some of the would-be assailants of the gentler sex, I began to notice, were now turning their heads as I passed. Then if I spoke my ready disarming smile seemed to do the rest, the rest being more attention than I'd been used to.

I began to notice unease in interactions with the more introverted of society while the more confident types responded to me personably.

I was at the cusp of life, well through puberty, all sorts of relationships at my feet – Romance, Writing, Business, Education, Philosophy, and now Psychology. The world was my oyster. Who'd have thought this possible?

My contemporaries were out chasing girls, playing football, going to dances, hanging around the streets in gangs, watching this relatively new innovation, TV, and seeing out their laboured school careers.

Some of course, a decided minority, were really studying and going for a full education and career. Some were destined to become sports stars.

All the family and office staff took me out for a birthday lunch on the day. I had requested a 'fry-up' at my favourite caff.

After the party had toasted my day they all went their separate ways – educators to the left and family to the right.

After an afternoon at the College Grandpa and I went along to Peter Hillingdon's surgery (a bit of a misnomer one might think) and took our places with the group members – two adults and three teenagers.

Basically it was a round-robin mutual opening of hearts which seemed to help them a bit in getting things off their chests.

Peter H asked lots of leading questions and let them answer in turn. What I noticed was that Peter H did not interrupt their dialogue, except to steer away from rambling and excessive repetition. And he made a point of really acknowledging what they said. This seemed therapeutic in itself and very different from what they experienced 'out there'.

I remembered the times I had spoken to Grandpa out on the veranda and was allowed to run down and have my view without criticism and given a really good acknowledgement, followed by prompting questions.

But that seemed to be it. How they would then fare back in the 'lion's den' of daily life was yet to be seen. This group was likely to become a safe haven for the subjects, mainly the teenagers. The adults were there to fortify the youngsters with tales of their similar youth. But one chap was still obviously scarred by his childhood bullying and was having similar 'bullying' from a relentless hen-pecking wife.

Later, over a cup of tea I said to Peter H, 'I learned something about communication skills today. So how about our reciprocal meeting at the College? I have a right challenging candidate for you to observe – educationally stricken this one really is.'

We agreed Thursday morning when Peter H had a gap in his schedule. 'I'll set it up,' I said. 'By the way, how do you suggest I get a look-see into a Psychiatric facility?'

Hmm, that's a tough one,' Peter H offered, 'You know I've never seen myself how they diagnose treatments. Maybe in my capacity as a member in the field, as it were, I could get to see 'a session' and bring you along under the guise of a career aspirant. Leave it to me.'

We two were becoming partners in crime, almost colleagues. That I was really just a youth had ceased to bother Peter H I think.

Sidney thanked Peter and we left.

I went back to the College and did my thing with the students and teaching assistants and had a conference with Ira G. She was getting on with her job of administration, with the cause burning brightly.

Here was a middle-aged housewife who had become incensed with ineptitude and failing Education, and fake experts. Her life up to this point had been rather mundane and half-hearted. She had a solid family life, comprising her husband and three children. But something had erupted in her to have her now being part of a sweeping movement which was giving her guided vent to her spleen. Family-only was not enough. She was a champion of causes, and a veritable business woman.

Peter H, the friendly Psychologist, arrived at the college first thing on Thursday, as agreed. I showed him around the place and then started explaining exactly how we set about assessing a student and determining which ones he could help, or not, as the case may be.

'It's just like in your clinic but these people have study 'traumas' behind them. These consist mainly of being left behind, exam and parental pressures, and feeling 'dumb' and somewhat inferior. In class they are not really there and fall easily into anti-social behaviour, mainly in the form of reactionary behaviour against the school or adult disapproval.

'These kids you see here have been revitalised by resurrecting or newly creating a purpose to learn; one that they can agree with, not an imposed one.

'Then you have to go back and unpick all their missed concepts, right back to the earliest. Then the light shines, their sparkle appears and their IQ goes up.'

I explained the study methods employed.

'Impressive,' Peter acknowledged. 'Show me an example if you would. I'd like to see you in action.'

I got hold of a new kid on the block and started in on him. Peter observed and was immediately noticing my patience but unswerving insistence on getting proper answers to my questions, employing lots of encouragement and validation.

I knew Peter H would be impressed with me not feeding 'the right answers' or telling the students what I thought, but rather letting them self- realise.

'I've taken some of your communication skills here Peter' I added. 'Let them unwind but not ramble. I've found you have to direct their attention consistently.'

'You said you had a 'right case' for me to look at,' Peter said.

'Oh, him; he hasn't turned up, and I don't think he will. It's part of the filtering process – will they turn up again, even with parental support?'

We were about to wrap up when I raised the subject of the Psychiatric Institution visit.

'Yes, I did have a chat with the 'Enrolment Secretary'. He thought it might fly; could I call back next week. He obviously needs authority from higher up'.

That was that. We parted with a hand shake. 'I'll contact you next week. Brandon you're a freak of nature. You've taught me something today,' Peter said. I like people like Peter.

With that he left and I got on with my day and gave some thought to the next, the confrontation with the powers that be. Was my little enterprise going to be shot down in flames or would we rise to better and bigger things? I am going to have to be at my best.

I gathered my team together and went through the likely scenarios and who would say what and when.

CHAPTER TEN

The 'Big Three' were all ready. We would show the 'Department suits' around the College (which had now expanded from four rooms to seven, having taken over another vacant floor).

And there were plenty of graphs and 'progress boards' on the walls, to show off the whole thing. Were we going to pay for our enthusiasm or live to fight another day?

At three pm on the dot a Mr James Hopkins and a Ms Audrey Melvin presented themselves, somewhat more politely than previously. After intros and a little hospitality we sat around a table in the meeting room and got down to it. Various students were lingering, by arrangement, to add credence to the scene.

Sidney 'took the floor' and invited them to present their case. Hopkins started off by saying, 'obviously it has come to our attention that you have started up an Education College here in Finchley, seemingly in opposition to the local school system. The Education Department takes a dim view of private attempts to bypass the school system, especially without any attempt to set up a bona fide private school – more like a rebellion of sorts.'

'There are children here who should be at their local school, getting a perfectly adequate schooling,' he added rather emphatically, with Audrey Melvin nodding in serious agreement.

Mrs G wanted to protest this straight away but I cut her short with hand gestures and 'that look'.

Mr Hopkins carried on rather verbosely and ended up by saying that the Department had in mind to close the College down. But he'd been allowed to wind himself down, hence the 'had in mind', which left a bit of hope I thought; at least an opening.

I chimed in here. 'Well that is what we thought. If I were in your shoes I suppose I might come to that action myself. However, let us give you our side of things Mr Hopkins. I accept this is an alternative establishment, as you say. If we could wind the clock back and do things differently we would of course have come to a course of action more aligned to the proper one. I must admit we became rather evangelical about our project, but not necessarily out of spite to the system. By the way, how did this all come to your attention?'

'Well, it was reported by your school here in Finchley,' Mr Hopkins replied rather hesitantly.

'By whom, exactly?' I asked.

'Well I don't know exactly, do you Audrey?' he replied.

Audrey was a bit startled, then got defensive. 'Does it really matter? The fact is you have an illegal Education establishment here which is taking away students from local schools and the Department can't, in all honesty, sanction it'. Serious lady, I thought.

I wasn't going to have this go in the direction it was going, nor have my carefully 'unwound' Mr Hopkins revert. Speaking to Mr Hopkins again (with Mrs G hardly able to contain herself), I said, 'all right we think we know who reported it, but it wasn't the HM. But, leaving that aside for a moment, we actually do have a very viable thing going on here. Kids who weren't learning are now learning with enjoyment. Let me show you around.

'There are students who I offered the same help to when I was at the school and I demonstrated to the HM a 'case study'. Mrs G here has a son who is part of the program. Tell these good people Ira, exactly what was accomplished with Nigel.'

Ira jumped in and expounded about her 'reborn son' and went on to describe my first 'prototype' who was presented to the PTA as a star example of my plan to help out the school with its recalcitrant and 'dumber' students. She struggled to hold back her venom.

I had to come in here. 'Look there is a problem at the school. It's a nigh-on impossible task to teach thirty-odd kids of varying IQ's, backgrounds and whatever. At least half of them get left behind and end up not wanting to learn. I, having no problem learning, decided that instead of being bored and idle I'd offer to help the teacher, Mr Casey, and the students, and hence the whole school.

'While the HM and the Deputy had decided they had their own scheme to improve things, I got on with more cases in my own time, to build up more credence. We suspected fudging by the two mentioned, and when questioned some months later at a PTA meeting there was no forthcoming program. At that point we embarked on this little project, bit by bit. Success bred success and here we are. We were on a wave, all wrapped up in our utter enthusiasm to continue and expand our success.

'Understand, we were not doing this to spite or revolt. We had drawn a line under the fracas with the school and had merely become rather missionary about the project. Most of the kids here still attend the school, but come here after hours. We have not poached any. A few are from other schools, mainly on the same basis.

'Now that you are here, quite properly to protect the system, I see we were a little carried away and naively ignored the proper registration demands of the Department. We wish to demonstrate to you how we operate and what we have accomplished, as part of our intended application for recognition as a bona fide independent College.

'Incidentally, when the kids are 'up to taws' we send them back to school with an enhanced ability to learn. We simply find out why they can't learn and fix it. You will find that this has all led to a marked improvement in the results, particularly at my old school.'

I think I had scored a few points here with Mr Hopkins. Audrey was stony and quiet but had let me take the floor.

'Let me see your graphs and speak to some of the kids for a bit, and I'd like to see how you fix them, as you say.'

Sidney and I showed him around while Ira took care of Audrey Melvin, by way of sounding out what the exact process would be to gain legitimate standing.

'This is unprecedented,' Audrey had told Ira. 'We just can't have an arbitrary syllabus and a school outside the Department's jurisdiction. I really do think you'll have to close this down and submit an application to the Department.'

Ira had now to exercise something that wasn't in her nature – a bit of diplomacy, a la Brandon. We had drilled this so she bit her lip and replied, 'yes, you obviously came here to do this and as we have said, quite properly. We agree with your premise of having proper jurisdiction. We will comply with your needs. I'd like to ask your help in exactly how we go about this.'

Audrey had then gone into the process and Ira had asked her lots of questions on the process and acknowledged her well for her help. Audrey was good at applying rules and regulations and almost enjoyed all this advice she was giving. She'd become quite a bit lighter.

Ira had played her trump card now. 'Now we have a few full time students here who are officially, I suppose, truants. I think we should send them back to the schools they came from for the moment, until such time we are legal. They can come here part time after school, to get brushed up. I hope a good look at our methods and results will satisfy you that we are not MIS-educating these youths.

'By the way, may I suggest, perhaps as a string to your bow, that you suggest to the appropriate Department that Brandon's old school be looked at by the relevant Inspectorate to find out why these kids are not getting the adequate education they deserve. The school is aware of the problem, as highlighted by our activity and the oft-repeated concerns of the PTA.'

Audrey Melvin was made for the civil service, her safe haven from life in general. She was not at all into ideas and innovation or practicalities, but simply following the rules, hypercritical of anything outside the loop.

'I think we should deal with this matter at hand as the first order of business. I may include some of what you have said in my report,'Audrey had offered.

'Well, that would be proper,' Ira had replied. 'After all this is all about keeping the educational standards of the area in good order, don't you think?'

Audrey didn't say anything, as Ira had quickly gone on to another subject. 'Do you have children yourself Audrey,' she'd asked.

'No,' she'd replied. 'I am single.' Just as I suspected Ira had thought. She also wondered if she was still a virgin. Who would go for the frumpy dress code and the manner to match? What sort of man would he be if she wasn't a virgin?

Ira had said, 'as a parent I worry about my children growing up, having a safe environment, and getting a good start in life, particularly in Education. I became a bit concerned about Nigel, my eldest, a few years ago. He started to lag and was becoming a bit disinterested in life in general. He's now thriving and I want to make sure others get the same. We're not a revolution here. I hope you can help steer us through the application process as soon as possible and we can get on with helping out the school and anyone else who wants educating.'

Before anything else was said, the others came in after their tour.

Sidney was saying to Mr. Hopkins, 'by the way, we had a Psychologist in here yesterday looking at our project from the viewpoint of the therapy side of what we offer. We had visited him too, not from the Psychology side of things exactly (we don't plan on being Psychologists) but to do with his communication techniques. He was interested in the fact that we were brightening up these kids, getting them back into life again and raising their IQ's'.

'That's interesting,' said Hopkins, quite sincerely. 'A bit of interest from the Psychologist. I suppose there is a bit of Psychology, speaking broadly, in Education.'

The denouement was upon us; time to conclude. Hopkins said, 'well I must say you have a pretty impressive thing going on here, even if a bit 'offline'. We'll go back to the Department and report what we've seen. You aren't actively abetting truancy I can see, but…' He left that hanging in the air.

'What happens now? I asked.

'We'll see' replied Hopkins. Audrey had started to walk out slowly, to encourage Hopkins to do the same. When she was out of earshot he continued, 'Between you and me I'll try and do the best for you but you'll have to legitimise this in the eyes of the Department.'

Ira was nearby and told Hopkins she had commandeered Audrey to help her with this process.

We shook hands and Hopkins said, 'I'll be in touch'.

Ira added, 'I think Audrey is bent on doing what you came here to do. Do you have any sway with her?'

'Easier said than done,' said Hopkins with a small grin. 'I'll work on it. I must say I thought as SHE did when I first came here. We were primed to do our worst, and yes, it was the Deputy Head who set all this up. The Head was the 'sheep'.'

He went on. 'Look I have my own kids in a West London school and they have the same problems. My kids are reasonably bright but I can't say they are jumping to learn – they are both sports mad, but homework, no way. It's a battle.'

I seized my chance. 'Here's an offer Mr Hopkins that you can't refuse. Let me do a casual interview on both of them, just as I showed you this afternoon and see if I can't kindle them. I may not be able to but you've got nothing to lose.'

'I may take you up on that,' Hopkins said politely, if not exuberantly. 'You'd have to come over to our place though.'

'Not a problem. Some time when there's no particular sporting activity on, or on a wet day or something,' I suggested.

With that we parted company on the doorstep. We three Execs sat down and discussed the meeting and agreed it had been positive.

Ira was busting to have her say. 'That woman will probably lean on him and try and stop things. However, she seemed to soften a bit after our little talk, and it wasn't the tea. You'd have been proud of me Brandon. I did it just as we drilled it. Then I co-opted her support in filling out and getting our application done. I think I am a fully apprenticed PR person now.' A big grin appeared over each face, as if to say 'we'll see'.

I couldn't resist – 'did you record the meeting Ira?' We all laughed and then I summed it all up. 'Well, we'll persist; full pedal to the metal. We're not stopping now. We'll get our application for legitimacy in ASAP. I'll leave that to you Ira. You and Audrey can become bosom buddies, even though you two are polar opposites. But I'm sure she's now putty in your hands. And Sidney you and I need to get hold of Peter H and see if he's managed to set up a visit to the Psychiatric Hospital. You are coming too aren't you?'

Sidney was a bit bemused as we hadn't really discussed his 'coming too'. 'Well, um, if you want me to; should be interesting.'

I called Peter H. 'Was just going to call you,' Peter said. 'They were a bit hesitant but I persuaded them that here was a chance to advertise their profession as a desirable career option for a budding enthusiast (you) and for increasing the knowledge of one of their closely related professionals, (that is, me).

'You ARE a budding enthusiast aren't you Brandon? Though I'm not sure you ARE enthusiastic about their subject, as far as you have ventured into it thus far.

'Anyway,' he continued, 'after getting over the initial surprise of our unprecedented request, they relented and agreed to a limited guided tour on Friday next, at ten a.m.'

I added, 'I'll bring Sidney along too as a representative of my family, which may add a bit more legitimacy to the proceedings. Where is this place?'
'It's in Kensal Green,' he answered. 'A bit of a schlep but I'll drive you there. I'll pick you up at my place at nine. Dress formally; suit and tie and shiny shoes. We'll make the first effort to gain their respect. I'm looking forward to this myself. Can't say I've ever been in a 'spin bin' before.'

'Maybe you should read my library books and get better set up for it,' I offered. 'Friday at nine at your place then.'

I put the date in my diary and wandered out into the classroom to find Ira G trying to interview a new prospect.

'Brandon,' she called out across the room whilst summoning me over. When I was beside her she went on. 'This is Joe,' indicating the lad beside her. 'He doesn't seem to be interested in learning at all. I don't know why he's here. His father sent him (maybe ordered him) here.'

I somewhat half interestedly said, 'well let's let him go then. He can go his own way and not learn how to know things, not gain a profession, not go anywhere in life or become anything, just like the majority of people out there.' Turning to the lad I asked kindly, 'is that what you want?'

The youth, a little bit younger than me, if at all, spluttered a bit and then muttered, 'I aint bovvered really.' He really was a bit of a scruffbag street kid.

'I don't believe you'. I picked up Ira's notes. This kid had been a petty thief, was a high school dropout in effect, and wasn't doing any work of any kind.

I continued quite gently but penetratingly. 'Tell me if you think I'm wrong

94

here. Your life hasn't been much up to now. Your mum and dad just nag at you and heap lots of disapproval on you. You don't study, don't really work, don't have much to get up for each morning. Your mates aren't much different. The future isn't promising you much. You may be easy prey for gangs, criminality; nowheresville. You're not bothered?' I was trying to be as factual as possible without appearing to be insulting– a hard thing to do when you are pointing out home truths.

When the youth started to squirm and show signs of leaving this 'barrage', as he was no doubt seeing it, I said, 'look, I'm not trying to make you feel bad, just to be straight. It's time to face the music. I could be all soft and beat around the bush, but we are here to help you, not disapprove. Your father has probably called you a no-good waster or words to that effect, and not with any kindness or understanding. When did someone last say a good thing about you and show you real respect?' This was left hanging in the air.

'I'm talking to you here, like this, because I can't stand to see a fellow teenager, on the brink of adulthood, slipping down the greasy pole.'

The lad sat there taking this in, actually beginning to look. I was impinging on him somewhat.

'I aint in no gangs, he said. 'Just 'ang around wif mates. They are like me I spose.'

I let him talk – the psychologist in me. He unwound about his life, with a few promptings. After a while I decided to spell it out to him. 'Well, Joe, if you want to change it you'll have to work hard. Sometimes it's tough, can be a bit boring, but lots of fun too. You have to work for anything you want. We show you how to do this. Learning is the key. To be clever you need to know how. We know how to do this. But you have to keep the flame burning, no matter what, even when there are some dark moments. Here's your chance. Think about this. 'Come here next Monday for an assessment and start on the program. I'll want to see your parents too.'

'If you don't show up I'll know what's happened. You'll have to breathe life into yourself. Nice to meet you Joe.' I shook his hand.

Joe, a little contrite by this, mumbled, 'Fankyou', and smiled just a bit and left.

After he'd gone Ira said, 'well if that doesn't get him in nothing will. It's up to him. We're not saving the whole world here. I learnt something there. I'm a bit intolerant of a whole lot of people, especially fools and dropouts.'

'Well, you don't mind saying what you think Ira, and that's all I did there, without the intolerance. You did it with Audrey from the Department. There wasn't much to work with in Joe, the life flame barely flickering. If he can see the truth without feeling small he just may come in.'

Ira responded, 'But I was about to discard him. You made a friend of him and sent him off to make his decision.'

'We'll see if it did him any good,' I responded. 'I guess the trick is to discern who's got the raw materials and who hasn't. I'm not sure about this one yet. There's a whole social thing behind this I fear. Best we get together with the parents and see what happens outside of here. When we assess him he may not pass the test, and we'll have to waste him. We're not here to save the youth of the world or be a social services club, but we have to try and ignite some of these educational lost causes, without beating our heads against the brick wall. Let's take the rest of the week off.'

'You do realise,' Ira said, 'it is six-thirty p.m. on Friday. I don't get paid for overtime here and just as well or the College would be broke. Besides Arthur and me and the boys are going up to Oxford tomorrow and are going to have a day of leisure.' Arthur was her husband and didn't see that much of Ira these days.

'Of course,' I said. 'Incidentally the correct grammar is 'Arthur and I…..' I let that sink in. She waved her hand dismissively. I then dismissed her. 'You enjoy the weekend, without even thinking about this place. You know I think I may join you… I don't mean in Oxford; I mean I'm going to have the weekend off too.

'Don't laugh but I've been meaning to meet with this young lady I met down at the library. My first date, eh? Then again I might chicken out. Of all the things I can do easily, sometimes I find you females a bit formidable. I've ignored this area of life, but of late it has sort of impinged on me a bit. You females are somewhat beguiling, as I'm beginning to discover.'

'Too right, Brandon. You go for it. And good luck. The lady is not going to know what hit her. Have a good weekend. See you Monday.' With that Ira left, smiling to herself. I followed her out not long afterwards.

———————————

On my way home I thought of Julia McDonald, this 'date' I was going to have at the weekend. I had set it up rather nebulously, that is, I hadn't really set it up at all. I had only told her I was coming back to the library on Saturday morning and she had said, 'I'll see you then'. Isn't that what was said?

She was a rather model example, physically, of the female body line. But what had mostly attracted me was her extroverted personality and confident response in conversation. Along with her looks she was captivating. Her looks? I'd scarcely regarded the opposite sex for their attractive or otherwise looks before. This had happened in an instant.

The interaction we'd had could have taken place between two of the same sex, but there was something else between us, like a pre-ordained extra something – not hormonal, nor laced with sexual innuendo, but a special affinity that only happens between two of opposite sexes. Maybe it IS hormonal. Had she been a really fat, unpleasant looking creature but with the same personality, would I have been attracted as I was? What was SHE attracted by? I wouldn't say I was hard on the eyes exactly, but I wasn't an Adonis either. Aesthetics was playing a big part in this, both physically and spiritually – a bit unfair for really skinny or overweight bodies.

Anyhow, I arrived home and had my heated-up meal out on the veranda, with Sidney.

'I hope to meet a young lady at the library tomorrow,' I told him. 'She's someone I met there and we had a brief spark between us. I don't have many friends actually, I being too busy with our project. I'm not exactly a socialite, but then again, if I took off time to go to dances or restaurants or parties, what value would I obtain from all that? It's not for me, so I'd rather make proper friends like Peter Hillingdon, or Ira Gibson and share meaningful activity with them.' Sidney jumped in and asked, 'what meaningful activity do you plan with this young lady then?'

Quick as a flash I replied, 'well I don't know yet as I don't know her. We'll see. I just like her unusual spark. Maybe she's shallow, though I hope not.'

Sidney smiled to himself. 'What…?' I asked feigning mild indignation.

'Nothing,' Sidney replied. 'It's just that you are on virgin territory here (well as far as you are concerned anyway).' He laughed at his own joke.

'You are being devilish, mentor. Perhaps you would care to enlighten me on your own exact same early brush with the fair sex, or were you still a….' I left it hanging and laughed lightly.

'Enough said,' Sidney retorted more seriously. 'I await a blow by blow report after the event or non-event, as the case may be.'

We left it at that and sidled off to bed.

I awoke the next morning with more than my usual rippling joie de vive. At breakfast I subdued myself a bit so Sidney wouldn't notice, I hoped. No more innuendos please.

I couldn't keep this up so I let it all out to all and sundry: 'today I am meeting a gorgeous specimen of womanhood who has a decent head on her shoulders. I am sure there will be a momentous meeting of minds. I am keen to see how this plays out,' I blurted out slightly unnaturally as I got up to leave the table. 'I think she is the lucky one though. Wish me good fortune.' I left pretty quickly before anything else was said.

The whole family were surprised somewhat. This was a new turn of events which had to come, I suppose.

Once at the library I went to the Philosophy section and picked out a few tomes on the subject, keen to get a little head start in my likely conversation with Julia. However no sooner had I sat down at a table than the very lady appeared opposite me and pulled up a chair and flashed her radiant smile straight at my heart so to speak.

'What is the subject of your attention good sir?' she challenged.

'Hullo Julia,' I responded in kind. 'I have heard it from a good source that Philosophy is the thing to study. Wouldn't you agree? So here I was about to embark on another Humanity when the very expert has arrived to explain it all to me.' I showed her the books I had drawn from the shelves.

'Oh,' she said leafing briefly through the pages, 'I can give it to you much more briefly than this. I have discovered that these Philosophy buffs are quite long winded, which makes me think already that they are padding it out to express their 'discoveries', or opinions more likely, to appear more erudite than they actually are.'

'Well here you go,' I offered, pointing to the books, 'save me some time and condense that lot for me, though I'd much rather you did it verbally. This is a subject for the coffee shop. Will you join me when I have condensed my study of this and rounded off a few other things of my own?'

'I'd be glad to,' she responded, 'and you can enlighten me on your Psychology/ Psychiatry subject, though I warn you that from what I know already I might have a reduced attention span and possibly a little tendency to doze, unless you make it fit my somewhat fixed ideas on the subject.'

I jumped at this. 'Be assured, you won't sleep. I will make it amusingly revolutionary, so much so that you will give up your Philosophy career aspirations and join me in my conquest of the world.'

'Sounds promising,' she almost gushed.

Then I asked her, 'what are you going to accomplish here in this hallowed space this morning? Don't tell me you are going to brush up on Psychology.'

'No, I'll let you do that. No, I'm here to complete an essay on the world's greatest nineteenth century Philosophers. I feel that doze coming on already, but it is a curriculum 'must'.'

I opened my first book. I looked up at her and she said, 'better get on with it then, and don't interrupt me anymore. I must concentrate. Besides I will need that coffee break very soon.'

'Ok. But if my head drops onto the table wake me up will you, or do you concentrate that hard that you wouldn't notice?'

I parodied this state by looking overly intently at the 'Table of Contents' with a studious frown on my brow. Julia smiled gloriously and got her stuff together and was about to begin. I began snoring loudly with my head on the table. She laughed, infectiously, and I lifted my head to communicate…... 'where am I, what…?' and laughed equally unrestrainedly.

We both became aware that we were potentially disrupting the space, and reined it in and got on with our thing.

About an hour later, having trolled through the chapters on ECT and Prefrontal Lobotomies I announced, 'enough already, I now feel brain dead.' Julia slammed her volume closed with a big bang and got up as abruptly. 'Let's hit the coffee drug store. I'm buying.'

We returned the books to the shelves and with notebooks under our arms, almost danced out of there.

As we advanced along yhe Finchley High Street I asked her, 'did you then finish your essay or precis on these philosophers?'

'Just about. I did my own condensing act and added my own two penneth worth,' she replied with a giggle at the end.

'I'd be more interested to read the cheap version then,' I replied. 'Are you sure you aren't being just mischievous towards your lecturers and hugely disrespectful to the experts of the subject?'

She explained, 'of course I am. I can't see that these learned gentlemen, (and they are all men I notice)....

'Ah,' I interrupted, 'so you are just a feminist really, here to put down these pompous old scholars and create a female uprising among the more emancipated of your sex. Or is it a revolution against men as such?'

'None of that,' she replied with a laugh. 'I'm a beacon of independent thought and an almost compulsive rebel against scholarly rather than practical knowledge.' She had her nose up in mock indignation.

We arrived at the café and took a seat in a booth in the window.

'Anyway,' she challenged, 'you don't strike me as a respecter of authority yourself.'

I put my hands up as if suddenly found out, 'ah, nowhere to hide. Wait until I tell you what I'm up to.'

'Yes, what's behind this holier-than-thou façade?' she butted in leaning forward.

'It's hardly a façade,' I corrected. Then, after we had ordered our coffees and buns I went on to explain my Education experience and new foray into the hallowed subjects of Psychology and Psychiatry. I made it brief and humorous, and there was much laughing, Julia teasing me all the way.

'So you are even more than 'the pot calling the kettle black'.' She looked at me more intently now, saying nothing, looking me over, so to speak. I thought I felt a surge of warmth and respect coming from her. This was not unusual in my experience, without being conceited about the matter. It was just a fact. In any case it was two way. Who could not warm to such a visage before me, and really listening to my story.

I went on. 'On Friday I am going to visit a Psychiatric hospital with my friend Peter, a Psychologist I have been swapping notes with. I want to know all about brains and see if there is any connection with behaviour. To use your disrespectful terms I want to know if these chaps are all fakes after all and that we are back to more like the gentler, but more truthful subject of Philosophy (though that may be more praise than yet deserved).' Julia gave a slightly offensive expression at this, but I went on.

'If patients are recovering and regaining their senses after having their brains drugged, fried and operated on, I'll go back to the drawing board. The most difficult thing to do, when a proposition assails your sense of right and wrong, is to remain impartial and look, rather than just be right. Then again, as in my Education experiment, there can be such a blatant absence of any credence that one just has to discover for himself the truth or the solution to the problem.'

Julia came in here. 'You are opening up such a can of worms here, aren't you? I mean what do you do if you find out it's all a fake, moreover a devious plan to quieten down the noisy nutters or unbalanced of this world and make some dosh out of it all?'

I said nothing for a minute and sipped at my coffee, then, 'or what if it is a control mechanism to get rid of the rebellious, the progressive and the artistic lights of this world? Already I have experienced a microcosm of this. There are some negative people in this world, like that DH I told you about, and the people from the Department. It's as if they are in danger from people of good will, and in the middle are a lot of sheep who sit on the fence and go along with the status quo, like my parents.'

Julia was thinking on this for a bit and after swallowing the last of her bun she said, 'do you really think the world is like that? Look at all the good things that have been created in the last few centuries – machines, mass production, standards of living for more people, planes, cars, proper infrastructure, opportunity for more people, mass education, medical advances, to name a few.'

I was enjoying this. I added, as if continuing the list, 'yes, of course, and war, hunger, mental problems, increasing crime, economic duress, anarchy of nations, an arms race to see who can destroy the earth quickest, social problems galore. But who is in charge of bringing common sense and solutions to these flaws, or, if you like, who is going to advance man beyond the physical? This is the domain of the Psychologists and Psychiatrists, or more exactly, it should be, but are they the chosen ones? I can't see from what I have examined so far, that they are. I really hope I am pleasantly surprised.'

'Blimey,' Julia responded. 'You really are an adult, and more. You are well into Philosophy here. I can see how you upset the Education Establishment. Fancy a teenager spouting all this stuff.'

Julia sipped a bit more coffee and then, 'Can I come with you on Friday?'

'Do you want to join my project? I'd be glad to have a fresh mind. You are very bright Julia. You can add something. But don't launch a takeover, will you? I'll check with Peter about Friday. Should be OK. I'll put in a word for you.'

'I'd love to. Enough of stuffy classrooms and libraries, and enough of not much else. I don't really know where this Philosophy is going. It seemed a good idea at the time, but there is no real result here. It's more intellectual than anything. I suppose it would need to be a practical subject, a philosophy that underwrites a useful application. I suppose I could make something up in the manner you made up your Education techniques.'

By this I was really energised. 'Come and meet my cohorts in crime. You'll love Sidney, my grandpa; and Mrs Ira Gibson – wait until you meet her! Come over Monday, say three to four pm. We'll be winding up the kids by then.'

'Kids? Here you are calling your peers 'kids'. Then again they are not your peers, strictly, are they?'

'Honestly,' I explained, 'I don't see myself as a kid. I've done my adult apprenticeship in full, except for growing older. I suspect you are much the same. Respect your elders? If they deserve it.'

We vacated the booth and I paid the bill. 'My treat next time,' Julia put in. She got the college address and leaned over and gave me a peck on the cheek. 'See you then,' she said quickly and darted off.

I stood there and continued to take in this new experience. I'd found a soul mate, but 'mates' don't peck you on the cheek, do they? But, whatever significance I could put on it, I enjoyed it.

Ira had pecked me on the cheek once, but it wasn't the same as this one. What's in a peck on the cheek, administered suggestively? Some automatic drilled-in response perhaps. Yes of course it is natural I can hear them all saying. There must be some genetic response though. Well, whatever it is, I liked it; definitely some sex-laden stimulus. If that's a tiny peck what would passionate sex be like, I wonder. I'm going to take this easy, I decided. I had given the subject of sexual intercourse a passing glance, from time to time, since the onset of puberty. That's a strange one; no thought of the subject before puberty. The body has undergone an 'upgrade' since then. It must be hormonal. Well, we'll see if this goes anywhere.

I wandered back home, my thoughts stimulated by my morning's intercourse with Julia. She wasn't the usual teenager. I wonder what she does when not studying. Plenty of grist to the mill for next time. If she's going to come aboard our 'train' I'd better know more about her, though I've definitely perceived a quality person here; a cut above the rest.

Come to think of it, I haven't really met, head on, too many of 'the rest'.

———————————

At home, I strolled in and plonked my books on the hall table and asked my mum what she was doing.

She wiped her hands on her apron and said pointedly, 'I'm putting away the uneaten food that I wasted. You can have it for dinner. You must have fallen in love and forgotten all about me.'

'Oh no, love of my life, that could never happen. But, without falling in love as you put it, I did get carried away with a very intellectual conversation with Julia (that's her name). She is coming to the Psychiatric Hospital with us on Friday.

'The things I do for a date – library and nut houses. What next; maybe the coroner's mortuary? Anyway, it was her idea, not mine. She's also thinking of joining our project. She's coming there on Monday to suss us out. We need some more hierarchy.'

Mother piped in and suggested I bring her home for dinner afterwards. 'I've got to meet my competition. Besides she's got to be vetted by the family.' And she went up to me and gave me a big hug and a pinch of the cheek. 'Got to know you are in safe hands. Nothing's too good for my boy.'

'What's all this then,' a voice from the far side of the dining room piped in. Sidney had been listening in all along but couldn't let on. 'Are we talking about a fair lady here?'

'Yep, we are,' I chirped, 'and so what? Jealous? And why so nosy?'

Sidney dismissed this with a wave of his hand, and a chuckle as he vacated the room and went out onto the veranda and continued reading the papers. Saturday was heavy reading time.

I joined him eventually. 'I have prospective staff member,' I announced. 'She's coming in on Monday afternoon to give us the once-over. We can all decide if she's suitable.'

'I'd say we,' means 'you', Sidney mused.

I laughed. 'Do you think that because she's young and beautiful I can't be impartial? Interesting question. Do you think these femme fatales are that powerful? It's strictly business I can assure you. If you don't like her then I'll find some other use for her ...' I left it trailing to leave the innuendo clear.

'Whatever you say. A new adventure anyway, eh?' Sidney added more seriously.

'Incidentally did you hear that the PM resigned today? Looks like we may have a change of government. But not a change of the status quo. They should all join one party or have no parties. There's a subject for you to get your teeth into Brandon.'

'Maybe, but I think you'd be the one to do that,' I suggested. 'Ever think of being an MP? Seriously, you'd be ideal representing our electorate. I can see you now standing up in the House of Parliament and questioning the PM or making suggestions, off the wall of course. 'Here here', I can hear them murmuring now.'

'I don't think so. Maybe twenty years ago.'

After some thought I replied. 'Seeing you energised in our little project, (or not so little), I think age has nothing to do with it. Many of those chaps down there in Westminster are longer in the tooth than you. And the Lords are even older. But then again they have been put out to graze somewhat. Why don't I come to your debating society and watch you in action. I would like to have a go myself. Then I can get an even better idea as to the suitability of your nomination for the constituency of Finchley.

'Not only that, it would be a great platform from which to enhance our Education project. What do you say?'

Sidney preferred to keep it jocular at this point because he could see me winding up here to another one of my prospective pronouncements. 'Okay, you come along to the debate tomorrow evening and we'll debate the subject of 'Comedians in Westminster'.'

'OK, you're on. What is the topic anyhow? I need time to prepare to blow you all out of the water.'

Sidney replied, with a smirk on his face, 'It's an impromptu night; no preparation. The subject is drawn out of a hat. I'll suggest that you go first. I will be writing down the subjects to go in the hat. Let's see….. ah, how about 'the joys of sex', or 'parental guidance to teenage relationships', or 'the value of teenage virginity'.

We both laughed. 'That might just backfire on you old fogeys.'

'Anyway, come along Brandon, It IS an impromptu night actually, so it will all have to be off the cuff.'
'OK, I'm in,' I agreed. 'Should be an interesting exercise, especially as you will be the one on the hotspot. Do you know I've never debated before. Are there any particular rules?'

'I'll tell you after you've spoken. Not really though. The key is in the word 'debate'. You can't ramble on forever though. Its ten minutes at a time. Do you think you can reduce yourself to such a restriction?'

'I'll have to. By the way, can I, as a new guest speaker, put a subject into the hat?'

Sidney rose to the bait. 'It will have to go by me first, young man.'

'Killjoy!' I protested.

And with that we disbanded as if going to our corners. I went to my room and sat at my desk and thought about the merits of being an MP. I'd only once been to the gallery at Westminster and witnessed the honourable members having a go at each other and generally raising questions and debating various issues. I had scant knowledge of what they all did outside of the House, and what they had to do to get elected.

As on many such occasions I pulled out one of my encyclopaedias and spent an hour immersed in the ins and outs of Parliamentary Democracy and Constitutional Government.

―――――――――

I awoke the next morning and indulged myself in some stretching exercises before dressing. I find this wakes me up for real, not that I need much waking up, what with the forthcoming debate that night and the new-found joy in my life. Both of these are a first for me, the latter pulling the hardest. I mulled over the likely subjects I'd be called on to pontificate about at the debate – all sorts of political subjects – the subject of right or wrong, mental illness, teenagers today, pre-marital sex (God forbid), the value of Education. The list could go on.

Should I be contentious or even controversial? I think I'll plump for the latter, I thought. I don't really have to hold a particular view personally. I can just make it up. This should be fun.

I bounded down to breakfast to be greeted by my brother Andrew commenting on the unusual spring in my step. 'What's got into you, mate? Or should I say WHO's got into you?

'I'm just full of the many joys of life,' I responded. 'But now that you ask with such innuendo you'll meet her tomorrow night as Mum has invited her for dinner. Think you can handle that?'

'Sorry I'm out tomorrow night. What a pity!' Andrew finished off his tea and left the table.

'Today I'm off to meet a few friends, including some fine-feathered of the species. We're going into town to visit a few sites and indulge in an art gallery or two and then some … well we'll see.'

'Ok, fare well Andrew. If you have time drop into the debating society tonight, Grandpa is going to be doing a virtuoso performance and there's a promising newcomer on debut. This is so, isn't it Grandpa?' I said this looking over pointedly at the oracle.

'He'll be eaten up by the veterans, Andrew, but it should be interesting,' Grandpa offered.

With that Andrew was off, and Grandpa took his tea and paper out onto the veranda.

Mother and father were clearing the table around the slightly tardy me. I sat there and decided, while sipping my tea and crunching my toast, what I could most profitably do today. I thought of College planning but decided to have a day off and do some work on my novel about the rags-to-riches sports star.

Yes, I should emulate Ira G and not even think of 'work' today. I pictured Ira wondering around the university town of Cambridge, or was it Oxford? I bet she can't resist thinking about these brains trust types there and whether they ARE getting an education. No, I think she'll actually have the day off and then tomorrow petition for more of the same in future, just to annoy me.

I decided to put my typewriter out on the veranda table and go for it.

———————————

The big debate was being held in a small meeting room in the Town Hall. I was introduced to all the dramatis personae and welcomed warmly and with a fair amount of gentle ribbing.

 The first subject for these impromptu performances was pulled out of the hat.

 There was an opening debate before my debut. This gave the opportunity to see how it was all done. There were a few formidable debaters, I noticed. These were experts at shaping an argument into a ten minute frame.

The subject drawn by the 'arbiter' for my debate was 'the merits of Socialism'.

I had studied quite a bit on this subject and chose to opt for the middle position of the three on my team. I'd read a bit about the Russian Revolution and the Communist Party, and the labour government previously in power here in the UK. But I had a paucity of detail, so I decided to go controversial, my team batting on the side of negative benefit.

Grandpa was on the opposing team and had chosen to lead out the argument having won the toss. He spoke articulately about the last labour government, citing the great advent of the National Health Service, the increase in unionism and the benefits to the working class, post war……

…….. Now it was my turn. I stood up and, after a quick nervous brush of fingers through hair, and a glance at Sidney who gave me an encouraging wink, I lifted my head and confidently announced I was going to cover the subject in its essence and in its world-wide aspects.

'Socialism is a political attempt to equalise the gap between rich and poor. I guess the rich and the poor have been at it since time immemorial. The poor want to have what the rich have and the rich want to retain their status. It seems true that those in power in society have somewhat held down and exploited the less well off, that is they have been less than charitable. So it was inevitable that somewhere along the line, as countries became more democratic and governments sought the support of the masses to stay in power, that agitators and champions of the downtrodden would arise. Somewhere along the way someone had to decide to call 'enough is enough'……..

…….At that point my brother Andrew came in and sat down in the 'audience, next to Sidney. I waved to him and nodded, and smiled. I went on.

………..'Therefore we must look at the great Socialist experiment in Russia. Has it led to an equalisation and prosperity for all? It seems not. In fact it seems to be more of a dictatorship and a suppression of freedoms than anywhere else in the world. The same goes for the 'Republics' attached to it. To enforce this 'equalisation' seems not to work at all.

'I say the merits of Socialism fall short of what is required for a harmonious prosperous society.'

'But somewhere along the line as a race we need to come up with smarter ideas than Politics the way it is, and for dealing with the illogics that are touted by our governments and their opponents.'

I sat down to a mild applause. Sidney slapped me on the back as a 'well done'. Andrew smiled at me too, disbelievingly, this being the first time he'd really seen his brother really expound on something.

The last two speakers concluded their summaries and it was left for the arbiter to decide who had won the day.

It turned out that I had given more than enough credence to our team's argument to sway the day in our favour.

The arbiter came up to me later and said, 'I think I'll become a capitalist now, but a charitable one. Well-spoken Brandon. You added plenty of weight to the argument. How did you manage to get a grip of all this stuff at such a tender age?'

'Thank you sir. I read a lot, beyond school stuff,' I explained.

The others all in turn welcomed me to the group as if they'd just elected me. We all went our own ways after tea and cakes, the next meeting to be in a fortnight's time.

Sidney and we two boys strolled home with Andrew and I seriously trying to influence Grandpa to become an MP for the area. Grandpa started to turn the tables and suggest that maybe I should become the youngest ever candidate.

'No way,' I protested. 'I think I'd rather join the mental asylum we are going to on Friday, though I think we should visit it first, before deciding.'

We reached home and went straight to bed, ready for the exertions of the coming week. I let my attention wander to Julia McDonald, tomorrow afternoon at the College.

———————

Sure enough, the lady breezed into the College at five p.m. the next day and walked up to me, put her hand on my arm briefly, and declared, 'well, here I am, impress me.'

I quickly responded. 'You bet, young lady. Good to see you too. By the way I have made an appointment, or should I say my mother has, for you to attend dinner at our place after the proceedings tonight. You game for that?'

'I AM curious as to who spawned you, and why,' she joked.

'Well, OK then. First I want you to meet the spawner of spawners.' With that I introduced Julia to Sidney. 'Julia, this is Mr. Sidney Waterman, my grandpa, mentor, debating protagonist, and prospective editor, and, soon-to-be MP for the Finchley area.'

Julia did a mock curtsy. 'That's a big mouthful, sir. Are you really all of that?'

Sidney replied with a mock embarrassment and quipped, 'he's understating it whilst outright lying. Pleased to meet you Julia.'

'Yes, I have noticed already that Brandon takes poetic licence to a new level.' She flashed one of those disarming smiles, with perfect teeth and sparkling eyes.

Just then Ira G sauntered in and, seeing Julia in full flow, couldn't help herself saying, 'so you are the cause of the cloud nine we now see around here.'

I quickly butted in and explained. 'Julia, this is our resident rottweiler, the formidable Ira Gibson, the scourge of the entire Education Department. Thus completes our triumvirate board of directors, partners in crime, hope of the future civilisation, revolutionaries all.'

Julia opened her mouth in mock disbelief and played the game too. 'You mean, Ira, you let a mere teenager loose on leadership and salvaging this mess civilisation is in? It IS men who have ruined this world, not so? I think I'll join this merry band if only to rebalance the issue.'

With that, the two women became instant pals, and hugged each other.

'Well, what cabal have you created here Brandon,' Sidney accused.

'We'll put them in their place, don't you worry Grandpa. Anyway, Julia hasn't passed our tests yet. Being female, and obviously a sexist to boot is definitely not going to help her qualify. In fact….'

'Enough already!' Julia interrupted. 'Take me round this project of yours and let's see who passes whose test.'

Ira G rubbed her hands together and enthused, 'oo, I like it,' and shuffled off with Sidney to deal with a few lingering students. I started around the College rooms and explained what went on in each, showed her the graph boards that monitored progress, and was about to end up in my 'office' when in through the main door came an unexpected event – Joe, the 'would be' dropout, and what looked like his father, Jim Baxter.

'Hi Joe, come in,' and turning to father Jim, 'I'm Brandon, I'll be with you in a moment. Take a seat, help yourself to tea over there if you want,' I said, pointing. So they sat while I eased Julia into my office and explained what had happened with Joe before, and went on, 'good then, this is an ideal opportunity to show you what we do. This guy is a borderline case. It might go either way. I'll introduce you as a new staff member learning the ropes, and you sit somewhat in the background and take notes, so to speak; but don't speak,' I warned with my own version of the big smile. The attracting game is on I thought.

'Come into my office gentlemen,' I invited. Joe was looking a bit subdued while Jim, the father, all eighteen stone of him in trousers and braces and striped shirt, took the lead.

'Joe tells me you have a program for him to learn things for a career, or something.'

We all sat down and I introduced Julia as a newcomer learning the ropes, and then told Jim, 'no promises here. It all depends on Joe. It will be tough for him, like starting life all over again. Some make it, and some don't.'

With that I turned to Joe and asked him, 'What did you decide Joe? In fact Jim, would you mind waiting outside a minute so I can talk to Joe by himself? We'll talk later.'

Jim left and I turned to Joe and asked him what had transpired at home. Joe said, 'well I told dad wha' we said lars time and that you could ' elp me ge' educa'ed an' stuff.'

'OK, how did you decide to come here tonight? Was it your idea or your dad's?'
' 'e said he'd drive me up 'ere, and all, and see wha' this was really abart. I said I weren't really sure I could go froo wif i', ya know wa' I mean. Bu' he grabbed me tonigh' and we go' in the car and, wairw, 'ere we are like.'

That's how Joe spoke – East London accent. I said to him, (with Julia well in the background) 'so, do you think you can go through with it, as you say, or does it look like a tall task?'

'It looks like its ard work,' Joe replied. 'I will' ave to see, wone I?'

'Tell you what,' I decided. 'We'll give you some tests to see where you're at, and then a small beginning program to give you a taster. But you have to keep a promise with me. You do the work and if we succeed together, we'll go and watch Tottenham at White Hart Lane one Saturday; my treat. If you don't like it you can go on your merry way and do whatever else floats your boat. But I'm not treating you for nothing. You have to do a whole regime here, and at home. We work all day, with breaks here and there, you go home and help around the house, stay off the streets, sleep at least eight hours per night. Reckon you could do that? We'll see what sort of a Tottenham fan you are.

'If you like it and want to continue, well and good. But no messing about. No turning up late. Eat a good breakfast and bring a packed lunch. Sounds like being in the army doesn't it? I think you'd rather this than the army though.'

Joe was wriggling about uncomfortably but had a small grin on his face. I went on, 'ask your dad to come in. Grab yourself a drink from out there while I tick your dad off a bit.' He laughed. Joe went out and Jim came in.

'Jim, we are going to test him and give him an intro program to see how he does. This won't work by forcing him. It's got to be his decision and he has to discipline himself. I've told him he has to stay off the streets and help around the house, get lots of sleep and eat a big breakfast.' I told him about the Tottenham treat and what the program would be.

'Encourage him. It's a new thing for him and maybe you too. He's on the cusp of either making a life-changing way up or to continue to fall further.

'You will have lost him if he goes down. You need to be his friend not just his disciplinarian or disapprover. You see, it's not just the education he needs but a whole new life around him. Given your support and encouragement and some new worthwhile experiences he'll make it. But he's starting from a low rung of the ladder. We are educators here, but there is a degree of environmental handling that comes into it too. Get the wife involved in this too. He's been a problem to you no doubt and you and the wife have got exasperated with him. It's a family situation though. Give it a whirl.'

'Gee,' said Jim, puffing out his abundant red cheeks and running a hand through his floppy hair. 'You are too good to be true. I'm not sure how me and the wife will do on this. But we'll give it a go. What choice do we have?'

I got into the logistics. I met again with Ira G and she did an assessment of the boy's literary and numeracy levels and did up a two week program for him, starting with simple English grammar and arithmetic.

Jim and Joe left and I went back to Julia and said, 'see how we do it? Joe is the bottom of the barrel, as far as we are concerned. Then there are simply good kids that need re-educating so they can learn how to know and do things.'

'I was impressed with how you spoke to him - very light, but firm. This looks like a good project Brandon.'

'Well, right now our project is to not keep Mrs Waterman waiting any longer, and get home and have some good old home-spun nosh. Nobody does it better than Mum. Shall we go? I'll get Sidney and turf him out of here too. He gets grumpy if he's hungry.'

'Show me the way, good sir.' And Julia flashed one of those smiles again.
On the way back to the Waterman's Julia and Sidney got more acquainted. He filled her in on the other schools they had on the go and the Tottenham experiment and spoke about the fun we would have at the Psychiatric Hospital on Friday.
Just as we were approaching the front gate I reminded Julia 'you'll have to behave suitably at the Psychiatric place you know. No remonstrations, no squeamish screaming when you see people being electrocuted, and no interrupting brain operations, ok?'

She shot back, 'it's not me one should be worried about. You seem to be the affronted one. You say you are an impartial observer. Prove it. Besides, what's wrong with a bit of sleep-induced rest and recovery from life's hard journey? What's wrong with a bit of shock to wake one up?'

'ohh, who's the cynic here?' I retorted.

We were all in good humour as we entered the modest portals of the family Waterman.

Mrs Gladys Waterman, my mum, was entering the hallway with her apron on, signifying her place here. 'You must be Julia,' she said with a big smile and gave Julia a big welcoming hug. I helped her off with her coat and hung it on a peg and we all made our way into the living room.

'He's never helped ME off with my coat,' Mum said in mock indignation. 'Make yourself comfortable Julia. Dinner will be ready in a minute.'

Julia was reciprocal with her greeting and as Mum slipped off into the kitchen to do her thing we others sat ourselves down. Unexpectedly Andrew appeared suddenly and Julia got up and introduced herself to him with a light hug. Andrew was awkward in his 'pleased to meet you.' He thereafter was entranced for the evening. Who wouldn't be?

I offered Julia a choice of tea, iced water, or lemonade. 'What about you, Grandpa, Andrew?'

Mum came in just then and said she had all those things on the table. 'You can come in now and sit down and help yourselves.'

While Mum served up the soup the others, including now my dad, Mr Cliff Waterman, were all bantering about the relative hierarchy of the household. Julia excused herself and slipped off to the kitchen and implored Mum to rescue her from the sexist company 'in there' and insisted on helping with the dishing up. She and Mum became partners in a very small space of time. They brought the soup plates to the table and, as if by arrangement, both iterated, 'you see a woman's place IS in the kitchen. Isn't that just wonderful?'

I looked at Julia and caught her eye and got one of those brilliant smiles in return, to send paroxysms of joy through my heart.

Mum announced dictatorially, 'you lot are clearing up all this after we have eaten. Julia and I are retiring to the veranda to recover from our servitude.' We men all went overboard in dramatizing the unfairness of this dictatorial edict. I was enjoying this. Julia was a hit.

During dinner Julia announced that she was now satisfied to have learned who had spawned the rebellious Brandon, and had decided that it was all Sidney's fault and that the parents weren't really to blame.

'Here, here!' agreed the two parents. 'He's been encouraging ALL the kafuffle that Brandon has caused us and the good people at the school and the Education Department. Why does he have to incite rebellion? God knows what else he's planning.'

Andrew added, 'I think Julia knows full well that BRANDON is probably the source of Grandpa's new-found inclination to become a rebel.'

And so the evening went on, with lots of laughter and bonhomie. The two women were as good as their threat and announced that they would now retire to the veranda and have a proper conversation. We men went into a mock-offendedness and started a sort of 'union cry' for equality and lots of 'how has it come to this?'

Julia talked domesticity with Mum for a while and then we all had tea in the living room. Julia did most of the talking as the family had lots of questions for her about her life. She held stage brilliantly and finished off with how she and I had met at the library and had decided the best way to save the world from itself.

It was time for her to be off. In her effusive style each of the hosts got a warm hug and lots of thankyous for the evening. I had told her I'd walk her home, which was a mile or two. We soon fell into a discussion about each of the family members. After a short while Julia took my arm as if it were the most natural thing in the world. 'I'm so glad I met you, you know,' she said. 'You have woken a real question about my life and its purpose. And you are not like the other boys, cum men, I've met. We stopped and she took both my hands and added, 'and I really like you.'

What else could I do? I instinctively took her closely but gently in my arms, one arm around her waist and one around her neck, and stroked her hair lightly. We stayed that way for many seconds as I drank in her femininity. 'Julia, you have spiked my life, and that's saying something. I have no experience with women but I feel completely natural with you.'

We kissed, not at all awkwardly, but now sexually charged. 'And you can kiss too,' she said softly.

'What a wonderful moment,' I said while holding her face in both hands and looking intently into those glorious eyes, and then that smile. I kissed her again, tenderly, still holding her head in my hands. I couldn't help myself.

We continued walking, hand in hand, both looking and smiling at each other, but saying nothing. Nothing needed to be said. Then we were a bit lost in our own thoughts for a little while. I thought to myself, so this is what it is between the sexes. It was just natural, like a seduction, but not unwilling, and an affinity stronger than usual, and an energy awoken in the body, much like goose bumps but better. I had felt the stirring in my loins. Well, I could see where this would naturally lead to. What an imposition the body had placed on me!

Julia told me she'd a few brief encounters with other men before but had felt sort of obliged to give herself physically to them beyond her comfort and so had frozen somewhat and backed away. I could see why this had occurred. I was the lucky one, or maybe even the chosen one.

We reached her doorstep and I asked her, while holding her, 'I would love you to join our group. Are you game for a laugh? You can make up your own philosophy as you go along. Don't we all want our own philosophy anyway?'

'Probably. What would you have me do?' she teased.

'I can't think straight about such an ambivalent question, right now,' I answered 'helplessly'.

'How much do I get paid? That's important. I can't live on nothing.'

'This would be a labour of love, as they say.' We both flashed our smiles again. 'Enough to get by at first (my definition) and more later as we grow. Probably more than you get as a pretend student right now.'

'Pretend?' She kissed me eagerly. 'Phew,' as she came up for air. 'I am going in now. Your turn to meet MY family next. See you at the college Monday.' With that she was gone.

I stood there and took in the most amazing feeling I had ever experienced – the 'cloud nine' syndrome. Then I whistled my way home through the empty streets and thought, here's another game. I wonder what the Psychologists have to say about this.

I reached home and the family couldn't wait to talk about Julia. 'You've scored a gem there Brandon', my mother said. 'So is she officially your girlfriend now that we've met her and approved?' she teased lightly.

Before I could answer Andrew chimed in, 'are you going to marry her, brother? She would have to be able to take the pace, wouldn't she? Or is it the other way round?

Then Dad added, 'I'll have to start thinking about grandchildren I suppose, and you, Sidney, about great grandchildren.'

'OK, enough already you lot,' I protested. 'Don't spoil a wonderful night. But you are right, she is a bit of a gem. I've hit the ground running, as they say. She's going to join our project, on Monday. She don't muck around, this girl. What I like about her is her ability to see what's going on and what we are doing about it, and so quickly. She's one of us, and I don't mean family lest you think I'm going to marry her tomorrow. Whatever else I like about her, and have done about it is none of your business.' Who's teasing who now I thought?

They were all reduced to smirky grins and carried on about their business.

I sought out Sidney on the veranda. 'Grandpa, on another subject, what do you think about Andrew being a potential member of our group? I've somewhat neglected him whilst I've been carried away with our project.'

Sidney was thoughtful for a moment, then, 'Hmm, I'm not sure. He's been bent on being a musician, but that's a bit nebulous really. Otherwise he's drifting while he finishes up his education, which is a bit of a struggle I think. Maybe we should have him as a student first.'

'Yep', I agreed. 'I'll get him aside casually and, more as a normal prospect rather than a brother, find out where he's at. Tomorrow I think.'

'Yes, you go and have pleasant dreams my man,' he smiled to convey the innuendo.

'Maybe my next book should be a romance,' I said, stroking my chin.

And we were off. Sleep beckoned, though more for Grandpa than me.

Monday morning, Julia arrived as the crew were sitting around a table in the meeting room, drinking tea and planning the day.

'Morning Julia,' I chirped as I gave her my biggest sparkling smile. She in turn gushed back. Sidney and Ira could hardly have missed this display and Ira looked at Sidney for explanation, and he in turn gesticulated with upturned hands and a mock 'don't ask me' expression.

I explained. 'Julia is joining the team. After a long interview the other night she decided to risk all. Is there any dissent in the ranks?' I was looking pointedly at Ira.
'Well no,' spluttered Ira somewhat. 'You know I don't recall getting a long late night interview, or even such a hot welcome, for that matter.' She continued with lots more mischief and 'hurt'. 'I only hope she has some power over the dictator in this establishment.

A bit more girl power is all right with me.' Sidney was enjoying this.

Julia was in fits by this and pointedly sat in a chair on Ira's side of the table. 'There!' she said. 'It's been officially designated. In the case of a deadlock, WE decide, on the basis that male dictatorship and sexism in the office is bad for rational decisions.'

'Good God, and you've only been here for fifty nine seconds,' I protested with much mirth. 'Is this takeover ok with you Sidney? I must admit I didn't see this coming; how naïve of me.'

Sidney came in on cue. 'Well we'll see how this goes. She'll have to start at the bottom and work her way up. No voting powers yet. I could do with another cup of tea actually. Ira will show you where the 'tea room' is Julia.'

Ira carried on the whole charade. 'We don't do tea, do we Julia?'

'No,' she replied. 'But in the interests of not rocking the boat too early I would be honoured to make Mr Waterman a perfect cup of tea.' She had him in her pocket, right there. The two ladies went off and Sidney and I looked at each other knowingly.

Ira took Julia aside and fielded all her questions adequately. 'I think it would please His Majesty if you got ahead of his plans and expectations and digested the Educational Program he has designed so you know where we are headed. She then became more earnest and gave Julia the whole story of how she and I came to be partners in crime and how I had revolutionised the subject of Education.

'He is a freak phenomenon, this boy, man. He's out to save the world I think. He's not content with rocking the Education Department, though I don't think he has really started on them yet. He's now going for the brain boys.'
Julia said, 'Yes. Do you know he invited me to come with him to a Psychiatric establishment on Friday? That will be interesting.'

'There you go. I hope they give him some kind of sedative, or whatever, to slow him down a bit. Tell me Julia, are you and Brandon now officially in a relationship?' Ira asked casually.

Julia was not in the least taken aback. 'Do you know Ira, we have gelled in the most natural way, as if we were meant for each other. There's no pretend, no normal 'teenage' games. We hit it off immediately. He didn't 'come on to me', nor me to him. He was just sitting there reading. I found myself (a bit unusual for me), just talking to him and he responded. I was immediately captivated by his easy natural manner and then his wit. He was voicing concepts about life and the world that fitted with me perfectly. And I saw a pure, untarnished persona. I can't imagine he ever gets ruffled or gets into any negative emotions. I feel so safe with him. And yes, there is a very clean sexual attraction between us.'

Ira put her arms around Julia and gave her a warm hug. 'I'm so pleased for you both. I was wondering if he'd ever get distracted enough from his purpose to even entertain the subject of women. But, who could not warm to that beguiling sparkling smile of yours. I should never have doubted him. It has come as easily to him as everything else has so far. I love him to bits. He's opened my eyes to life, and Sidney is revived as if from a life slumber. Sidney has been his mentor and seen him through the early rougher times, such as they were, but now it's almost the other way round.'

They were cemented as friends already. Ira set Julia up with the 'Book of Education' and went off to attend to the students who were beginning to trickle in by this. She ran into me and came up and gave me a big hug. 'You have surpassed yourself there young man. Congratulations. The rest of the field can give up trying.'

I was touched. 'Yes, I think she's special and I don't know much about her really. I'm now into another subject aren't I?'

'Ah ha,' Ira agreed. 'I've got her reading the gospel for now. Then I'll test her on it. When she gets to you again she'll be as good as us. Why don't I assign her to Joe, if he shows up?'

'Good idea; in at the deep end. Just warn her not to be too upbeat with him. He's pretty downtrodden and might get overwhelmed by her bright personality.'

CHAPTER ELEVEN

Joe did arrive, dressed as a typical fifties street kid, with the latest stove pipes and loud socks and rock n roll haircut, all brushed back with a curl at the front. His Mum was with him. Julia took up the challenge and with natural aplomb had Mrs Baxter eating out of her hand in no time. She had a written starter program for Joe, the most basic in the whole project.

'Joe, tell you what, while I talk to your mum for a bit, write me a short composition on your life. Here's a pen and there's a bit of paper. Take your time, go for it. Back in a mo.'

Julia, after having been in on his original interview, explained to Mrs Baxter, 'this is a life-changing exercise for Joe AND for you and husband Jim.' She went over the drill we had organised for home activities.

'Whoah! This is quite a thing, isn't it?' This woman was a sort of born housewife. If she'd had her apron on it wouldn't have looked out of place. Her manner was more that of a kindly old lady. Confrontation was not her thing. Husband Jim was the opposite. He erred too far the other way as more of a disciplinarian, though a failed one at that.

Julia drilled her on various situations that might arise, until she felt more comfortable. 'You have nothing to lose and only your son's future to gain. It's time for you two to have some parenting success here, don't you think? We'll tee him up each day here so he's got it from all sides.'

With that she handed Patricia over to Sidney to take care of the registration. Going back to Joe she noticed he'd written hardly anything. 'OK Joe,' she said sitting down beside him, 'let me help you here.'

 Where do I start she thought? As if on cue in I came. 'Hey Joe, you turned up. That's gutsy. We are at the bus stop on the way to White Hart Lane. No journey, no arrival anywhere, yet. See what I mean?'

Joe smiled wanly, not entirely sure what I was on about, but he liked the compliment, something he'd not been used to in his life of paucity.

Julia explained that she'd asked for a composition and Joe, listening to this conversation said, 'I'm no good at writin' fings. I can't fink of wot to say.'

Brandon asked him, 'are you able to talk about things rather than write them?'

'Probly.' He replied.

'OK. So, where were you born, and when?'

'Wew my mum said I was born at ome when we were livin in Artfordshire, in ni'een for'y-six.'

'Rightio. Write down exactly what you just said. Doesn't matter if you spell it all wrong.'

Joe wrote it down, and though his handwriting was scruffy and his spelling a bit off and there was no punctuation, there was a sort of story there.

'There you go, we'll make an author of you yet'. We all smiled.

Turning to Julia I explained, ' If something is too hard or they stumble, you have to look for a lower level that CAN be done. Proceed like that, asking him lots of questions about himself.' Now turning back to Joe I said, 'Julia will help you through this. We need to know where to start so we don't have you falling on your head on the first day. But promise me you won't write a whole book.'

Joe smiled a little less wanly this time. He was almost up and running.

As I left the room I winked at Julia and suggested, 'small bursts of business, then lots of little breaks, and fun.'

She beamed back and, turning to Joe, 'OK my man, you've got to make me look good here. One more sentence then we hotfoot it to the drink machine.' Joe was loosening up a bit.

And so it continued during the week with Julia bedding in beautifully, Joe becoming almost a proper student, and me casting my eye over the burgeoning chain of Education establishments. Ira was doing famously with Audrey from the Department and had the application for legitimacy well on track. Sidney was administering behind the scenes like an old fashioned jobsworth but without the restraints normally associated with that breed.

I suspected that the progress made with the Department might be credited to Mr Hopkins, the head of the 'delegation' that had visited us in the last week or so. Mr Hopkins had rung me and set up a meeting with his sons which occurred during this busy week. I went to them as arranged and, in a nutshell had diagnosed their 'cases' and written up a program for them to do, a sort of correspondence course, if you like.

I had the father, James, operate the program after I'd covered the methods as outlined in my publication. I'd inspired the two young tyros to learn and James to see that it was done. I would operate the whole thing remotely.

Having spent a good few evenings at the Hopkins home I'd had little time with Julia. But needless to say she'd been in good hands with both Ira and Sidney.

On the night before our Friday visit to this Psychiatric institution I took Julia to a fancy restaurant in Hampstead where the conversation naturally turned to the interest I had in this subject. Julia was in startlingly good humour. Her long dark hair and naturally beautiful features and complexion and perfect teeth shone out to captivate any would-be wolf on the prowl.

'So your idea of a romantic date is to take me to a Psychiatric institution?' she asked tauntingly.

'No, but these guys are the experts in what goes on in the head, so I have planned to have yours examined, and treated if necessary. So the pressure is on. Will you pass the 'sane and rational test'? Will you come out of there a different person? You see, I've been thinking about us these past few days and what I really want is a homely, malleable, compliant wench who just makes life easier for me.' I was putting on a mock serious demeanour.

'Well then,' she responded, playing the game. 'I've got you all wrong. I thought you were the more liberated type; the free thinker. I think I WILL submit to a head examination. How could I have been so wide of the mark?'

We both cracked up and sat there looking admiringly at each other for quite a few moments. The waiter came over and took our order, including a small glass of wine each.

'Boy', Julia exclaimed after having chosen her meal, 'can we afford such extravagance? I'm out of touch?'

'Don't worry about it,' I said. 'I've decided, arbitrarily, on a new company policy – all new staff are to be indulged with a slap up wine-and-dine of their choice. The tab is on Sidney. You can take him the bill and tell him that you thought it would be OK on this occasion.'

'You are mischievous Mr Waterman, junior.'

'Miss McDonald, you are worth it. Let's celebrate our coming together. Let me say, you look absolutely beautiful and radiant tonight and I am so glad our love of libraries has led us to where we are now.'

She offered her hands which I took and squeezed affectionately. 'And just where ARE we now?' she asked, beaming at me.

'During my busy week I missed you,' I said.

'I missed you too,' she replied.

'Well that's where we are. 'We came together so easily. It has seemed like a natural progression. Let's drink to us and what we can do together in the future.'

And so we did and then got into tomorrow's prospects. Julia started asking me how I was going to approach it all. 'Do you really have an open mind on the subject?' she asked.

'Well, you observant little thing, I must confess I'm not impressed with what I've read. It seems quite a bit of nonsense to me. I just can't conceive that such harsh treatments as electro-shock and brain ops, let alone drugs, can help someone become better. It goes against my grain. But I will take it all in and ask lots of questions. Peter hasn't been into one of these places either, you know.

'Maybe you should do like you said and try out a bit of shock and see if you feel better. You do that and I'll sample the drugs.'

Julia retorted with, 'I'm going to go for a diagnosis first. If they recommend shock, I'll do it,' biting her bottom lip and frowning at the thought.

She continued, 'but what is your interest in this anyway if you're not expecting to be converted?'

I answered her quickly. 'Well, despite my views and what I've read I promised myself I'd get out and expand my horizons. This is a big subject. I'm looking for something that does for the character of Man what I've done in my own little way for Education. I've barely scratched the surface.

'My brief examination of Religion didn't fill me with much hope, though I haven't looked at Eastern ones muchl. My experience with Psychology is also brief and gives a little hope, but is it cutting the mustard in a broad way as yet? Let's at least have some fun at tomorrow's venue. We can't just criticise it from reading a few books. But who knows, we might have to go in a totally different direction and end up forming an anti-barbarism front group.

'Anyhow I can't wait to see you psychoanalysed and how you respond to a little electricity to the brain.'

She responded quickly enough. 'How can you talk in such grand terms for Man and yet be such a sadist?'

'I've got to vet the female partner somehow. How do I know if you aren't what you seem to be? I'm told women can be so devious. Look at history.'

'Well, you'll just have to find out for yourself, Mr male chauvinist,' she replied. Lots of joyous emotions flowed between us as we set about our sea bass and posh vegetables. We talked about the day and Joe's experience 'out of the box.'

As we waited for pudding I asked her what her aims were in life. 'Well,' she said, 'I've been making it up as I've gone along, really. I recognised a long time ago that what I saw around me was not much of a life. Before I reached the milestone of teenager I was a happy-go-lucky little girl just doing school – reading a lot of books, playing with my friends and doing a lot of sports, particularly athletics and gymnastics. My mum and dad were all very supportive of me and my elder brother.

'My elder brother Dan and I are very close. He is a few years older than I but we like and do the same things. I often thought, in more latter years, if he wasn't my brother and best friend he'd be my model for a boyfriend. Actually he IS a lot like you.

'Anyway, as teen years progressed I continued to do lots of sports and did really well at school and of course as the hormones kicked in I began to notice that boys were more interesting in a somewhat sexual way, but, apart from a few dalliances with the odd member of your race, I became rather disillusioned with the normal banal boy/girl thing and found myself too much as prey to nearly all of them, who seemed too interested in my body rather than in me. I feel uncomfortable with the predatory game. A lot of males my age were also quite immature; still kids really. My brother is neither of the above.

'My girlfriends have always seen me as a bit aloof toward boys. I've become almost a loner of latter years. So I had become rather more and more confused as to what it is all about, this growing up and 'maturing', as they say. So I decided to further my education on completing my schooling last year, and so there you found me studying Philosophy and becoming rather disillusioned with that too as it wasn't really moving me toward any purpose or career.'

She was silent for a while, looking down at her now empty plate. I had been listening with full attention, and filled the silence with 'that was a very good summary of your life. You are describing a void which I am very familiar with.' I described my school experience and deciding to do something about it which led me to where I am right now.

'Exactly', she said. 'This week, working at the College, and with Joe, and looking at Sidney and Ira, and you and this whole project, I came alive. I was doing something meaningful, with concrete results. Maybe I'm meant to be an Educator. I got such a buzz out of it. Joe came right out of himself. He's doing so well, although baby steps so far. But he is smiling, even laughing, just about. Well he's turned up on time every day and stuck it out. It's as if he's just come out of the desert and found civilisation. Ira and I get on so well and Sidney is a version of you – so calm and helpful and he's got a wicked sense of humour.'

I paid the bill and we caught the tube to Finchley, chatting about the college and all the people involved. Lots of jollity – two new lovers hand in hand, all the way to Julia's house.

'I think this is a good time to meet my family 'she stated. 'I've told them all about you. It isn't too late; they are still up.'

'OK. I'm curious to see who produced this work of art I have here in my hands.' With that we kissed, as we had done here and there on the way home. Julia fumbled for the keys to the door and we entered a very bright, homely hallway. Julia's mother, Delia, came out from the rear, a very young looking mother with that wonderful big smile and rather effusive manner – Julia, Mark I.

'Hullo Mrs McDonald,' I said in response to her welcoming greeting. 'I can see where Julia gets her shining personality from, not to mention her beauty.'

'Not another flatterer!' she almost blushed. We went into the living room. Gavin McDonald, the dad, was on his feet to greet me. We shook hands warmly and everyone sat down. Brother Dan was not at home.

Gavin started the conversation. 'So you're the cause of our daughter's endless ebullience of late.' He was a tall, lean and strong-featured man, also with a rather youthful face like his wife, and a full head of dark hair, and that characteristic personable manner.

'Not guilty,' I replied, putting my hands up and shaking my head. 'Your daughter, it seems, is quite capable of such emotions without provocation from me. I'm sure it runs in the family, from what I can see already.'

I was very easy in their company. I have no problem in these social circumstances.

'I hope you don't mind,' I went on, 'but I am taking Julia to an insane asylum tomorrow (to have her head examined). Maybe that will bring her back to earth again. I'm not sure actually if it qualifies as a nut house. I should be more respectful shouldn't I and call it a Psychiatric Hospital.'

I went on to explain briefly my project and what I was searching for to enhance the Education side of my operation. They seemed impressed and asked lots of questions. We drank tea and scoffed some scones, and then it was time to go. They saw me to the front door and invited me around for dinner next Friday.

Julia went to the gate with me and we arranged to meet tomorrow morning at eight at the College.

'Thank you for dinner Brandon,' she whispered as she kissed me goodnight.

'Julia, you are welcome. I'll see you tomorrow. Be on your worst behaviour.'

We let go of each other slowly and I was off into the night in high spirits. I'm really enjoying this liaison, I thought. It definitely adds another dimension to my existence. I thought I was already switched on but now…….. another level.

Julia went back inside and her mum gave her a big hug, as if to say 'you've scored well there, my girl.'

Her dad was equally enthusiastic. 'We wondered who you would pair up with, or even if there was anyone around good enough. I must say he seems like a special individual. How's he going to fit you into his life, being so ambitious?'

'Well,' Julia replied, 'it looks like I will become equally ambitious, and in my own right. I feel like I've woken up from a slumber and that there is a big bad world out there to put to rights.' She told them about her week. They had not seen her so energised for some time.

CHAPTER TWELVE

The three hospital tourists got things started at the college, grooved Ira in on one or two things, including Joe who needed pretty well one-on-one attention. 'We'll be back around lunch time,' Sidney told her.

'So you lot are leaving me holding the baby and running this whole show by myself. Do I get four times the money?'

Ira grabbed this opportunity for a bit more light ribaldry. 'You are all going to the right place. I think it's ME who should have my head tested. I heard they incarcerate anyone they suspect of having 'loose wires'. So, if you aren't back in a few hours or so I'll assume full control of this place, and if time then allows me I'll come and visit you. On your way then.'

With that we WERE on our way to Peter's surgery.

Peter loaded us up in his car and off we went. 'I don't know how much access they will give us to their facility. They seemed very cautious. So we are career people, right; budding Psychiatrists? You already, Sidney, look more the typical Psychiatrist. A white coat will fit the bill nicely. You can be one of my associates, and these two student types among us can be the would-be acolytes.'

After a lot more joshing we arrived at the hospital in Kensal Green, North-West London. We parked and walked up to the front doors. Whilst waiting for someone to answer the bell I glanced around at the building and grounds. There were a lot of lawns and pathways, with scattered benches. The buildings were somewhat typically school-like. They were not as well-cared for as the grounds, with peeling paint on the windows and some moss-covered brickwork, all giving the place a rather severe appearance.

The doors opened and a rather officious older lady, obviously not expecting us, enquired with a curt 'yes?' Peter explained our visit and without further words she ushered us in and led us to a waiting room. 'Take a seat,' she ordered, and walked off.

The four of us looked at each other as if to say, 'what a friendly woman,' and sat. The room was quite austere, as was the hallway and what we could see at a brief glance down a corridor. The walls were gloss painted in a buff colour. The wood was of dark natural wood, gloss varnished, and the ceiling a faded white. The floors were all in a dull-coloured shiny linoleum.

After about fifteen minutes a middle aged man, dressed in a grey suit and grey tie and with rimless glasses low on his nose, came in and sought out Peter H. 'You are the Psychologist I understand? You two young people are the ones interested in a career in our field?' We nodded.

He looked at Sidney as if about to ask who he was when Sidney, sharp as a tack, introduced himself by name and explained that he worked with Doctor Hillingdon.

'Very well,' he went on. 'What would you like to see? You understand I can't take you into all spaces, but I can show you a few of our wards and perhaps one of our treatment rooms and introduce you to one or two of our resident Psychiatrists. But on no account must you talk to any of the patients. I will give you each a white coat so you blend in better with the surroundings.'

'Got it,' Peter responded. 'That seems fine.'

As we were putting on the white coats our guide introduced himself as the Chief Registrar. His name was Mr. Braithwaite, seemingly not a doctor but having the presence of someone important. We were led along a corridor, the landscape continuing its earlier style, not enhanced at all by the dim lighting.

We entered what seemed to be a large common room where patients, mainly dressed in dressing gowns and slippers, were sitting rather blankly in lounge chairs. Mr Braithwaite explained, 'the better-off ones are allowed the freedom of this room for a few hours per day. Some of them are also allowed into the gardens, especially at visiting time.'

Nearly all the patients, all men, were either talking quietly to each other, or just sitting there gazing around. Brandon was struck by the blank expressions. He had to ask, 'Mr. Braithwaite, are these people here on medications?'

'Of course. Everyone here is on some drug regime, depending on their condition. It's part of the treatment. And it keeps them from becoming agitated as some of them are prone to be,' he answered. 'These people arrive here mostly in a neurotic or psychotic state. They are observed for a period and quickly diagnosed, and put on a prescription of anti-psychotic drugs. Some need more advanced treatments but all have the drugs.'

I continued my questioning in a way that didn't brook any challenge. I was the sincerely interested tyro. 'When you say they arrive in all manner of conditions, what would be some of these?'

Mr. Braithwaite answered in a very learned manner. 'Depression, schizophrenia, manic or compulsive states, some raving quite out of control. If they are not manifesting any obvious psychotic condition at the point of arrival their referral case folder will have been studied and taken into account at the diagnostic stage.'

I probed a bit further. 'Who does the diagnosis? Is it possible to see a diagnostic session, or speak to one of your clinicians to explain what happens? I have become very interested in trying to work out what the various mental ailments are and how they can be treated,' I added earnestly.

'You can't see a diagnostic session but we'll see if we can detour one of the doctors to explain it to you. No promises though.'

Julia asked, 'Mr. Braithwaite, there are no women here. Is there a separate ward for them?'

'Well,' he answered, 'there's an entirely separate block for them. We'll come to them.'

We all followed Braithwaite along another corridor and came to a room marked 'Diagnostics'. It was occupied by a man sitting at a desk perusing some papers. He had a sign on his desk labelled 'Doctor D.W. Fitzgerald'. He looked up when Mr Braithwaite entered. The 'train' stayed outside.

'Doctor, I have these people doing a tour of the hospital.' He indicated to us standing in the corridor, now moving closer to the doorway. Doctor Hillingdon here and this other older gentleman (indicating Sidney) work in Psychology, and those two young people are interested in career possibilities in our field. Could you spare a few moments to answer their questions on diagnosis?'

I'll give it a go,' he said, He straightened up his desk and stood and walked round his desk while Mr. Braithwaite beckoned them all to enter. On the walls were a few large-scale diagrams of human anatomy, particularly the brain and all its parts, and there was a typical medical couch in one corner, with curtains for privacy. They all shook hands. 'What would you like to know folks?'

Peter H began, 'you are the first port of call so to speak, for all entrants, I presume?' he asked.

'For most, yes, but some arrive in a mid-psychotic break, that is, very disturbed, so they go upstairs to the acute ward first. They mostly need to be isolated until we can calm them down and then be observed further. To question them at that point would be futile. Their behaviour is worth more than their words. But the majority I see here first. I study their notes, usually from medical doctors or from Psychologists. They are given a verbal standard questionnaire about their history, their environment, their treatments at the hands of other fields – like your own, sir.' He nodded at Peter H.

He went on, 'for example a patient might have been referred here, having had a nervous breakdown. I ask for the patient's version of this, when it started, for how long it has gone on, and so on. He or she tells me he can't cope with family life any more. His wife and kids are giving him a lot of trouble and he can't control them, or something similar.

'His solution is just to separate himself from them – sit in the garden, go for a walk, or just stay in bed. He's lost his job maybe, due to his mental state. We usually find him quite nervous, maybe shaking a bit, or even just sitting very rigidly or fidgeting excessively. His doctor may have prescribed sedatives.

'This gives us an opening. We place him in a ward of people with a similar state, that is, not severe, but nevertheless disturbed. They are given an opening dosage of one or two drugs which are aimed at calming them down.'

'We have here,' pointing to a shelf of many books and extracting one in particular, 'a guide for diagnosis.' The book was titled DSM 1 (1952). 'This is the Diagnostic and Statistical Manual for mental disorders. It lists all the various categories and describes them. We can label a patient using this manual, coupled with our interview questionnaire and any observations.'

Peter asked, 'do we know, mentally, the source of their travail?'

'Not precisely, but the brain is a rather complex entity, and it takes a bit of trial and error to find which drugs work best on which patients. Most Psychiatrists are trained in diagnostics and can operate the drug regime themselves, or in consultation with the Head Psychiatrist.'

I took my chance. 'Doctor, is it that all these mental phenomena are all brain related?'

'As far as we know to date, evidence points to this being the case.'

I went on, 'do you expect these patients to recover to their normal states with drugs?'

'Yes and no,' he answered. 'Some calm down enough to be released again into society, with their supplementary drugs to help them. Others don't respond enough for release and may be recommended for electro shock treatment. In really extreme cases they may need an operation, such as a lobotomy. These usually don't revert to their former selves but can, in some cases be released back to their homes, if that is functioning.'

Julia came in here. 'So we don't cure them but quell the demons somewhat, so they don't need hospital attention all the time.'

'More or less, yes. But we have come a long way since the 'early days', thank God. We are still working on it.'
Sidney asked, 'Do the drugs have side effects?'

'As with all drugs, medicinal, or mere alcohol, there are side effects. But they are not extreme. Drug treatment is in its relative infancy and new ones are being developed all the time.

'I must be off now to do my rounds. I hope I have been of help,' he said, looking at his watch.

We all said our goodbyes and proceeded further with Mr. Braithwaite, who indicated he could take us to a typical ward.

'Is it possible to see an electro shock machine, do you think?' I asked

After a pause and a slow shake of the head he answered, 'I don't know about that young man'. Another pause. 'I'll see what I can do. This is highly unusual. I'll ask our Consultant Psychiatrist, if we come upon him.'

We went up a flight of stairs and entered a ward full of beds sectioned off by curtains. Probably twelve beds made up the ward. Some were occupied and some empty. 'Presumably this ward is for less acute cases, where patients could come and go like the ones downstairs?' Peter asked.

'Yes.' Mr. Braithwaite replied. 'There are three wards in this block, just like this; the same upstairs. These here have just had their medications and so are rather less active than they might be. Each ward is supervised by male nurses who attend to everything, like toilet requirements for some, meal times, any patient troubles.'

The patients were a mixture of those preoccupied with their internal troubles, just lying there or sitting on the edge of their beds, some rocking backwards and forwards, others talking to themselves. Some were talking to each other normally.

'They are visited by one of the doctors every two days. Once a week they may have an assessment which goes more thoroughly into progress, or deterioration, whichever is the case.'

Peter asked, 'If I were to have a conversation with a selection of these people, how would it go?'

Mr. Braithwaite replied, 'some would be somewhat coherent and apparently normal, and many would be non-sequitur, or even just silent, but it would have to be fairly calm and simple conversation.'

I asked, 'Are we able to visit the more acute ward, or the one which restricts patient movement?'

Braithwaite hesitated. 'Well this will be pot luck, though it is probably the best time of day for it. I will have to talk to the Consultant on that floor first. If we are lucky we may at the same time be able to visit the Shock Room whilst we are there.' We walked out to the stairway and were told to wait there whilst he went into a nearby office and made a call to the ward.

Julia somewhat whispered, 'I don't see a picture of health and happiness here, but I suppose one wouldn't, in any sort of hospital. Nevertheless I get a picture of troubled human beings hanging onto their sanity by a thread, monitored largely by drugs. I was looking into the eyes of a lot of these men and not seeing much of them 'at home' so to speak.'

The other two were heads-down and looking rather serious.

Mr. Braithwaite re-appeared and ushered us up the stairs, explaining, 'we will have to be quick. Doctor Cusack will be free in a moment and can give you a few minutes.' We went up two flights and entered another ward which contained small rooms rather than open plan.

Doctor Cusack, a rather stern looking individual with a bald head, a red face and a bushy moustache, appeared out of the first room we came to and without a greeting he almost ordered us to follow him.

Ahead, out of one of the rooms on the right, a patient, flanked by two nurses supporting him, shuffled along the corridor. We glanced quickly at the patient as we allowed him to pass. He looked semi-conscious.

Julia and I glanced at each other with concerned looks as Doctor Cusack led us into the room from which this poor chap had just come.

'This is what we call the 'Shock Room' he said. 'Electro Convulsive Therapy is administered here, by means of this machine here,' indicating what resembled a large wireless, with a glass face and a number of knobs and dials. Plugged into it were two wires at the end of which were electrodes in the form of a headset. The machine was mounted on a table at the side of a bed. The doctor explained, 'the patient is strapped down to the bed and these electrodes are placed on his temples and the machine, monitored by the instrument panel, delivers a current to the brain. The patient does convulse, hence the reason to strap him down, to prevent any injury. The process is quite quick as it is electricity, after all. The amount of current is relatively light considering the voltage that comes out of the socket.

'The idea is to pass the current to the brain, especially at the areas considered to be associated with thought and emotions and thus relieve the patient of his surplus stress, depression, whatever.'

Peter H asked, 'do you give them an anaesthetic?'

'No, but usually a sedative, especially if we are dealing with a severe case of psychosis, such as suicide, or mania.

'Mostly, after a recovery period, the patient experiences some relief from his symptoms, at least at first. Thence repeated treatments are required at particular intervals.'

The four of us were fairly stunned by what we were seeing and hearing. We were led out of the room and led along the corridor. I asked Doctor Cusack if these machines were available to the general public or other clinical establishments. 'And what would happen if a normal well person, such as yourself for example, were to submit to this treatment?'

He stopped and looked at me as if he thought I might be winding him up. I assuaged this notion with a perfectly straight face and genuinely enquiring look. 'Well firstly, one has to be trained in their use. It would be dangerous to let loose this device to random hands. Even Psychologists wouldn't use it, a) because it isn't their field, or shouldn't be, and b) they aren't trained. The device is easy enough to use but how to administer it, and on who, is more involved.

'And as to whether I would submit to this treatment, the answer is 'no'. One has to be mentally ill to qualify. You wouldn't operate on a patient's heart if there is nothing wrong with his heart, would you?' There was a bit of sting in this remark.

'But what would happen if you WERE given a shock, though normal?' I persisted.

The doctor looked at me and then turned away, leading us on. I thought I would have to use my imagination to answer that one. And I did. I suspected the doctor hadn't thought of the answer before but nevertheless I thought it was a good question.

We stopped at a random room, with its usual viewing panel. Doctor Cusack told us that he could show us two or three rooms and then he would have to get back to his tasks. 'This fellow here came to us quite disturbed and suicidal. He was immediately put on a course of drugs and after a few days, after having created quite a commotion, we started on his shock treatment. He has calmed down quite a lot, but is still on suicide watch. His door is locked. You notice there are bars on the windows in this room.'

We each looked in and saw a man slowly pacing the room and occasionally sitting on the edge of his bed. He was sometimes holding his head. We then moved on to another room and were told, 'this one suffers from severe mood swings, known as 'manic depressive'. At the moment he seems to be quite level, the shock treatment having seemed to have worked somewhat.' The man was prone in a sleeping position.

The door of the next room was open and the patient was sitting at a desk drawing a picture on a note pad. 'This one is probably due for discharge, after a bit more observation. He is able to move about, and even go outside at visiting times. He looked at us all and announced, 'so there I must leave you. I'm sorry I didn't have more time. We are really busy here.'

'Thankyou Doctor,' Peter acknowledged, and he was off.

Mr. Braithwaite told us he could show us briefly the female block. And off we went down the stairs and outside again. We were shown the female block which was not that different from the male one. We did comment that a lot of the nursing staff were male. There were some females. On the whole the staff seemed like a caring bunch of people. Not an easy job.

After they reached the gardens again and whilst strolling back to the entrance, Mr. Braithwaite asked the two 'budding Psychiatrists' if they seriously contemplated a career in this field.

I answered first (thinking, not on your nelly). 'Well it is a bit early to decide that yet. We are at the beginning of our search for a career. I am a little disturbed at what I saw, to be honest. Is there any part of your treatments that doesn't rely on drugs and the other treatments?'

'Well yes, but in combination with drugs. But these are 'talking therapies', much like what you would be familiar with Doctor Hillingdon. In this hospital we don't do much of this.'

Julia asked, 'Is the upper floor of these buildings tantamount to an asylum? I mean what happens to people who are obviously lunatics? What happens to people who are insane by virtue of their harmful behaviour towards other people?'

He became a bit patronising at this point and rebuffed the question. 'We don't really talk in those terms young lady – lunatics and madmen. These people are sick for sure but we address them professionally as just patients with various levels of psychosis. There are establishments, usually attached to prisons, who deal with the very extreme cases that society throws up.'

'Well thank you for your time Mr Braithwaite,' Peter said as we reached the entrance door. 'We'll be off now. It has been very enlightening.'

We walked off to our parked car and decided we needed some sustenance after all that. We went to a café around the corner in Ladbroke Grove.

We sat and ordered bacon and egg sandwiches and tea. Sidney started the discussion. 'Well it all looked normally hospitally but it all seems much like a dressed-up prison for the mentally afflicted instead of for criminals. I don't see the cure fitting in here; make them quiet and manageable.'

I offered my opinion. 'The thing is, their 'technology' IS based on the premise that the brain is the organ of thought and behaviour – correct a malfunction by tinkering with the mechanism. They are trying to do something about a theoretical chemical imbalance which is causing the problems.

'We already know, do we not Peter, that we can improve behaviour by directed communication or simply by study techniques. But what are we directing it all at? Whether the brain has anything to do with it is conjecture at best and unprovable at worst. When a person loses his rationality we say he loses his mind. We know that people are at various levels of rationality. We know that traumas and continual failure result in some deterioration in ability to think and make rational decisions and tend to take people out of life bit by bit.

'Look at Joe for instance. He's now reversed that trend just a bit, just from a little TLC. Has this got anything to do with the brain? It seems a theory, not a proven technology. How do you examine a brain and observe these processes? You can't.'

Peter was next. 'Do you know, I had some idea that they actually did things this way but today has opened my eyes. You have articulated it very well Brandon. I'm so glad I have not actually referred anyone to a place like that.'

Now Julia, who'd become uncommonly serious in the last hour pounded her hammer. 'I think this subject is fraudulent. I'm disgusted with what I saw, and we only saw a snippet. Unless people are coming off the 'assembly line' cured of mental illness without drug maintenance, in the same way as broken bones are healed or infections handled, it is a pretence. How could people like us ever come close to contemplating work in that field? We wouldn't. It is repugnant.'

She now lightened up a bit and spluttered into an apology with a laugh. 'I'm sorry. It's out of my system now.'

'Well it wouldn't be the first time we've encountered pretended knowledge would it? Sidney added.

We finished our butties and tea and headed out and back to something like normality. We travelled back mostly in silence at first and then started talking about our afternoon plans and activities.

———————————

I had been given much food for thought. Back at the college I took a moment to survey our domain, i.e. what we had going in all – our now five branches, their degree of establishment, the future of our Education plan. Up to now I had been busy expanding in this one vector, and although it had succeeded exponentially and could probably continue so, it was nowhere enough for my ever-burgeoning ambitions. Would I be satisfied with this? I had opened Pandora's box and looked inside. I definitely could not continue so hands-on if I were to pursue other paths as well.

After business Julia and I went home with Sidney and the three of us gathered on the veranda over Mrs Waterman's pie and mash.

Julia and I had earlier been discussing the subject of the mind and the problems facing society, spurred by the plight of the unfortunate but encompassing the average specimens of humanity too. Now here we were affronted by the existing solution to the matter.

'Julia, I noted your outrage at the fraudulence of Psychiatry. I am going to go a step further and call it criminal. To somehow convince a hierarchy in government and establishments, over at least a century, that they are the experts in mental matters and so gain financial support to the extent they presumably have, and in the face of such shallow evidence, this has been the cleverest con trick of all time, which doesn't say much for the ones duped.

'There is more to this than meets the eye. So I think we have two avenues to explore here: one is what's this farce all about, and the other is what IS the right solution to improving thought and behaviour?'

'I'm with you there. I'm glad you said 'we'. I could wholeheartedly get into this.' We had already tacitly agreed to be partners in this crime.

After having downed the delicious fare I said to Sidney, 'Grandpa, I need to extricate myself from the college somewhat and go out and tackle the bigger problem, as I have expounded to you before.

'To do that we need a more proper and trained setup. I would concentrate on training the existing teachers more fully and training MORE of them and add a few of the best of them to the management so that you and Ira are better able to run the place. I would still be present but more as an adviser if needed. That all assumes of course that you are willing, and Ira too. It's more responsibility but better than being a political lackey down there in Westminster,' I added lightening it up a bit.

Sidney looked at me and smiled. 'Of course I'm willing my boy. You are MY project in many ways. How can I say 'no'? I'm sure Ira will take up the challenge as well. Don't tell me our bright new star here is going to sit on the side lines though.' He was awaiting a smart reply, and got it.

'Brandon and I have decided to become new-wave Psychologists and Psychiatrists,' Julia pronounced, 'though we won't tarnish ourselves with those titles officially. You could call us Philosophers or protagonists. Watch this space.'

I looked at Sidney with a look that said, 'how about that then?'

145

After a little discussion about logistics I changed the subject. 'We still haven't got hold of Andrew, have we?

Sidney answered. 'Well I did have a bit of a discussion with him about his education. He just scraped through his exams and wasn't too happy. I suggested he come down to the college and get an assessment and see how the other students were advancing. As yet he hasn't responded. I'll have another go at him over the weekend. He's actually quite bright but he's unmotivated.'

I suggested that maybe Julia would be the best person to motivate him and that though I had spent a fair amount of time on Andrew over the years I hadn't done anything since leaving school. 'Like to have a go Julia?'

'Sure. You best tackle him on the actual study though.'

'You mean you aren't up to doing this yet? I'll take this as the final part of your study apprenticeship.'

'OK. There's the gauntlet.'

With that we were done and I walked Julia home - my 'quality time' with her. We discussed our project together. I was very impressed with Julia and how she had jumped into it all with such clear vision. 'I'm so glad you've joined us. Maybe I should go back to the library and see who else I can pick up. We are going to need some more manpower.'

'Don't you mean girl power?' she responded.

We were so comfortable together and the excitement of our newfound relationship was ever heightening. The sexual attraction was coming close to a peak. Both of us had been raised in fairly moral surroundings, and society, though loosening up on sexual freedom, hadn't exactly reached revolutionary proportions by a long chalk. However, though our hormones were in good order they were rather tempered by the spiritual plane that existed between us, as from the beginning. We could hold each other close and just be together in each other's spaces and laugh and joke and discuss creatively plans ahead. There was no 'taking it one day at a time' or 'we'll see where this goes to'. It was off and running.

I announced, 'I want to travel and explore other cultures, especially their religions. I don't hold any further hopes that Religion as WE know it can lead to the answers we want. Nepal and China and Japan seem like fruitful sources from what little I have learned. I am going to read up on things like Buddhism and Shintoism and others. I think another trip to the library is in order, to give me a start. Who knows what adventures await me,' I teased.

Julia asked, 'How do you suggest we go about doing our expose of our favourite doctors?'

I thought for a moment. 'The daily practitioners, like we met today, are the disciples, the adherents of the whole movement, just like the teachers in the schools. There will be a few diehards in their ranks, and a few bad eggs, (like the DH at the school) and then a lot of probably well-meaning troops who have swallowed the dogma and can't face what is really going on (like Casey and the Head at the school).

'But somewhere at the top of the Psychiatric tree there must be some founders or instigators, who are pushing the whole process – the powers behind it all. I think we should look there. Before doing that I think we should broaden our knowledge; speak to ex- patients, or victims, talk to more Psychiatrists, gather information that backs up our initial findings, if that's the way it goes.

'You can bet that the Education Department Establishment is rather benign compared to what we will confront with this lot. Also, what do we want out of this?'

Julia didn't pause at all on this question – exposure on a grand scale. The public has to be educated as to what is going on in the name of Mental Health. It's no good going half-baked into this. But I agree, more data and facts are needed; lots more people interviewed. They probably have an annual convention or something where they all congregate and announce and discuss things. I may start there while I'm swatting up and advertising for victims to come out of the woodwork.'

It was now obvious that Julia had taken this on as her baby. 'Yes, all or nothing. I like it,' I agreed. 'I will work on extricating ourselves from our enterprise here on a more or less full time basis. This project must continue to expand as part of the solution I am looking for which somehow could supplant the existing lack of viable solutions. Good God, what are we into here? It looks daunting. Oh well, one step at a time.'

Julia hugged me and added, 'To think I was living a life of ease, quietly studying Philosophy in quiet places, minding my own business only weeks ago.'

'Well you are actually 'to the manor born', so to speak, my love, as am I. Just a few years ago I was sitting in my classroom sleeping my way through school and reading my books. My teacher woke me up would you believe, by slamming a book on my desk. That was the catalyst to get moving. I suppose I should give him some credit for whatever I achieve.'

'And you woke me up,' she added, 'by lacing my coffee at the coffee place that day.'

'Oh no, you were ripe for the picking as they say,' I protested. 'Actually, you seduced ME, not the other way round, and I am still under your spell.'

'And may you remain so,' she ordered.

We then went about our normal activities. But not for long.

PART TWO

CHAPTER ONE

Another year passed, time having speeded up, represented by concertinaed accomplishment.

Julia was a natural star executive, having taken on the reins of overseeing all the six Colleges and now grooving in Peter Hillingdon to take over her job so she could concentrate on the subject of Mental Health.

Peter gave up trying to help lost causes, as he had come to view them, and was now only a part time Psychologist. Julia had recruited him after she had unbugged his own education flaws using the 'Waterman method'.

Sidney, the revived grandfather, was the organisational wizard behind the expansion of Colleges, having used his influence to gain investors and see that finances allowed this expansion. Even Julia's parents invested, having seen the two stars in action up close. The whole entity would become a limited company soon enough.

Ira took the strain and ran the day-to-day logistics of the main College in Finchley. She had now legitimised the whole entity, using her 'friend' Audrey in the Department.

She attended PTA meetings and entertained herself there by subtly but somewhat sarcastically validating the school for its improved performances. Her son Nigel had completed his schooling and had joined the College as a tutor. Her other two boys were flying along at the now greatly improved Finchley High.

I wasn't idle either in all this affluence. I had devised a method of study whereby a larger number of students could study together in one classroom instead of one-on-one. A trained tutor would supervise their study with each student doing their own tailored course, often in pairs.

One-on-one was never going to expand anything. Eventually we'd have to penetrate the mainstream Education system and use our Colleges for more remedial hard core cases and for training teachers.

Using James Hopkins I'd managed to enter the front door of his institution and make some useful allies. My publication was being distributed throughout the Department and in some schools.

Television had introduced me and Julia to the masses on a program called Young Entrepreneurs – not peak time, but it was an intro. Some of the Nationals got hold of it too, some hypercritical, some favourable. All free advertising.

I took charge of who would run the branch Colleges and trained them up to be 'clones'. My own novel was taking shape and I continued to attend debating sessions with Sidney.

CHAPTER TWO

The Minister for Education, newly ensconced in her lofty office in Whitehall, had a lot on her plate. She flicked through her ministerial briefcase, loads of files on her desk and her more pressing 'in' tray. Then she saw the 'pending' tray and after glancing through this she was hit by the true impact of what she had inherited from a not-too-successful predecessor.

'What have I inherited here?' she said to her Aide who was delivering a cup of coffee to her.

'If the press and airwaves are anything to go by, there's a bit to do. If anyone can do it, you can,' Alison answered supportively.

Diane McAdam had been promoted from junior ministerial ranks and was known throughout the Department as a no-nonsense Executive.

She sat back in her seat with her cup and saucer in hand. 'Show me the press cuttings would you Alison,' she ordered. 'Let's start there. Then I will see more clearly the way ahead, or maybe sink into apathy perhaps.'

She studied the cuttings as she sipped her coffee. There were a few high profile legal cases on the go, reports of failing schools and teacher shortages, plus the usual storms of privileged versus ignored.

What's new, she thought? She called in Alison again. 'What would your predecessor have regarded as his first port of call in all this, do you think?'

Alison sat on the edge of her chair opposite her new boss and thought briefly and then adventured to suggest: 'well, if you ask me, he would usually start by working out a way to put a fair gloss on things, such as preparing press releases which would appease the media, at least temporarily. As you can see by the stack on your desk he was rather trying to balance a lot of plates at once and, well, frankly drowning in the overwhelm. He was a very considerate man but probably too mild for ministerial office. I felt sorry for him.' She carried on with more pre-history and opinions.

Half way through Alison's narrative Diane had resumed shuffling through the press cuttings and had stopped at a particular bunch of articles regarding a rogue College in North London. She was particularly taken by the invective heaped on its 'teenage upstart' head teacher. She read through a few of them and then tailed off.. 'hmm, interesting'.

'Ok, Alison, I've got the picture there. I think I'll start off by doing the opposite. I can't stand the games we politicians play, especially with the media. I think I'll spend my day looking through this stuff here and work out what's important in order of importance, if you see what I mean. Thanks Alison.'

While Alison turned and started to leave, Diane asked her, 'by the way what is it about this young chap that the media seem so much up in arms about?'

'He's some bright kid who seemed to have created a lot of trouble at his school, you know, stirring up the PTA and then encouraging truancy. He's set up his own College as an alternative to us. That's the short story anyway. Who knows, he might be on to something.'

'OK, thanks. Do I have any meetings today, apart from the Cabinet meeting?'

'No, today you are lucky. You can be a desk jockey after the Cabinet meeting.. I'm going to go out there and get the rest of them going.'

Diane added, 'Perhaps I should call a staff meeting and introduce myself to the civil service that matters.'

'Good idea Diane. Is it OK to call you that?'

'If you manage the whole place efficiently, as I'm told you do, you can call me what you like. She smiled. 'I'm fine with that.' Alison left. Meeting over.

I was happy enough with what I had established educationally, but was it about to revolutionise the mainstream system I wondered? I decided I would have to stoke up a 'movement', somewhere between a revolution and an evolution.

My immediate opportunity came on a TV Debate program. It was an audience of all-comers from various backgrounds, mainly middle class-ville, taking on a panel consisting of Education hierarchy, a headmaster or two, a professor, and an outsider.

The program consisted of an MC who had a selection of questions submitted priorly by members of the audience. More or less, each panel member got an opportunity to answer the question in turn (although that wouldn't happen exactly like that because the usual panel members couldn't resist talking over each other).

There was an open period toward the end of the debate or at the tail end of each question where random members of the audience could ask un-vetted questions of whomever.

So, off it kicked. Right there on late night TV each panel member was introduced by name and profession or interest. I was to be the last to be put on the spot (how not to be the least I was figuring)

I sat quietly, listening interestedly to each speaker in turn. The penultimate speaker to my 'baptism of fire' was an ordinary teacher. He agreed that it was impossible to cater to all abilities. 'My class is thirty-five. The brightest get on with it and the bottom of the class struggle. Although I try and co-opt the help of the parents with special homework drills I am worn ragged and feel I have to soldier on and do the best I can knowing it is nowhere near enough. After all we can't provide a one-on-one system. We'd have to have almost as many teachers as pupils.' Mild applause.

'Now we come to you Mr Waterman,' announced the MC. 'I expect you have the answer for us,' he added a little sarcastically.

I passed this off as if it hadn't been said like that. 'Thankyou Mr Shelley. We have a number of opinions on this panel as to whether class sizes is the reason behind falling standards, teachers' difficulties, and so on. There are a few very valid points. But may I say, the situation of inadequate education for the masses goes on, so if we could correct a few points, tinker with it here and there, would it resolve? As our teacher here admitted he is being worked to the bone to try and improve it, which tells a tale all by itself.

'To cut a long story short, what I have done, I think, is undercut the whole problem. Yes, half, or more students fail in their studies, not because of the teachers alone, but because they stack up too many failures and are left behind. The failures don't get undone. This is more a matter of learning techniques.

'Of course, they could all be shunted over to my schools and I would become the first Education magnate, and the latest millionaire.' The audience giggled a bit at this. 'But I have other things to do and it's not what you pay your taxes for.'

I felt I was getting them onside. 'Because I, relatively recently, was an unchallenged top student in my school, and learning nothing I hadn't learned by myself, I offered to help the school bring the slow learners up to the mark, even in my own time.

'I had, having left school, a truant indeed, taken a few of the lagging students and worked out why they were failing and corrected it. I did this by evolving a technique of learning which bypasses the need to fail. It is simply a new way to educate which circumnavigates failure and rote learning and further, misbehaviour.'

The MC was going to interrupt at this point, but I put my hand up and ensured him that I was winding up. I continued, 'I had two or three examples by this to present to the school, but my whole project was not taken up. I contributed to the school with no thought of revenge as you put it.' I said this looking the guilty party straight in the eye.

'To finish, it is improved teaching methods, even in large classes, that will solve this situation. It would involve getting by a number of egos, because you see, I am only a teenager, a young neophyte, who can't know what Professors and Heads know. I am not even an adult technically, but let me tell you I have done my full apprenticeship in 'not being an adult' and perhaps there are some even twice or more my age who are still in their apprenticeship.'

At this the crowd decidedly expressed their approval. When it had all died down the MC invited random questions. One was from a very serious looking man, directed at me. 'Aren't you just climbing on the bandwagon here and trying to boost your ego and make some money all the while?'

I looked at him directly. 'I invite you to my Head College to see for yourself. Bring your children along too. It's results; these speak louder than words. My whole credence is in results. Those parents who wanted results have stayed with me because I give them results.

'Now we have seven schools, all getting results. Yes, it is private remedial Education but I'd love to see it instituted into the system. That I've been rejected thus far is perhaps the more basic problem here. It's a pity I am young, but even if I was a wrinkly fifty something I think I would still struggle. It's an institution, an establishment which is so conservative and stuck in its ways it can't change. It needs fresh, looser minds.'

Again more eager applause. The MC went onto more mundane and less vital questions which the rest of the panel largely answered, I perhaps having 'shot my bolt' already.

Towards the end, one in the audience asked me if there were any students that couldn't be handled. I jumped in. 'Yes, at this time, the really socially disadvantaged or damaged and the anti-social or psychotic members of society. But, I am looking into that too. And that's not Education.'

The program wrapped up. There I was, being surrounded by members of the audience who wanted more information.

They soon 'had their fill' and I was approached by Mr. Tom Shelley and congratulated on what he called an 'exercise in stage presence'. 'You certainly handled that with amazing skill, given to only a few in my experience. You should become a politician. I can see you now in the House. We'll have to have you on again, maybe WITH some politicians. Sorry about the sarcy intro there; that was out of order.'

'Thank you for that Mr. Shelley, and thank you for letting me finish my piece,' I replied.

Of course I had been on a few smaller programs before but this was prime time TV with a lot of ratings. Perhaps I had created a more formidable stage for myself. The cogs were turning. There was a big splash in most of the big nationals the next day, with my picture loud and prominent.

———————————

When I got home that night Grandpa was there to greet me and ask how it went. There was no TV in the Waterman household. We didn't even have a telephone. I hugely understated the experience so Sidney didn't have a sense of what had really happened. I also described my buzz at mixing it with the adults and bigwigs.

But the McDonald household did have a TV and Julia and family had seen the whole thing, so that in the morning when I arrived at the College the whole staff had the newspapers spread out on a desk and were reading the articles. On my entrance they all cheered me like a conquering hero. Julia jumped all over me with hugs and kisses. Sidney just sat back and grinned with pride. Andrew was patting me on the back and after the initial outbursts and greetings Ira came up and gave me a warm hug. I love this team.

I asked if the articles were accurate and was told to look at the headlines. 'I'll read these later'. Ever pragmatic, I added, 'it's good to get some free publicity. I've been sort of invited on again. The MC, Tom Shelley, was very positive. Expect some enquiries from this as I spoke with many of the audience after the show who all had problems with their kids' education.'

I had seen Julia only in passing in the last few days so we went out to the café around the corner and I related my tensions and buzzes to her on the whole TV program. 'You have these learned eyes on you, and these big cameras, and this rather expectant audience. It took me a few minutes to really feel comfortable but then I began to just speak my mind. I could tell they were all listening. When I got the big cheers elation set in.'

Julia said, 'I think you were wonderful, particularly when you stuck it to the toffee noses on the panel. The audience loved you from then on.' She leaned over and kissed me again and then added, 'my parents and my brother were watching. They were gobsmacked. My father said that we were well worth investing more into, now that he'd seen the action side of you. And my brother wants to talk to you. Maybe he's another resource.'

'Alright,' I began. 'Now is the time to get onto our next project. By the way, I meant to ask you how are the newer schools going – Westminster and Kensington?'

'They are an interesting bag, a bit different from the others in that we have more demands from the posh and famous. For that we charge more money,' she joked. 'But on the whole they are doing fine. We have this ace 'Head Master' in Westminster. He's very posh himself but is a free spirit, and so funny. He uses humour to handle all   situations. Anyway, he's on the ball and won't take any prisoners when it gets down to it.'

'Good. Anyhow I was thinking that having become a TV star, as I have, maybe this is our opening platform for a bash at the Psychiatrists. Wouldn't it be interesting to be invited onto a program that deals with Mental Health. We still need to study up on the subject some more, visit lots more practitioners, and get lots more victims to come forward to complain about their treatment. This is your baby, baby,' I said humorously. 'You suggested it. I'll rustle up some Psychiatrists to interview or pretend mental illness to and do lots more research than I could manage in the library with you distracting me and all. When we have enough together I'll write a book about it, and put myself forward as a protagonist.

'At the same time I'm going to take you out on a date to that Annual Mental Health Conference you mentioned once. It is being held in Brighton next week. I'll find out if I can get tickets. Or how about we gate-crash it?' I added mischievously. 'Also there are various bodies that represent the profession, and there are some that represent patients too I think, or patients' rights. Let's get into these.

'I dare say I should start using my newfound stardom to try and further push the Department into using our methods. I'd like to start a revolution against this Establishment, but I'm not sure if that would work, especially if it goes the way it went at my old school, with the frightened parties begging off when push came to shove. Let's call it a ground swell of public opinion.'

We two lovebirds then had five or ten minutes of our own, outside of projects and plans. We just jousted back and forth and cackled a lot. I asked Julia to invite me for dinner at her place so that I could talk to her brother.

On the way back to the College I popped another surprise. 'I'd also like to invite you for a date at a Hindu temple. I've been researching Eastern Religions, in particular Taoism, Buddhism and Hinduism. I want to speak to their head honchos and see some of their stuff in action.'

'Oh', she swooned. 'I've always wanted to eat chapattis in a proper temple. What a romantic idea. How should I dress? Full sari?'

'Who said you were going to get fed?' I responded in mock severity. 'You see I set out to discover if the Psychologists and Psychiatrists could enlighten me further on what it is that holds the key to being able to improve human behaviour. What is it that we are addressing here that seems to have resisted all attempts by man to accomplish so far, beyond moral codes, like the Ten Commandments?

'Anyway, I've read a few interesting things so far, and, rather than take you to a 'who dun it' or a football match I thought you'd much rather do something new and educational.'
'At least it's not an insane asylum,' she said, trying to have the last word.

Dan McDonald was one of a few more additions to the expanding staff. After I'd met him for dinner he was a convert.

Talk about two peas in a pod. Dan was the male version of Julia in that he was physically striking and as personable. He joined the project keenly and picked it all up quickly.

Dan was to be the Peter Hillingdon of South West London. He spearheaded the College of Remedial Learning into Chelsea and Fulham. These are two middle/upper middle class, more inner London suburbs with quite a population. Dan, with the help of Ira and Sidney at first, took up the mantle and more than served his apprenticeship in these two areas. Sidney just about managed to create the finance until fees could ease the burden. My exposure on TV had served us well.

I decided to use my TV success by using Tom Shelley, the anchor man from the panel show. Tom seemed to be an ambitious young man but as yet not fully untied from any dogma from his seniors. Independent Television competed with the BBC and ratings begat advertisers and advertisers begat money, and money begat ITV, all in a circle.

A new controversial star like me, very young, charismatic and very believable, was just what the doctor ordered. In fact it was Tom who approached me to do a follow-up. As soon as this approach had been made I decided to utilise this TV opportunity to the maximum.

I arranged a meeting with Tom at the Finchley HQ. I showed him around, introduced him to the main protagonists present (Ira, Sidney, Andrew, and a few of the teachers). I had Tom look in on an introductory pupil analysis, (just like the one he had done with Joe some time back now) to see exactly how we sifted the wheat from the chaff and how we organised an individual curriculum for each pupil.

'This is impressive Brandon.' Tom said, 'I didn't realise this was as up-and-running as it is. I have an idea for a program.' There was always a hint of humour or mischief lurking behind his expressions.

Before he could launch into his idea I jumped in and presented MY plan for TV. 'Let me run something by you and see if it fits at all with yours. You could do this as a documentary on our operation. You could call it 'an Upgrade on Education' or, more controversially 'The Education Innovation the Department Turned Down', or something of the like. It could be a live demonstration of how to turn a struggling, underperforming student into a high flier.

' I would take a randomly selected pupil from wherever, maybe one from an average school or from any of your colleagues' families, interview the parents and the pupil and see if they are up for it, and do it on live TV. What do you think?'

Tom replied, 'I like both ideas. My idea was more like your first one; a documentary. This is like free advertising for you isn't it?'

'The thought never occurred to me,' I 'innocently' responded. 'But equally it has to be of interest to the public and hence your advertisers. Sometimes these pupils we get are quite raw to the bone and would be good TV.

'See that guy over there, the guy with the weird haircut (pointing at Joe). He came in here a year or so ago, a complete drop-out, completely inarticulate, barely 'home' at all. We got his parents in on it all. We had to do a big number on them too as part of the problem was that they were failed parents.

'We got through to him enough that he actually turned up on the first day, with his Mum. I promised him a trip to White Hart Lane to watch Spurs if he turned into a proper student. He played the game and changed his habits of a lifetime. I keep meaning to take him to watch Spurs play Arsenal, as promised.

'Look at him, he's a different kid – all smiles, talkative, sociable and more to the point, he reads proper books and is actually enjoying getting educated. His parents are over the moon and are learning how to parent properly.

'You see, this branches over into lots of fields – Parenting, Psychology,

Sociology, and, watch this space, a whole new subject.'

'What's that?' Tom couldn't resist asking,

'Well, I can't tell you that yet. It's my secret for now. It's definitely a dead cert to lift your ratings off the chart. But you see Education is only part of the answer to making a successful citizen and helping to put our youngsters (and adults) onto the right life path.'

Tom Shelley couldn't believe what he was hearing coming out of my teenage mouth (though he was ceasing now to view me as such). 'Why don't we do a documentary on you? It seems like you've crammed enough into your brief life so far to warrant such a thing.'

'Well, I suppose we need to mix a bit of life story in with the Education thing. It could at least be an intro to the learning live shows. Maybe I could become a TV screenwriter, or producer too,' I added teasingly, with a wink.

Tom Shelley wagged a finger at me, mischievously. 'I'll tell you what,' he went on, 'I'll write a 'screenplay' for a program that I think might fly and then run it by you.' He was excited.

Just then Sidney and Ira entered the room, it being the tail end of the day now. They couldn't help noticing the enthusiasm oozing out of Tom Shelley. They'd seen this 'star-struck' look before. They looked at each other and then at me. I was leaning back on a table edge casually sipping a cup of tea. 'Oh oh, what are you up to now Mr Waterman?' Ira piped in.

I looked at Ira innocently and explained, 'just throwing a few ideas around with Tom here. He's planning on making a TV show about you two, the powers behind the throne.'

Tom found this funny and joined in the fun. 'Yes, I've been wanting to write a TV comedy for years. You look like you'd be perfect for the part Ira. And I'm sure Mr Waterman senior has a great sense of humour too. Must be off now,' he added, backing out of the door. 'Thanks for a great afternoon and I'll be in touch, boss.' He winked at me and I smiled broadly and gave him the thumbs up.

As if on cue Julia breezed in and flung herself at me in mock romanticism and ordered me to take her out and lavish on her something other than Education and something that tasted scrumptious, and then… let's see.

She picked up on the atmosphere that had pervaded the office and looked at Ira and Sidney. 'What am I missing here?' I shrugged my shoulders.

'Mr. Waterman here, our benign and totally ineffective MD has been plotting some TV stuff with the TV producer you must have seen leaving as you came in,' Ira accused, 'and I think it all means more work for the rest of us.'

I defended myself as if hurt to the quick. 'How could you say such a thing?'

Sidney decided to side with me. 'To be fair to my boy here, we haven't given him a chance yet. He can't get a word in edgeways.'

'Yes,' I said, 'you are very presumptuous here Ira. What an attitude! I should have you disciplined. For that I am banning you from the workplace tonight. Get home and have a go at your husband, or someone more deserving.'

With that Ira huffed off in mock indignation, muttering 'we'll see …' but with a broad grin on her face as she got outside the room.

I now rounded on Julia. 'And as for you young lady, before I lavish anything on you, you have to do a crash course on the rules of football and the Tottenham Hotspur team because this weekend we have a date at White Hart Lane with Joe and his parents.'

'Oh no, another Waterman date. You are such a romantic! What's a girl to do?' What an actress!

With that we all packed up and waited for the majority to leave and left a few teachers behind to clean up.

Julia and I waltzed out of the building arm in arm. 'This is all such fun, isn't it?' I enthused. 'And everyone is playing the game.'

'Julia agreed. 'I suppose, if I really try I could enjoy this football match date, but do I have to study it first?'

'Up to you. I could easily explain it all when we're there, or better still I'll get Joe to. He'd love that. You've got to admit that the 'dates' I take you on, as you put it, are far superior to any other life experience you've had up to now – stimulating, educative, and lots more, all with a superb meal afterwards.'

Julia couldn't help herself. 'I challenge you …..' I stopped walking and cut her short with a finger to her lips, gathered her in my arms and kissed her tenderly. That shut her up. She swooned and surfaced for air and just put her head to my chest and stayed there while I stroked her hair; two young people comfortably sharing their space. The passers-by all looked and smiled.

'She looked up at me and said, in submission, 'You've got an answer for everything.'

'Is that so?'

We disconnected ourselves and continued walking and found an Indian restaurant which promised good ambience and a decent enough fare. We sat and ordered. 'Tell me about your day, my love.'.

'Well… oh yes, I haven't told you this. You know you were talking about the Psychiatrists having their annual shindig next week, in Brighton. I bypassed you and looked into it. It's a three-day gathering of the faithful. I also found out that we can go along if we get someone in the profession to sponsor us. Enter Peter, our resident Psychologist. He's going to arrange it. He's such a good guy you know. He's like a man possessed doing my old role. I've spent a bit of time with him this week. He's found his vocation. He wants to come with us on one of the three days. I think one day will probably be enough. He's going to choose which day and get the tickets.

'In the meantime I've been searching around for ways and means to pick up on victims of Psychiatry. I've discovered there are opposition groups, even opposition Psychiatrists. There are publications of journals, books and miscellaneous articles on the general subject. This subject, you know, as we've studied, is open to a lot of opinion as to its basis of operation and, if I were to listen to its knockers, especially the ones inside the profession, it certainly comes out as a pseudoscience. But we know that anyway.'

She continued, in between giving me the odd peck. 'And as if to add insult to injury, it is closely tied up with the Pharmaceutical industry of course. Which is the horse and which is the cart?'

I sat there totally in admiration of this person in front of me, and took her all in. The meal arrived and Julia proceeded to eat with her mouth mostly open as she continued her animated dialogue. 'Anyway, I got the names of some of these publications from my new-found partner in crime at the aptly named 'Society of Anti-Psychiatry' down in Queen Anne Street in Central London, right on the door step of the home ground of the Psychiatric profession in Harley Street. We can pore over these together. It's a sort of comedy class.'

I jumped in. 'It's a date then, nine a.m. at the library on Saturday morning, to educate ME. Today is Thursday.' I put my thumbs up in victory and flashed my biggest smile.

Julia didn't waste any time for a bit of play. 'I'm sorry, sir, I have the hairdresser at nine and my beauty therapist at ten; maybe after that.'

'Maybe?' I protested.' You don't need all that pampering; you, in your natural state are simply gorgeous. Cosmetics are for those who need enhancing.' Julia smiled and continued with her 'events of the day' and then we wrapped up and I walked her home, both of us in glorious harmony.

CHAPTER FOUR

The date at the Hindu temple came around quickly. In fact it was the day before our chosen day at the Psychiatric jamboree. The temple was in Southall in West London. We pitched up at the friendly hour of eleven a.m. and knocked at the big front door.

'I thought these places stayed open all day for people to come and go,' I commented.

'I think they are getting our samosas and chapattis ready, don't you think?'

The doors opened and a grandly dressed 'swami' style gent appeared in the doorway and gave us a big smile. 'You must be Brandon Waterman I presume,' he said.

'Yes sir,' I replied. 'This is my colleague, Julia McDonald.' She gave him her most winning smile as she greeted him.

'I am the priest of this temple. My name is Mahal Patil. How can I help you good people?'

I explained. 'We are Educationalists primarily, but our search for personal improvement has led us further afield, most recently into Psychology and Psychiatry. But enlightenment has not shone from these latter areas and in our quest to try and resolve normal living problems we are venturing into religions, particularly eastern ones, such as yours. We are hoping you can steer us through this one.'

Mr. Patil ushered us into the inner sanctums and, after shoe removal, sat us down cross legged on a plush carpet. I expanded on what I was looking for.

'In Christian religions the answer seems to be finding God and worshipping and praying to Him for guidance and power, and in reading the Bible for His word.'

'I see,' said the priest, a swarthy man with a rather pock-marked face and a covering beard, moustache and glasses to complete the stereotype. 'And you want to know if there are answers in Hinduism?'

'Well, that's about it, sir, I answered. 'We are particularly interested in what practical steps can be taken to improve one's mind and behaviour – the reasoning power.'

'You really need a library,' the priest replied. 'But on top of that I can briefly run through our practices here and you can try them out for yourself. Of course we have scriptures, as in Christianity. And we have a number of Gods, but each is a subdivision, if you like, to an overall God, or life force. Over a series of lifetimes a person develops, or not, and becomes a higher or lower tier being. His development is dependent on his deeds in each life. The idea is to get to God or be at one with God.

'To do this is a search for wisdom or spiritual enlightenment in the practices of meditation and yoga. Yoga includes exercise, diet and breathing techniques. You could say that by such techniques one is seeking a oneness with God and the universe.'

'So your God is not worshipped as such?' Julia asked.

'Yes and no. It is a personal worship, not a group one. The term 'God', though meaning the Divine, is not like your Christian God. There is one essence of the Divine, a senior God, Brahman, which is everything created but 'via' other Gods. The three main Gods worshipped are Brahma, Vishnu and Shiva, There are many others representing different things. The worship is to a selected God, via an image, such as you see over there, (pointing to a statue of a God in the adjacent room).

'The idea of the image is to tap into the energy of the real God via the image. One might do this by offerings such as flowers. This practice can be a bit diverse, that is, there are quite a number of variations of the practice. In the end one is seeking to be in personal communication with the Supreme Divinity.

'The essence of our religion is that it is a socio-religious movement which binds its adherents together in a search for a better life. The caste system fits into this and regiments society to that degree. To be a better person you have to try and elevate yourself to a higher spiritual plane and work out what deeds you need to live by to help achieve this. Obviously it is understood that a person is a spirit and goes from one life to another in a different body and maybe caste.'

We wandered through the building which was done out rather ornately with lots of figures of gods, intricate decorations and subtle lighting. 'Perhaps you two would like some refreshments. We have an eating place at the back of this hall.' He led on.

Julia whispered to me rather irreverently, when out of earshot, 'I hope they have chapattis.' I kept a straight face, just.

Mr. Patil reappeared with a plate of goodies and a colleague brought a teapot and cups. We went into a side room and Mr Patil led us in sitting again on the floor (a rug) around a table. 'So you see,' as he poured green tea and passed around the plate of food, including chapattis, 'it is a voyage of self-discovery. I will give you your first lesson in meditation shortly, to demonstrate.'

He asked us about our own beliefs and practices. I told him that we don't believe in the idea of a God who guides, forgives, and rules one's life and that putting one's life in this God's hands is a) hard to achieve and b) negates one's own powers and responsibilities, and c) is so open to abuse and blind following.

While sipping my tea, I told of our ways of improving intelligence and state of mind through proper education. 'We are looking for a technique of undoing and preventing failure and at the same time boosting one's ability to behave rationally, beyond Education.'

Julia, having consumed a number of chapattis and their dips and had her fill, chimed in. 'I like the idea of the spirit finding God, not as a deity but as a concept of enlightenment and freeing the mind of negativity. Somewhere in this may be the answer to our quest.'

The priest came in again here. 'Well that leads us nicely into our meditation because that is precisely what we are trying to do here as a practice - to tackle compulsory negative thoughts and realise more fully the present. Now what we do is simply sit here as we are, close our eyes and repeat an optional mantra. The idea of the mantra is to concentrate one's mind on what one is doing and cause the random thoughts and concerns and worries to subside. It doesn't matter much what the mantra is. One does this for twenty to thirty minutes at a time, a number of times per day, optimally.

'If one is very disturbed in the mind on starting, this is harder to do. But it will take a conscious effort to do the whole thing anyway. If one does this well a great amount of peace may result. As a long-term practice one maintains this peace more and more.

'Are you ready to do this?' he asked. We both copied the priest's position. 'Close your eyes and repeat aloud the mantra 'Om namah shivaya', which is the name of a particular peaceful mantra, but we will just say these words. It's not what the words mean that counts. But don't go into automatic; really chant it over and over.'

We did. After about fifteen minutes the priest stopped the proceedings and asked for our feedback.

I said, 'I found myself wandering off at first but with a bit of will power found myself doing it here and now and nothing else came into my mind and I wasn't really concentrating too hard.'

Julia frowned and said, 'I was all over the place and was distracted by my stomach turning over and over and Brandon's voice, and yours too. I almost got there in the end.' I think she lied.

We 'acolytes' asked a lot of questions and Mr Patil answered them all very patiently.

Our time was up and we rose and thanked our host for his time. I promised to meditate every day for a week or so to get a more full experience.

We left and went towards the main Uxbridge Road bus stop and headed back to the College.

'How were the chapattis and samosas?' I asked.

'Not bad, but whatever I ate with them got my innards working,' she replied.

I looked at her knowingly, 'I guess you were more impressed with the feast than the med.'

'Well yes,' she agreed. 'It's not like physical technologies that have a definite series of steps you follow every time which fix the problem, or it's not like our learning techniques which quickly fix the problems, relatively. It's an exercise in waking up and being all there where you are, ready for whatever comes. I can see that might be valuable. But I think you could accomplish that more easily by going for a stroll and looking at what is there in front of you.'

'Hmm,' I added. 'I'm still struggling with this spirit concept. The thing is, a spirit is not a something. It's a no thing aware of or operating a some thing. Some entity creates an impulse, decides to do something, initiates a series of actions, whether in the world around us or in the mind. It can then decide to change the action or stop it. Interesting though that this spirit is apparently a being who doesn't die, ie, goes from one lifetime to the next. I wonder why there's no memory of past lives. Maybe it's just a supposition.

'Whatever this spirit is it doesn't really matter. We get our students to follow our instructions and eventually change their minds about themselves. We just get them, with our steps, to rub out the past and replace it with some ability to not get into that trap again. And it brightens them up and strengthens them.

We were at the bus stop and along came our first bus, from west to east. We went up to the top tier and sat at the front and continued our conversation.

'All we have to do is find out how we get the same students to change their mind about themselves and drop old habits and not live in the past. It seems to be the same principle.'

'Piece of cake, or should I say piece of chapatti,' offered Julia. 'But not now. Where is that meal-after-a-date you bragged about earlier?'

'Ok. When we get to Marylebone station we'll pop into a caff I went to once in Seymour Place and have us a feast of protein and fat, before going onto the next lap of our journey. Or do you fancy some more curry? It's buttered toast and fry up or chapattis and curry.' I sat back and waited for her to bight.

She couldn't get the answer out for a fit of the giggles.

———————————

We had our three pounds worth of dietary hell and caught the tube to Finchley and walked to our home domain, strolled into the College and set about our separate tasks.

Factually we were spending less and less time in the College and more and more time out and about. Talking of out and about, Peter H strolled in from there and found me in my office. You could say it was 'my' office but it was used by anyone who needed to use an office at any one time.

There were no pretensions about this crew. We didn't require plush offices or a Board room even though we were now seven schools large and counting. However space was becoming a matter as each of our schools was expanding and functional rooms were becoming a requirement, such as a staff room, a meeting room, a couple of interview rooms and much more room for the burgeoning customers.

We needed a bigger HQ. Quite often me and Julia worked at the my house not far away, just to avoid getting tied up with Education stuff.

Peter H collared me before I could get down to my next task – proof of the pudding. 'Tomorrow is our day at the temple of the Psychiatrists, and I think I know what we should do to maximise the experience.'

He proceeded to outline how it would go. I listened and then said, 'Peter I think you should go over all this with the Psychiatric guru. She has some ideas and is actually more up to speed with all this than I. But tell me, are we planning some mayhem amongst their establishment?'

We amused our way through some scenarios and then both went off to share it all with Julia. Peter went first while I made a quick visit to both Sidney and Ira.

They were in what was just passing for a canteen cum office. 'Well hello boss,' Ira chirped, just a little too falsely. 'Have you two reached the state of nirvana yet?'

I bowed my head and placed my hands in a normal prayer pose and with the best Indian accent outside of Bombay, pronounced reverently that heaven was just around the corner, but Julia got a small dose of Bombay belly because she didn't have breakfast and pigged out on eastern 'delicacies' and scoffed too many chapattis.

'Ah, not good for the figure then' Ira surmised.

'Not only that', I went on, 'she then had a full English fry-up on top of it. If this was an antidote it seemed to work. The whole visit was interesting and has given me some food for thought, if you see what I mean.'

Sidney chimed in and asked, 'which room in our house is now to be set aside for meditation or yoga? Are we to be invaded with incense and candles?'

We then sat down and went over the state of the nation of Education. It all seemed to be going swimmingly

I looked at Sidney and asked him what we could do about the cramping of space we were experiencing.

'Oh ye of little faith' he grumbled. 'I'm on it. I'm looking for a space nearby, a bigger building with a separate adjunct to serve as a Head Office. Here in Finchley there are a few options. When I get the logistics assembled I'll let us all know. Not only that, we need some expansion in a few of our other schools, so that means we need an Estate Office and Officer to operate out of our HQ.'

He was on a roll. 'Ira knows a chap who is a surveyor at one of the local estate agents. He may be willing to make the jump to our new post, while I take a long deserved retirement.' He said the latter statement in a serious manner, after a pause.

He looked at Ira and me dead pan, and just stood there.

I looked at Ira, who shrugged as if in disbelief, and then at Sidney again. I put my hands on my hips as if taking this in seriously and then blustered 'nice try Cyril. I'll sue you for breach of contract.'

Sidney and Ira creased up. 'We had you going there for a second or two, my boy. That is a victory.'

They both went on about their plans and I was amazed at how much they had grasped the nettle. If proof were needed I saw I was almost redundant in the administration of our enterprise; very satisfying. I could quite comfortably devote myself to the bigger picture.

CHAPTER FIVE

Time came to pass, the Psychiatric gathering had been held, the College was running 'on auto pilot'. Julia and I took Joe and parents to White Hart Lane, the Jerusalem of North- East London football (which was a howling success) and now I found myself in a new TV studio with Tom Shelley.

We had organised a brief story of my life so far for the first half of the show and a demonstration of my Education methods for the second half of the show; a double forty five minute program, on prime TV.

The story has been told already. I was really in fine fettle. I fielded the questions well and added a lot of humour to the recounting of particular events. To help matters (or so I thought) there was a live audience. I got them well on side at first until a heckler surprisingly interjected into the proceedings.

'You are a fake, Waterman,' the heckler shouted, and then proceeded to rant on, half heard by the TV audience at home and fully heard by the studio audience. I sat silent for a minute and looked expectantly at Tom for an intervention to deal with this. It didn't happen. Tom was a bit frozen.

I said casually to Tom, 'Was this in the script?' The man came even closer to the front of the audience and shouted even louder. He was calling me an opportunist and a right-wing upstart. No TV staff were interfering at this point. A few in the audience were shouting at him to sit down and be quiet.

'OK Tom, I'll handle this,' I said, and promptly disconnected my wiring and jumped down off the stage and walked right up to this man and invited him calmly to introduce himself. By then a huge boom had appeared over our heads. It was loud and live.

'Do you know sir,' I interrupted, 'I've been accused of this before. Perhaps, now that you have taken the stage, you would like to tell the good people your view. I'm sure our host won't mind. I won't mind.' I then beckoned him toward the set at which point the man got cold feet, especially when more of the crowd began to heckle him.

He stormed off uttering obscenities and it was only then that the TV 'bouncers' escorted him out.

As I turned back to the set the TV channel went to an ad break. I told Tom that it was all good and I was ready to carry on. They wired me up and sat me down again, ready to go.

Tom sounded a little aghast. 'You certainly diffused that Brandon. You were your own bouncer!'

When we were back on air Tom apologised to the viewers for the interruption and asked me to comment.

I seized the opportunity for some kudos. 'You know Tom, just like that Deputy Head I was describing, these blowhards, bullies, whatever you call them, are basically cowards when you face up to them. I've learnt that to argue with them is to fuel their fire, but all I did was give him a chance to blow in full view, without opposing him. He wasn't expecting any of that.'

'What would you have done if he'd taken you up on your offer to come up here and tear into you?' Tom asked.

'Your producer willing, I'd have let him,' I answered.

Tom looked at him queryingly, 'You mean you'd have stood for that?'

'Look, I know who I am and what I stand for, so it would be no skin off my nose. He'd have been as embarrassed as hell, especially as the audience would probably have had a go at him too.' I said all this looking at the audience.

At that point I got a big round of applause. I nodded modestly in acknowledgement, and continued, 'You know, most of the trouble I've had I think is because of my youth, which makes insecure adults feel uncomfortable. I keep saying to my students 'don't wait until you are twenty-one before you become an adult.'

This was all good unscripted TV and I had showed more about myself than I could have otherwise.

'Are we still on script?' I asked in a by-the-way manner.

'No,' Tom responded, 'but we couldn't have written a better one than what we've had. But now I will finish off my original questioning, briefly. I'll just make it all up, like you did.'

I took a sip of water and Tom continued to question me about my romantic life and my next project. I tackled the subject of Julia and our unconventional dates and unconventional life with complete equanimity.

'As for my next project,' I said, 'I've given you a clue here – 'Psychiatric Hospital' and 'Indian Temple'.'

Tom decided to play with this. 'So you are introducing Hinduism into Psychiatric Hospitals?' The audience liked this.

He tried again with a few equally ridiculous suggestions. I just shook my head. 'You can book this slot here for a more controversial program. Anyway, changing the subject, who have you got lined up for me to tackle tonight? I hope it's not that same chap we nearly had on just now, is it?'

Again, more laughter.

'Well, as it happens we have a young lady from a local school. She's thirteen and has been selected as a bright girl but underperforming and not that interested in school life, except for getting into a bit of trouble here and there.'

He stood and invited her in with, 'would you please welcome Francis to the show.' The audience applauded and I stood and invited her to sit in a third chair, opposite me.

Looking at the audience I explained, 'with this young lady's permission we are going to expose her reasons for being a tearaway at school.'

They all laughed lightly. Francis, feeling more at ease, slightly, smiled and adjusted herself a little.

I went on, 'you may think I'm joking there when I say that but I've met no students yet who make the school frown on their so-called bad behaviour who aren't also having trouble with their education. Wait and see.'

I started by bantering a bit with Francis. I thought it worth the time to put her somewhat at ease. 'See all these people out here Francis, they are only here as extras. Take no notice of them. See all these cameras and staff here, they are just stage props and busybodies. They are all just lazy geezers who have nothing better to do. We'll just ignore them. And our host here, well he's become redundant. He can fetch us coffee and cake or whatever we fancy. That just leaves us two, do you agree?' She replied in somewhat more relaxed tone, now giggling.

'I promise you we'll not have any hecklers. Ok?' That caused a little mirth. 'We are just going to have a casual chat about school, teachers (don't be too hard on them), and what your plans are. You might just really not want to learn things or follow any particular career path. You know, just take it as it comes. Well that's OK too.' I left that one hanging.

Then I went into my thing, my 'party trick'. I asked lots of questions and got a lot of problems about learning - the failures.

I talked to her right at her level and we concluded that she did have a few aspirations, under the learning detritus and agreed that there were things she should know to achieve these, if she could only get motivated.

I demonstrated that she had to have a will to learn and somewhere to go with it. I promised that in a separate program I would demonstrate the methods I use to get to the bottom of the failures and help her be rehabilitated and even more keen to learn.

I said to her, just as Tom came back into the conversation, 'you are now a TV personality. Who knows, you might see your picture in the paper tomorrow, or people will be stopping you in the street and saying 'aren't you the girl I saw …'. More laughter.

I left it hanging and then, being more into the spirit of things she joked, 'I think it's more likely you will be the one in the papers.' I grimaced. And the audience cheered lightly.

Tom came in and agreed. 'Yes, I think you're right Francis. Are you game for the next show then? The Education mechanic is going to find out what's causing the motor to not operate on all cylinders.'

She smiled a little wincingly and said, 'Yes, I suppose so. This is embarrassing.'

Tom took this as a cue to invite the audience to give our brave young lady, and myself, a big hand. With that we were done.

I gave Francis a big smile and a thumbs-up. 'Well done. You handled that very well. See you next week.'

Tom came up and told me that the show had exceeded expectation, especially with the unexpected participant. 'Next week will be plainer sailing I think.'

'Well I think you are right,' I agreed. 'But you never know. If there's any emotional breakdown, which happens at times, be ready for an ad break.'

'Did you like the interruption we turned on Brandon?' Tom asked.

'You guys will do anything for ratings', I accused.

Tom continued, 'You know I've just got another idea for a show, further down the line. You talked about your girlfriend during the show. How about we have you both on to discuss your romantic-cum-business life together. We could make it a real slam dunk and have you propose live on air.' He looked at me as if he was just closing a deal.

'Now you have damaged our TV partnership beyond repair,' I replied with an almost embarrassed smile on my face. 'I think you are serious, aren't you?' I continued when Tom didn't respond or look away.

'One thing at a time,' Tom added, to let me off the hook. We went off to the canteen and chatted about how well the show had gone. Tom asked me what was likely to occur in the next show.

'Depends on what unexpected guests appear. I think you are trying to set me up for a fall; very devious. No, well it should go fairly smoothly. I think she'll hum and hah a bit and maybe get a bit upset when we get to the nitty gritty.'

'Is that usual?' Tom enquired.

'Quite, especially with girls, who are less worried about showing tears than are boys. But truthfully, a lot of emotion builds up around misconceptions about words and concepts, so much so that when you start to get to the truth the emotions build and, like a pressure cooker, they just blow.'

The two of us wrapped up and went our ways.

I went round to Julia's place and found her 'horrified' that she'd been mentioned on TV. 'How could you?' she protested (just a little too dramatically).

'You haven't heard the worst of it yet,' I told her rather mischievously. 'I've booked us to appear together to do a program on teenage true love. How about that for another one of our now-famous dates?'

Dan was there too, and as Julia backed off with a horrified look and hands to her cheeks, he silently mouthed 'YES!' while he pumped his fist. 'I like it, he said. 'Bring it on.'

Mrs McDonald came into the living room and greeted me effusively and congratulated me on how I'd handled myself on the show. 'Your evening was not exactly boring was it?' We all sat and chatted about the show and what would be on next week.

'Seriously,' Julia had to ask, 'did you really mean that about us appearing together?'

I took her hand and tried to 'comfort' her. 'Don't worry sweetheart, you'll deal with it in your customary way. You'll become more of a TV star than I, especially when Tom announces that you are going to appear on your own on an expose of Psychiatry.' I was so deadpan. Julia was on the hook.

Dan could hardly contain himself.

I noticed this and quickly came in. 'Don't worry Dan I haven't left you out of this. Why not make two McDonalds famous for the price of one. You I have ear-marked for an extension of the Education series – 'Inside the College of Remedial Education.'

Mrs McDonald suggested, smiling, as if being left out of all this, 'I suppose next it will be 'Life in the McDonald household'.'

Julia cottoned on at this point, and punched me on the arm in outrage. 'You know what makes it so believable is that you are so capable of all this. Why can't you just take me to the pictures or for a cruise down the Thames, or something?'

With that I put my arm around her and she responded and was back to normal. Mrs M was obviously enjoying her daughter being in such challenging and loving hands.

Dan piped up and said, 'I'm sure glad you didn't earmark me for the TV screens.'

'Actually Dan,' I responded, 'I didn't, but now it's come up I think you would be ideal for this.'

Julia piped up quickly and put a stop to this. 'Oh no you don't Brandon.

You're not going to play with us McDonalds anymore.'

'OK, well at least not for tonight,' I agreed, with a wink.

As the 'party' broke up and I was putting my coat on in the hall, out of earshot of the rest I said quietly to Dan that Tom had suggested I propose to Julia on live TV.

'Really! We better keep that under our hat.' He was enthused. 'Could you really do that?'

'You mean propose, period, or do it on TV?' I replied.

Julia came in and took me by the arm and led me outside playfully. She looked back at Dan and told him, 'he's being banished now from our house.' Then that big smile.

Julia walked with me along the street for a little while and then stopped and, in my arms she told me how she so admired my TV performance. 'You were stellar my darling. I'm so proud of you. I can't wait until next week.' With that we kissed our goodnights and I disappeared into the night and Julia skipped lightly back to her front door.

CHAPTER SIX

Diane McAdam was working late one night at the Department. She happened to stroll through the large open-plan office where a few of the staff were gathered around a TV set. She strolled up to the group and enquired about what they were doing. One young chap said to her, 'look at this, Mrs McAdam. Look at this guy dealing with this failed student. He's like an old pro'.

McAdam looked over at the screen. She too was taken with the performance in front of her. 'Is that this chap Waterman I've heard about?'

The young chap replied, 'yes, he runs an alternative College in North London. He's trying to rescue this girl here. Looks like he's getting somewhere too. I've never seen anything like it. He's only sixteen I hear.'

McAdam watched a little longer. 'Tell me when the follow-up program is on will you?' She then returned to her office.

She looked up all of the Press cuttings again, more thoroughly this time. She noticed there were visits by the Department to the College premises. I wonder what all that was about, she thought.

It was time to call it a day. She gathered her coat and handbag and left.

CHAPTER SEVEN

The next instalment of the TV show came around very quickly. This time the two 'stars', me and Francis, were set up opposite one another from the beginning. There was a quick video resume of what happened last time and then Tom invited us to go ahead.

I had primed Francis before the camera rolled, by having her look at the audience and the cameras and then walk amongst them briefly, just to get used to the whole scene. We had talked to the cameramen and Tom and the Producer.

Now that we were on, it was as good as we would get to being relaxed. I was not that advanced a 'campaigner' not to get a few butterflies.

I established what her worst subjects were. I selected English as the one to tackle. 'Why should you study your own language for goodness sake?'

'Because we have to, I suppose,' she said.

'Why do you think high schools go on about English though, when you can already speak it and write in it?'

'Well I guess,' she began stutteringly, 'they want you to be able to ....' She hesitated, and couldn't really answer the question.

 Brandon spoke to the audience. 'Do you see there is no self-generated purpose from the start to do grammar, composition, let alone reading the classics. It's a sort of imposition.'

I turned back to Francis and asked her what she wanted to do when she left school, or even before that.

'I don't know really,' she answered. 'I've not really thought about it.' I didn't interrupt as she was still looking at the question.

'I don't know, I've more or less thought I'm a bit dumb, you know, like there's not much I could do   ....except maybe be a waitress or shop assistant, like my mum, or something like that.'

Brandon asked her, 'what if you weren't dumb, as you say? Can you imagine for a minute what you would go for, if you could?'

She thought and then said, 'maybe I'd like to be clever and do stuff like being a newspaper reporter, or maybe even a lawyer, but ....'

I jumped in and finished the sentence for her '... but you aren't bright enough, yes?'

'Yeah,' she concurred.

'Ok' I continued,' 'so you really are too 'dumb', as you say. Did you ever think you might have BECOME dumb?

'No,' she said, 'not really.'

'OK,' I said, gently admonishing her, 'from now on the word 'dumb' is not in our vocabulary any more, you understand? And we will show you why, OK?'

Francis hesitated and said 'y..yes,' now expecting a sort of moment of reckoning.

'Now those things you said you would like to do if you really could, ok, where do you think you would learn these things from?'

'In books I suppose,' she replied.

'Good, and how will you learn these things from books if you can't read them properly? If you've ever looked at a book of law or anything like that ....' I invited her to come up with something.

'Yes, I've looked at encyclopaedias and they are double Dutch' she realised.

'And if you were to write a story as a reporter, what would you need to know? I asked.

'Lots of words and fancy writing?' she tentatively suggested.

'Aren't they teaching you all this at school then?'

'Yes, but it's so hard. I can't understand it, like, all them terms like, subjects, objects, clauses, and stuff,' she answered. She became sad at this point and burst into tears.

They took an ad break.

On returning Francis had recovered enough to go on. I opened up by turning to the audience and indicating, 'You see there are failures here and it gets compounded if it's not picked up. How can teachers know when their forty pupils are losing? Pupils don't just put their hands up and say 'I'm lost.' Even if they did how can they remedy that forty times over every day? Anyway pupils aren't that honest, or even aware of it when it happens.'

Turning back to Francis I asked, 'What other things in English do you find hard?'

'Well, some of the text books have got long words in them and when I go to write a composition I can't think how to say what I want without being lost for words except baby words.'

'I'm surprised you are still standing,' I said in a humorous way.

'Well I'm not, really,' she laughed.

'Ok. You are doing great, incidentally. Not every student can stomach an examination like this. We are going to end this particular period soon, but not before I give you some hope.

'Can you see what effect this has had on you? Can you imagine how a pianist would struggle to play the tune if he, or she, couldn't read music?'

'Yes, and you know I tried to learn the piano once and lasted about two lessons and gave up. I just remembered that.' She was 'coming to.'

'Well, we have established that to learn something you have to know how to read and spell, and have a vocabulary and know the grammar, yes?'

She nodded.

'And we have found out that you got left behind a bit, early on, and it went from bad to worse and you more or less gave up, AND became…… don't say that word, it's been banned …. You simply failed to learn.'

'Yep,' she agreed.

Tom was motioning for me to start wrapping up.

I saw this but continued. 'If we can pick up when you got left behind and learn the things you should have learned, and advance from there, would that sound like a better place to be?'

'Yes,' she said more hopefully. 'It's hard though.'

'Yep, it can be, but our concert pianist didn't get to be so good without doing lots of scales and things, and the famous opera singers didn't rise to their heights without lots of 'doh, reh, me's' for hours and hours. Learning English isn't that hard luckily. But you have to want it. A few lessons will have you flying in no time. Then you may want it more.

'Also, my mum used to say, 'hard work never killed anyone.' Is that right everyone?' I asked turning to the audience.

The audience vocalised their agreement and clapped.

'Francis, you do have to work at learning things but English and a technique of learning is the tool to use. Can you see any hope in all this?'

Francis nodded almost enthusiastically.

I concluded. 'We'll make a piano playing lawyer out of you yet.'

Tom came in here and ended the show, to big applause.

After the show I explained to Tom, Francis and the Producer that I couldn't do the whole exercise in one program. Speaking to Francis now, 'what we would do next is actually at home or at our College; that is, go over all the grammar terms you didn't get, square them away, check out a few spelling rules, learn how to use a dictionary, and then come back and do a last program on how successful you have been and how it makes your future look from there. I'll be with you all the way. Do you want to shake on that?' I offered my hand.

She took it and asked when and where this was to be done.

'We'll work that out now with your parents. Here come the devils now,' I said as the said mum and dad approached them.

We organised the logistics and everyone was happy.

I left them and went back to Tom and worked out that it would be a good idea to do a follow-up program to showcase the results.

'Good job Brandon,' Tom said. 'You brought her right out of it. Can you actually rehabilitate her IQ here, as it were?

 'I think so. She's got the IQ, basically. Miseducation makes people stupid.'

Tom continued, 'that program we talked about, going into your College and recording what goes on, we could include the rehabilitation of Francis in that, and finish off the program in the studio with Francis talking about her new life. What do you think?

'Yep,' I agreed. 'I think you should include a few of my key personnel too. You've met them already, but they are very much to be validated in this whole project.'

'Way to go,' Tom agreed, in the new vernacular used by show biz people.

Tom's producer was standing within earshot of all this and asked, suspiciously, 'What's going on here? You two been hatching new plans? Spill it.'

They did and there were no objections from the Producer. His name was Vincent Maklin, a tall undistinguished-looking man, but with a ready dry wit. No bombast or dramatics from this man.

He told them, 'I'll run it by the programmers and check with the advertisers, and then give you the green light, or not'. The latter he added with a wink.

Tom said to him, 'You are a genius,' and slapped him on the back, lightly. He turned to me and said, 'we may as well 'do the screenplay' now, eh? Any suggestions?'

Of course I was full of them. This was to be my advertising coup. This was to set me up with the credibility I needed to tackle the Department. To convert the Department to our Education methods would be far easier than setting up a private Education chain of schools in opposition, wouldn't it?

A few doubts crossed my mind. Notwithstanding the progress we had made in getting legal accreditation and making some inroads into the Department's bureaucracy via James Hopkins, I wasn't that naïve to assume that this would be plain sailing. In fact I expected choppy waters realistically.

However, TV and newspaper exposure was all good stuff. We needed as much exposure as we could get and as many allies as possible

---

Alison Burns was in the office of Diane McAdam telling her boss about the TV show on Education. 'That Waterman chap is a genius,' she said.

'Oh hell,' McAdam replied loudly. 'I meant to watch that. I gave instructions for one of our staff out there to remind me when it was on.' She was more miffed at her instructions being ignored than about missing the program.

'Don't worry boss, Alison cut in. I believe we have it on tape. We can replay it for you.' She quickly exited and went searching for the recording.

Half an hour later she returned and brandished the tape with a victory smile. 'You will have to come into the main office Diane. There's only one VCR in this establishment.'

McAdam tutted and came from behind her desk and followed Alison to the outside office. She sat at a desk in front of a monitor and waited for Alison to put the tape on.

The monitor sprang to life and there was the opening studio scene, with Tom Shelley announcing to the live audience that Brandon was about to demonstrate his techniques to the nation.

McAdam sat passively through the whole program. 'Quite a performance don't you think?' she said to Alison.

'Indeed. What do you make of all that Diane?'

'He's a phenomenon alright. Our teachers aren't all like him unfortunately but there's a technique there. I don't see yet what he does to actually rescue her apparently failed education. The next program I must see. Will you please take charge of reminding me when it's on and tell that young chap, whoever he is, that I don't take kindly my instructions being ignored.'

Will do,' Alison replied.

———————————

Talking of exposure, prior to the TV show me and my cohorts and I HAD made a bit of a splash at the Psychiatry do. It didn't just 'come and go'. Far from just sitting there in the audience and being good spectators, (as we had done in the morning session, whilst listening to various professorial dronings from the leading lights), we had vigorously joined in the Q and A session half way through the afternoon. We really put the cat among the pigeons by asking for demonstrations of analysis sessions and explanations of the theory behind ECT, for the relatively uninitiated of course.

This had been stone-walled.

The evening session was split off into seminars at which Julia, Peter and I divided our attentions in a three-pronged attack.

Julia and I attracted a lot of attention as our presence was rapidly creating more and more consternation among the more elite of the gathering. The newspapermen had soon cottoned onto my presence and notoriety, and their buzz for a story fluttered up to the organisers who decided to come down on the disturbance. After much exaggerated protestation from we self-appointed public-spirited watchdogs of Mental Health, we were ejected from the venue.

Consequently, the media representatives created a bit of a circus outside the building. They surrounded we trio and pumped us with questions about our quest, which in turn got splashed across the main papers the next day, with pictures.

The upshot was that my positive notoriety had taken a dip from bright white to a light grey. Of course the reports were inaccurate and had made us appear as imposters rather than exposers. What were we teenage pretenders trying to pull off here? Education was one thing but Mental Health? Who were we to question the gurus of the subject whose names were elongated with lots of scholarly capital letters and full stops?

At Peter Hillingdon's place the next night we had sat around and discussed the events of the previous day.

'What do you think Peter? I had asked. I had perceived Peter to have been a rather reticent activist. He wasn't a shy man but he was more inclined to the conservative ranks than to ruffling feathers. He was safer in his more academic duties.

'That was a bit hairy,' he had offered. 'To be honest I felt really uncomfortable. I've never done anything like that before. I felt all the eyes of the world upon me.'

At that his wife, Mary, had entered the room with a plate of sandwiches. She was a kindly sympathetic sort of lady, in a slightly bent and frail body. 'Here's something to keep you all going,' she had said softly, in her manner, as if she was at her church social.

I had decided to risk it and introduce her to the newspaper. 'Mary, have you seen who's in the paper this morning?' I had chirped, spreading the paper out on the table.

She had looked quickly and come out with just what was needed but nevertheless unexpected, 'Oh that. Don't you all look great! I saw this this morning. At first I was taken aback, but you know I just can't abide those cruel things they do to those poor patients. It's like the bad old days. I'm really happy for Peter to help you to expose it all. But I thought you were all Educationalists.'

At that her thoughts had simply returned to the immediate tasks she was involved with.

I had looked at Peter who seemed rather relieved. 'This is our appointed mission, if only by default, Peter. It's uncomfortable for each of us. I've got to say my heart was going somewhat faster than normal when we got up and asked the uncomfortable questions.'

'I couldn't believe this was the normally more polite me, going hell for leather at those reporters,' Julia had added.

Peter had concluded, 'well, I guess I need to toughen up. It would have been much more uncomfortable for our brave servicemen to be shot at and bombed in the last two wars. Brandon, what are you doing to me?'

'To us,' I had corrected. 'But don't you feel alive out there in the 'trenches'?'

With that we had tucked into the sandwiches and then re-ran some of the more humorous events of that day.

'Now we need to convince Tom or ITV to do a program on this, unless we have overstepped our welcome and blown our PR. I can't believe this bit of controversy wouldn't make great TV.

Tom HAD gotten hold of the Psychiatric event. He was meeting with me at the TV studio in West London. 'I see you lot have been living a quiet life then Brandon. One of my Executives raised this revolution you perpetrated at the Psychiatric Jamboree. It had escaped me. When I looked it up in our newspaper files I was rather amused. But this Executive of ours is old school. He wasn't amused. He said that if he'd not been away at the time of our initial programs he'd have pulled them. His deputy has taken the fall, so to speak, and been transferred to 'Siberia'.

'Which leaves us where?' I asked, a bit deflated.

'Well, I'm not sure. He recognises we are incomplete on this series and, on balance, should complete it,' Tom replied a bit seriously. 'But Brandon, if your next project is on the shrinks then you may have blown it with him. Me, I'm all for it.'

'Wait until I outline my plan,' I replied. 'Give it a bit of time. In that time we aim to expose some actual criminal activities which will make the exposure irresistible. I'm sure I can sell it to the top dog.'

'I hope so. Actually, apart from my own vested interest in you, I would enjoy exposing these charlatans to broad daylight.

'Enough of that,' Tom continued. 'Now to our final show. I think we should set it up like this: we home in on the school at opening time and...... Then we should film the various stages of Francis's resurrection.'

I told him about the likely students, and their parents, and at what stage each had reached in the process. 'OK, when? I suggest we strike while the iron is hot; I don't want Francis to fade here by time lapse.'

'Well, Monday first thing then,' Tom suggested.

'It's a date Tom. See you then.'

CHAPTER EIGHT

Julia was sitting in the lounge room at home, leafing through various publications she'd picked up, when her father Gavin came in with his paper. 'What you up to daughter?' he chirped.

He looked over at what Julia had spread out around her and sat down at the opposite end of the three-seater settee. 'Ah, I see you are at your new favourite subject. It didn't escape me that you and Brandon appeared in one of the papers last week or so. Are you two taking on another part of the Establishment?' His tone was not exactly jocular, more hinting at disapproval.

'Yes we are, and this is as much my baby as Brandon's. You remember we went to a Psychiatric Hospital not long ago. It started from there. What I saw and heard there 'pricked my ears' and all other senses. This was a run-of-the-mill Mental Hospital. The specimens of humanity we saw there and the treatments outlined disgusted me, so much so that I was aboard in looking further and seeing where this led to.

'I couldn't believe this was what mental technology had evolved into in the twentieth century. These patients were all highly drugged. Those less well-off were submitted to the ECT machine, which we saw, and I believe there are those who get to have their skulls opened up to cut out the 'ogres' that haunt them.'

Gavin had listened to Julia and asked, 'so at the meeting of Psychiatrists you attended, your purpose was to cause trouble and vent your outrage?'

'Well,' she replied, 'basically to find out what they talked about, how individual Psychiatrists operated, and see if our questions could be answered. We weren't there as a protest movement, though the way it worked out we may as well have been.'

'Julia, do you not think you are getting in too deep here? Aren't you following Brandon's lead just a little too blindly? You are a teenage girl not long out of school. How believable do you expect to be?' Gavin was talking down to her. He was being a bit like a judge sitting high on his platform. His bearing was even a bit like a judge, looking at her over the top of his glasses.

'Dad, let me put you straight here. I can understand you find this whole way of life Brandon and I lead is not the usual. But, you know, lucky for me, we are not usual people. You saw how Brandon got trashed at first by the Education authorities, mainly because he was 'not long out of school' as you put it, and because he exposed an unpleasant truth about the system and mediocre results. And he didn't just carp about it. He did and is still doing something effective about it. You've seen the TV shows!' Julia was getting some purchase here.

'Your daughter, young though she is, has become a live, awakened, thinking citizen. I wasn't before. I only need to be able to look, observe and evaluate what's in front of me. I have a keen sense of what is right and wrong. And there's a lot wrong with this society, and Mental Health is one of them, as I'm finding out.

'Don't tell me to rein back my zeal, take it easy, get a normal job or anything other than support my self-chosen path. Let me fall on my head if I must. You know I'm in good company and that we are not trying to be reactionary, but are, rather, evolutionary here. The broad plan is to find a way of improving our students beyond Education and help people behave better and manage their lives better.'

Gavin felt like he should put that in his pipe and smoke it.

Julia continued. She wasn't affronted, not defensive, but really trying to get him, a bedrock in her life, to see what she was about. 'It just so happens that Brandon started to look at existing subjects that should know about these things. It started with Psychology, then Psychiatry. Also, did I tell you, we went to a Hindu temple as our first inspection of Eastern religions?

'It turned out that our visit to the Psychiatric Hospital made it so obvious that we weren't going to find answers there. Instead we were so incensed that their whole stock-in-trade treatments are brutal, and so pretty well flawed as to basic theory, that we thought we'd look further into it all, and here we are.'

Gavin leant over and hugged his daughter. 'I'm sorry. It's just that it's hard to keep up with your development, you know. You go for it girl. Let us know if we can be of any help.' The 'judge' had been given his own judgement.

Julia responded and said, 'thank you Daddy. That means a lot to me. Actually, there is something you can do to help, you being a solicitor. I have a few cases that I'd like to take to task in the courts. I need to know if they are going to be worthwhile.

'While Brandon is concentrating on his TV show I'm getting into all this. Dan is doing so well at the College that I'm more or less an overseer now. It's been a whirlwind hasn't it? Not so long ago I was a carefree College student blowing around in the breeze. And I've found my partner in life. So much for being a teenager.'

'Well this teenager,' Gavin responded, 'is an adult teenager. Let's drop the 'teenager' bit shall we? I'm sorry I brought it up like that. Run over one of your cases with me and I'll give you some idea of what your chances are in making mayhem for your chosen target.'

Julia produced one of the booklets she had there and turned to a page which was an article about the downward spiral of a patient who'd been hospitalised and drugged over a period of six months and then let out. This had left him unable to cope by virtue of the effects of the drugs and having no means of support (he having lost his job on being taken to hospital and kept there).

'Well,' Gavin said, 'if he was kept there against his will there may be a case. If he went there voluntarily and had adverse reactions to drugs and is now relatively disabled, one would have to prove clear negligence. It depends what symptoms of mental health he was exhibiting too.

'You see, you can't just make a case against any practitioner who makes an honest mistake, otherwise no one would risk becoming a doctor. It would have to be some clear violation of standard practice with considerable ramifications, and it may be a suit against an individual doctor or a particular Health Authority or Trust.

'You would need witnesses, paperwork and clear evidence, to make a case. Otherwise all you have is a broadcast of the case, such as you have there in this booklet.'

Julia looked at him, frowning a little and thinking. 'Mmm, it seems I would have to be a bit of a detective and I'd have to put my outrage aside and think legalese.'

'Yep,' Gavin confirmed. 'But you get one of these cases and get all the gen you can and run it by me and we will know better what can be done.'

Julia was silent for a moment then said. 'This could all get very involved. We need to be able to bring about some reform in this field and bring particular practitioners to book in the process. We have to become whistle blowers, champions of the disadvantaged, whether we like it or not, without losing site of finding something useful and workable to use on normal average people.

'Food for thought, but not right now. I need some extroverting activity for a while. I think I will go round to Brandon's and talk him into treating me to a proper date for a change.

'Unfortunately he is likely to take me to the library, or do some meditation, or something exciting like that. Well at least I'll get to see him. Maybe he needs a trip through the art galleries or the British Museum.'

Gavin asked, 'Is he seriously into meditation?'

'Well, yes, in that he wants to see if this offers anything supplementary to the arsenal of knowledge. He gets a bit of a kick out of it in fact. I've got to admit it is a way of extroverting one. It's not what people think it is. You don't just sit and think. In fact you don't DO anything. It's like separating oneself out from one's environment and thoughts and being comfortable about it.

'Anyway, maybe I will try seducing him. What do you think of that, father?'

Gavin felt just a little uncomfortable with that but soon recovered and replied, 'whatever turns you on, as they say.'
They both looked at each other amusedly for a few instants and took each other's hands.

Gavin said, 'you really love this man don't you?'

'Yes I do, wholeheartedly, and not in a mushy romantic sense. It is real mutual 'admiration society'. We see the world the same way and are excitingly tackling life together. We don't fritter our time like others. We don't play games, if you know what I mean. And it's not all just 'business'. We make it fun and keep it light. We complement each other perfectly.

'Of course we turn each other on, but we don't have to jump into bed to, what would you say, consummate the relationship. I know we will one day. You know there are more desirable thrills than having sex, I think, such as the thrill of creating real change in people, or the joy of bantering each other wittily, and of winning against the odds. I suspect sex is overrated, maybe an anti-climax, so to speak. How about that from a virgin?'

Gavin was so enjoying the maturity of this person in front of him and thinking how lucky he was to have her as his daughter. For that matter, how lucky she'd chosen wisely in Brandon.

'Well have fun seducing Brandon while he is meditating his way through the galleries.' He kissed her on the forehead and she lay her head on his shoulder for a brief while.

Julia soon sat back and started gathering her things and then, as a deliberate after-thought said to Gavin, 'you know Dad you must join us and be our President, or Legal Counsel. Why not put your skills to proper use, for a good cause. I can see you on TV too now, champion of the downtrodden, scourge of the Establishment.'

Gavin changed the subject with a grin. 'I came in here to do something, what was it? Oh yes …' and he picked up his paper and pretended to study it seriously.

 When he looked up Julia was standing there shaking her head, and said, 'seriously, think about it. And you could become a property magnate and invest in our buildings and make huge profits.' Then the big smile, upon which she danced out of the room and left Gavin a happy man.

I, meanwhile, and unsuspecting of what was to come that afternoon, was indeed working at home on my final TV performance. Tom and I had done the preliminary filming at the College and Sidney, Ira and Peter had all been interviewed and 'starred' in their own way.

Joe, our most unlikely success, and his two revived parents had set the scene for the resurrection of the educational life of Francis, the recalcitrant student.

This was a trickier 'screenplay' to do so I decided that we should film it ALL, from start to finish and then edit the key bits into the final time span. This was going to be an hour-long program, including five minutes of follow-up to show the aftermath of it all.

This main body of the program was to start the next Monday coming.

Julia arrived on the Waterman doorstep at around lunchtime and after greeting the family she went out onto the veranda to find me concentrated into a notepad. I looked up and broke out into a broad smile and got up and hugged Julia, almost as if I'd not seen her for some time, which was true if you considered two days as 'some time'.

Anew, I was struck by how much this model female delicacy had become so much part of my life. 'I was just thinking of you my love, and here you are.

Are we becoming telepathic?'

'Of course, darling,' she beamed. I had suddenly put my hand to my chin in thought, and Julia held me more at arm's length   and looked at me and almost predictably wondered what was hatching in my head.

'Yes?' she posed. 'What is your next great announcement?'

'We sat and I explained, 'Telepathy. What exactly IS that?'

'Oh no, just when I was about to suggest a frivolous afternoon together, doing something diversionary, I now fear we are going to pay a visit to the 'Telepathy Museum', if there is such a thing. Could this not just be a coincidence or a likely happening, me turning up like this?'

'Oh, don't worry my fair one, I don't think there is such a thing as a 'Telepathy Museum' or research facility, but, you know, …that gives me an idea…' I became thoughtful, but couldn't hold the stance for long.

Then, well into this playful game, I suggested, 'perhaps we could go for a walk on Hampstead Heath; you go clockwise and I'll go anticlockwise and we'll send thoughts to each other and meet up at the ice cream shop at the southern end and swap notes. If we get good at this we won't need to meet or talk to each other and can have the first sort of cyber space relationship on the planet. And we can sell it to the TV producers and become stars, and can make a pot of money to boot.'

Julia tapped her fingers on the nearby table, put her feet up on the veranda rail and yawned with great exaggeration. 'Whatever. Is this your latest idea for a date?'

'Yep, otherwise I will get totally consumed and seduced by your presence that I will lose control and all perspective.'

'I thought you had an endless capacity to experience anything,' she retorted.

I didn't let up 'Who knows, abandoning the physical plane might be the new exciting game of the millennia. Did this never occur to you?'

'Of course it did, I am way ahead of you,' she lied in mock reprisal, as she got up and sat in my lap and gave me the full flavour of her femininity.

After a full clinch she drew back and asked, 'what do you think of abandoning the physical plane now?'

My erection had come between us and I looked at her adoringly and told her, 'I guess that proves I am mortal after all. I could get bored with telepathic communication.'

She looked at my bulge and said, 'I can see that. It's a pity we aren't in some remote corner of Hampstead Heath right now, to prove the point.'

We sat there for quite a while, then she went back to her chair and fanned herself in exaggerated, but real excitement, just as Mum appeared with a plate of cakes and a tray of tea and cups.

'You are just in time mother,' I spouted. 'I am indeed in need of some relief from my exertions, and Julia has distracted me so much that I think a cup of cha and the best cake in the land is perfect right now, after which we are going to go out. I won't say where. It's a surprise.'

Gladys said to Julia. 'Bring him back to base, I mean normal, will you? It's all work and no play with him.'

'Oh I wouldn't say that exactly,' Julia said, looking at me mischievously.

'Oh, I see,' Gladys added, sensing what was going on here. 'You obviously know something I don't.'

Tea and cakes were had and Julia and I sauntered off up the street, indeed heading for Hampstead Heath, a fifteen minute bus ride away.

Brandon said to her, 'Seriously though, what do you suppose telepathy is?'

'Well, it's obviously a transfer of thought or concepts between minds, in some way. Don't you get the idea that you and I often know what the other is thinking, even without physical mannerisms to assist?'

'Yes, but how do the thoughts travel? Hmm… some finer wave length of energy perhaps.'

Julia was onto this quickly. 'Does it really matter? It happens. Who cares about the mechanics? We are so closely attuned to each other, mentally, that we can do it. Others do it too, but more often with bodily mannerism clues I suspect.'

'Yes, how simply you put it,' I replied.

At that we had arrived at the northern end of the Heath and got off the bus and entered the gates.

I said, 'How about you go left and I'll go right?' I was struggling to maintain a straight face.

Julia said quickly, as if deeply offended, 'now I think you are trying to get rid of me,' and put on a sulk. With eyes down and arms tightly folded, while kicking her feet.

Then she ended that little drama, just in time to curb my pretended protestations, and said to me challengingly, 'we don't need to part company to do this. Let's just walk along together and see if we can project thoughts to each other. For instance, without looking at me see if you can guess what I am thinking'.

We continued strolling down the pathway and among the shrubs and trees. Julia thought of something (probably the ice cream she would buy at the other end) and tried to send me this thought somehow, as if willing me to get it.

I concentrated on her, without her looking at me, trying to perceive what she was thinking. 'All I get is a blank,' I said. 'Is your mind a blank?'

'Don't be silly,' she responded. We tried back and forth with much joshing.

Eventually we decided we weren't going anywhere with this and that we would really have to be in the groove to do it properly, if at all. We spent the rest of the afternoon talking about the TV show and Julia's proposition to her dad, and generally had a wonderful time looking about and enjoying doing nothing in particular, an activity rather unusual for us, and with a limited threshold.

That threshold having been reached we went on to have dinner and went to see a movie, which was a re-showing of 'Gone With the Wind' starring Clarke Gable and Vivian Leigh.

'What a fabulous movie', Julia remarked afterwards. 'Such a big production, and brilliant acting. A story of indomitable spirit. After so many misadventures the heroine just put it down to experience and decided to just get on with it. And,' she added as an aside, 'what a hunk!'

Hearkening back to our earlier activity I said, 'I knew you were thinking that.'

'Oh did you now?' More fun.

CHAPTER NINE

The filming of the final program, with young Francis as the heroine and me the hero, concluded after a lot of takes and condensation. Francis wasn't going to be turned around in 'just a few takes'. The editing took time.

As a final 'scene' to our program I asked her, 'Well, my dear, do you consider your education now resurrected and ignited?

'Sure do. As a matter of fact I have decided to pursue a career as a barrister (via being a magistrate).' She received a big ovation from the TV audience for that. She was chuffed. And so was I.

For that she indeed needed command of her language and a real interest in life outside of a previously meandering school life.

I had become her opinion leader, but in truth, in that role, I actually was becoming quite redundant as Francis was developing a mind of her own, a consequence partly of real education, as opposed to rote exam-based learning.

I had given her a 'sliding scale', or more exactly a 'rising scale' of books and miscellaneous publications to read while she completed her high school education, which was now about the next four years ahead of her.

She was now fixed regarding grammar and I presented her, on live TV, with a reward for her accomplishment – a trio of chosen dictionaries, from simple to more complete, without killing her off with the more complex ones.

Her parents, who had appeared on the show on film at the College, were so impressed they couldn't have been more of an advertisement for me and the College if their words had been scripted for them.

Tom was over the moon. Vince, the Producer was ecstatic, and even the power that was couldn't deny that I was a godsend for ratings and revenue. No modesty applies here; I was.

Tom even closed the show with a humorous invitation for viewers to watch for the next instalment in the Waterman Series, as he put it.

———————————————

'Don't forget the TV program tonight Diane.' Alison felt sure she'd gain some kudos for having remembered.

'Oh yes of course.' Diane replied. 'I'll watch it here I think. How about we watch it together over a glass of wine, or two.' This was tantamount to an order.

'I'll get the wine,' Alison replied. This would give her an opportunity to score again, she thought. I'll simply get an expensive white Sauvignon. 'White ok?'

'Beautiful, and maybe a treat to go with it; something sweet and creamy perhaps.'

'Cream donuts do?' Diane was already back into her papers. Alison took that as 'anything would do'.

And it did. The pair sat at a table by the TV in the main office, the rest of the staff having left much earlier. Normally only top Execs worked on late in the civil service.

The wine was poured and the donuts were served. Their feet were up on the low table. The program had now started after the adverts.

There was Tom Shelley inviting Brandon to demonstrate what he had done to totally revive young Francis. This was a new approach to Education, McAdam thought. It was indeed remedial. How could a teacher do all this without having to do it one on one? But the idea of tuning up the desire to learn towards a definite goal and then rubbing out the past failures was enlightening.

'This girl Francis is revitalised, Diane. It's taken a bit of work, many months in fact, but he's done it.' Alison said.

'Yes, food for thought,' Diane replied, licking the sugary cream from her fingers and swilling the last of the wine. 'Well, I think I'll look into this a bit further.' She got up and thanked Alison for the spread and returned to her office where she sat and surveyed the piles on her desk.

How would it go down, she wondered, if I were to groove these methods into our system here? How many corns would I tread on? Perhaps this chap Waterman was having the same problem? He doesn't appear to be anything else but an interested teacher. I certainly don't see a malevolence. I must find out more about him. Things do have to change.

I was becoming renown beyond my expectations and comfort. I had reporters knocking on my doors, at home and at the College. Business was rolling in at a rate that was extending the group's business acumen. I was being offered invitations to speak at various venues, such as Rotary clubs, University campuses, political meetings, and further TV appearances.

At the moment I was regarded largely as a teenage prodigy and an Educationalist. My 'side-line', as a Mental Health reformer, was as yet not so prominent, but I was managing to slip this subject into conversations, promoting the fact that I'd become a reformer and activist.

Consistent with my experience with establishment conservatism in Education I was attracting more than just opposition to change per se. There was a class within that class that were opposed to success or winning, period.

As an example, one national broadsheet reporter had taken on the mantle of being my antagonist and 'opposition ego'. He had written a few articles since I had come to prominence and each was scathing of my character, totally cynical about 'the pretentiousness of this opportunistic juvenile', all without a single visit or conversation with 'the accused'.

He had though been in the TV audience of the Francis program and had paid a visit, apparently, to my old school and interviewed the Deputy Head, Jake Levison. He quoted him broadly in his articles.

I was thinking had Tom been the Chief Editor of this rag this guy would not have been put into print. It was interesting to note that few positive articles, on ANY subject, had appeared in this paper either – little if any good news. In so-called statements about everyday events many 'facts' were presented as generalisations and depicted as calamitous.

This particular reporter, Denzil Appleton, wasn't the only culprit of smear. The whole publication had an agenda which was to stir up its readership and/or feed distortion and lies to a certain portion of the population.

I was talking to Sidney, Peter and Ira at the College one afternoon after normal business, discussing the burgeoning business we were experiencing, and the cans of worms that were being opened.

Ira told me, 'that's what comes of being a prominent figure, my boy.'

Peter added, 'more like what comes from success.'

Sidney said, 'I remember reading a book by Ernest Hemingway, 'For Whom the Bell Tolls', in which he refers to the originator of the concept of the book's title, Jon Donne of the sixteenth century.'

Sidney paused and they all waited for the punch line. 'Seek not to know for whom the bell tolls, it tolls for thee', or words to that effect.'

'What does that mean?' I asked. 'I am the chosen one?'

'Think about it,' Sidney suggested. 'You are on this ride now, what are your choices?'

'Hm …' I thought, seriously at first, then more whimsically, 'I just did. It's all your fault for humouring me. You are all in it now, so it tolls for ye.'

That got them all going, and as was our way, we splurged on it all.

'By the way, I'm giving you all a head's up here. If a reporter called Denzil Appleton from 'The Observer' calls here or slinks around outside or even tries to tap any of us or the staff he is to be given short shrift. You may not have read this paper but he's been printing very negative stories about me and our outfit.

'I will write an article which can be used as a template for any visitor who wants to look around. It will be about our origins and program and progress. If he arrives here, invite him in and give him my article to read and tell him he can print it as-is and that we are so inundated with all-comers that we have had to curtail any further interviews due to time constraints. Don't offer him tea. Then politely show him the door, no messing.'

Ira came in here, 'I'll be the bouncer. Then I won't have to try and be diplomatic, just myself. That should sting his tail.' Much mirth.

'I'm saying nothing. Just don't give him anything to latch onto, though he will anyway if that's his wont, which we know it is. Go home team. Fill the rest of the day with extra curricula activity.'

Ira couldn't contain herself. 'Do you know what time it is Brandon?'

I held up my hand defensively, warding off any further smart comment.

I went and typed up the article for visitors and ran off fifty copies on the Gestetner machine. Then I packed up and, as arranged, met Julia in town, in Marylebone High Street.

———————

Why Marylebone High Street? Well, it was the nearest shopping centre to Harley Street and Queen Anne Street (if one wanted to avoid the more grandiose Oxford Street, THE shopping hub of the entire city).

And what was Julia doing in this neck of the woods? Shopping? Though she dressed with a tasteful clothes sense, she had no wish to be a society girl or a model.

Her morning was spent in Queen Anne Street talking with her 'partners in crime' and hatching plans for more widespread disruption to the overseers of national Mental Health. She had decided to try out a few of the shrinks, on spec. She laughed her way through telling me all about this devilment, as we sought an eating house fit for rumbling innards.

'And, pray tell, you modern day Emmeline Pankhurst, what did the Psychiatrists of Harley Street tell you about your sanity?'

'Listen,' she quickly retorted, half expecting such a comment. 'You should know me by now…'

I continued her explanation, 'Tell me you were challenging THEIR sanity.'

'How did you guess?' she answered, and with ME rolling MY eyes. 'I managed to find a few of them willing to see me without an appointment. None of them twigged who I was (which tells me what little impact we've made so far).

'Though some of them are high-fliers in the profession, many are just rank and file. It is the latter category who deigned to see me I suspect.

'This one guy accepted me upfront as a patient. I told him I was experiencing depression as a result of academic pressure and domestic unrest. I told him I had been a happy-go-lucky child and early teenager but in latter years had come to worry about losing it – experiencing sleepless nights, hallucinations at times and mood swings you wouldn't believe.'

I couldn't resist it. 'So you blew it and told him about me and the pressures of a new-found romance.'

'Don't kid yourself, big boy, I don't think he would have heard of you either, and in any case I think the 'pressure' is all on you.' I could see she was doing, mentally, another footballer's fist pump.

I put up my hands submissively. 'So you laid it on thick and you had him on the hook. Do go on.'

'I was the epitome of a perfect patient. He asked me a few more questions and took notes. You know he didn't even ask me how I managed to arrive at HIS door step or why I didn't approach my normal doctor first. But, I was to find out about this a bit later.

'Anyhow, moving on. Don't interrupt.' We were interrupted anyhow by me leading her into one of these newish innovations of a coffee house restaurant. We sat and ordered. Then I looked up at her expectantly and made the motion of zipping up my mouth.

'As I was saying,' she said smilingly, 'he said I was suffering, it seemed, from depression and a milder form of mania, I suppose manic depression. He'd got that from questioning me about my mood swings. You can read between the lines here, I'm sure. He then took a bit of time out and looked in some volume, which turned out to be the DSM.

'I asked what it was he was reading and why. He stumbled a bit and then told me he was looking for the exact drug dosage advice. At that I looked horrified and went into my objection about drugs of any kind. 'Do I have to take drugs for this?' I asked him. 'Might this not just disappear with a bit of maturity or something dietary?

'At that point he told me that I'd come here for professional help and now I was protesting the treatment. Then I asked if there were any other non-drug treatments, like counselling or group therapy or something. He said that my symptoms were a bit beyond that perhaps but I could try a Psychology therapist if I chose, meaning it was all up to me.

'Then I started questioning him about the mechanisms of the brain and how drugs deal with mental problems. I was very close to the bone here and almost got carried away with my disbelief. He gave me the same theories we have come across before. When I asked him if these were cast iron science he became vague and gave me the 'its still developing' line.'

I feigned drowsiness and nodded my head a few times as if dropping off.

'OK,' she responded, 'well this will wake you up. As I was leaving he told me that the fee for the session (forty minutes in all) was twenty five pounds. If I'd been more of a rowdy I'd have just charged out of there noisily.

'As it was, after a bit of polite protest, he became quite disgruntled and haggled it down with an offer of twelve pounds. I paid it, just managing it down to the bottom of my purse. I should have expected this, to be honest (the payment I mean). I don't think he wants to see me again.'

I unzipped my mouth and then was about to speak for once when she put a finger to my lips and asked, 'can I take it out of petty cash?'

She then reached over and kissed me tenderly on the mouth as we got up to leave.

I responded, 'do you think such sorcery will turn my head?'

As we left the café she carried on. 'Well just in case you aren't immediately coming up with an acquiescence, I repeat.....' and she kissed me with much more seduction this time, and I responded unequivocally. What has happened to me?

I carried on fighting the losing battle. 'I must say I quite enjoy losing these little battles but I somehow must install a contingency plan to finance such instances. You wouldn't make much of a financial manager. What would you do if the boot was on the other foot?'

Sharp as a tack she replied 'I'd kiss you right back and tell you that flattery (but in this case blackmail) will get you nowhere and stand firm and enjoy the results.'

I sighed and said, 'you leave me no choice but to appoint you Financial Manager of our enterprise and confine you to the office and pay you only on profit. And I'll make sure I see you regularly by coming in for petty cash requests and a passionate kiss each time.'

'Well I'll enjoy the battle then,' she said, finalising the repartee. We continued north up Marylebone High Street.
I suddenly asked, 'oh, by the way who was the other Psychiatrist you saw? You mentioned more than one.'

'Oh yes, (glad you were paying attention). Yes, I was standing in the Reception of a rather important looking building which listed all the practitioners in the place, and I was taken with a large chart on the wall which was a 'map' of the human skull with all the parts of the brain shown in different colours. This was largely double Dutch to me so I asked the Receptionist who had appeared what all this meant. Sitting nearby was an Asian gentleman who got up and started to explain it to me.

'After he had, (with me none the wiser), we chatted for a while and he told me he was a 'junior' Psychiatrist and was here to meet Professor Weber for an interview as an assistant or apprentice. So here was this chap, rather smart looking and quite articulate regurgitating his university course but with barely an ounce of understanding, I came to perceive.

'I put him on the spot with lots of questions and he gave what he thought to be the right answers but when I asked him how this and that actually worked he fumbled. When I asked him if the treatments of Psychiatry cured people he responded just like the chaps we interviewed at the 'Shrinks Ball' that time – "we don't really cure insanity but make the patients more comfortable", bla, bla, bla.'

I asked her how she explained her being there.

Well,' she answered, 'I told him I had come here to book a consultation with someone about my own situation but now I had second thoughts and that he'd put me off. Then I bade him good morrow and thanked him for his time and trouble – perhaps another time.'

I couldn't hold myself in, listening to my revolutionary partner 'in battle'.

'Well, Harley Street will never be the same again, and so are you never going to be the same as you were once – wiling away your time in libraries and sitting under shady trees on university campuses reading Philosophy. I'm proud of you my love.' I squeezed her hand.

We wandered along Marylebone Rd toward Warren Street tube discussing the next steps of our foray into mental health.

Once on the tube Julia concluded, 'so our activities outside the school ARE really financed by petty cash, more or less.'

I agreed. 'Well if my pocket and yours are the source of finance then it IS petty cash.' We smiled at this.

I went on. 'Well at the end of my searches I will have evolved a saleable technique for self-improvement, just like at the College. In the meantime we will do our jobs at the College and live off that. The colleges together are generating enough now for expansion and some profit. We pioneers are worth our pay so you and I, and Sidney and Ira are now worth a decent reward after a few years of relative privation and monetary sacrifice.'

Julia asked, 'do you think people in the public, or even our own staff will start thinking of us as money grabbers?'

'What public? Who could deny us eventual recompense for a decent service? Only the cynical and hypercritical would raise such an objection. Our teachers and administration staff now earn well in comparison to their counterparts in schools and offices. That's how we've set it up. It's a fully-fledged business and is answerable to our directors who are answerable to shareholders (your Dad and Sidney being both).

'The Education Department is answerable to whom? They are financed by the tax payer ultimately and run by a distant Minister of Education and local Councils, but this finance depends on the overall condition of the economy, which is down to the government as a whole and to some degree on world conditions.

'Look what happened in the thirties, and the following world war. But, leaving that out of it for a moment, we sink or swim according to the value of our commodity, which is a student able and willing to learn. Now compare that to our school system, which just gets money thrown at it whether it does educate the population or not, as we well know.'
'Where are you going with this?' Julia asked.

'Basically, people who can do things and make successes should be well and truly recompensed in addition to the self-satisfaction they get. And by reverse logic, those who can't or won't do things and who fail should not. We are in the business of creating success. 'Psychiatrists are in the business of numbing at best the less fortunate and doing them in at worst. And they get a lot of money thrown at them. Should they be financed only to the degree they produce success? Probably, but that would take a revolution which, now that I think of it…

'We are doers, and succeeding; we've earned our bread and butter, so I declare petty cash open, and our pockets a bit too.'

We got off the tube and started walking towards Julia's house. Julia raised a point from her visit to the Psychiatrist: 'Do you know, I'm not sure who is doing the wagging – the donkey or the tail. If the Psychiatrists are dependent on drugs for their treatments then the drug companies must see the Psychiatric profession as a huge cash cow. What vested interest is going on here?

'I suppose the same could be said of the medical profession to some degree, though you CAN see a result in many instances, such as with penicillin, body repairs – actually, many things.

I came up with a big question. 'I wonder what would happen if someone came up with a real cure for mental illness, that wasn't based on extreme treatments. Would the drug companies pack it in and revert to the new discovery? Or would they oppose it or even try and get rid of it? This would be the true test of a vested interest and the degree of objective interest in discovery.'

Julia came in here opportunistically. 'Ah, before all that we will have gotten rid of them.'

'Or they us.'

'Life is exciting isn't it Brandon?' came Julia's response.

———————————

We reached the McDonald abode and entered to a nice welcome from the parents, Delia and Gavin, and Dan too.

We sat in the lounge room. Dan asked, 'What have you two been up to; the usual Waterman date?'

Julia answered up. 'Well almost. Actually we had a meal in town. Before that I decided I must visit a Psychiatrist in Harley Street to get an opinion on my sanity. On account of my rough upbringing I had come to mistrusting my decisions in life and was wondering if I was imagining things, you know, and maybe I was hallucinating.'

Dan interrupted her, 'Yeah, come to think of it, I have often considered my childhood was positively laced with lack of care, deprivation…'

It was Gavin's turn now 'Well, times were hard, we did our best. You two weren't our immediate concern so we left you to get on with it. You don't appreciate the freedom we gave you.'

Delia now decided to cut this all short. 'Well what did the Psychiatrist have to say then? Send your parents down there to be analysed? What a business.'

I chimed into this circus. 'Actually, according to Julia (if she's not hallucinating) he listened to her ramble on for an hour about how hardly done-by she's been and ended up prescribing a large course of hallucinatory drugs which she has to take every hour. Do you see the paradox there?'

They were all laughing now and Julia finished off without the jollity. 'Actually he did recommend a course of drugs. I had gone there to pry and test him – not him in particular – to see what he would do. I declined the drugs and after all that he gave me the bill.'

Now back to the fun. 'I told him to send it to my father. It's his fault, so he should pay.'

Gavin said, 'fun and games then. On another subject, I looked over that case you gave me and decided there ARE grounds for legal action. The practitioner in question is criminally liable. We need to get all the papers together and work out the procedure.

'And, talking about bills, I'll send you the bill, eh, daughter?'

We drank tea and downed a generous amount of Delia's chocolate cake. Delia announced that Dan had recruited her to the College, on which news I got up and gave her a big squeezy welcome.

'Well done Dan,' I said, 'Come to think of it we'll give Delia the job of recruiting MY mum Gladys, too. Then it becomes very much a family affair.'

Julia was enthusiastic about this. 'Yeah, more girl power. Ira will be so pleased.'

I exaggerated being tired and announced I was off to get the sleep I'd need to cope with such goings on.

With that I suitably embraced Julia on the doorstep and was off into the night.

CHAPTER TEN

I had become even more busy – TV appearances, debating, writing texts, overseeing, boosting teacher training, meditating, studying Eastern religions, my novel. And of course there was the Waterman/McDonald partnership, the love affair of the century.

I was also now tackling the bigger picture in the Education field – the Department itself. With the help of James Hopkins I had managed to arrange visiting a few select schools to give lectures to the staff on our methods, giving demonstrations using their pupils.

James had stuck his neck out here. He used private schools for these demos and lectures, utilising his contacts 'in the business'. It was a bit 'off-piste' but he'd felt he'd seen such a change in his own boys that he wanted to help this project along, a bit under the radar as it were.

But, it went exponentially well with each Head Master concerned asking for the texts and a trial program. It seemed that private Education didn't solve the learning problem. Maybe the classes were a bit smaller and the school environment a bit safer, but the learning problem was much the same.

In concert with James, I continued the project in the private school sector, one school leading to another, mainly by word of mouth. These independent schools were under the general umbrella of the Department, particularly as regards basic curricula. Critically they weren't under the financial constraints or dictates of the state school system. They were 'independent' after all. This included religious schools too.

I'd indeed end up revolutionising the whole system wouldn't I? Well that was by no means a forgone conclusion as the Jake Levison types in this world soon got into the act. James Hopkins was soon to learn he'd stuck his neck out just a little too far; so much so that he was suspended by his hierarchy, pending full investigation.

He and I began circling the wagons to defend the ground gained. We met at one of the Independents in Hammersmith, West London. The Head there had received a letter from the Department stating that utilisation of the Remedial College of Education was strongly advised against on the basis that although we were officially a registered establishment it was against the Department's policy to sanction 'alternative practices'.

It wasn't an order as such but official enough to cause this particular Head to demur.

The same letter had been sent to all private schools. More than fifty percent backed off and cancelled their programs with the College. The remainder, under more progressive leadership (and probably in more dire need of the service) decided to stay firm and give the program time to work.

We were seated in this Headmaster's office. David Samuels, the Head, was waiting for me and James to finish reading the letter before announcing that he'd decided to stall on accepting the program.

I began to point out some facts. 'You do know David that the Department has granted us legitimacy. James here was instrumental in granting this. We have shown you the success rates of our program and methods. You said you'd seen my demonstration on TV not so long ago. Almost half of the Independents we have signed are sticking to their decision to utilise us.'

David Samuels was a tall thin man, with brown thinning hair combed back off a receding hair line and flattened down with Vaseline. He wore a pinstriped suit with a waistcoat, a bit like the gentry of the earlier part of the century.

'He replied, 'Yes, I know all this, but I have investors to answer to here; Trustees if you will, and we aren't really prepared to upset any Department boats. It would be curtains for us if they were to come down on us and it all ending up ruffling their feathers and those of the parents too. You do understand, don't you?'

'James entered the fray here. 'Between you and me there is more to this than meets the eye. As you know I have been suspended for encouraging all this. I don't regret it either. I know enough to recognise a cabal when I see one. Someone is stirring this.

'I would understand it if there were complaints and failures, but there is none of that. I even had Brandon perform his magic on my own boys before I got into all this. I will be challenging this decision and trying to clear my name. We are up against an encrusted system here and likely some bad egg at the bottom of it all.'

Before he became wound up any more about this he decided to desist. 'I understand your position. When this clears over we can talk again. In the meantime you have the texts on the learning methods. I encourage you to pick out a few specimens and try it all out on them yourself. That way you won't get into any trouble with officialdom. And when you win, let us know. Brandon is always available to help out and advise. You've had a demonstration and that particular student is on the improve, not so?'

Mr Samuels shifted a bit in his chair and hummed and hawed a bit. 'Yes, but it's not just me involved here. I have a number of people to please and I don't feel comfortable spending the school's limited resources on this and having to explain to everyone.'

He was rather entrenched and as is the nature of the conservative personality, not inclined to take risks, no matter how logical the reasoning.

I put in my weight. 'Mr Samuels, take your sample student, (Ken?) and continue the learning technique on him until he is right through the process and a shining example. This way you will have a better chance of getting this by your colleagues and you'll have more first-hand experience and certainty that this works. Remember, failing students, mediocre results, all began some time before now and will not revert unless you do this exercise. You do have quite a few of these students. Your Trustees and parents deserve better.

'Please call me for any help with Ken. I know you really have to be confident of all this before continuing investing.'

We all rose and shook hands 'Thanks for your understanding. I may very well do as you suggest,' he said as his parting comment (which meant he'd breathe a sigh of relief and put it on the back-burner).

Once outside and whilst sitting in James's car, we discussed this matter. I asked him, 'what are you going to do about your predicament James?'

'Well. I'm on full pay for the moment while this matter goes to a tribunal – trial if you like. The worst that can happen is that I am dismissed or if not, demoted.'

'I can see you are worried about this,' I told him empathetically. 'Well, look, if the worst comes to the worst you can work for us. A burgeoning adventurous soul like you is right up our street, and your financial security will continue. But it would be better to defeat this decision from the inside and you live on to fight for better Education.

'In the meantime, let's find out who is at the bottom of all this. Do you think it might be Audrey?'

'No,' he replied quickly. 'She might be a stickler for proper process and following the rules but I don't think she has that mean streak that's in play here.'

I thought for a moment, then added, 'yes, after all she did end up processing our legitimacy. You know, this may be more about me, me having this higher public profile. I'll look into it my end.

'Onwards and upwards,' I spouted. 'You know, let's not baulk at opposition. Reason and smart action has to prevail not so? If not, what then?'

With that we left and went our ways, agreeing to stay in touch at any eventuality or discovery.

I had some serious thinking to do. I knew instinctively that this was more about me than James Hopkins.

It had been Sidney who had alerted me to a few newspaper articles recently, both highlighting the 'publicity seeking Brandon Waterman', with his TV activities and his appearance at the 'Shrinks Ball'.

Sidney had said to me, 'My boy, you have been attracting the attention of the more sensationalist section of the media. These articles are going for your throat. There are many repetitions of the terms 'jumped up teenager', 'pretender', 'fortune seeker' 'opportunist'. And, to prove the point, there were no attempts to find any positives in your work.

'One writer even suggested an enquiry into your activities, 'before more damage is done to lives'. I think you already know that when interests are threatened or winners speak loudly the negative and downright anti-social come out of the woodwork, albeit under some camouflage.'

'Yes,' I had added rather pensively. 'These types must feel personally threatened by success. They could, if otherwise disposed, rejoice and investigate and broadcast successful projects or discoveries. But they seem to only want one topic.'

I planned to go on expanding and fighting just causes; drive these carping critics mad. I reasoned that there were probably more people like Tom, of the Independent TV network, and surely wide broadcast of good deeds would defeat a few yapping cur dogs.

Perhaps, as an experiment even, I'd investigate one of these Jake Levison types and see what the 'microscope' showed up. Maybe I could get Tom to invite one of these guys onto a suitable TV program and so show him (or her) up for what he (or she) is. Maybe best to ignore.

A few days later though a Sunday paper printed an article with me and Julia pictured and featured as a likely teenage love double, dabbling into affairs (on this occasion, Mental Health) beyond our station.

Somehow we had been pictured together on the day of our stroll through

Hampstead Heath. The import of that alerted me to broaden my vision in public places. Not that I was about to become paranoid about things, but just realise I was somewhat of a public figure, and more latterly a controversial one.

Julia was a target now and I predicted, as anti-Psychiatry stuff began to appear more in the public eye, that she would be subject to more invective.

We were getting well into the subject of Public Relations now.

Well, she and I, with our senses of humour well stirred, would have a field day with this one.

I had come across another article, this time alerted by Ira. It was in a magazine so it had escaped Sidney. I bought the magazine at a newsagent. I took it around to Julia's that same night.

Me and the whole McDonald family were sitting out on their rear terrace when I chose my moment to introduce the family to the article. They passed it around, all protesting the gall of all this.

'Good God, Brandon, we're being stalked!' Julia exclaimed, half affronted and half amused.

I let the family outrage subside a bit and then asked Gavin, 'is there anything illegal about this?'

Gavin explained, 'I wouldn't think so. It's a grey area. You may call it invasion of your privacy to a point but the Press enjoys quite a bit of freedom. If this guy was trailing you consistently and you were to document it, with witnesses then you may have a case.'

Delia, no shrinking violet incidentally, decided to write a letter of protest to the magazine, specifically about her daughter being followed for a publicity picture, in her leisure time.

I wanted to lighten up the subject a bit. 'Actually it wasn't leisure time. We were conducting a telepathy experiment IN our leisure time.'

'Don't take this so lightly', Julia protested, with a smile on her face and looking at her parents with a 'he can never be serious' look.

Dan came in here. 'Don't you two ever go on proper dates and outings?' How many people were going to ask this question?

I continued. 'Actually it's quite a good photo of you Julia. He (or, more likely, she) has captured your very essence. There's that devastating fun smile which could only have led to the photographer being envious of me.'

Gavin decided he'd side with me. 'I agree with Brandon. Who is not going to simply ignore the article itself, and Brandon, and be captivated by the beauty of your radiance, (only matched by my good wife here)?' He leant over and put his arm around Delia and gave her a loving smacker on the cheek.

I announced, with some fanfare, 'I have a plan. Don't worry. I'm way ahead of you.'

'Oh, oh, now I am really worried. Pray tell,' Julia said.

Dan said, rather drily, 'he's going to invite the photographer on their next outing.'

I gave her the bones of it and then added, 'as a coup de grace we will invite all the snipers to our very public wedding and have the TV there and all. They can take all the pictures they want.'

The four of them were aghast. Julia looked at me with her mouth wide open, then said, 'is this what I think it is? Really?'

With Gavin and Delia hanging on my every word, Delia quite excited, I announced 'yes, this was part of my plan. Well, it was my plan before all this. It just came to me at this moment, what with you Gavin and you Delia right here to witness this, and hopefully give me your permission to marry the most wonderful woman I could ever have hoped to encounter. That picture sparked it off.'

I turned to Julia. 'Julia McDonald, you are the most beautiful person in the world.' I took her hands and continued. 'I admire you greatly and I think we fit each other like a glove. I want us to share our lives, (as if we haven't been doing that already really).' I looked at both parents and asked, 'do you agree with this plan?' They nodded, excited by this event and its spontaneity. Dan whooped.

Then I squeezed Julia's hands and asked her, kneeling down in front of her, 'will you marry me Julia?' She flung herself at me and we kissed full on for many moments.

'Yes, yes,' she said. 'You are the most wonderful man I could have found. Yes we do fit together. I look forward to more of that.' She then burst out laughing at what she'd said, as did we all.

We all stood up and Gavin decided it was well worth a toast. The two parents and Dan went inside, rather diplomatically, and left we two lovebirds in each other's clutches.

'Brandon, that was so lovely. I bet no one has proposed like that before. True to character.' We stood there in each other's arms for quite some time.

The family returned with a bottle of bubbly that had been conveniently chilled at the back of the fridge, five glasses and a large plate of the inevitable cakes.

Gavin filled the glasses and proposed a toast. 'To a magical couple, and a huge welcome to our newest family member. I couldn't have conceived of you being anything other than family Brandon. May you both continue to tread your chosen path together with fulfilment and happiness. Delia and I now consider our job done and Julia in good hands.' The glasses clinked and everyone was jolly.

Dan raised his voice above all the hubbub. 'Now a toast to my future brother-in-law, boss, and friend. If I'd known you before you met Julia I'd have certainly made sure you had met each other. You Julia, deserve him. You are a perfect sister, and I'm so happy for you.' The glasses clinked again.

The toasts went on until the champagne had been drunk. We even began to toast with cake.

Delia asked, 'Brandon, do your folks know about this?'

'No,' I replied. 'As I said, it was all spontaneous. How about we go round now and tell them, my love?'

She nodded enthusiastically and Delia agreed. 'You must. In fact why don't we all drive there and make it a complete family affair?'

With that we all crammed into the family Ford and did just that. Not everyone had a phone; not the Watermans anyway, so this would be a very impromptu visit. It was getting a little late for normal social visits, but needs must in this case.

When we got to my house we bowled in and just about caught Gladys and Cliff and Sidney before they retired.

Hugs all round, Sidney suspected something extraordinary was afoot, especially if Julia's state of excitement and the whole McDonald clan's presence were anything to go by.

I took Julia by the hand and stepped forward, facing Cliff and Gladys and said, 'Mum and Dad, meet your future daughter in law.' The two parents were gobsmacked, Gladys soon in tears. She hugged Julia excitedly and Cliff and Sidney shook my hand vigorously. Julia got hugs all round.

The McDonalds joined in and the family was as one.

Sidney asked, 'what brought this on? Don't tell me,…. Brandon had an epiphany. But if I know him, he has a masterplan, and this was all in a day's work.'

Gavin told him, 'a bit of both. There we all were, relaxing in the evening dusk, and there he proposed in family public, as if he had just thought of it, more or less. I don't think he came to our house tonight intending to propose to Julia. But he does have a plan. This man knows what he wants. By the way there is no ring. That's how spontaneous it all was.'

'Ever the maverick' said Sidney, still with a huge grin on his face.

'What are the plans?' asked Cliff.

'About the wedding?' I asked. 'There are none yet.'

Dan told them about my plan to invite this photographer to the wedding. They all looked nonplussed at first but nodded knowingly when Dan expanded into the article (which he had brought along fortuitously).

Delia added, 'Brandon claimed that picture was the epiphany moment.'

'Well,' I explained,' I think I should invite this guy along to give him thanks for inspiring my decision, and give him a nationwide exclusive. Smother him in gratitude and goodwill and see what he does with that, and convert this snide journalism into something spiritual.'

Sidney couldn't stay quiet on this. 'Brandon, you have mischief afoot methinks. I'll debrief you later.'

Everyone laughed and the gathering went on for another half hour or so. The McDonalds left, with Julia giving me a world class goodnight kiss. As they were all stepping into the car I suggested that she call Ira with the news when she got home.

'It's time we had a phone connected, don't you think?

Another kiss and they were gone.

Plans began to be discussed. We two lovebirds were still in our teens, early to be married by society standards in that year of nineteen sixty-two, but we weren't two ordinary youngsters. We had both done a short time of living but really packed it in, by most peoples' yardstick, particularly me, but with Julia now hot on my heels. We were observing and absorbing the harsh realities of life and tackling them head on and were leaving the more frivolous or mundane aspects of life to others.

We were in no particular rush to have the wedding. We were bonded anyway, we reasoned, and other activities were demanding our attention.

However, those around us had absolutely welcomed our decision. Ira in particular was over the moon. She and I were joined at the hip from the beginning and Julia was the cream on the top. Ira was a natural 'partner in crime' for Julia, with her natural antipathy toward pretenders and baddies and total willingness to front up to opposition. She was becoming more and more involved in Julia's anti-Psychiatry researches without dumping her responsibilities at the College.

She and Sidney were effectively the directors of operations at the College, with me 'off on his search for the perfect human', as Ira put it.

Sidney was revelling in the whole project. Nothing was too much effort for him. He and Ira were determined to keep the expansion going and leave me to my PR activities and other researches.

Peter was in charge of the Inner London Colleges, and Dan was in charge of the burgeoning West London group. Andrew was being groomed for the North London group which was currently being overseen by Ira. He was a bright boy (part of the gene pool) especially since he had been loosened up in his education by the 'Waterman technique'.

Even young Nigel, Ira's boy, had shown interest in teaching, and so was being prepared as such. Her other two children were a bit young as yet, but had been at the College as students needing some remedying.

Delia got nowhere with her letter to the magazine (called 'Out and About').

She even went to their offices and was stone-walled rather expertly but not without creating a fuss and threatening legal action. So she joined the College and became Ira's administrative assistant. Two peas in a pod, once again.

My henchmen and I had attracted some very upscale staff. There was not a hint of a bad egg among them. I had noted that they were all motivated by the cause, and not the need of a job, but in any case were good quality personalities.

I pointed this out to the group at network staff meetings and made it official policy that they were all responsible for the quality of staff employed. Bad eggs and negative personalities, even the glum- faced, were automatically refused or sieved out quickly.

Was this all too good to be true or just so good?

CHAPTER ELEVEN

I was probably close to being fully grown by this. I was reasonably solid in physique, six feet one inch in height and fourteen odd stone in weight (one hundred and ninety five pounds/ eighty eight kilograms). I considered myself fairly clean-cut and well-kempt in a more conservative way – shortish back and sides, hair brushed back with a part down the middle, clean-shaven. I was definitely not a poser. I had a modest wardrobe with a mixture of casual, office and going-out clothes.

I was aware that I stood out from the crowd, but with some modesty I might add. I'd worked on developing presence, by observing obvious role models in public life and had filtered it all down to the necessity to stand tall so to speak, and to project one's communication penetratingly and in an upbeat manner. Listening and making others comfortable in one's space was a gold dust quality.

I'd always had a good attention span, whether concentrating unblinkingly on whatever was in front of me, and for long periods of time or taking in many details and goings-on in a wide periphery.

With such a strong purpose burning in a number of fields now and with so much success to date, I was tireless. I had noted that tiredness was not just a symptom of physical exertion but more of a blunting of purpose, which was basically accumulating loses, not just in learning but in any project in life.

My meditation activity definitely added to my armoury. I made a point at the end of each day to do twenty or thirty minutes of undiluted meditation. In discussing this with others I realised that the subject of meditation was largely misconceived by almost anyone who wasn't a practitioner (and among quite a few who were, it must be said). It wasn't just a matter of emptying one's mind or cogitating on some thought or subject, or one's navel.

When I began a period of meditation I would sit (it didn't matter how and where I sat) and merely perceive the space I was in but with my eyes closed.

My attention scanned the present area without scattering or fixing. If I began to day-dream or wander off, which I did occasionally, I'd quickly, by sheer mental effort or by chanting a mantra, drag myself back to the now.

Usually after five minutes into a period I'd begin to quite comfortably sit there silently in peace and experience an amazing quality of awareness. If someone had tapped me on the shoulder I would have been right there, without surprise. I supposed that someone with a lot on their mind would have trouble doing this, or would need the mantra as a kind of crutch.

On one occasion I did an extended period of meditating – about an hour. I experienced something quite new, a what could only be described as a widening of space and a perception of the room as if I had my eyes open. I'd heard of 'out of the body' experiences and could only surmise that this was what it was. It was very comfortable and uplifting. When I'd opened my eyes I was 'floating on air' and on some sort of remote control of the body. The state did not continue for long though.

This experience hastened my research into other Eastern religions, namely Buddhism Hinduism and Taoism. Christianity and Islam, I concluded, were monotheistic belief systems largely, there being an overriding belief in an all-powerful God, whereas the Eastern religions were essentially saying that the truth (which all religions are trying to get one to, whatever that is) is within oneself and is a journey of self-discovery, arriving at a more satisfactory state of mind for humankind.

Buddhism and Taoism talked a lot about being in the moment and finding 'the way'. Meditation was a big part of the means to this and the teachings of their founders were largely describing how to attain the goal, rather than dictating what was right or wrong. There were many advices to creating harmony and being at one with the world or nature.

Buddha described 'the promised land' as Nirvana. This was a state of being awake or enlightened.

Well, I thought, was this what I had experienced in my meditation or was I just on my way to something higher?

More importantly, was meditation workable for all, or was Man too far gone for an evolution by this means only?

It would be easy if he could eradicate the gremlins of our students and the population as a whole by something this simple. Had it done that for the teeming millions of the East? Surely one would expect a highly civilised culture in these places and a resultant command over the environment and progressive standards of living. From what I'd read the East was a largely underdeveloped and deprived area, living largely in abject poverty. This can't be enlightenment for all.

Then again all religions had undergone changes over the centuries and perhaps had been altered or varied so as to lose their true nature. There were opinions in each as to what was really true, witness the variations of Christianity and Islam.

Overall, I began to conclude, somewhere in this hotchpotch of efforts to change and maintain a healthy mind-set, there were some useful clues. For sure Man's attempt to improve his moral fibre and spiritual enlightenment was to no small degree down to religious practices.

I decided also, by reverse vector, that some urge, in probably a minority of society, was the cause of the worst inclinations and destructive actions that passed as life on this planet, and that these were IRRELIGIOUS.

Whatever the case, my search would go on. Before one could get to a higher state of reason something had to be done about 'the spanner in the works'. Sanity is the ability to tell right from wrong, and then again, by what yardstick?

Yes, I thought, reasoning power is what it is all about – the ability to reason without the spanner in the works, and, 'on the move'.

CHAPTER TWELVE

Diane McAdam, the Education Minister had indeed initiated her own little enquiry on the subject of Brandon Waterman. In return she learned that one of her senior Inspectors, James Hopkins, had been suspended for allowing Waterman's influence to infiltrate the Private School sector. He was being dealt with by a Hearing which was under review.

Reading the submissions before the Hearing she learned that apparently a fairly newly-appointed Inspector of School Standards, one J.C.Levison, had known Waterman at his previous school and had experienced first-hand the trouble created by Waterman at that school.

She read various scathing reports about Waterman and his 'College', and that it was he, Levison, who had, indirectly, instigated proceedings against Waterman.

The Private Schools were adopting Waterman's techniques outside of Department jurisdiction.

'Hmm, I'd like to meet with the Hearing's convenor,' she said to Alison who was seated expectantly opposite.

'That would be Mr. Ben Downs,' Alison informed her.

'And, Alison, I've got to go up North this evening so could you seek out this new chap, …what's his name again…?' she asked looking for his name amongst her papers. 'Ah, yes, Levison. Get him to tell you all he knows about this. In fact you interview Downs too and find out what he's doing about this. We'll talk again on Monday.'

'I'll do that. This will be fun. Are you a bit suspicious of his suspension?'

'I don't know yet. Let's just say this seems to contrast with the impression I got from the TV shows.'

CHAPTER THIRTEEN

As I had intended I'd been looking into this matter of James's suspension, and discovered that the fly in the ointment hadn't changed that much; well, not at all. It turned out that Jake Levison, our past nemesis, had graduated (if that's the right word) to the Department itself, and had been busy poisoning minds there, or just as likely, finding like-minded cohorts.

I'd found this out by questioning Ira about things at the old school and she had recently noticed the absence of said snake at PTA meetings and had enquired about the matter.

Levison hadn't wasted any time. He had been promoted by positioning himself as the source of the school's much improved standards over recent years. He must have applied for the new job to get it ahead of the Head.

You'd have thought he'd gain the kudos and let sleeping dogs lie. But no, not only had he gotten at the Department hierarchy but also the TV bosses. He'd found a few like-minded characters there too and now he had a bit of a 'plot'.

Now newspaper articles were appearing in some parts of the media belittling the College's work, and especially my motives.

This trickled down to some of the ground gained in the private schools and resulted in the beginning of some more withdrawals from the program.

I knew what the propaganda line was and who it appealed to most. I thought I had the more adventurous private Heads well aboard, but even they fell prey to threats of investigation and status withdrawal, not to mention anxious Trustees and the odd parent creating a fuss.

I met James at his home in West London. James was spending more and more time at home since his suspension.

His wife, Cindy, (a big fan of mine by this), cooked up a big slap-up meal for the two mavericks of learning.

She was an attractive woman, now in her middle ages, but wearing well. She was a little in the mould of Julia with her ready wit, adventurous spirit, not to mention that dark featured face and a frequently displayed set of teeth.

She sat down at the table too after she'd dished up the meal and promptly announced that there was only one thing for it. 'I am going to go out and work, just to cover all bases. And if James's Hearing doesn't go well then we don't fall into any financial problems.'

'You won't do that,' I put in. 'I've already offered James more than gainful employment in our enterprise. In fact, now that your boys are flying along you could join us too Cindy. We need as many progressive rottweilers as possible at our place.'

James added, 'We couldn't do much better than that could we Cinds? But just for a little while longer I think we need me in the Department. I think it would do you good love, to get your teeth into something.' And now looking at me he nodded. 'Thanks for the insurance policy though Brandon.'

'What could I do at the College Brandon?' Cindy asked.

'The world is your oyster,' I replied. 'We have two schools in West London now, still burgeoning. You could start in one as a teacher and learn the ropes, and if you fancied it you could run one of them, or two even. I know you have domestic responsibilities but give some of that over to your two great lads. You could work part time while you groove in.'

'That could work don't you think James?' she added, enthusing all the while.

'Up to you love. I'm all for it, myself. You are under-utilised.'

I closed that discussion off. 'Well one thing you can't dispense with here James is this cooking.' I ran my tongue around my mouth and put my knife and fork together on an empty plate. That went down well with Cindy.

I turned to James while Cindy made some tea. 'I've been poking around to find out where all this heat is coming from. It turns out my old Deputy Head who you know caused a lot of trouble at the outset, has been elevated to the adverse press and some private sector withdrawals. Bit of a coincidence don't you think?

'Maybe you could sniff around and question a few of your decision makers about who has said what to whom, to bring your suspension into force. You might talk to the people on your Hearing and ask them what information they are acting on.

'This guy Levison will be very clever and sound really reasonable and believable, without coming out from under cover. You know your associates well. Use your more upbeat contacts and bleed the info from them.'

James was listening and thinking and nodding his head.' Ok then. I'm not taking this lying down. No reason to be cautious, just clever.'

Cindy came in with the tea and sat down. 'What are we talking about?' she asked.

I explained the whole situation. 'We are going to go on the offensive, quietly at first, and then noisily if we have to. A lot of lives and livelihoods could be affected here, and a lot of good work undone. Call it counter PR.'

'You are a freak Brandon' Cindy said. 'I'm thinking I wouldn't like to be YOUR enemy.'

'Do you know,' I added, 'an investigation into the personal activities of this Levison character wouldn't go amiss, if it comes to it. If he's that bad a character I'm sure there will be dirt to be found in his private life.'

'How would you do that?' asked James.

'Maybe I've been reading too many detective stories or something, but I think there are PI's who do just that sort of thing. Anyway, before we get to that, but quickly mind you, we'll try and smoke him out into the light of day and maybe he'll disgrace and suspend himself.' I couldn't help rubbing my hands together in some sort of anticipation.

'Thanks for lunch, you good people. I'm off to talk to the TV chaps and see if we can arrange something positive there. Let me know what day next week you want to start, Cindy. I'll set it up at Hammersmith to expect a bright new spark.'

'What's the pay?' she asked with her hands on her hips.

'Duty is above mere money,' I quipped, and waved them goodbye.

———————————

I called Tom to sort out our next TV venture. I was a bit surprised Tom hadn't been onto this before now.

'Ah, Brandon, I'm glad you rang,' he said a little hesitantly. 'Something has come up, which you won't like.'

'Say no more, old chap,' I got in quickly. 'I know what's come up. We should meet and swap notes and I'll tell you what I'm doing about it.'

'How did I know you'd be right in there on this?' Tom replied. 'Ok, your place or mine?'

'Can you come here to the College this afternoon, say about six? I have another surprise for you too.'

'Mystery sandwich! Ok, I'll bite. See you then.'

Tom sauntered into the College bang on six pm and the first person he ran into was Julia. 'Hullo young lady,' he chirped provocatively. 'So you are lasting the distance I see. How much of your man has rubbed off on you?'

'Wrong assumption Mr TV.' Julia never missed an opportunity.

I joined them from a nearby office. 'Hi Tom.' I put my arm around Julia's shoulders and said to Tom, 'have you met the future Mrs Waterman?'

Tom was gobsmacked. 'Well, no, not really; only in passing, not that long ago come to think of it. You don't mess about do you? I should have a camera tail you wherever you go. That would make a series all by itself. Anyway, congrats. Is this the news you hinted of when we spoke earlier?'

'Yes, and don't think you can automatically have first rights to the wedding ceremony. I know how your mind works – ever the opportunist.'

The three of them walked off into the nearest office and sat around a table. 'We have a fly in our ointment,' I began, 'and I suspect he's gotten into yours too.'

'Yep,' replied Tom, 'the powers that be, that is that same Director we've managed to just about keep onside up to now, has pulled the plug on our next program, at least for now.'

'Do you know what precipitated this?' I asked.

'Not exactly. But someone has whispered unfavourables in his ear. He hasn't just come up with this. We were all green light for the next program after our runaway success with the Francis program.'

'Well, here's a co-incidence Tom. I've had a few Heads pull out of our program in the private sector of schools, having been leant on by the Department. James Hopkins, the man responsible for helping us gain recognition and getting a foothold into these schools has been suspended.'

'Nooo!,' Tom responded. 'That MUST be a co-incidence.'

Julia chimed in here. 'Not if you hear the rest of it.'

I continued. 'There's that character, Jake Levison, the Deputy Head at my old school. He's wangled a promotion to the Department, all in these few weeks we are talking about here.

'He's been at the head of any and all trouble I've ever had, from my program with the school pupils to the hassle we had setting up our Colleges.

'And here we are again.'

'What's your plan Brandon?' asked Tom.

'Well I've got James on the inside of the Department ferreting around for info and if we don't get immediate actionable data from that, I am going to have him investigated. I think I'll start that anyhow.'

'Wow!' from Tom. 'This is serious, isn't it?'

'Yep, up to now we've had nothing but pretty-well uninterrupted success. We've done nothing else but expand, with great success and without any direct advertising costs – all word of mouth. We won't have a bad-mouth spoil that. There are a lot of lives and livelihoods on the line here.

'The hardest part about all this is getting into the Department and instilling good educational methods into the mainstream. It's an intractable object. We don't need it to be counteractive to us. We could do with your help here Tom.'

This was the closest Tom had seen me come to being anywhere near phased. 'What can I do to help?'

I told him very directly, almost as an order. 'Use your contacts and influence to sniff out who's said what to whom within your station. Kick up a fuss if you have to.'

Julia said to Tom calmly and with a hand on his arm, 'Aren't you enraged by this Tom? You stand to lose here too. You have some pull by virtue of having delivered some prime time TV ratings and advertising sponsors.'

Julia was looking at Tom and detected some reticence. Is this guy all PR; a lightweight?

She continued, 'you can only be driven by your own integrity here. If it's right to get involved and damn the flack, then it's right. Or you can sit on the fence and let it all happen.'

Tom was getting a lecture here. I added, 'We don't need to talk you into this Tom. Talk yourself into it. If you really think it's not worth getting involved then of course don't. We'll leave you to decide, but quickly if you will.'

Tom felt very much on the spot and was wrestling with his conscience. He wasn't used to confrontation at this level. His ambition only went so far.

Julia and I started to rise. I said to Julia, 'I have a driving lesson now. Give me a quick test on the Highway Code.'

Tom got up and said, 'I'll see what I can do when I come in to work tomorrow.' I knew this was a conscience appeaser but just said, 'fine Tom. Let me know what you find out eh?'

I had a pile of papers in my hand and, having almost forgotten why, said to Tom, 'By the way, here are some ideas and scripts for further programs. Look them over and see what you think.'

We shook hands and Julia gave him her big smile and another touchy-feely gesture. Tom disappeared into the night and me and Julia went to the staff room and over a soup and bread snack got into the Highway Code.

I spoke individually to all my senior staff and all the Heads of Colleges. I impressed upon them that not one student could be allowed to lag, not one student to be admitted that didn't pass our criteria after their trial period. 'When a student slows down or gets disinterested, or fails to attend – ANY non-optimum sign – there's always a miss somewhere. Dig it up and repair it, get the parents in on it, whatever. Absolutely NO standards must slip or falter.'

I gathered my area managers – Peter, Dan, Ira (still doubling up to a small degree) and Andrew. Sidney and Julia joined the meet too.

I began to speak. 'You've all heard about the Levison disease by now. It's contagious you know.'

They all laughed. I continued. 'Not to get too serious and stop smiling, but I want you all to closely inspect all Heads and how they are going about their jobs. I've spoken to them all, as you know. Our results will make us unassailable in the end, but sometimes the public can be spooked and easily follow the sensational, and easily believe all sorts of lies.

'If you get any parent in and they raise any media stuff simply pour the coals onto 'results'. Ask them are they really happy with the results. They should ALL say they are happy. So leave it at that and re-iterate that that tells them all they need to know.

'If anyone presses for more info or they become critical about us, or me, refer them to Ira or Julia. You do get hypercritical parents too, and kids too sometimes.

'If anyone from the media shows up at any of our colleges then refer them to Head Office here. No conversations, no explanations. We here will deal with them.

'For your information we have someone in the department, James Hopkins, doing some sleuthing for us, and with a bit of luck we may find out some more skinny from Tom at the TV station. Interesting times.

'Carry on doing what you've been doing. It's all about standards and results. With every student you rescue you should get a referral. That's where our future business comes from. Media attention like we've had up to now is the cream on the top.'

CHAPTER FOURTEEN

Alison Burns, in the Education Department, visited Ben Downs, the man dealing with the Hopkins Tribunal. 'What Can you tell me, Mr. Downs, about this James Hopkins thing? I hear he's suspended for, well, what exactly? The big boss wants to know.'

Ben Downs immediately felt the need for a toilet break. 'Well, ah, Mr. Hopkins it seems, has, um, exceeded his brief and allowed this chap Waterman to, ah, get his methods into the Private School domain.'

'Well, has it amounted to any damage, do we know?' Alison asked, expecting her boss to browbeat her about this.

'We, ah, don't … well I haven't gone into that. It's not, ah, really the done thing to bring in outsiders .. well, you know, it is against Department policy."

'Is that what this is all about then?' asked Alison

Ben was sweating mentally and physically. 'He has a history of, what would you say, um, disturbance in his area. There are reports of his earlier misdeeds at the, um, Finchley school he was at and his illegal, ah, establishment of his own school. There were incidents of aiding and abetting truancy, to, er, gain students.'

'I see,' Alison responded. 'That seems pretty damning, but who did these reports come from, do you know?'

'From the…Finchley school I think. James Hopkins and Deirdre Moore also visited the Waterman College. That's how Mr. Hopkins got involved in all this.'

'Is this College still illegal? Tell me they are now properly registered.'

'Well, ah, at least it was in the pipeline. I, I'm not sure to be honest.'

'Mr Downs, would you mind forwarding to me a copy of all the reports you have on this matter. As soon as you can please.'

'Ah, certainly. Right away.' Downs started rustling papers as he stood up.

Alison left and sought out Mr. Levison. This was not a simple expedition as he seemed to be constantly out of the office.

'Mr. Levison I presume,' she said after eventually getting through to his extension. 'I am Alison Burns, Education Aide to the Minister. I need to speak to you about this Hopkins Tribunal. Could you come up here to the 4th Floor around 4.00 pm?'

'Ah, yes Alison' He was thinking fast on his feet. 'Do I need to bring anything with me?'

'No, not at all. Just yourself please.' She hung up not quite abruptly.

I had retired to my office – yes a new office at Head Office, all to myself, and with a phone and a typewriter. The whole Head Office had a general secretary who helped arrange things for the Execs and typed letters and kept files. This was Veronica, a small stocky, short-haired blond lady of still teenage years, just. She was the daughter of one of our investors. She was also on the educational program (every employee had to go through it).

She was a godsend, lightening the load a lot. She was so bright and efficient she anticipated what to do before being asked. I benefitted by her having my favourite coffee in front of me on point (tea was going out of fashion?) and a list of people I had appointments with and a whole host of messages, in order of importance.

Sipping my coffee I wondered who else I could get to rally around and help nip in the bud this infestation that had occurred.

Immediately I lifted the phone and rang Jim Naylor of the Hampstead

Gazette. I hadn't spoken to him for a while now even though his daughter and son had been enrolled at the College.

'Jim, its Brandon Waterman here,' I announced cheerily. 'Tell me how fabulously your two offspring are now doing.'

Jim replied, 'all is good Brandon. Good to hear from you. To what do I owe this pleasure?

I told him about the little problem that had arisen and asked him if there was anything he could do his end to help, like an article singing our praises.

'Something like, 'six months after the treatment' type of thing. Maybe a picture of you and me at the College, or you and the kids – you know.'

'Yes, good idea. It all went down well last time didn't it?' He had splashed me and the College in his pages when his kids had begun their re-education.

'Good Jim. I'll leave it with you. Let me know what you are going to print if you would.

'No problem Brandon. Talk to you later.'

I hung up and thought of another idea – a College magazine to all the parents, investors, and anyone else we had spoken to on the fringes. Maybe a copy to each local newspaper editor.

The magazine would have lots of pictures and stories and testimonials in it to broadcast our progress. It could be a monthly or quarterly issue, I thought.

When Veronica came into my office again with some letters for me to sign I decided to play. 'Veronica, how'd you like to become famous?'

'Oh, oh,' she replied cautiously. 'You want me to go on TV or something?

I sat back and put a hand to my chin, as if to stroke a beard, and peered at her. 'Hm, what an idea. You are just busting for it aren't you?'

She said, 'I think I can see where you are going with this.' She opened her mouth and put a hand over it, waiting for the inevitable.

I laughed. 'No, just toying with you. I've decided you are under-utilised doing filing and making coffee and so on. I want you to become our in-house magazine editor.' I just looked at her, taking a sip of coffee, and let it hang until she absorbed what she was hearing.

'Oh, you are not kidding this time are you? What would it entail, on top of my normal over-worked/under-paid duties?'

'Veronica,' I responded quickly, 'I see you have joined the club of women in this place who somehow believe me capable of extorting cheap and unfair labour and in the process being sexist.'

She was warming to this game. 'Never let it be said. I think I am a free spirit.'

'That's more like it,' I encouraged, with a smirk on my face. 'Didn't you know that the best way to choose someone to do a job for you is to find out who is the busiest, and then give the job to him or her, in this case her?'

'How does that work?' she asked, somewhat playfully. 'Sounds like cheap and unfair labour to me.

'Ok, take it that way and report back to your leader,' I said somewhat mischievously. 'Actually it's a big compliment.'

This girl had a great sense of humour. I went on to explain my idea. 'Make it nice and glossy with lots of pictures. Add in a map showing our Colleges and the ones that aren't there yet. Let's have a few mottos, like, 'normal education could make you stupid', or more positively 'get inspired by learning', 'school doesn't have to be a drudge'. Maybe you can better those. You can become a journalist, editor, publisher, investigator, reporter, author – all of those things, all rolled up into one.'

'You are playing with my ego,' she replied, putting on a mock faint.

'Take it like that if you must. Map it all out in a draft copy, as if ready for the printers, and let me see it before you completely take over. We'll see about the TV bit when you've driven all this new business down on the College,' I teased.

She skipped out with a chirpy, 'okaaaay! Watch this space.'

I liked this girl. She was another 'shades of you know who'.

I lay back in my swivel chair, with one foot up on the desk and with thoughts buzzing round in my never-idle head and said to myself, 'yes, we'll consolidate an impregnable image – all good news and accomplishment. We could of course put colleges in all major towns and cities, but wouldn't it be easier to just get my methods into the existing infrastructure?'

Talking about the latter, I decided it was time to check on James Hopkins and Tom Shelley. I glanced down at my appointments list and messages. Sure enough there were messages from both Tom and James to call back.

There was also an appointment with a leading journalist from 'The Observer'. He had been pre-vetted by Ira, meaning he'd stated an intention to write a pro-College article.

Just then the said lady breezed in and plonked herself down in a chair at my desk and promptly put her foot up on the desk and sat back with both hands behind her head. 'It's good to take a break from the busy-busy sweatshop out there.' She looked up at the ceiling, smiling and sighing.

I was quick, looking at her as if noticing something for the first time. 'You know Ira, you're looking younger by the day. How do you do it? Must be all the busy-busy stuff and being worked off your feet by an insensitive and unrelenting boss. Do you know Veronica has the same disease? She just now finished complaining about it, AND she demanded more pay! Wherever did she get that attitude from? Strange, this disease is peculiar to the women in this office. How much are the Union fees? Do you need quarantining until it's all over?'

'Sorry boss,' she responded, sitting up normally again. 'We women have been persecuted and subjugated for centuries on end and are on a pendulum swing. You'll just have to go with the flow and hope there's not too much collateral damage.

'I came in to talk to you about this journalist who's coming in shortly. I know you didn't want to be talking to them really but this one seemed different. He knows all about your psychiatric interest too. What do you think?

I replied, 'words and stated intentions are one thing. Do we have any examples of his regular articles? Would he be willing for his children to undergo a re-education (if he has kids that is)? Did he digest our general piece for journalists?'

'You don't trust this breed do you? He's been given our information piece. Don't know what he thinks of it, but good idea to answer his questions with a suggestion he subject his kids to our treatment and, on that basis, see where we go with that. I'll get some back copies of 'The Observer' for you.'

She continued. 'Why didn't I think of that?'

'Because you are too pre-occupied with women's rights and female inferiorities to see the woods from the trees,' I retorted.

'We'll see,' she answered. 'I'm going to take on this guy myself. You keep your feet up and enjoy, from above, me slaving away on your behalf.'

'Good idea,' I said. 'More seriously, Ira, how are you, despite my compliment?'

Ira knew this was not just a social question. I am always very interested in my friends and staff (well almost all my friends WERE staff) and I'd do ANYTHING to help them. Then I reckon she thinks that's me somehow managing to get them all to 'slave for me for next to nothing'.

'Well,' she replied, 'if you really want to know, I couldn't be doing better. Nigel finished his schooling with flying colours, loves reading, and now LOVES working here. Bertie (my youngest) is following close on Nigel's heels and will pass out of school another credit to the school (they're looking really good on the back of us, aren't they?) and my hubby couldn't be happier with his family because properly educated and purposeful kids and wife beget a happy family. He deserves it.

'I'm so happy here Brandon. The game gets bigger doesn't it?'

'Certainly does Ira.' I replied. 'And when you are winning there is always someone who doesn't like it. But I'm so glad you are here with me Ira. I have total faith in you and am proud to have you as my friend. I couldn't think of anyone else I'd rather have as a founding member and fellow Exec. We are a rare breed us lot.'

We both got up and came around the desk and hugged. This was a common show of obvious affection between us. I get plenty of acknowledgement from people around me but I appreciate that all my staff need a huge expression of appreciation from those who count most, that is, me.

As Ira was leaving I said to her, 'by the way, I've given Veronica carte blanche to devise and send out a monthly/quarterly College magazine to all parents and anyone else who has the vaguest association with us; and the media.

'This is part of our strategy to combat any bad news coming from the Department and TV quarters; total good news, and for real. Maybe you could just cast a surreptitious glance over her shoulder here and there, but you know, I think this little lady is another star and won't want or need much advice.'

'You are right there,' Ira replied. 'And I might say she's a great member of the female takeover club. Julia loves her too. Sidney has no chance. And you, well…… good luck,' and she swished out of there with me open-mouthed, no time to have the last say.

What a gang, I thought. How could it be that I am so lucky to have such good people around me?

Well, without any false modesty I reckon I attract them like bees to the hive. I am aware of the effect I have on people and know what I have that works well. But I dont seek to be admired. My motivation in all things is to be effective and succeed in what I see is right, not to seek notoriety or popularity (the latter being hallmarks of insecurity).

I went to get on with my 'in basket' when the next important cog in my wheel, Mr Sidney Waterman, knocked and entered.

'I see you knocked Grandpa, I mean Sidney (we are at work now). The women around here conduct their campaign in rather underhand ways and just stroll in. By women I mean Ira, Julia and now Veronica, their latest recruit.'

Sidney replied. 'Never mind, let them continue where the suffragettes left off until they get it out of their system. It's you and I. If the world over the centuries has been ruined by men maybe it's time to give the women their heads.

'I was wondering if you and the lovely Julia McDonald, soon-to-be Waterman, were going to attend the inter-borough debating championship this evening.'

'Well I am. Let me find out what the lovely lady IS planning that could be more important than this. Its good publicity you know; get onto all the avenues of society and spread the news by example. I have a list of things here to do first.

'How are things in your neck of the woods?' I asked.

'Well, as you know we are looking for premises for our Highgate branch. If it proves too expensive we might have to morph that into Hampstead and Finchley. I would then go looking for another catchment area, perhaps Mill Hill or Edgware.

'Delia McDonald is definitely the co-sire of your missus. We have another member of the 'club' to contend with. She's already re-organising me. Now I don't know where anything is. She's a godsend though; glad to have her to lighten my load.

'By the way, young man, do we intend to take over the whole country? Are we going to be the next big conglomerate?'

'You can't stop a speeding train too easily, eh?' I replied. 'but, good point. The shortest and most effective way to export our product should be to use the Education system that exists but it wouldn't be under our ownership would it? Would it survive without our care and attention and under lesser lights? It must all be in the training, like any craft or technique.

'I suppose we could be subcontractors to the Government and train all the teachers ourselves. Would they allow that? If not, I fear it would get watered down and maybe changed or modified.

'This works here because we are all very like-minded people. Were we to go nationwide we'd suffer the same dilution as under Government control. Just shows, what we do is very special, even when compared to other middle-to-large scale businesses of any description.'

Sidney added, 'well the private schools will give us some idea of how well things would go in an establishment outside our closer jurisdiction. But even there we have offered them our own inspection and some supervision, as part of the service. This could only go so far.

'We have to deal with this Department blip first, or we go nowhere in the grand scheme of things.'

'Yep. I'm working on it, which reminds me I need to call James Hopkins back on this very subject. How are YOU doing? I haven't spoken to you for a while at any length.'

'Don't worry about me. I'm very much alive and well and enjoying the game. We are financially fine. Our fees are at about the right balance of affordable versus viable. And we are a boon to the society around us.'

I took in this deceptively efficient man anew. His health looked robust, he was afire with the project and could be left to get on with it – a brick. Retirement hadn't previously been kind to him really, so now, in full flow he looked even younger and more alert, and still the wise old bird of the family.

'Thankyou Mr Waterman. You are my foundation.' Sidney left after we arranged the logistics of the night. That reminded me to call Julia. She'd be out and about most likely, but with a bit of luck I could leave a message with one of the family (that wasn't here working already). I rang and there was no answer so I sought out Mrs McDonald Senior, who must be in the building somewhere.

I thought to myself, I must invent a phone messaging device, or better still a roving phone. Someone must be working on that. I'll leave it to them.

I cleared all my 'in basket' including calls to James and Tom. They weren't available, so I left messages with their respective staff.

As I was about to leave, right on cue, my leading lady breezed into my office, and closed the door. She came right up to me and enveloped herself in my arms. 'Hi stranger,' she oozed. 'Haven't seen you for at least forty eight hours.'

'Unhand me wench', I said, stroking her hair. 'We need to go to dinner; we have a big debating competition tonight, didn't you know?'

'So Sidney said. Sounds like a royal command. I didn't know it was on the horizon.'

'Me neither until an hour or so ago. Either way I was planning on taking you to dinner. I'm so glad you showed up. I missed you.'

That dealt with any residual surprise at the lack of any prediction. We pecked again and left for our most commonly visited restaurant on the

Finchley High Road.

Having eaten and gotten ourselves up to date we moved onto the venue for the debates, which was 'at home', in football parlance.There were to be three boroughs, or Town Halls, involved in the debate – Islington, Camden and ours, Barnet. So there were to be three debates in the evening. The subjects, unknown to any of the teams were put into a hat by an arbiter.

Sidney and Julia and I were separated, each in a team with two other members of the Society. As it happened, each of the 'big three' were chosen to be the final summarisers.

There was quite a crowd there, maybe thirty altogether. There were three diverse subjects – Politics, Religion and Social problems.

Sidney was dealt Politics, I got Religion and Julia, Social problems.

We each acquitted ourselves well and there was nothing much to choose from the three. Sidney and Julia extracted a draw and I a decisive win.

On the way home, Julia, a tad miffed at her result said, 'if only the subject had been Psychiatry, I'd have killed them.'

'I thought you killed them anyway Julia,' Sidney announced. I nodded too.

Julia bowed and continued. 'Brandon you utterly slayed them, especially with your knowledge of Eastern religions which none of them had any knowledge of. You weren't helped by having an atheist on the positive side of the argument.'

'Yes, that chap struggled for our side of the argument. He's a rather intense chap that one. I had a brief chat with him afterwards and he brought up the subject of my TV program. Turns out he thought it was all a bit canned. He was oh so polite about it and threw in a few almost imperceptible compliments, (more as a softening action rather than sincerely meant). Not in so many words he thought I was trying to seek notoriety and pulled apart the program make-up.'

'How did you deal with that?' Julia asked.

'I told him I would take note of his comments and thanked him for them, and that was it,' I replied with a smile.

Sidney knew what this meant. 'You didn't give credence to it all but made a note that this chap was one to be wary of.'

'Yep. George Smithers is one of THEM; the polite on top and slimy underneath. What does he do for a living Sidney?'

'I think he's a solicitor, or a magistrate of some sort,' he replied.

'Hmm,' I mused. 'That pricks up my antennae a bit more. How long has he been in the group?'

'As new as you two,' answered Sidney. 'What you have told us about him is a lot more than we knew up to now.

'He was rather articulate tonight, if a bit illogical. On another subject, you two, when is the big wedding?'

Julia fielded this one.' It so happens we haven't decided if it's going to be the 'big wedding' or a small family-only affair. What do you think, Sidney?'

'Well,' he answered, 'do you want it broadcast widely, and shared with all and sundry – I mean, all staff, people we've befriended, students, even reporters?'

I answered, as if on Julia's behalf. 'Julia wants the whole world to know. She's becoming a society girl. And I suspect she wants everyone to contribute to a huge wish-list, to get us off to an economic and logistic-free start.'

'Oo I never said any of that,' she objected mildly, 'but now that you mention it....'

'There you go,' I butted in. 'It's all decided, except for where and when. All that has to be confirmed is whether either of us are free on the day.,... or evening.' We two lovebirds looked at each other in happy mirth.

Sidney spoke again. 'That tells me nothing. I'm going to call a family meeting without you two and a day will be decided and you WILL be there; probably on a Saturday or Sunday. If you don't turn up, who will be embarrassed most?'

Julia and I looked at each other as if to acknowledge the challenge. 'We can decide to be embarrassed or not, can you Grandpa?'

I walked Julia home as Sidney branched off to his resting place, and rest he would.

First thing the next morning I had a call at home from Ira.

She started in on her reason for calling without much ado. 'That reporter who turned up, I hadn't had time to vet him as we discussed, but I'm not sure we will need to now as, after a bit of obfuscation, I finally got out of him what rag he represented.

'Do you remember the paper which wrote the rotten article about us around the time of the big TV program? It's him. I hadn't immediately put him together with The London Observer. Say no more – a bad rag.

'He said he wanted to write a different article this time. We talked for only a minute on leopards and spots and as soon as I gave him short shrift he showed me his spots. I don't feel sorry for leopards so I gave him another copy of our Press spiel and ordered him to print that.'

'I've got the picture, even though you didn't say how polite you'd been in 'shrifting' him. You didn't just call me to tell me this, did you though?'

'You perceptive man,' she replied. 'Here's the thing: remember that picture in that sneaky magazine, 'Out and About'? You know, the one that inspired you to propose to Lady Julia?'

'How could I forget that? I responded. 'I owe him so much for that. What about it?'

'Well I talked to Delia about it. She said she went to their offices and confronted the guy who took the picture. She said he was so memorable for being obese and having a really pimply face. There was a guy with a camera, a little way off from our front doors when the Observer guy left. He was taking pictures. I gave him the big stare and had time enough to take notice of his obviously repugnant appearance. The way Delia described him I twigged who he must be. Birds of a feather stick together, eh?'

'I hope he got a good shot of you kicking that creep off the doorstep. You'll be in the nationals tomorrow Ira. Welcome to the bigtime. Well done for all that. We'll keep our eyes peeled for this guy. Do you think I should invite him to cover our wedding?'

I heard a loud sigh at the other end of the line. 'You're welcome,' she said chirpily.

'Goodbye Ira, enjoy the rest of your day.' What else could I say?

'I will. No overtime chit today; I have to go early today.'

Time to get some good press. I immediately thought of Jim Naylor. I better get him to hurry this up. Also I decided to acquire some independent journalists; those that acted on their own and submitted articles for publication in the leading dailies. I'll get Ira and Veronica onto that tomorrow, I thought.

I went to my room and started about my meditation. I hadn't quite reached the heights of my epiphany of a few weeks ago but I was so relaxed that after reading for five minutes I went into what must be the real definition of a beauty sleep.

The next morning I awoke early, full of the joys of life. I danced down the stairs whistling and, meeting mother in the kitchen, I grabbed her and whirled her around the floor and ended in an exaggerated backward hold. 'Good heavens,' Gladys exclaimed, whilst laughing. 'Do you think this old bird is made of plasticine?'

'Not so old, but made of all things good under God's firmament,' I quipped. 'Talking of all things good, point me to the best breakfast in the land.'

'You are a bit early but help yourself to the teapot and if you want something more solid let God help you by helping yourself. You know the saying. It's on the table anyway. You'll have to wait for the main course. What did God say: patience is a virtue?' She was wide awake now and enjoying this chirpy interchange.

'Not sure God said that,' I corrected, 'but it sounds right. How are you Mum?' I gave her the usual piercing scrutiny to pick up anything equivocal or merely social as she responded.

She talked while she pottered in the kitchen. 'I'm fine — a few achy joints, nothing serious. Did you know Delia (she's a great lady that one), she asked me to join her at the College? Was that anything to do with you, my boy?'

'Would I ever? Expect you to go out and work when you have we men to look after?'

'Yes. How do you think this suspicious thought even occurred to me?'

'I can't imagine at all.' I replied innocently. 'What did you decide?'

'I haven't yet,' she said. 'What do you think I should do?'

'Well, after you've finished in the kitchen sit down with a notepad on your left and a small bit of paper on your right, and a big pot of tea in the middle. In the notepad write down all the reasons you can imagine why you should. Then by lunchtime, end off that by quickly noting down on the bit of paper all the reasons why you shouldn't. This will decide you. Then come in with the notepad and bit of paper and I'll interview you just to make sure you are up to standard and to check you've told no lies in the process. How about that?'

'So it's an order then,' she replied resignedly, then bursting into a big laugh.

I went over to her and took her in my arms 'You do what you think is best all round, my love. It may not be the most convenient or most comfortable, but it would be perhaps the best benefit to the most. We'd love to have you. You could work out your own schedule. Soon you won't have to put up with me as a sort of lodger, or maybe not even Andrew, in time. You could come in and go through our learning procedure while you work this out. Everybody does this.'

She immediately raised this subject. 'Yes, Delia mentioned this. I was no good at school. Aren't I too old to learn? Could I take the embarrassment?'

'Never too old. You might even become hungry to learn. Treat it as a renaissance. Ask your father-in-law; he who thought he knew enough. He'll tell you. I embarrassed him quite a few times.'

With that I kissed her on the forehead and let her go. I sat at the table and tucked into my cereal and glanced at the paper.

Smack on the front page was a picture of Ira standing on the front steps of the College with one hand on her hips and the other waving off the almost-cowering reporter. That determined look on her face I'd seen before.

The headline read 'Abusive staff at Waterman College'. The article went on to describe how with all good intentions the reporter had gone along to write a favourable article about the College and Mr Waterman, and had quite paranoidly been ejected by this woman.

It then accused this Waterman of currying favour with the media to gain notoriety and business and been entirely unwilling for a prospective 'ambassador' of goodwill to spread the word. Was this all a sham and an exercise in self-glorification?

It claimed a paradox in intentions by citing the matter of me and my woman having been willing to try and shame the honourable profession of Psychiatry, digging up the dirt on our visit to the Shrinks Ball. 'What is this organisation really,' it proceeded to hammer?

I wondered if Ira has seen this? I decided to finish my breakfast and go and have my driving lesson, booked for eight a.m., and then go straight to the College.

The driving instructor pronounced me ready for the test (not at Brands Hatch, but at the Licensing Department, on the same streets as everyone else, obeying all traffic laws and speed limits). This was now booked for one week hence.

Having been dropped off at the College by the frayed instructor, I bounded in and promptly walked into Ira's office and congratulated her on her national media picture. I spread out the picture on her desk. She hadn't seen it and sat there agape and stared at it for many moments. 'He did get the press release didn't he?' I asked.

She nodded, still a bit taken aback.

Ira eventually found her tongue. 'I thought I exercised considerable restraint yesterday. I've got to say that photographer takes a good picture. I'm going to frame that. Maybe it's just that Julia and I are so photogenic. Jealous Brandon?'

'Yep. But you and Julia have a head start on me, being naturally beautiful and distinctive. I think I need to make up my face each morning in case I get taken off balance. Watch this space. Anyhow, good work. I'm sure it didn't happen exactly like it was reported.' My look was fishing for a response.

'What you mean is I've exercised some poetic licence in my version of this and that old habits don't die easily,' she overly protested. 'I'll have you know I swallowed my pride and became ever the professional PR person, just like you taught me.'

She was about to go on when I put a finger to her lips and said, 'dont change your nature one bit.'

She liked that. I told her, 'I'm off to rustle up some good press,' and left and went to my desk and rang Tom. This time I got through.

'Morning Tom. You seen the Observer this morning?'

'Yes. That rag has it in for you. Or at least that reporter does.' Tom sounded much more up-beat than the other day, and went straight to the point. 'I'm sorry for being a bit reticent the other day. I decided to get on board and go for this. I've got some ideas for our next programs after reading your scripts.'

'Good man Tom,' I acknowledged.

Before I could say anything else Tom carried on. 'My producer, the one you've met (Vincent Maklin), is all for some more of the same but he told me he is being restrained by the big boss, the one who wasn't keen on our last series. So I got this guy, Barry Lancomb, to agree to a meeting with you, me and Vince. Can you be here at the studios this afternoon at four o'clock?'

'I'm impressed Tom. How about we meet in your café for a bit of lunch and some preparation for the meeting?'

'I'm sure Vince would accommodate that, Brandon. See you at, say, two?'

'I'll be there,' We signed off and I called James next.

James was at home which got me wondering if this was good or bad news. 'How's the upstart from Her Majesty's Department of Education?'

James was in reasonably fine fettle. He was generally coming out of his mild nature but this whole matter had still put him out of his comfort zone to some extent, so he was treading a little cautiously.

He explained to me that a certain amount of smoke screen had been put over this whole matter as he enquired about the origins of the smear campaign.

'My Hearing is tomorrow Brandon. My fate is to be decided. But I do have a meeting with the Deputy Inspector of Schools this afternoon, to have a frank discussion about my situation. The Hearing recommendations will go to him.

'Also, I discovered that this Levison chap has the grand title of School Standards Director. I ran into him in the canteen and introduced myself, in a rather cold manner. I asked him about his input into the decision to warn off the Private sector.

'He hummed and hawed a bit and then denied he had any real interest in the matter. I pressed him a bit and asked him what he'd reported, on you in particular. He became quite vague and said he'd just commented to a few casual queries made by others here, from his knowledge of you. Then he scarpered.'

'That sounds like him,' I commented. 'Ok, thanks for what you are doing James. Have you any taste for how it will go?'

'Not really. I'm not exactly holding my breath though. But I'm going to fight for justice here; and my job. You've opened my eyes to the limitations of our Education system. Let's try and reform it from within before I make any bold moves, or unless this change is forced upon me.'

'I like it James. Good luck this afternoon. I'm tackling the TV hierarchy now. We both have a challenging afternoon. Let's talk this evening, eh?'

'Ok, young man. Until then.' We hung up.

Now I was in full flow. It was mid-morning and I had lots to do. I had a quick chat with Veronica and gleaned that she was well into the layout of the Magazine, and I was playfully told to butt out until she was ready. So I did. Who is in charge here?

Before I could get started on my next task Sidney and Delia summoned me to morning tea. We went to a café down the road. What's this all about, I thought? Delia told me, on the way, that Julia was working at home with Gavin, on this abuse case. At the cafe Sidney announced to me that all the family seniors had met and the wedding was all planned for two months hence.

'You really meant it, you old devil,' I said.

'Yes, your future has been taken out of your hands. You can't have us all wondering and waiting so it is ordained that you shall have a day off two months hence. It is a Saturday, July thirtieth. This happens to be the start of the summer break (for kids at least). You can even arrange a honeymoon without much disruption.

In a mock patronising manner Sidney told me, 'the word 'honeymoon' means a sort of long date, usually at least a week in duration; a holiday. The word 'holiday' means doing something together as a family away from the normal day to day existence, often at some sort of resort. You can add to that 'private communication in various forms; you know, bonding. Maybe that is the clincher for you.'

I went along with this amusement. 'In that case this would be an opportune time to do our tour of The East.'

Delia quickly chimed in. 'You are wasting your time Sidney. I've noticed that these two workaholics have fixed ideas on what to do in any spare time. I'm sure that these ideas would extend to honeymoons, tours, breaks, excursions, or any similar concept. They aren't normal.'

She went on, in dramatic dictatorial tone. 'Be that as it may, Gladys and I are in charge of this day. You will do what your parents tell you, with no argument, do you hear?'

I looked at Sidney and got no change from him. 'Well, I just lost my independence. I thought I was gaining some.'

Delia went on to explain where and when and in what form, who was invited, and that type of thing. 'And you can't dress casual. Everyone will be done up to the nines. The press will be there. We've arranged for Jim Naylor to cover the event. He will distribute pictures to whatever other media show up. We can't stop them from being outside the venues but they won't be allowed in.'

Sidney asked, 'who will be your best man, my boy?'

'You of course, Sidney,' I declared without hesitation.
Sidney immediately protested. 'You can't have ME! I'm your grandpa.'

'Give me just one choice here in this affair,' I retorted. 'You don't have to do anything, except look proud. Oh, you can give a speech if you want to, but I won't hold you to that.'

Sidney grinned at me whimsically. 'Ok, it's all decided then. Delia finalised the 'discussion' and quietly reminded me to put the date in my diary. She had done it anyway because she didn't trust me to do it. 'I don't want my daughter turning up and in front of all those people finding you not there, or that you are at some mosque or Hindu temple.'

I sighed in resignation and changed the subject. 'I'm meeting with Tom at the TV studios, after this.' I looked at my watch – plenty of time yet. 'It's crunch time for our future TV programs.'

Delia got in quickly. 'Don't think Tom can get inside and profit from the event. You are a schemer Mr. Waterman. I'm going to get Gavin to keep tabs on you on this day.'

Delia and I had bonded nicely in our short relationship. She loved the play that was always available between us. And for my part I couldn't have prescribed a better mother-in-law.

We departed and went back to the College. When in my office I glanced at my diary and, as I suspected, July Thirtieth page had been crossed out, and the following week as well.

I smiled to myself, largely in satisfaction at my family and team.

CHAPTER FIFTEEN

At the TV studios, in Ealing, West London, Tom and Vincent Maklin were sat at a table in the corner of the very excellent canteen. I strolled in and shook hands and sat down with my buffet lunch and we small-talked for a bit before talking shop.

Tom started. 'The problem is Barry Lancolm, our Controller of Programs. Whereas we see ratings and advertising money as the main driving force, he is more concerned with broad public respectability, shareholders, and balance of subject matter. A bit contradictory for his role, don't you think?

'We have a number of Documentaries going at the moment, and quite a bit of Current Affairs. But I think 'having enough of that' is a smoke screen for some other problem he has with our style. For instance, he wasn't impressed that we attracted a heckler (totally missing the real good TV moment). And he's not too impressed with celebrities and their laisse faire attitudes, if that's the right expression.'

Vincent (Vince, to most people) came in here. 'He's been there for quite a while now and is quite stuck in his ways. He's very straight-laced. He likes to stick to his format for how it should all be run.'

'I see,' I said, while finishing off my chicken salad. 'Hmm, we have the same thing in the Education Department. It's a Civil Service-type thing – almost a requirement.' I sat there for a few moments, thinking. I sensed the other two waiting for me to spit out a suggestion or something. 'Maybe we should set up our own TV Documentary station.' I looked at them for a response. They didn't catch the smallest smidgen of a sparkle in my eye. 'Just kidding.'

Vince responded to this. 'I'd go for that,' he said enthusiastically.

Tom said, 'careful you two, you'll talk yourself into this before long.'

I made my real suggestion. 'Maybe we should sell the idea to one or three of the biggest advertisers.

Explain to them what our plans are; lay out the screenplay as it were, and get them to insist on the program they'd prefer to sponsor.'

Vince thought for a moment and then added, 'that's rather going behind his back a bit, isn't it?'

'Well, at the least it's going AROUND him,' I sort of agreed. 'But it might get the job done. Or you could just lay it on and then put it forward to Mr. Lancolm, saying you've got the sponsors really keen, the cast is ready, the time slot is prime time. It might brook some controversy, but that is what gets viewers. Sell it to him as a big coup for the Network. We don't want me to go to the competition with this proven formula. I'd do just that if push came to shove. You two will have to really push your point. Tell him how much recognition he'd get from all this. What do you think?'

'Blimey,' gasped Tom. 'What exactly have you got planned as the topic and content?'

I was away now. 'Getting off the subject of Education in the first instance I want to expand from that into how I am looking for a solution for everyday people (not nutters or the mentally handicapped), to improve their character, their emotional problems, their limitations.

'For instance, that young guy, Joe, at the College who was virtually a life drop-out. We got his parents aboard and between us all we got him revitalised to learn, and thence to see the opportunity for a career and a better future. But the guy has limitations – he's flaky and prone to be a bit moody. This will hamper him. The education has got him off the runway but it won't get him to soar, or stay soared without possibly crashing.

'I have been looking for some ways of developing such solutions. I started with Psychology, then got into Psychiatry. Well, this turns out to be the biggest load of nonsense you ever heard of. You know about the Shrink's Ball, don't you? Well, between that and the Psychiatric hospitals, lots of study and now handling of psychiatric abuse cases, I have amassed quite a lot of fodder for more programs.

'Are you wanting to expose this subject on TV?' Vince asked.

'Yep, that's my idea. For instance can you imagine the scene: I go over the brain theory behind it all, then I get a sheep's brain and put it on a slab and demonstrate what happens when you drug it, fry it or just cut it to bits. I get the audience to imagine their brain being electrocuted, or drugged continually, just to deal with their everyday behaviour.'

The two TV guys were rapt at all this. 'What else do you have in mind here?' asked Tom.

'Well, there are the abuse cases, which will shock you. Then there is the subject of Religion....' I left them hanging.

Vince came in here. 'That subject won't fly – too close to the bone, not my bone but that of the culture. I can tell you that now.'

'I thought I might get this reaction,' I said, smiling. 'I'd present it as a good thing, a pillar of society. I am in the infancy of formulating my solution to human bad behaviour. I have been looking at Eastern religions and found that their practice of meditation has some very concrete benefits. This is one of the areas to look at. From there, a little bit further down the line, I will develop my own sort of Psychology, just like I did with Education.'

'Whoah, there's some fodder for us, 'Tom commented. 'That will take some getting through to Barry.'

I continued. 'We can make it as controversial as you like, depending on the backlash and any possible legal challenges. We can't have the Network being sued .. or could we?' I added mischievously.

Tom had been picturing the presenting side of this, and Vince had been looking at all the production nuances.

Tom said, 'well that dwarfs my program plans. But I can see the potential here.' Then he added with a smile, 'you understand, Brandon, we'll have to charge you a huge fee to provide the opportunity for you to have all this free publicity.'

'That's ok,' I retorted. 'My bill for the creativity, screenplay and cast, would more than pay your bill.'

On that happy note we finished our coffees and decided on the next meeting. I was to bring my 'screenplay' and Vince and Tom were to start in on the advertisers. They actually did need some more of these, and some revitalisation of the rather monotone fare the station had been dishing up of late.

Meanwhile, Julia was at home, trying to wrap up her abuse case evidence after a long meeting with Gavin. Gavin had agreed, part time for the moment, to act as the Legal Officer for the College. The whole enterprise would now be formalised under a private partnership called Macman, a composite of two surname syllables of Julia and me.

I called around after my meeting at the TV studios.

'I heard you were in, Julia,' I said as we kissed on the doorstep. 'I have my spies from within, you know.'

Julia was so glad to see me. 'Let me show you what we've got here. Dad and I have been going over this case. It looks like a promising one; so much evidence.'

I speed-read the two page document. It was about a man who had had a marriage break-up and whose wife had fled the scene leaving this chap with their young five year old son. He'd left the country with his son for a few months to visit his parents, in America. On coming back he stayed with a friend immediately and applied for social housing from his local council. Because he was unemployed and had no fixed abode he had been reported to the Social Care people who promptly took his son away from him outside his son's school. The father had kicked up such a fuss he was taken away by the police to a Psychiatric facility in South-West London.

There, he was drugged and then sectioned. He was allowed a phone call to the friend he was staying with who tried to visit him, but who wasn't allowed into the wards to see him.

The father was still there some months later. His plight was alerted to Julia's contact in Queen Ann Street, by the victim's friend. This part of their office was now known as 'Friends of Psychiatric Abuse'.

Julia explained, 'I went to the hospital to visit this chap. I was allowed ten minutes only, at first. The poor guy was pretty much out of it but I managed another visit in the afternoon a few days later when he was not so recently drugged-up and I got all the skinny I needed, that is all the names, dates and events; the whole details. The poor guy was busting to get out of there. I was tempted to just walk him out of there myself.

'Between myself and Dad and Beverly at the FPA we managed to get him released with threats of legal action if we were denied.

'This guy is now living in a hostel temporarily, but has visitation rights with his son, nearby, until he can get a job and a fixed abode of his own.

'We are taking legal action anyway. This is how a lot of people end up in an institution, quite apart from the fact that they are ostensibly made into drug addicts, in a lot of cases.'

I had listened intently. 'Wow, falling between the cracks, eh. Well Gavin is the man to deal with this. We must drum up some media on this.

'Talking of media, I was discussing with Tom and his producer my expose of this nefarious organisation. Once we remove the blockage at the top of the TV hierarchy they are keen to go. Somewhere in all this we can incorporate this case, or others like it.'

I took her hand and told her of my meeting with Sidney and Delia. 'We are actually being summoned to our own wedding!'

'No,' Julia corrected, 'YOU are being summoned. I am all set to play ball and be glad I don't have to arrange it all.' She threw that out as a challenge. 'By the way, what did you have in mind for a honeymoon, my dear?'

I suspected she had somehow some idea of this. 'Well I told the conspirators that where and when we were going to consummate the marriage was none of their business, but that we might take a trip to the Orient and check out the local sites and cultures, to broaden our experience and minds. What do you think?'

'Why do I detect an undertone of 'work as usual' here? Wouldn't you rather just go to a decent library and be done with it?'

'Library? You know what I think of those places,' I replied. 'I thought we could check out the Mental Health scene in a few places like India, Nepal, maybe Tibet. They might just have the answers there to our problems here.

'We could check out the old historic sites and see how the other half lives, in between romantic dinners.'

Julia finished this for me. 'You mean we will eat chapattis in numerous temples and shrines and have this spiritually sublime coupling, above mere romance.'

We loved this little game. Julia never objected to my whims or even my off-the-wall plans; they always ended up really entertaining and stimulating. She loved that about me. But occasionally she liked to be the instigator.

'I'll book the itinerary', she said. 'I can see it now – Bombay, Agra, Delhi, Amritsar, Kashmir, Kathmandu, Lhasa. I can have you all to myself for months.'

'Now, that's what I'd call a honeymoon,' I exclaimed. 'We'd cover quite a few mental hospitals in these places. We could set up 'Abuse Cases International.'

'I'll do a bit of research and find out where all the various holy or retreat places are. I know Agra is a sort of holy city and Amritsar is the centre of the Sikh religion. There must be some famous lamaseries in Nepal and Tibet. I think these are very old Buddhist lands. Spoilt for choice eh, not to mention the mental institutions en route?

'Whatever blows your horn,' she sighed resignedly. 'I bet we end up hitch-hiking and making it up as we go.'

'That's my girl,' I responded. 'Adventure! Let's go and tell the caterers.'

They went out to the back of the house where the family were, by this, preparing for dinner.

'I have a surprise for you Brandon,' Gavin announced. 'Come with me.' He led me outside to the front of the house. Julia followed, very inquisitively.

Gavin produced a set of keys and promptly handed them over to me. 'These are yours – a wedding present in advance. Not too many buses and trains for you in the future, and I want my daughter chauffeured everywhere from now on (but not until I check out your driving habits first).'

I looked at him quizzically.

He pointed to a sparkling Ford Consul car, parked on the kerb. 'It's second hand of course, but your reputation precedes you and the insurance premiums are high for newly qualified drivers. Jump in and turn it over.'

I did just that and checked out all the dials and knobs and switches. I turned it off and got out and walked over to Gavin and gave him a man hug, and Delia, who had joined us by this, was given a son-in-law hug. 'Thank you so much you two. This is so generous, don't you think Jules?' I said, putting my arm around her. 'Did you know about this?'

'No, but I did wonder what this car was doing parked outside our place.'

'My test is next week,' I explained. 'I better make sure I pass it. I'll have to back-pedal a bit as, if my instructor is anything to go by, these licencing people are sticklers for exact rules and proper road etiquette.'

Delia said, 'I take it you haven't been following his instructions to the letter Brandon. You've probably been trying to pass some advanced test or even Formula 1 qualification.'

We went inside and had dinner and talked about weddings and honeymoons and legal cases. Everything in the garden was rosy, wasn't it?

I called James Hopkins after I left the McDonald 'farm'. James had met with the Deputy Inspector of Schools and was initially told that he would more than likely be dismissed 'for abuse of position'.

James more or less pre-empted the Hearing's findings to follow, and laid it all out for this man (who had the unfortunate name of Ben Downs). His outrage got the better of him apparently.

Mr Downs was a bit flabbergasted at this unusually mild-mannered man being so forthright and somewhat emotional.

Mr Downs merely said that he'd take into account what James had told him when the Hearing findings came to him.

On that note he had walked out and strode down the corridor and out of the building.

Having relayed all this to me he added, 'Actually I felt really good when I left. It must be how you felt when you left your school and did what you knew to be right. I'm not betting my house on the outcome of this.'

I responded quickly. 'James there are a few things we can do. I'll consult our Legal department (yes, we have one now) and see if there is a case for unfair dismissal, if it comes to it. We can also threaten to (or actually) defame the Department in the Press, or at least Levison. We can make his life so unbearable he'll cry for mercy. In fact, I was considering investigating him, to see if there is any dirt to dig up that can be used on him. He deserves it. He's caused us some hassle here, and slowed down our rate of expansion. Meanwhile we are taking other counter-measures to ensure we don't lose ground; full steam on the purpose.'

'Brandon,' James put in, 'You are indomitable. We'll see what comes tomorrow. I feel a lot like you now – affronted at the attack on my good intentions and results.'

' Let's talk tomorrow' James You are tailor-made for our project, you know'

Now, I thought, I need to know what is going to eventuate with Tom and his hierarchy.

CHAPTER SIXTEEN

Levison wondered why he'd been summoned to the Minister's office. The meeting had been postponed by a few days due to an urgent Cabinet meeting McAdam had had to attend.

Now, with his wits alerted, he entered the outer office and a secretary led him into McAdam's office. She greeted him pleasantly enough and asked him to sit at her desk. 'I have been looking into this matter of James Hopkins and his suspension. Word has it you are very familiar with this chap Waterman who Hopkins has set loose on the Private domain. Tell me what you know about all this.'

'Oh yes, of course,' Levison replied, as if he had just put together the unexplained reason for this meeting. 'It all started a few years ago when Waterman proposed ....' He then proceeded to tell the story with heavy emphasis on this Waterman's cleverness, ego, and wily manipulation of the PTA.'

McAdam listened until Levison finished his story. 'That's about it, I think. I had tried to deal with the concerns he raised but eventually, in order to head off a PTA rebellion I had to unfortunately suspend the lad. He then became what I suppose you would call a professional truant.'

'How does James Hopkins fit into all this?' asked McAdam.

'I don't know the man, actually,' Levison replied. 'But I believe he befriended Waterman after a visit to his College. The next thing I know he and Waterman seemed to be in cahoots in the Private School sector, disseminating Waterman's methods there. It would be quite a profitable operation I would have thought. I don't know if Hopkins is benefitting financially from all this. The Tribunal will no doubt look into that.'

'I see,' McAdam said. 'That seems to concur with the reports I have on this.' She paused in thought for a moment and then asked him, 'tell me Mr. Levison, how did you come to jump from Deputy at Finchley High to your current post here in charge of standards?'

Levison was caught slightly back-footed but after some lag, not unnoticed by McAdam, he explained, 'I have always been career-minded and was looking around for opportunities. I saw an advertisement in the Department magazine for the post I now hold. I applied for it. The school had done rather well due to the Head and I instituting some remedial programs, so I landed the job. I must have done rather well at the interview I suppose.'

Levison looked at McAdam who was giving nothing away. He smiled in his ingratiating way. 'Is there any other way I can help you about this Minister?'

'Not at this moment Mr Levison, but I know where to find you. Thankyou for your trouble.' She rose and he considered himself dismissed.

McAdam, after Levison was gone, sat and pondered the facts. Indeed, what were the actual facts? She decided to let the Tribunal do its job, for the moment, not entirely happy about something in all this. She couldn't put her finger on it.

Tom and Vince decided that they would ease this controversial topic onto their viewing public, calling it, unofficially, the Waterman series, which followed on from the Education programs.

Officially, they would call it 'In search of the answers.' The first program would deal with my problems with 'the uneducatable'. This would include the more apathetic and then the anti-social sections of society and then move into the remaining problems of the actually educatable, including the searches for answers in Psychology and Religion, granting these two practices as having some useful tools toward the big answers.

After a few programs of this, including live audience participation and demonstrations and 'experts' in this field (to bring in the controversy) the bombshell of Psychiatry would be allowed to explode on the airwaves.

Then it would be down to my newly proposed techniques which could begin the real answers to the problems of bad behaviour and faulty reasoning.

The two 'journos' did indeed sound out the likely advertisers and they, provisional upon being given the actual program formats and content, would be aboard. More than that, they were dead keen.

Our boys met me at our Head Office and explained all of this before confronting Barry Lancomb.

'Sounds like a plan, I agreed as we met in the College's 'Boardroom'. So, how do you think it will go down with 'Sir Barry'?'

'We'll put it to him as soon as we get back. Do you have anything to add to it, Brandon?' Vince asked.

'I would like to be there, ideally, but maybe we should keep that up our sleeves if he baulks at first. The main point is that we'll have to make sure he understands that we are not going to do a rallying cry overtly against Psychiatry, but rather just present the facts starkly and let the audience make up their own mind. The subject of Psychiatry is so flawed and, I might add, so unknown in detail by the broad public, that they will welcome the information.

'We could then do another program with the Psychiatrists invited on, with me as their counterpoint. That would help them dig their own grave and might be a good bridge over into the abuse aspect of the subject.'

'What do you think Tom?' Vince asked.

'Yep. Let's hit the Execs,' he said eagerly.

And so we all shook on it and left. On the way out we ran into Julia. Tom teased her with, 'just mapping out your TV career with our star performer here. Are you ready?'

Julia with all of her personability to the fore retorted, 'at last he's got me into the action. I have some very tasty abuse cases for you. Are YOU ready?

CHAPTER SEVENTEEN

Ben Downs, the Education Exec with the unfortunate name, was sitting at his desk reviewing the findings of the Tribunal on James Hopkins. He scratched his bald head and then put his puffy hands to his forehead and elbows on the table, wincing and frowning, trying to join the facts James had assaulted him with, contrasted against the relative indictment this Tribunal report was giving him.

If he were to go against the Tribunal's data and recommendations there would be one hell of a backlash and accusations of cronyism, he thought. Then again he didn't want to be the one who ruined the career of one of his long standing and well-liked staff.

He'd seen how incensed James had been that this matter had arisen at all. Maybe James would appeal any negative decision and this would drag more senior Execs into all this. Perhaps I could downgrade the 'verdict' to demotion. Would that satisfy everyone? Hmm, not James I suspect, but it would give me the best way out of this dilemma.

He decided that he'd break it to James gently and encourage him to lie low in a lesser capacity for a while and make his way up again. I'd encourage him to sever his association with Waterman, who, after all, was the cause of James going down this adventurous side road.

So he called James in and sat him down and, with lots of humming and hawing, tried to break the news to him. He gave him a copy of the Tribunal's findings and sat there uncomfortably while James read it.

James by this had been resigned to the worst. After reading the report he sat there while his gutless superior tried to rescue his conscience and salvage some integrity.

'Well,' James said after a rambling 'sentence', 'is that it? How come I didn't get to have my say? Did you question the Tribunal on its so-called facts?'

Ben Downs was sweating noticeably now. 'Er, well that's not how it goes with these hearings. I, um, of course wrote my own report to the Tribunal, but, ah, that's all I can do. You see, it's a decision by a section of your, um, ah, peers. Ah, I can accept it or not. In this case, ah, I've tried to be fair and keep you in the Department, um, for recognition of your longstanding service, and give you a chance to work your way up again. This will all blow over I'm sure.' He wiped his brow with his pocket handkerchief.

James was getting the picture. No sense arguing the matter with Downs. 'Well, I shall appeal this decision. I consider it grossly unfair and flawed. How do I go about this?

Ben Downs explained how it worked.

James stood up and before he stormed out asked, 'And what is my new title and job description, in the meantime?'

Downs stood and replied, 'well we'll go over that once the whole procedure is over. In the meantime wrap up your current cases. We'll get this appeal business done quickly.'

James left without further ado and Ben slumped back in his chair and tried to convince himself he'd done the right thing, while all the time feeling a bit embarrassed but not inclined to do anything about that. He could pretend. Torture.

———————————

Back at the TV studios, Tom and Vince had met with Barry Lancolm and after a bit of to and fro between the latter and his other associate directors they decided, on the basis of the advertising revenue and the demand of a few provisos, that the programs could go ahead.

Tom was on the blower to me as soon as he heard the news. 'What a coup mate. We did it.' Vince was on an extension, joining the call.

'Hey, that's good news you two. Money talks in independent television. Eat your heart out BBC. By the way, did you find out who in the Education

Department whispered in their ears about me?'

Nope. I think that goes up higher than Barry Lancolm.'

'Ok, I sighed knowingly. 'Alright. What are these provisos?'

'They want to see the 'screenplay' of each program before it goes out, and reserve the right to pull out at any time. And they want increased security in case there are unrulies in the audience,' he replied with a strong hint of cynicism.

'OK, we'll make it consumable for the cautious. Let's hope some of our protagonists make some drama,' I added. 'I wonder will this go out before my wedding day. I'd rather it go out later.'

'Why is that?' Tom asked.

'I'd rather not attract any demonstration at the wedding venues.

'What on earth are you going to do with our 'screenplay'? Are you going to incite a mental health riot, or something?' Vince asked.

'Well, wait until we get to the abuse cases. You never know,' added. 'You see, you can't write an exact script for these things. You can't train the audience or interviewees to say a script. It has to be spontaneous.'

'What do you know that we don't, Brandon?' Tom asked.

'I'm not saying exactly. I'll endeavour to stay within the caveats of the big nobs, I promise. But don't try and have these programs pre-recorded. That will just get edited to hell.'

Just in time Tom cottoned on to my little game. 'He's yanking our chain Vince. Don't take any notice of him.'

'What an accusation,' was my too-protesty response. 'Anyway, when do we get down to the nitty gritty?'

'Well, let's do it right away,' answered Tom. 'The first program will be largely you Brandon talking about your bigger plan and how you got into looking at Religion, Psychology and then Psychiatry. We can get straight onto that. Let's say we do a dummy run of that on Monday and get it programmed for as soon as possible, the earliest being probably a number of weeks after that.'

Vince said, 'we could actually pre-record this one as it's without an audience, isn't it?'

'Well we could pre-record it but it must have an audience. There should be some audience questioning.' I was actually insisting. I wanted impact.

'Ok then,' agreed Tom. 'Let's meet here on Monday afternoon and we'll do the dummy run.'

We wrapped up the call just as Veronica bounded into my office with a smug look on her cheeky face and plonked down on my desk the artwork of the magazine to go to all our customers and contacts.

I looked it over while she sat there swinging her leg from a crossed position and twiddling her pen, waiting for my verdict.

Then I cast my verdict. 'Veronica, you surprise me. You left out a full stop on the last page. Otherwise it's fantastic. To the printers with you.' I got up and handed it back to her.

She took it, as chuffed as she could be, and started to leave, looking for the missing dot. She hesitated in the doorway, put her hands on her hips and turned to me and wagged an index finger.

I winked and she floated out of there. In actual fact Ira had helped her measurably with suggestions here and there, but Veronica had excelled and was now a multi-faceted career girl.

I then sat and called James, who promptly told me the verdict on his future and his plan to appeal the decision.

'How do these appeals go? Is it one person you appeal to or is it a body. And do you appeal in person?'

'Unlike the Tribunal Hearing it is one person and I think I can have an opportunity to state my case and pull apart the evidence in front of me,' he replied.

'Well, let's go over that report in detail and highlight all inaccuracies and injustices and thus be as prepared as possible. Do you know who the senior person is that deals with the appeal?'

'Yes,' James answered, 'but he's a relative new boy but I don't know much about him.'

'Hmm, you can only do your best,' I said. I thought for a moment and then asked James, 'Even if you were cleared it would do you no good to be back where you were but still unable to push our cause again; do you think?

'I see what you mean,' James replied. 'However, maybe I could if we can ferret out this Levison character first, and then push our cause, officially this time.'

'Yes, good thinking James. It would save me a lot of time setting up alternate schools all over the country. After all why should people pay their taxes AND pay again to have their kids' education remedied? And think about all the kids whose parents couldn't afford to have the remedy. It's best to be accepted as part of the public Education program in schools.'

James was aboard with this idea and we agreed to talk after the appeal. In the meantime I was decided on investigating Levison. James could tackle him from his end.

CHAPTER EIGHTEEN

There was just enough time to squeeze in the TV program before the wedding, so Tom and I got straight down to it. We did the dummy run and submitted that to Barry Lancolm, as agreed. It was OK'd and then the first program was set to be recorded, but with an audience.

It was well advertised, with snippets of the previous Education program highlighted, along with the bit about the heckler and a 'come on' invitation to not miss the next revelation of Mr. Brandon Waterman.

The program began. Tom was asking me how our schools were doing and touching on the reluctance of the Department to adopt my program.

'Why bother including the Department at all if things are going so smoothly? Think about the empire you could create and how rich you could get.'

I was in my element. 'Well,' I began, 'in a nutshell, I have other fish to fry. My aim isn't to get rich, but to get my program into the existing schools so I don't have to supplant the Education Department. What you have suggested would be a lot of work you know. They could, though, pay our organisation to 'subcontract' to the public schools or simply just adopt the program under a proper retraining of their teachers and I could get on with my 'other fish frying'.

'Well, to continue the metaphor, we are all biting. What are these fish?' There were a few cackles from the audience.

I answered. 'I noticed, not so many years ago, that a lot of crazy things happen on this planet of ours. We aren't a harmonious thriving species. With all the discoveries and physical advances that have brought improvements to our lives, mainly in the West, we are nevertheless pretty-well a disagreeable bunch of nations who are inventing bigger and better ways of destroying each other, and the planet itself. We have war hovering over us ready for some spark to push the button.

'Though we have a United Nations organisation it is contradicted by bigger

Powers being above this which means it is only really a pretense. A hundred odd nations cannot agree on enough vital co-operations to ensure a sane and peaceful progress for mankind.'

Tom interrupted him here. 'Are you saying we are doomed? This sounds very pessimistic.'

'Well, if one points out the obvious that is just saying how it is. One can't live in dreamland. Not more than a few decades ago we had a world war which rocked the whole of Earth's societies, and a few decades earlier we had another such event. Since then we have determined to INCREASE our nuclear testing and capability to destroy life on this planet and begun to increase armaments worldwide. So the guns and bullets and bombs get bigger and more nations have more war capability.'

Tom asked, 'But that's the idea isn't it? With weapons being so planet-destroying no one dare use them without self-destructing. So there will be peace and no war.'

Tom was feeding me the right lines. 'So peace is a state of arming enough people against each other with weapons of mass destruction with all of their disagreements in full cry? I had another understanding of this.' The audience could see his point and applauded and whooped.

Tom asked him, 'so where does your project come in here?'

I smiled. 'Well, let's see if I can perk you up a bit here. There are microcosms here, in everyday life. The newspapers feed on them, from drunkenness, family feuds, unemployment, to a panoply of crimes and considerable social problems.

'This reduces further to where I came into this. Take a class of children. Some can learn and some can't. So, as I have discovered, you can help the learning and increase the IQ to a point, but then you run into the mental problems that are intrinsic in our species; the imperfections. These are serious enough to be outside the capacity of Education to deal with.

'For example, we have a pupil who was having trouble learning. We fixed that but this pupil was still very mouse-like and was inclined to be bullied. We couldn't fix that. On the other side of the class there was the bully, who wasn't interested in learning, only disruption. He could only fly off the handle and undermine. We couldn't fix that.'

'I see where you are going with this,' Tom said. 'You are saying that there are various grades of rationality in society, there not being enough rationality in all of it to make society a thriving entity.'

'You've got it. I have been looking for a way of dealing with these flaws in human nature. Even the so-called brightest among us aren't really bright enough to do any more than what we have seen over the centuries as regards in-fighting and destructive intent.'

'But isn't that just being human? You know how the saying goes – it is human to err. It's normal.'

The audience gave Tom a small hum of agreement and some smattering of applause.

I went on. 'You could say it is USUAL but is it normal or acceptable? After centuries or millennia of erring one could forgive the conclusion that this is the norm. Well it was normal to have pestilences and epidemics but man sought and found solutions to these. Man went from subsistence manual farming to huge sewing and harvesting solutions, to handle mass feeding.

'I maintain that THIS is normal – seeking advancement. I am merely saying that Man has not advanced his mental technology along with his scientific and other technological discoveries and applications, and this is his Achilles heel.

'This is what I am looking at. I want to help people to think and behave better. Education is a good start, but we need to go further. Let me ask the audience, by show of hands: how many of you have children?' About two thirds of them put up their hands.

'Ok, how many of you have trouble and strain in getting them to where you want them?' Most of them did.

'How many of you know dysfunctional families that have out-of-the-ordinary problems that you don't have? About half of these raised their hands.

'See what I mean? I said to Tom. 'Look, to summarise this, let me give you all a little exercise here. Imagine someone came from out of space somewhere and ran into Earth, let's say, on his space holiday. And let's suppose he came from an orderly society which didn't have the situations we have here. What would he see? Not what you would like him to see, but what would affront him?

'I can see him saying: 'wow, these people are stacked to the hilt with nuclear weapons primed to use on each other, a majority of them live on or below the bread line, they have police forces to deal with a lot of crime, there is an enormous amount of economic duress. What are they trying to do to each other?'

'I don't want to be doomsday here. I have a lot of optimism. I just do not accept non optimum conditions as being normal. That's not how we advance.' The audience gave me some mild applause here.

Tom came in. 'We have to take a break after which we will get onto what you have been doing to solve the problem.'

When we came back Tom asked the question. 'So Brandon what have you come up with so far to deal with Man's big problems?' Tom wasn't being snide here. His tone was quite serious.

'In Education I soon noticed that a student, once he'd missed the boat in a subject, or subjects, once he'd failed in essence, it was necessary to rub out the failures by going back to where he first failed or got left behind and smooth them out, one thing at a time. Then he would get back to battery and could learn, and WANT to learn, providing you taught him how to learn. Just like in our previous program with young Francis.

'Families, governments, nations also have a string of failures behind them. Every time there is a failure they get a bit more extreme in their solution, or a bit more desperate, AND there is missing or incorrect data in the solutions.

'So here we are with two world wars and lots of other wars before that and we have our current answer to these big mistakes. Everyone hopes that the bombs are too big to use without wiping everyone out in the process, so they won't use them. Does that not sound like a somewhat desperate solution? What about abolishing armaments altogether? That just highlights the real problem – Man has had so many failures in solving his disputes over land and resources that only force will do. If a bit of force doesn't work, use more and more until we are where we are.

'Take that down to classroom level – the pupil doesn't learn, the teacher and the parents try and force the issue. The kid still doesn't learn and rebels and maybe starts acting anti-socially, so he gets the corporal punishment, or he gives up in apathy and becomes a dullard. Of course those in better shape survive ok.

'We don't know what to do with the anti-social when they commit crime so we stick them in jail and they come out still none the wiser and in most instances continue where they left off. We don't have a solution to bad behaviour, nor any real rehabilitation techniques.'

Tom repeated, 'So what is your plan here?'

'My first searches took me into Religion. It is probable that Religion these days has a positive effect in society. It's certainly not without its leaky holes but overall with its insistence on striving for better behaviour and more social improvements it is a civilising force.

'Of course there is a big element of blind belief in much of this too. Christianity has had a good innings and it doesn't look to me like it is going to win. Teaching Ethics or Morals is good and is part of the solution. I would enter more reasoning into it all and less preaching.

'I started looking at Eastern religions, particularly Hinduism, Buddhism and other similars. These are not monotheistic religions like Christianity and Islam, which means they guide one to a self-discovery of greater awareness and spirituality.

'My fiancé and I visited a Hindu temple and learned how to do meditation. I have found it positive as have many of its practitioners I am sure. But like Christianity it can become ritualistic and also prone to blind faith. But again, it leads to something toward the solution. That's a work in progress.

'I am getting married next month and my wife-to-be, (who also may appear on this program later), she and I are going for a 'honeymoon' to India, Nepal and maybe Tibet or Thailand; an extended trip to research this subject, among other things.'

Tom asked him at this juncture about Psychology and Psychiatry.

'Now we get into some really interesting territory, I thought that those who deal in mental matters would be worth investigating too, so I looked into Psychology. When I say 'look' I mean study all about it and meet some Psychologists and see what they do. It's a little confusing as the word means 'study of the soul' but they don't mention the soul. It is a misnomer and would be much better described as an attempt to work out what makes people tick, especially in relation to irrational or problematic behaviour.

'At the end of the day it doesn't matter about the terminology. There are some useful bits I learned from this. Some of it tries to go back into one's past and get the subject to talk about it in order to try and come to terms with various traumas, just like in my Education methods. They have group therapies and analysis.

'Communication is a big part of it and this is a really key tool. Psychology is a work in progress too and again the jury is out on this. It has been around for some time and doesn't seem to have made much of an impact. But, it is associated with another subject which is where it all gets controversial.'

Tom decided to take another break here and during the break he primed the audience to ready their questions to me when the time came.

We returned and I continued. 'Myself, a friendly Psychologist and my fiancé attended a Psychiatric Convention. We listened in at first, joined in the various seminars that took place and asked lots of penetrating questions, so much so that we actually were asked to leave. You may have read about it in the papers.

'Not long after this we visited a Psychiatric Hospital where we saw what goes on there. These places are where the failed Medical and Psychology cases are sent, or, more exactly where society sends its more extreme cases, from nervous breakdowns to the outright insane AND in many cases those that are maybe just a bit odd and aren't really that sick or harmful. You could call them insane asylums if you want to be flippant, or they are the 'not yet necessarily mental but might end up mental' asylums.

'What we saw there was definitely not helpful in our quest for answers. In fact you could say it exemplified my earlier description of the continued use of more and more force to try and solve what isn't working. As you will hear in another program this is a very interesting study in where we are as a society.

'Make no mistake, it has always flummoxed leaders of all previous generations and societies – how do people go mad and how do you deal with it? When you are confronted with a raving psychotic how do you deal with it? It is the same question when confronted with a misbehaving child or an irrational parent, only of course these are not as extreme. There are shades of grey of irrationality, from minor to heavy.'

'OK' said Tom. 'Now audience, are there any questions to Mr Waterman?' A lot of hands went up. 'Oh my God, what have you awakened here Brandon?'

A middle-aged lady in the second row stood up when chosen and asked, 'I hear you are a teenager Mr. Waterman. How are you qualified to solve the problems of Man. Do you have a degree?'

I rubbed my metaphoric hands and started in on this one. 'I am indeed a teenager and I don't have a degree madam. How am I qualified otherwise? Well I am fairly bright and have an enquiring mind and a thirst for real knowledge, which are the prime qualifications. There are plenty of folk who have academic qualifications and who have lived life longer than I but the problem goes unanswered.

'I offer my Education methods, well demonstrated on TV and in my schools as credence of my ability to look and solve. I have only skirted the edges of it all at the moment. At the end of the day credence will only come if I come up with anything.

'It does affront many that a mere adolescent is talking like this. It is what it is. I'd be happy for any likeminded takers to chip in and join in the quest.'

I got some applause for this, even if a bit conservative.

The next question came from an elderly gentleman at the back. The studio boom swung round to him so he could be heard.

'What sort of recognition do you hope to gain from all this young man? You do seem to have a considerable ego.'

'I would contest the latter part of your question, or statement, sir. I have no interest in self-glorification. I am a confident person. If that comes over as ego, as you put it, it is not the case. I only hope to get self-satisfaction out of anything I do, and positive results. I guess that sounds too good to be true, for most.'

'One more question,' Tom offered. 'Brandon will be available for further questions after we are off-air.'

The final question came from a man in the middle of the audience. 'Mr Waterman, I am a Clinical Psychologist. I have been one for more years than you have been a teenager. It seems that in a very short period you have had a cursory look at my subject and dismissed it as being inadequate. How do you justify this?'

'Simply, I don't,' I answered quickly. 'It is very much an ongoing work. I take advantage of any discourse I can find with professionals like yourself, to extend my knowledge. I'd be only too pleased to swap notes with you and gain what I can from your experience. I seek it. In fact one of my colleagues is a practising Psychologist.

'But, be warned I am underwhelmed so far and I reserve my right to reject out of hand any pretended knowledge or any ineffective methods, as you will discover in a future program where I do even more than just that. We are only just getting warmed up.'

Tom wound up the program with a call to give me a warm round of applause, which they did. And he invited them to tune in to the next episode which would be a panel discussion comprising me, some leaders in the fields of Education, Mental Health, and Social Services. The subject would be around the burning problems of mental health and social problems.

I did indeed answer further questions after the program and then Tom wheeled me off to meet with Vince to have a pow-wow about the night's events.

I was elated to find Julia backstage. 'Well done my darling. Superbly handled.' We embraced. We then all retired to the canteen and sat down with Tom and Vince.

'How do you think that went?' I asked them.

'Just the right amount of balance and an easing in to the forthcoming programs,' Vince said.

'What did you think Julia?' asked Tom

'Well, apart from me being dragged into the dialogue, pretty damn good. Do you know, it was a bit above the audience in that not many people even think about Man's big problems and aren't really confronting the big picture. They were fairly subdued, as audiences go.'

Tom said, 'They did a pretty good clamour for a go at Brandon, you know, for a subdued audience.'

I added, 'Yes, they took a while to warm up. But they were getting there.' Then I asked Tom and Vince who they had in mind for the panel show.

'That's not decided yet. We've put out a few feelers among the hierarchy of Psychology, maybe a Board member. Then we have the Minister for Social Services lined up, about seventy-five percent. A top Philosopher, one Anthony Cribbens, has yet to come back to us. With Brandon, four might be enough. Three against one ok for you Brandon?'

'Bring them on. I think we should have an Educationalist too, say, someone from the Department, or maybe an executive of the Private Schools Association.'

We chatted humorously for a while and then called it a day.

Julia and I drove home. This was our first outing in our first car. I couldn't wait to pick it up that very morning after having passed my driving test with flying colours.

'Well Mrs Waterman, where doth thou desire to be chauffeured to?' I asked her.

'I am already there. 'I am in dreamland. How's the car?'

'It's good. Sure beats the bus and train. When are you getting your licence, my love?'

'It's booked for three week's time, the week before our wedding. And I have booked my teacher to get me ready by that date.'

'He'll have his work cut out, won't he?' I added.

'Yes, you will,' she replied and looked at me with that big smile 'Look, I have the L plates right here.'

I pulled over and took them from her and got out of the car and fixed them back and front and opened the driver's door for her.

'No time like the present. Your introductory lesson begins now. I am well insured.'

She sat in the driver's seat and we got down to it. That saw out our night.

CHAPTER NINETEEN

I entered the building at a doorway to the side of the ground floor shop on a High Street in Hendon, North London. I walked up the stairs and found a door on the second floor which had 'Michael Stone, Private Investigator' written on the frosted glass door, just like in the movies.

I entered and was confronted by a Secretary at the desk, a young busty thing with newly permed blond-streaked hair and with a cigarette burning in the ashtray. 'Hullo', she said cheerfully. 'How can I help? Oh, you must be Mr. Waterman,' she remembered.

'That's me,' I chirped with a big smile. 'I'm here for Mr. Stone.'

The secretary strutted over to a doorway and stuck her head around the door of an office and announced my arrival.

I was ushered in, with the busty blond being noticeably busty and not allowing much room for me to pass. Well, she was doing the passing.

I shook hands with Michael Stone and was invited to sit.

He was a rather large, broad-shouldered man with a messy shock of dark but greying hair. He wore an open waist coat with his shirt collar open and tie at half-mast. His face was rugged and well worn. I thought that maybe he'd been a rugby forward in his day, which wasn't that long ago.

In a quite personable manner he asked what I wanted of him.

I explained.

'Yes, I rather thought you may have attracted a few bothersome flies Mr Waterman,' he said. 'I've seen your programs on TV and read the papers. It's good to know a bit about who one is dealing with you know.'

'I agree,' I responded. 'That's precisely what I want to know here too.

This Levison character is not what he appears to be methinks. Is this task up your alley?'

'You want a bit of real dirt on him, do you?' Stone asked.

'I need to sideline him at least, or get him out of the picture completely at best. I need some ammunition. Right now he's shooting at me from behind cover.'

'I see,' the detective replied. 'So, let's see, you want financial, legal, sexual peccadillos (these are the usual things one can dig up).'

'Is this feasible?' I asked.

'Depends how far you want to go and how much you want to spend,' he replied.

'Hmm, well let's see how it goes. Start with the most disreputable and damaging area first, and we'll see if that's enough. As he is a coward, by demonstration and is secretive and devious, and a first class liar, again by his behaviour so far, I'm reckoning he has much to hide under his 'respectable' smokescreen. I'll leave it up to you as to where to start.

'I have a man on the inside of the Department, a man who has, since this character's arrival there, been suspended from his post, from a trumped up case. He is going to stoke Levison up a bit with controlled harassment, and see what we get from that side.'

'Wow, you should come and work for me,' Michael Stone offered.

'We have a good thing going in our project,' I stated. 'We don't want our progress smeared by anyone.'

'It is not usual for someone running an operation like yours (and it being relatively fledgling at that) to come so quickly to someone like me. Usually they just take a hit. You are being pro-active. I like that.'

I liked this man instinctively. I questioned him further about his avenues of approach and where they all stood legally.

Stone told him, 'I don't need to go out of business, you know, by being too cavalier and risking the wrath of the law. In fact, I work quite closely with the Met (London's Police force), so I have a few friends in good places. We look after each other, if you see what I mean. Nothing underhand mind you.'

We talked money and then I 'placed the order' and went on my way, passing the saucy secretary on the way out, she making sure she was as prominent as she could be.

CHAPTER TWENTY

The second TV program came around in a few weeks. I was pitted with (or against you might say) the opinion leaders mentioned.

Needless to say I was the butt of quite a bit of belittling and discrediting of course, because of my youthful status. However I dealt with that early on and put it all to bed. I curried a lot of agreement with them and the audience on the subject of how Man advanced his knowledge on human problems and that it was a good idea to question existing theories and practices, especially those that were particularly lacking in results.

I cited the example of Government and its struggle to run solvent and effective economies and deal with problem citizens. I got the audience to agree that social problems were becoming more and more prevalent.

At the end I asked the panel and the audience was it not a worthwhile activity to try and improve Man's lot, just as I had done with Education?

There was much applause, and the show ended with Tom giving the viewers a taster of the next planned program: 'Next week we are going to have Brandon look at one of his research areas, the subject of Psychiatry. This is going to explore the brain theory. On this program Brandon's fiancé is going to be joining him and revealing some stunning cases of mental therapy, as it is in the twentieth century.'

He bade the viewers and audience goodnight after thanking all of the participants.

After the show Tom, Vince and I went to one of the reception rooms at the back of the studio and discussed what had occurred on the show that night and what was next.

Tom said, 'so far we have done two relatively safe programs – nothing to upset Barry or anyone else upstairs. Brandon, I liked the way you generated some begrudging respect from your participants. I think we have the teenager on equal footing now, intellectually.'

He continued. 'It is what comes next that worries me. I'm not sure Barry will allow Julia to bring on her abuse cases. For you to expose Psychiatry as faulty is one thing but to have it lambasted as fraudulent and dangerous might be a step too far for our Barry.'

I thought carefully about my reply. 'It's hard to tiptoe around this one, to appease your masters. It IS shocking and will be all news to your audience. Do you two believe in the message we are bringing? Do you not think that TV media, just like the Press, should, in the interest of the public, expose what is shameful or disgusting or controversial?'

Tom and Vince agreed that it should but.... the powers that be might regard this subject as potentially litigious.

'Ok,' I said. 'I think what you need to do is present this as a new look at an accepted (well not really) subject, which is to be presented without emotion, just matter-of-factly, with the audience asked to make up its own mind about it. The abuse cases will be just to highlight what can go wrong when mental health staff are presented with patients who are stirred up and are very difficult to control. It's not to be a rant at this stage, but we must get the subject out there so people can know what the subject is and what goes on in the name of ' mental health', and, more to the point, why we should row back on certain practices and develop better ones.

'On the legal side, somehow I don't think we'll get any serious challenges because I doubt the Psychiatric fraternity will want more publicity. It is so blatant it is indefensible. I think they would go more in the direction of merely trying to defame your station and ridiculing myself.'

'Yep, that's a good way to go. After all we are a public information service,' Vince agreed. Tom nodded too.

'We will have to record this program Brandon, at least as a show to the bosses of how it is going to be LIVE.'

I sighed and said, 'It will get scrapped, I'm sure. Let's write out the format and the information that will be conveyed and let them see that. The program should be LIVE I think, so there is no chance of it being overruled. This is our chance to do mankind a big favour. What's the worst that could happen?'

'Well, we could be on the dole, or in the courts, or, FAMOUS,' Tom laughed. 'Your call Vince.'

Vince slapped his hands on the nearby coffee table and as he stood up and pronounced decisively, 'Let's do it.' It only remained for me to produce my 'screenplay' and have it presented to Barry Lancolm.

CHAPTER TWENTY ONE

It was now Saturday, three weeks to the wedding. Julia and I were sitting out in the garden at her place, along with Gavin and Delia.

'How're liking the job at the College, Delia?' I asked.

'It's great. I've learned the process, and in that process had my own learning experience exposed and brushed up, and I've done the same with a few new students. Now I am helping out Ira. That woman is a powerhouse. She does the work of three people, you know. Is that how I have to end up, Brandon? I think you are trying to get cheap labour.'

Julia replied for him. 'the modus operandi is that if he can do it, you can.' She smiled at me, then added, ' Not only that, he believes people have all been conditioned to perform well below their native best, and we staff, partly by re-education and partly by whip cracking, can be brought up to a whole new expectation as to what can be done.'

I was about to speak but Julia prevented me. 'Actually it is an economic thing. Sidney rattles in his ear each night about finances and Brandon executes the Waterman plan – slave labour. Ira has become inured to it, as she soon did from the beginning. Her husband has become long suffering. Your turn Dad,' she said looking at Gavin.

'I can feel myself getting this disease,' Delia put in. 'Should I resist it?'

'Well, Delia,' I edged in. 'You can become more able and efficient or you can choose to be a slave, like these women in our organisation are protesting about. You lot spent all of your previous history being slaves, so you claim, so might as well be productive ones.'

Gavin joined in. 'I guess I am on Brandon's side here, by natural selection. He's created a playing field for you all to really learn how to dominate the male species. Go for it. But bear in mind, once you get there you will find there is a downside to being the dominant species.'

They could see where all this was going and much to their enjoyment.

Gavin asked, 'what are you two planning to present to we mindless public on your final program?'

I explained. 'We have the outline plan ok'd, just, by the TV hierarchy, but are having to tone it down a bit, which means just a matter-of fact perception of the subject, no outrage (unless the audience gets outraged all by themselves – who knows how they will react to the display we will give them).

'So we will have to present the abuse cases as 'what can happen' in this minefield of a subject because of the extreme nature of patients' behaviour at times; or something like that.'

'Exactly,' Julia replied. 'The audience will be left with making up their own minds without our personal feelings or bias added to it all.'

'I just thought of something,' I said. 'Where do I get hold of a sizeable, all-intact brain? Do they sell such things at butcher shops or would I need to go to an abattoir?'

The women looked at each other, as if asking each other the question and not knowing the answers.

Before they answered I saved them the trouble. 'I'll get our latest bright spark onto it – Veronica. I'll need to find some sort of machine too that resembles a shock machine. I will need a hospital trolley and some straps. There you are Delia, you and Veronica can get onto that one and have it all sorted by ten a.m. on Monday.'

'I don't take orders on a Saturday, Brandon,' she responded, quite dismissively.

'There's that office disease showing in full view, Gavin,' I replied.

'There's some research for you to get your teeth into,' he replied. 'Good luck with that one.'

Julia cuddled up to me and finalised the matter by saying, 'don't be fooled. He has it all worked out. we are simply putty in his hands, can't you see?'

More tea and light conversation and then Julia and Gavin went off to discuss the abuse cases and Delia and I talked about the wedding plans, not that I was that interested in them, really. I was just going to turn up on the day and make it up as I went along, wasn't I?

Young Veronica, my gopher, indeed sought out some brains, and a chiropractic pulse machine, with lots of electrodes. The studio provided a hospital trolley and some straps and other theatrical props.

The night arrived with me dressed in a suit, covered by a white medical coat. I was, to all intents and purposes, a Psychiatrist. Tom introduced me to an audience of about two hundred people in the studio.

Tom opened with: 'you may wonder why Mr Waterman is dressed like this. I will let him explain. Over to you Brandon, doctor.'

'Thankyou Tom. Good evening everyone.' I was speaking to the audience and then directly into the camera. There was no autocue; straight from the hip.

'As you will have been informed from the earlier programs I have been involved in, I am looking for a way of improving Man's power of reasoning or thinking; his bad behaviour. By 'bad' I mean any behaviour or reaction to life's situations that gets him into more trouble.

'I am not immediately interested in curing the more severe mental problems that you would normally associate with insane asylums, just improving the ability of normal people to think more evenly and clearly -- such things as blowing one's top, being shy or introverted, losing confidence. The list goes on.'

I definitely had the studio audience listening.

'As I said in the last program I'm looking at Psychology, Religion, Philosophy – anything that helps in the solution.

'I came across Psychology and then Psychiatry in my researches. These, I presumed, should be where I'd get the most answers. I found this interesting, in more ways than one.

'Psychology is an attempt to explain and rectify mental problems. It uses communication to get the patient talking about his past in order to analyse the problem, either one on one or in groups. It is thought that the source of human travail lies in earlier traumas, which, if brought to light can help resolve things. Not too unreasonable, I thought.

'The Psychiatrist treats mental illness, beyond, usually, what the Psychologist cannot deal with. They have a diagnostic manual which lists a whole parade of conditions, some of which you will be familiar with (Schizophrenia, Mania, Manic depressive).'

I held up a copy of the manual. 'It's pretty thick. There is a name for any possible errant behaviour –scores of them.' I started reading the list of conditions. 'But, largely on the basis of this book and an interview, you are diagnosed and given whatever treatment applies.

'You don't have to be crazy to get diagnosed; you just have to have an acute or chronic problem which is obvious by deviant or irrational behaviour, or even any 'feeling down' conditions. This can be a very opinionated area.

'Let's suppose your life was giving you quite a lot of stress and you weren't managing it well. You have what is perhaps termed or diagnosed as a nervous breakdown, on the basis that you start taking days off work, get shaky perhaps, stop socialising, you struggle with everyday situations of family and work. You just can't get it together.

'Your General Practitioner doesn't really have the answer as it's not usually a medical matter. He refers you to a Psychologist or a Psychiatrist. If the

Psychologist can't help then it goes to a Psychiatrist – something like this, putting it simply.

'He, or she, gets out his manual, after a consultation, and you will then start on the treatments. So far so good.

'Understand I am giving you this simplistically. We don't have space here for a university course on Mental Health.' A murmur of agreement followed.

'Now, I better explain the basis of Psychiatric Theory here. Of course it derives from the same genus as my own subject in that it is an attempt to solve or improve human behaviour albeit at the more extreme end of the spectrum.'

I had a display board on an easel with a large-scale diagram of the human brain. I went over to it and explained what the chart was. 'You will find this sort of chart in Psychology clinics, and in Psychiatric diagnostic spaces, and in nearly all Psychiatric books.

'The theory is that the brain is the thinking mechanism of a person. It is supposedly the intelligence and emotional monitoring organ.

You've all heard the terminology – 'he's got no brains,' or 'use your brain, man,' or 'he's got a loose wire in his brain' or 'he's brainy'. Not so?'

The audience generally agreed, with a low-key rumble.

'Now, we are going to have to take a break, but after the interval I am going to examine this theory. I warn you this might be a bit squirmy for you. Had my search for a humane and ever-reaching solution been rewarded or not?'

Tom came on and we took a break. 'Reasonable enough, so far Brandon,' he said as if it was not going to stay that way.

I rubbed my hands together. 'I am having a ball.' Julia was backstage and gave me a light hug. In a pre-recorded section of the program two abuse victims had been filmed exposing their Psychiatric experience. Julia didn't think the victims would hold up in the full glare of the cameras, lights and audience. This was to follow my piece.

'Now for the gory bit,' I said. I took a quick swill of water, gave Julia a peck and went back to the set, which by this had transformed into a hospital room, with a bed and restraints, a 'shock' machine, and a table containing a needle, and various other prop instruments that one might use in surgery. And there was a small table with what looked like the innards of some creature or other.

'The countdown finished and Tom faced the camera and said, 'Welcome back. As you will see we are now going to hand back to Dr. Waterman. Over to you.'

As imposingly as possible I stood in front of the audience, with half of my attention on them and half on the camera.

'As I was saying, in Psychiatry, and as widely understood in society generally, the brain is the key organ here. It is deemed that when behaviour deviates it is the brain that goes wrong. That chart over there shows all the bits of the brain – the prefrontal lobes, the cerebral cortex, and so on. Each part is deemed to have a function. Psychiatrists have worked out that, like a car engine, if you can find which part is faulty and what chemical is not feeding properly (that gas, oil or water) then you can fix it.

'Of course, the brain is more complex than a car engine, but you get the analogy. So, if this theory is right, we should be able to cure people of their mental ailments, right?' More or less silence.

'Now, hold your hat. The first treatment one gets, (unless really serious) is chemicals, that is, drugs. These are specially formulated drugs from the big chemical companies, like Glaxo Smith Kline, and others. These drugs have mostly long names, like most chemicals anywhere, so I won't bore you with all that. They are called anti-psychotic drugs.

'The thing is that these drugs are strong, but depending how much is administered. The general effect is to quieten down the gremlins in the brain and supposedly adjust certain chemical imbalances that have occurred to cause errant behaviour.

I walked over to the brain display. 'I have here a brain, taken from a recent execution victim at one of HM prisons.' The audience was mixture of sharp breath intakes and uncertain laughter. 'Just joking' I said, followed by a bit more real laughter, though a trifle restrained.

No,' I went on, 'it's my sense of humour. Maybe that syndrome is in that book.' The audience laughed again. Holding it up, I explained. 'You see, even though it is a cow's brain, it looks much the same as a human brain. I did ask the producers could I supply the real thing and they said no, would you believe.' More laughter – they were warming up. 'But really, this is no laughing matter.

'Just imagine this is your brain, for a moment. Yes, it is offal, but it's your brain.' More laughter.

'In here,' I said, pointing, 'are the prefrontal lobes (very important as you will see if you are still conscious later on). I was keeping it light. 'Over here …' and so on with all the parts of the brain and their function.

'So, the Psychiatrists work out what drugs to use, from your history, some observation and their interview in the diagnostic room. So the chemicals make their way into the nervous system, the brain being the head of this system, and you are supposed to improve as a result. It may take some time, so you can usually expect to be hospitalised for weeks or more.

'If you seem to be calmer you walk out of there with a prescription of one or more drugs to take at home. You are told to take these drugs and come back at a later point, to see if you have improved, or can be taken off the drugs, or are to be, essentially, a drug addict (on drugs forever and a day). My 'matter-of-fact' portrayal was slipping.

'So, with our brain here, now coursing with mental adjusting chemicals or behaviour enhancers, or simply numbing agents, according to theory your behaviour is held at bay or it isn't. You may not be responding. In this case you are given higher doses or different drugs.

'Now remember I am looking for a treatment/therapy that will improve behaviour, on the order of medical treatments – you go in sick, get the treatment and walk out cured, back to yourself again.

I held up the brain. 'Here is a question,' I asked the audience very matter-of-factly 'Imagine this is your brain. Imagine the effect. These aren't aspirin you are taking in.'

I picked up a bottle of pills. 'These are the ingredients' I read them out and got half way and said, 'this is like reading from one of those lists you see on some supermarket products.

'I won't go on with this list and I'm not going to give a chemistry lesson here. And, I haven't mentioned side effects yet. There CAN BE side effects. 'Are you feeling this? Do you feel better already?'

The audience were a mixture of amused and bemused.

'This is where I really started to ask questions. You ask them too.'

'I want you to imagine the sheer genius of this contraption here,' I said, holding up the brain again. 'It's made of flesh and blood, and it thinks and emotes. Right now, listening to me you are supposedly using this to take in what I'm saying, and compute with it and store memories. Take that – store memories! This is a piece of meat, essentially and it does all that.'

I was really winding up here. I had to contain myself to keep it less like a ridicule, and was losing the battle.

'As an aside, note I said 'you' are listening and computing. Who is this 'you'? Who is the 'my' in 'my brain'? I paused. 'More of that later.'

'The greater genius is how was this discovered and proved? I have searched high and low and can't find the answer. I can't find how someone proved that this thing does what it says on the can.'

The audience were getting their money's worth here.

'After the break I will demonstrate what the next technique is to persuade this brain here to behave properly.

'I have to say that I can see the efficacy, in some disturbed cases, of prescribing a 'quietening drug', in much the same way as giving a pain killer for someone in acute pain. But it would be only a stopgap to prevent someone from harming themselves, or others. Anyhow ...'

Tom chimed in and said, 'don't go away, we'll be back.' And they cut to the ads. The audience murmured amongst themselves.

Vince was there and looked worried. 'I have a few restive Execs back there. I think they want to pull the plug. One of them is talking on the phone to someone upstairs. I hope we can get back on before anything goes awry.' He was fretting.

We made it back on and I was into the next segment.

'Now, when the case becomes too extreme, that is, it hasn't worked or the whole behaviour is highly acute, there is an additional step to the drugs. Once again, going back to our brain, the idea is to up the volume of the treatment. This is done by what is known as ECT – Electro Convulsive Therapy' Note that – 'therapy'. You will know this as 'shock treatment'.'

On came a stooge patient, walking in as if he was in a stupor, guided by a 'nurse'. He was placed on the trolley bed and strapped on tight. He was primed to be a bit anxious so he tried lifting his head and straining on the straps. I went over to him and mock injected him with a sedative drug . 'Now we are going to get this brain into shape and shock it into submission as it were. The theory is, in loose terms, you shock the system into adjustment. Keep your imaginations running.

'He is strapped down because, as the name applies, he may convulse when he is fed the blasts of electricity from this machine here. So we attach these electrodes to his temples and apply the juice.

'Imagine this is you. As I said the idea is to kick start the mental machinery in much the same way as one would kick start a heart that had stopped beating. Again this is simplistic, but it's done. Whether it works is another point – you decide.'

'Now this machine, in case you were wondering, is not attached to an electric point, and this machine is actually a Chiropractic pulse machine, not an ECT machine. Nevertheless imagine now you are about to receive your carefully worked-out electric current.'

The brain was on its table and had electrodes on it too. I flicked the switch for a few seconds and the stooge made a good imitation of a convulsion. The nurse held him down. This was repeated. This time the brain on the trolley began to smoulder and give off fake steam. The audience reacted and shifted about in their seats.

The nurse let the stooge out of his straps and he was helped up and looked at the audience trance-like and then shuffled off under the guidance of two nurses. It was pretty convincing and the audience weren't sure if he was a good actor or he'd actually been shocked. But he re-appeared and bowed to the audience and shook hands with me and then left the set. I smiled and said, 'I warned you it might be squeamish. He looks cured doesn't he? I hope you are still with us.' One lady had actually fainted and was being treated by the medical staff. I told them, 'I was going to demonstrate the next weapon in the Psychiatric armoury but it may be too graphic. Yes, there is more. If the ECT doesn't work (and it only seems to really 'work' by quietening down the patient so he is not agitated.) then he gets a number of doses of this and/or he now gets into brain operations. There are a few of these but in essence they involve a surgical fiddling with the lobes of the brain. It is called a lobotomy.

'So you see the treatment gets more extreme. You can only decide for yourself,' I said looking into the camera and then at the audience. 'Do our scientists have the right theory? Does it make sense to you? Would you submit to this even if you were desperate? Are these practitioners onto something here or is it bad science or even fakery? Are we getting results along the lines I explained I was searching for?

'Is this a big cash cow? If so, how have the rulers of this country, and others, accepted this subject? Do they have evidence that this is worth investing in or advancing? They wouldn't let this loose on we public, would they?' I paused for effect. I'd overshot my 'no ridicule' brief.

'I have been graphic here because it became very apparent to me that this subject needed a good looking at, either as a bona fide therapy or as a representation of how far awry we may have drifted in our humanities and science… well maybe not science.

'To sum up this segment, I asked you who is the 'you' and the 'I' and the 'my'? It's not just semantics. But it may lead to another way. Let me give you a little drill here.'

This bit was unscripted. Talking to the audience I said, 'I want you all to close your eyes, you at home too if you like. Now get a picture of a cat. Have you got that picture there?'

They all acknowledged. I continued. 'Now make it black, now blue, now in a tree, now sitting on your lap. Nice pussy cat. Keep your eyes closed.'

The audience were enjoying this. 'Now, where is that picture? You can open your eyes. Where is it?'

Someone in the front row said, 'in my brain'. Another said 'in my head'.

I said, 'we could go on all night, but ask yourself, if you hadn't been told repeatedly in your life that you were a brain and it is 'in your head' would you say that? Can you prove it? Are you sure? Has anyone found that it is in your head or brain?

'If it isn't where is it? This is your mind we are talking about. Mental treatment is, or should be, by definition, treatment of the mind. I am saying all this because the chemical and electrical and surgical route, as I have illustrated, treats a physical organ, a piece of flesh and blood.'

'I ask you to consider this: when a person dies, what happens? Does his brain break down or wither? If he is diseased or has a heart attack, the body packs up. But what is the difference in the previously live body and the dead one? Or, if you are religious or spiritual, and you believe one goes to heaven, or another place, this can hardly be the brain that goes there, can it?'

'You know, the therapy I am looking for may be as simple as getting people to talk out their problems, if directed properly. Many Psychologists seem to get some results from this. My point is you are talking to the PERSON, the live force that is operating this body. You know, you can listen to a little kid talk about his upset with, say, his mum, or brother, whoever. He 'runs down' and soon gets over it, if you are really listening to him.

'It doesn't seem to matter what label you put on it – mind, person, being – it works. But brain? Question mark?' The audience mumbled a bit as if trying to answer it among themselves.

'As a final question, get that cat back again. Now, who made the picture? Who is looking at it?' There was silence, then lots of 'I am's'

'My contention so far is that maybe it has nothing to do with the brain or head. Is a person a brain? Or is he just a person, a live entity, a spirit, whatever. Maybe that doesn't matter, but I'll tell you this, I defy anyone to convince me that when I educate a person and increase his intelligence and better his emotions, that I am changing his brain. The brain is a wonderful device as a shock absorber and switchboard for the nervous system. It is the fulcrum for the nervous system. It's the switchboard for action and glandular messages. But who gives the messages?

'I look around the world to see if we could be seen to be on the right track as a species, and is the brain theory helping or hindering?

'There is more to this subject, which I was hoping to present to you tonight but perhaps we are out of time,' I looked over at Tom who had come on to set.

Tom told everyone that time was up and maybe we can cover the results of Psychiatry in another program. He thanked the audience and they gave me a 'tad above conservative' round of applause.

Tom told me, as soon as we were off air, 'We can't go any further Brandon. The top brass are not happy but I'm not sure why. Brilliant job though Brandon. The switchboards are jammed.'

And so they were. Tom later reported that half of the people ringing were those on medications and wanting more information, some wanted to know if I was affiliated with any protest organisations. Quite a few wanted further information and discussion. Of course about ten percent were up in arms and wanted to have a go at the TV station for sponsoring such a program.

Julia joined me and gave me a warm hug and said quietly in my ear 'I think we have them rattled. They are not going to do my segment.'

Vince and Tom were summoned into the inner sanctums and Julia and I were free to call it a day. Many studio staff came up and gave me a warm pat on the back and lots of 'good jobs' and 'sock it to thems'.

'Good to have you here my love.' I had stopped beside our car and was opening the door for her, but not before one of our world class kisses. Then, 'time for another driving lesson?'

'All right then, I'm game. But don't you want to wind down after your heroic performance?

'If I need relaxing you can do it with your driving,' I responded. I stuck on the L-plates and off we went. It was about nine-thirty pm. 'Let's drive to somewhere we haven't been to before and see if we can catch one of those coffee houses that stay open late.'

'You're out of touch my dear. We would have to go to Soho probably. Do you think I can negotiate the traffic and narrow streets there?'

'You can do anything, especially with me as your navigator.'

'Alright. Soho here we come. I'm really getting the hang of these gears now; that's one thing you don't get on go-karts.'

Tom and Vince and I had arranged to meet on neutral territory the next morning – a café in Chiswick, West London.

We had a handful of national Dailies with us and had them spread out on the table we had occupied at the back of the café, awaiting our orders.

'Wow, sensational! Vince exclaimed. 'What have we opened here? Seems like you have stirred a viper or two in high places, Brandon.'

'It's your fault guys,' I suggested.' It's your media, your program, your decision to run it. I was just the mouthpiece.'

Tom came in here. 'Ah, he's backing out. Such cowardice from the prime mover. Are you the cook that's getting out of the kitchen because it is too hot?'

'You know chaps, its exactly what I was hoping for. Think of the revenue you could garner from follow-up abuse cases, panel debates – lots of controversy. What was the scene backstage last night? I take it they weren't licking their lips like I am.'

Vince answered. 'Apparently Lancolm's senior got a call from one of the top dogs in the Royal Medico-Psychological Association, their HeadOffice. He threatened to take legal action immediately and take the TV station to the cleaners. It got quite heated there at one point. Barry told me to wind up the program at the next break, especially as he revealed that we were going to show abuse cases.'

'Good,' I put in. 'Let's have the Psychiatrists on the program and we can hear their side and then shoot them down like sitting ducks. Nothing I presented tonight is inaccurate. I did cover myself by making it simplistic, for brevity. They don't have a legal stand. In fact we can go to them and present the abuse cases we have and invite them to explain why legal action shouldn't be taken against THEM. I say hold the line. Milk this for all that it is worth.'

'You don't work under these guys, Brandon,' Tom explained. 'These aren't mavericks we are dealing with. They'll protect their jobs before taking risks.' 'This is not something I don't know, Tom,' I replied. 'Let me have a word with them, whoever they all are. I have a legal man too. He will have watched last night's program and he will back up what I have said, I'm sure. Consult your own legal beagles too.'

I looked at my two partners in crime as they looked at each other, considering what I had said. 'Look, these Psychiatric guys have a LOT to hide. They have become a law unto themselves, making spurious decisions about Mental Health, meanwhile wrecking peoples' lives. Look at those abuse cases. Look how dramatic the response was even while the program was still playing.'

The two TV guys couldn't disagree but this was perhaps above their pay grade. After all we were up against the big boys.

'Ok,' Vince decided. 'We will give it a whirl via the legal guys. Meanwhile let's tuck into our grub.'

While we tucked into bacon, eggs, chips and beans, at ITV expense, Tom asked, 'Brandon did you see all that when you visited the Psychiatric Hospital?'

'You mean the drugs and shock? I didn't see the moment of shock but I saw the room and the machine and the immediate aftermath, which you wouldn't want to experience – by what I observed in a patient who had to be carried out of there. I also saw the effects of drugs on patients; that is, I saw a lot of stunned and nervous-looking patients who weren't about to walk out of there and live normal lives. I saw the diagnostic room and spoke to the man who did the diagnosing. They do it by 'The Book', which was there, handy.

'Peter, our resident Psychologist, was seeing all this for the first time. He and I visited a couple of other establishments too, through his Psychology connections. We hadn't been barred at that point but I'm sure we probably are by this. Of course we weren't able to see a lobotomy; just ask about it. I didn't volunteer to have my brain poked at by sharp instruments or by ice picks. You can imagine. But it all happens.

'One of these days someone will make a film about the inside of the mental institution. There's a project for you guys.'

'Heavy duty!' Tom commented. 'What is worse, Bedlam or this?'

We finished up our meal and agreed to get our legal teams in touch with each other and meet again later in the week.

CHAPTER TWENTY TWO

James Hopkins was sitting in the Department of Education cafeteria minding his own business over tea and crumpets when none other than Jake Levison appeared at his table, armed with a tray of fare. 'Mind if I join you? he asked. I'm Jake Levison.'

'Yes, we have met before, briefly,' came James's tapering reply, half stunned that his chosen adversary didn't seem to remember.

James soon gathered himself and pointed his open hand at the opposite chair.

'I was sorry to see you being found reprehensible for the private school business,' he said after settling himself comfortably. 'These hearings can go either way, can't they? I'm sure you were trying to help the schools involved.'

James was going to take this opportunity to glean what information he could. He was looking quite pointedly at Levison over his cup of tea, as he spoke. The look on Levison's face was an apparency of empathy but he was laying it on a little, just a tinge too unnaturally as he spoke further.

'I knew this central character, Waterman, at my last school. Clever chap. Unfortunately he didn't fit in at school – a bit of an oddball, you know, a misfit. He ended up truanting and causing strife with the PTA. But I guess he was just trying to blame the school and the teachers for his situation. I met his grandfather too. He's a piece of work. I wouldn't be surprised if he was the one behind all that.'

He carried on with his story. 'Then he ended up on your plate. You know he's got a big money making machine going on the back of all this. I don't blame you for being hoodwinked by him; he's a sharp operator I think. You are best off out of all that.'

James was wondering whether he should antagonise Levison or try and string him along as the 'innocent' victim in all this. He decided on the latter.

'You certainly seem to know more about all this than I do, Mr Levison. Perhaps you are right. Maybe you can help me a bit here in my predicament. Do you know how all this came to the Department's attention?'

Levison was evading his direct gaze and smiling, dithering a bit while he prepared his answer. 'I'm not sure, I having only recently arrived here. I heard comments from various personnel, and I was asked what I knew about Waterman, which I just told you. Then I thought no more about it until I saw the office news broadsheet about it all.' He then put out both upturned hands, and shrugged his shoulders in all innocence.

'Hmm.' James said. 'That's a pity. You should know my whole career has come to a shuddering halt. It's like starting all over again. I feel hardly done by, as you can imagine. I appealed the decision of course but that's not justice for me. I'd like to get to the bottom of it all. What do you think?'

Levison was on home territory here. 'I understand, really, but you know big organisations such as this are minefields for chatter and intrigue, and mighty slow, if not over-bureaucratic in dealing with cases like yours. I get the impression they'd rather sweep such matters under the table and let time wear it all down to nothing. You know how the saying goes: time is a great healer.'

James was about to respond but was interrupted by a ringing bell, which sounded like a fire alarm or something.

Levison cut in above all this. 'That's probably a false alarm – someone testing the system. You know Mr. Hopkins, if I were you I'd take the hit, get your head down and rescue your career by sheer hard work and results. It won't be too long before you have worked your way up the tree again and all will be as it was.'

James nodded his head as if deciding to take this advice.

Levison continued. 'You appear to be a good man. Just get on with it and, if I were you, stay away from that Waterman chap. He's not what he appears to be. He's even now ruffling feathers in the very respectable Psychiatric field. Did you see him strutting on TV last night? Whatever next. I think he wants to take over the world.'

James said, 'perhaps you are right. Thanks for your advice.' James rose to leave. They left with a handshake but James thought he'd just heard the pot calling the kettle black. THIS man is definitely not what he appears to be, and he hardened his determination to expose this snake.

What appeared in subsequent daily newspapers was astounding, even to my unshockable disposition.

'Waterman Charade on National TV', and the Observer came up with 'ITV Turns Mental Health Watchdog'.

I was depicted again as an upstart whose feasibility had sunk for good with this painting of Psychiatry as a sham subject. Who was I to pontificate on a respected institution?

They were clamouring for me and our whole organisation to be investigated, not to mention ITV to be sued for misrepresentation and libel.

It was all over the airwaves and BBC TV, the latter not being more than a lackey to the Establishment and its press dogs.

Of course there was only scant coverage of the details of the program itself and what was reported was a twisted version of actual events.

I called Tom. 'Have you seen the rags today Tom?'

'I sure have. I think we are in real trouble here my friend. Maybe we should not have been so brazen on this subject. I expect to be carpeted this morning. Vince agrees.'

I replied, 'that was my first reaction, but after my first cup of tea (amazing what this stuff does) I decided we'd been a great success. Having the cur dogs yapping at us this loudly means we have really hit a nerve, and really close to the bone, as it were. The advertisers must be rubbing their hands for more.'

'Brandon,' Tom replied, 'you don't half put yourself above the parapet don't you? We are going to be slung out! You WILL be investigated. I can't see any way out of this. It seemed like a good idea at the time, but naïve, I reckon.'

I cut in quite decisively here. 'Now listen Tom, remember why you agreed to all this. Just because there's a lot of noisy reaction is no reason to back off. This is all to introvert us and your station. They want us to react like we've offended the hierarchy or something and should just stare into the headlights and be shot down. Now is the time to stand up for what is true and right and NOT back off.'

Tom, as usual, was a bit of a captive audience here. I continued. 'What we portrayed last night was, if anything, a watered-down version of what goes on daily in our mental institutions. These chaps are a public menace and not enough people know it. There should be a hue and cry to have THEM investigated. And I'll tell you, Julia and I already have enough information and cases to do just that.'

Tom was listening and having his somewhat tenuous grip on his integrity shaken. 'You are a brave man Brandon. I don't think I can take the heat in the kitchen like you.'

'Tom, now listen. Is it not true you felt great about us advancing on this escapade?'

'Yes' he admitted.

'You thought it was the correct thing to do, not so?

'Yes, I did, and I still do.' Tom was in the wringer.

'Alright. Nothing has changed,' I continued. 'You have to stand up for what is right, even when opposed, not so? Or else what happens to you?' Like it or not, you are an investigator.'

'I suppose,' said Tom, not quite there yet. I could see he was churning.

'Look you can walk away from this and subside into some place where you can't get into danger, you don't upset anyone, and everything is nice and calm. Is that living or dying? Take a cold look at it no matter if the nerves are fluttering.'

There was silence on the line for a few seconds then Tom showed the first signs of coming round. 'So, charge on and take the bullets and die fighting for the cause. That sounds like the charge of the light brigade' he said, lightening up.' Hmm, I see your point. But I'll probably lose my job, what then?'

'Yes, and I'll maybe lose my whole organisation and all those good people, and Julia might declare she can't live with this, and … except none of that is going to happen. I'm clean, and I will fight whatever comes my way. I won't die. You won't die And we won't feel like heels for giving in. And, just by way of an aside,' I added with emphasis, 'what about all those patients, what do they lose?

'We are in the sphere of public information and entertainment. We aren't in the field of undermining and backstabbing, and cheating and telling lies. We are a force for good, Tom. So you lose your job. You'll eat beans for a few weeks and get another one. You are good at your job.'

I thought I'd give Tom a bit of space on this one now. I switched subjects. 'Incidentally, my plan was to get our legal teams together and discuss the whole thing. I don't think they have a case of libel or anything close. We can invite them on to refute our program and expose themselves to scrutiny. They won't accept. They have too much to hide. It would be bad publicity for them, especially if Julia and I were their inquisitors.

'Once we settle your seniors down about these legal matters they might even feel inclined to do the next program. What revenues for that one!'

Tom came out of listening mode. 'I can't refute any of what you said Brandon. I'm being a bit of a chicken aren't I?

I was going to finish him off. He'd either see sense or not. I'd given my best shot. 'Tom, you decide. You'll have to live with whatever you decide. I'm going on the attack. I'd prefer to have you on my side. We may not be able to make more programs on your station anyway. But I'm going on the attack. I'm going to get onto these hacks and find me a few better ones, if they exist, and get my stories out there. And if we can inveigh upon your tenderfoots there at ITV, all the better. I want a discussion with them. I would hope to turn them around. I'll bet they haven't come across this situation before.'

'Brandon, I'm going to discuss this with Vince and Barry and see what the day brings about. Either way I wouldn't want you as my adversary. You've got guts man.'

'Ok Tom. Let me know what you two come up with.'

That was that, for now, but I was straight into the Office to make sure they hadn't been blown away by the Fleet Street cannonade.

CHAPTER TWENTY THREE

Diane McAdam walked into her office on the Monday morning following the TV show on ITV. Her Aide, the ever-faithful Alison was just walking out.

'Morning Alison,' McAdam almost chirped. 'Did you have a good weekend? What's new on the agenda for today?'

'I'm OK Diane. There's the usual on your desk. I included a copy of the Guardian as well. There's a big splash on Page Three about that Waterman chap. I thought you'd like to see it.'

'See it?' she exclaimed. 'I saw it all on TV over the weekend. This young man has branched out into Mental Therapies. I have to say I was impressed, especially with his reasoning.

'I missed it,' replied Alison. 'It has certainly stoked up a bit of a furore in the papers.'

McAdam sat down and said, 'I spoke to this Mr. Levison last week. He explained what went on with Waterman at his school and then since. There's something about this man Levison. I can't put my finger on it but it's as if he was telling me what he thought I should hear.

'If I study this Waterman alone I get a very logical, unemotional picture of what he's about. If I add the media and our staff to the picture it gets muddled.

Sure enough, when I got to the office, at about nine-thirty a.m., I was assailed at the doorstep by a cavalcade of reporters – newspaper and radio and TV.

As I approached the front steps of the office building the mob descended upon me, a bit like you see in American movies, all pushing and shoving for a sound bite. I saw Ira at the front doors. She had obviously corralled them outside and had been pressed a bit.

I expected to see a rolling pin in her hand. This was right up her alley.

I was all smiles and good nature. I fought my way to Ira's side, looked at her quickly and said, 'good morning, isn't this fun?' and then turned my attention to the rabble. Ira rolled her eyes as if to say, 'predictable'.

I raised my arms in the air as a signal to get their attention, which it did in reasonably short order. 'Good morning to you all. I dare say you all have stories to write or broadcast. I'm sorry I can't invite you in and offer you tea. This is an Education establishment and I don't have a press room as such, so this is it here. I will take some questions for a while then I will issue a broad statement which will cover a range of points you will probably want answered.'

I knew there'd be some carpers, maybe even some hypercritics (if that's not the same thing). There may be some that are more like Tom. But I was exuding considerable self-confidence and elan and would take it all in my stride.

I started off with 'the rules'. 'I will select the questioners one at a time. Tell me your name and which outlet you are from. Keep it brief, and I'll be brief so I can get to as many as possible. Ok, this handsome lady at the front.' I looked at her and prompted her to ask her question.

'I am Lilly Franks, BBC News.' I smiled at her expectantly. 'How have you come to being a Mental Health expert from being an Educationalist?'

I answered her with a question, at first. 'I thought I covered that pretty comprehensively in the program last night. Did you watch it?'

'Yes I did,' she answered 'but aren't you off the main road a bit here?'

'It's still covered in my programs. I am a concerned citizen, as I imagine you are too. We probably have a lot in common in that we look for items of interest in life, look into them and report on them. If you had a tip that there was something awry in our Mental Hospitals, wouldn't you look into it and report on it, for the public good? Or perhaps you think there's something awry in ME doing this. Is that fair? Your only answer to that dilemma is to go and have a look for yourself.'

I moved quickly onto the next inquisitor, a middle aged chap with a typical reporter 'uniform', from The Daily Mail.

'Some say you are unqualified to do programs like this and that you have an axe to grind, or perhaps a monetary interest in all this.'

I went for him, not antagonistically, but forthrightly enough. 'Who is 'some say' may I ask? Give me the names of the worst of them.' I smiled at him. 'Did you write such comment in your paper today?'

The chap tried not to get flummoxed and avoided the questions, but I didn't let him go on. 'Look, if these are your heart-felt opinions (and they ARE statements, not questions), then print them. Make sure you can back them up with good research and true information that will stand up to scrutiny. Anyone who has an accusative question like this doesn't need to ask it. I'm not on trial, nor will I be getting my knickers in a twist by such accusations.

'I dare say the most objectionable things about me are probably that I am young and that I have the temerity to put myself out there. If I was forty-five or something, looked professorial and had some fancy letters after my name, things would be different. I'll take a few more questions and then I will go and prepare my news report.'

A chap from a fairly obscure radio station asked, 'was it you who disrupted the Psychiatric Convention a little while back?'

'I'm not sure there was much disruption actually. You could have been there yourself and noticed nothing, but the head guys thought we were 'from outside the bubble', as polite as we were. It was a fact-finding event for us. We didn't get many FACTS beyond the fact that they didn't like being questioned about their protocols or practices. You'd have enjoyed it if you'd been with us. Next question.'

This was about Julia and her involvement in all this. I answered this with equanimity, but basically 'none of your business, she's not on yet.'

Then came a question from a softly spoken lady, not from any particular organisation, but she had a small recording device and microphone in her hand. 'May I ask your interest in this?' I asked. Her name was Ivis Knightly.

'I am a freelancer. I pick up on any out-of-the-ordinary subjects that come up. This is definitely in that category,' she smiled.

'What would you like to know?' I asked her.

'Could you explain further how this subject of Mental Health meets up with your quest for answers on human behaviour?'

I noted that this was the first apparently intelligent and genuine attempt to learn something from me.

'Well,' I began, 'further to what I explained in the program, and more of an extension of my work in the Education field.....' I explained again my program.

'You can't say that despite Education we are great communicators and thinkers, as a society. I am judging society by its products here. Put it this way, if our reasoning powers and ability to prevent and deal with social problems were as good as our sciences, we'd be a lot better off. Do you see what I mean?

Ivis nodded and continued. 'So where does Psychiatry fit into all this?'

The other members of the corps were taking this in. My answer was in two words. 'It doesn't. Simple as that. Well, let me rephrase that – it shouldn't. In my research into answers I found that rather than be a source of help Psychiatry was very possibly adding to the problem. Watch the next program if they let us run it, and you will see why. Didn't you think last night put that in the spotlight?'

'Yes, I did,' she agreed. 'I want to know more'. I nodded at her with an encouraging smile.

'I'll just flick around now and have you ask your questions briefly and after I consider myself bombarded I'll try and 'shotgun' the answers.'

So it went like this: 'How old are you? What is this organisation actually? Don't you think you should have given the other side an opportunity to defend themselves? How much money do you make out of all this? What are you going to expose next? I believe the Psychiatrists are considering suing you for last night's program. What is your response?

I held up my hands. 'OK, enough already' I said smiling. 'I think I have been quite fair and candid here this morning. I'll try and sum up the last fusillade now and that will be it. Leave your cards with Ira here and I'll be sure to send you a nice big juicy release.

'Now, I am nineteen, as you know already. I am primarily an Educator which is what this building is all about. This is a college and a Head Office for all our other colleges, of which there are seven or eight – I've lost count. How much money I make is not the point. I am a humanitarian more than I am a businessman. We make ends meet and expand and everyone gets paid a decent living wage. We are not finished exposing Psychiatry yet. Watch the next program which will be an expose of the end of their assembly line.

'Then, after lots more research I will expose what I find in the direction of real solutions to human problems. Incidentally, if the Psychiatrists are considering suing me, I welcome it. We will invite them onto the next program. I don't think they will come.

'Thank you for your attention. May truth reign in your ranks. There's many a story out there to be written and shown with all the power you media have.'

I went inside and left Ira to collect their business cards. They all got more than they expected probably.

When I went inside I was met firstly by Veronica with a mug of tea. Ira sauntered up and said, 'Glad that was you doing the talking. It was brilliant.' 'Thank you,' I replied. 'But I don't think that lot are really part of the sharp point. Keep vigilant. I don't expect the Mental Health boys are going to leave it at that. I need to talk to Gavin, today. Incidentally, give me the card from that nice young lady who asked the only decent question. I may be able use her.'

Ira did and by stuffing it in my top pocket.

At this I went into my office and rang Julia. 'Hullo my love,' I said quietly and intimately. 'We just had the media circus on our doorstep. They are at bay for the moment.'

'Hullo gorgeous,' Julia greeted. 'It's all over TV already. I saw you there enjoying yourself and performing like an old pro. I thought you dealt with them amazingly.' She is surely my biggest fan.

'Julia, my love, invite me for dinner at your place tonight. Apart from my prime interest I need to speak to Gavin about the legals of all this. In fact, invite me for lunch. As Delia is at the office, why not demonstrate your wife-worthiness and lay on a spread for us. Do you think Gavin could be available?'

'He's actually at home right now, as it happens. I'll pass him onto you. In the meantime I'll go into the kitchen and see what worthiness I can rustle up. I do hope it passes the test. Otherwise you will be the cook or we'll spend our life eating out.'

She put Gavin on. He and I discussed the bones of the thing and we agreed to meet for lunch. Gavin got the urgency of it all.

I then went and touched base with all the key players in the office, as usual.

'I must speak to their legal team,' Gavin told me. We were sat in the conservatory munching on a seafood salad Julia had concocted. Between mouthfuls Gavin was giving us his appraisal of the legal standing, only on the basis of his watch of the TV program.

'On the surface of it I'd say you are on safe grounds. As for the TV corporation, they would seem to be safe too but at a fair cost of fees, being that they would have to, if sued, go back and forth with the opposition on proofs and counter-proofs.'

I asked, 'How does this work? Would they sue for misrepresentation and libel and if so how would they prove it? I'd have thought, considering the amount of ruined people laying in their wake (and we'd only need a few I'd have thought, and we have half a dozen or so) and the results of any inspection they'd have to somehow defend, that they wouldn't dare exacerbate the already damning evidence.'

'You have a point there.' Gavin replied. 'It depends on what charges they made. The TV corporation might decide that the expense would render it not worth defending and they'd just take it on the nose. Or, if the suit were inordinately prohibitive, they might retract and run an apology or a corrective program to obviate a ruinous situation.'

'If they were courageous they might invite the Psychiatrists on to 'put the record straight'. If this were the case you could put it to the TV guys that you and Julia could present them with the evidence of mistreatment and the accuracy of your own data, as given on the program. And see if they accept. By the sound of it they have too much to hide and, might I say, too little ammunition to best you two stars.'

I said, 'I was going to go to the TV Execs, with Tom and Vince, and with you and their law boys, and put just that case. They'd need to be convinced that they are on a sound legal footing to present truthful, incontrovertible exposes, without having to provide a mile of legal defence.'

'As I said,' Gavin repeated, 'we need to bang heads and see what we are actually up against'

'Ok, I'm onto it,' I said, rubbing my metaphoric hands together. I rose and then turned to Julia. 'That was the best seafood salad I've ever tasted, my love, and thank God I don't have to eat out or cook myself.'

'Well, actually, I am planning a revolutionary marriage. I will be too damn busy to be a domestic housewife, if that's your expectation. In fact I plan to have a live-in housekeeper-cum-cook. You can order from the menu at home.'

With that she cleared the table and left we two men to choke on that. We resigned ourselves to losing.

I got onto Tom at the TV station. 'Tom, I've spoken to Gavin. We want to meet your Execs and legal team. We have worked out how to prevent the opposition from suing. Can you organise it on that basis? They have to be interested in that.'

'Ok, Brandon, I'll give it a go. I'll come right back to you.'

I then went to find Julia. 'What say you, gorgeous, shall we have a little 'us' time?' We melted into each other's arms and the 'us' time began.

'How about we have a driving lesson,' she suggested. 'I can drive you to that nice café in Richmond Park. By then I'll be ready for my test. Just one more drive. Did you know I am booked for my test next week?'

'No, you don't tell me anything,' I teased. 'If I were the examiner I'd give you a flying pass through the post – a mere formality. Let's go.'

We drove over Putney Bridge and into Richmond Park via Roehampton Gate. We didn't bother about the restaurant. We had stopped in Lower Richmond Road and bought some picnic things.

We found a quiet peaceful yet panoramic corner of the park and spread out a blanket and tucked into our snack picnic.

'Well Mrs Waterman, this is an unusual event for us and outside our home turf. It's a nice area. I've heard that Putney, Sheen and Richmond, and, further south, Wimbledon, are quite affluent areas. We must drive around these later and have a look.'

'Well Mr Waterman, I have no idea what's on your mind. Could it be that you are actually at work under the guise of having some down time?'

'Always,' I replied. 'You know that one can span one's attention quite readily. I mean I can take in the beauty immediately in front of me, in full detail and technicolour and I can be very aware of what's around me peripherally, and plan our life ahead, all at once, though I must say that what's immediately in front of me is by far the most attention-grabbing and appealing.'

'Is that so? Well that's all right then.'

'So why did you drive me down here to South West London. Have I been taken for a ride?' I asked her.

'It is a beautiful place, isn't it?' Julia looked around her – nothing but trees and grass, blue skies, and an external elevated view of Central London including Westminster.' There were a few deer grazing not too far away.

She asked me, 'have you ever been in a park like this? I dare say you have lived such an enclosed life, barely six inches from a book page and a few students. Only of late have you ventured into a TV studio to break the boredom.'

While chewing on a stick of celery, I looked about and then told her, 'Yes you are right I haven't really lived have I? Well, we'll fix that on our honeymoon and make up for lost time.'

Pointing to the north-eastern horizon of inner London I said, 'life is going on there where I've been sheltered as you say. There, within our eye span, more of this planet's adventures have been perpetrated than in most places on earth, and we are doing more than our share of adventures to add to them.'

'I wouldn't be doing anything else,' Julia said, while cosying close to me.

'Where is all that life over there and around the world going?' I sort of asked. 'I can't help feeling it is bumbling along, through all its catastrophes, interspersed with just enough successes to keep it going, most people living or barely surviving from day to day, wrapped up in their own little worlds, a step or two above subsistence. As a species, if reports are to be believed, the majority are living only just above the animal kingdom, that is, abject poverty chased by disease and premature withering.'

'We are into Philosophy here,' Julia said softly. 'Here in the West and some privileged pockets of the East, there have been great minds and some monumental achievements, and some civilising factors, though that is relative. We are finding that there are gaping cracks in it all, covered by a thin social coating to make it seem better than it actually is. How long do you think this civilisation will last Brandon?'

I thought while snapping a few random twigs I'd picked up. 'I don't know. This planet has had other epochs I believe. Man is a Jonny-cum-lately event in all of its history. Ten thousand years ago there was virtually nothing going on beyond flora and some fauna. Through the Ice Age, almost nothing. Maybe there was human life at other times, but I believe we are hurtling to a day of reckoning, unable as yet to determine a favourable result.'

'I know you are not doomsday Brandon, but it's hard, when looking at this matter, not to be negative or even apathetic. I suppose we have to be truthful though and name the game.'

'Yep, life is in us as we speak, and life changes things. I believe it is our mission to get more and more people living; not just surviving, but really alive, and all singing from the same hymn sheet. In another few centuries or a few thousand years on, which are not great time spans, what will we see out in front of us?

'Just take the playing field, for instance – the physical planet itself. Apart from population explosion, finite resources and so on, will we have ravaged the physical environment so much that it becomes uninhabitable? Will we take it to the tipping point before something to reverse it will work?

'The flaws in our species do not, to me, show signs of anything but a headlong tipping to an irreversible crisis.'

We sat there close together, silent, with a light wind ruffling our hair and clothes. It was harmony amongst disturbance you might say.

I abruptly disentangled myself and got up and helped Julia up and pronounced, 'Enough. Let's play.'

This had been a definite exterior look at things. We continued looking around, Julia driving and me navigating. We did a tour of East Sheen, Richmond, Ham, Kingston and Wimbledon, all choice residential areas, and confirmed it all territory for future forays. We even visited Wimbledon Tennis Museum which we happened to pass on our way back north.

We then carried on through Battersea and over into our patch in Chelsea and Pimlico and through Kensington and Hammersmith. We visited all our establishments in these areas, our staffs being pleased to see us. A quick inspection and chat to the staffs in each saw us more than pleased enough. We headed home, Julia now concentrating hard in the rush hour traffic.

'You have mastered it, my love,' I told her. 'Roll on the test next week.' We ended up in Finchley and found all the key staff still working beyond normal hours.

When we rolled in, everyone gravitated to the canteen. I told them we'd decided that the staff should know we'd been out reconnoitring the next areas for conquest.

Before explaining what we'd been doing all day Ira asked 'What's happening with the TV programs, Brandon? And what about the Education Department?'

'Sorry people. I haven't kept you up to date, have I? We are at the crucial stage in both, determining what to do next.' I expanded a little and told them about the new virgin areas Julia and I had just scoped.

'I realise the labour union in this establishment are about to plug for a sixty hour week, without us adding to the spread we have going right now. You'd have thought it was slavery the way you lot go on.'

'Haven't you heard that some unions in this country are talking about forty hours per week?' Ira continued.

'Might as well not bother going to work, at that level,' Sidney said.

I kept the banter going as Veronica refilled all our cups. 'There's only one thing for it: Sidney becomes Minister for Employment and bans all unions and thus doubles the production of the nation and becomes a national hero and then moves into Number Ten and runs the Education Department himself and gets us what we want. Then you can retire, Ira, and become the housewife you've always wanted to be.'

'No, I think I would help Sidney with the Education portfolio. But he has the Watermen gene, which is a disease. I'd be worse off than ever before.'

'Stop moaning then girl,' I concluded. 'You don't know how lucky you are. Any more revolutions on offer?'

The ladies, who were Julia, Delia, Ira, Veronica and their latest arrival, Cindy Hopkins, all started to speak at once in mock protest whereupon I got up and placed my hands over my ears and signalled for Sidney to follow me out of there, into the peace of my office, but chased there by volumes of laughter coming from the canteen.

'I did find some new areas in South West London,' I told Sidney. 'Just as good as the North, maybe better. But I would like to make a coup at the Department; save us a lot of organising.

That reminds me, I must get hold of the PI that I hired and see what dirt he may have dredged up on you know who.'

'You actually went ahead with this?' Sidney asked, mildly but pleasantly surprised.

I looked at him 'Gee, I hadn't mentioned it to you had I? Yes, if James is to succeed in the Department he has to be rid of the latest vermin attack. This chap is on the case.'

'I'll get back now to my servitude under the other species in there and hire me a bunch of bright men to balance the odds.' Sidney said.

'Ah, we Watermans don't need that. They are under surreptitious control, really. Besides there's one of them who is rather attractive, the rest are all spoken for, so I guess you should hire an attractive older lady for yourself even if that means adding to the odds.'

Smiling to himself Mr W senior strolled out of there. I picked up the phone and called Michael Stone, the PI in Hendon.

Having reached him and done the pleasantries, I asked, 'I know it's only been a week or less, but any progress?'

'Gee you ARE in a hurry, aren't you? As it happens I managed to find out where he lives, where he banks, who he associates with, what organisations he belongs to. I even followed him for a few days. How about that for service! But that's only the beginning. However, I found he does visit a questionable establishment in the East End. So I'm going to follow up on that next. In fact I'm going to follow him in there. Hope I'm up to such dens of iniquity.'

'Good work Michael. I can already see the Department of Education issuing his P Forty Five (job-leaving tax certificate). I'm in a hurry for this dope so have fun. Hear from you later.' I hung up and swung into my next task.

Michael Stone was beginning to enthuse about his project with us.

CHAPTER TWENTY FOUR

'Ah, Brandon, you really are a mind reader,' Tom said. 'It must be all that navel contemplation you are doing. You'll have me at it soon.'

'You could do worse, Tom.' I replied. 'But before that we have to work some magic on your upper reaches there first. What's the latest?'

Tom turned a little more serious. 'They were at first a little entrenched, but after Vince and Barry and I parried around with them a bit they said they'd look at it again and at whether or not they'd meet with you about it.'

I thought for a moment and then asked Tom. 'Do they ever go into your canteen to eat or have a break?'

'Yes they do, as it happens,' he realised.

'Well, it takes me twenty minutes to get to your studios, the quick route. Keep an eye on their movements, use a mole for this if necessary, and give me a call when they are there. Best at a lunchtime, to allow enough time.'

'OK Brandon. I'm with you. Pray tell what is the short route here may I ask? Or should I use my imagination?'

'Yep, just that. Then I'll not have to tell any lies, or confess to any impropriety with the rules of the road.'

'God, and you've not long passed your test. Ok, speak to you, hopefully tomorrow. Have your hot rod ready to go at a moment's notice.'

Tom was about to hang up, but then asked, 'by the way, your wedding is next Saturday isn't it? I'm arranging a shoot of it for our news program. You better remember to turn up.'

'I'll be there but remember Lady Julia is the star attraction. This will warm her up for her nationwide TV debut.'

We rang off and I rang James next, and told him to get ready for some sparks, explaining the PI information.

James was pleased. He was expecting his Appeal to happen any day soon. Maybe he'd be let off the hook but in any case he'd want to rub it all in with a juicy expose.

I got the call from Tom the next morning at eleven. I was at home and dashed out of there and into the little Ford and wound my way through and around the traffic to the studios of ITV. I parked and hot-footed it to the canteen where I was met at the counter by Tom and Vince, and the in-between guy, Barry Lancolm.

We grabbed a plate of snacks and a cup of char each and found a table close to the unsuspecting targets. After a few minutes of tactics talk and scoffing we four got up and approached the two Execs who seemed to be winding up their break and about to leave.

Tom introduced me to both gents who were standing to shake hands. The lead Exec, the Deputy Director of ITV, one Alistair McIntyre, not quite impolitely, offered us seats, after I had asked for a few minutes of their time.

Quickly I got down to it. 'I believe you gentlemen have been mulling over whether to follow up on our last program, which has stirred the hornet's nest more than a little bit.' I was a little conspiratorial in manner, as if they were in on it all along.

The second Exec, who was the Director of Programs, one Ken Crofton, said, 'that's an understatement Mr Waterman. How do you think we'd survive another program of Psychiatric bashing?' He was reasonably personable, a sense of humour not far away, probably in his mid to late thirties.

Alistair McIntyre, a fairly dour Scot by all appearances, added, 'and that's assuming you were to rein it in even fifty percent.' He looked like he'd been fashioned from the archetypical Scottish cauldron. He was probably in his early forties – still, a young one for a top Exec.

I sized them up rather quickly. 'Let me ask you this,' I said looking at both of them: 'do you agree with the content of the program, not from a legal view but just as factual information? Were you sold on it?'

Ken Crofton answered. He was the looser of the two. 'I must say I was glued to it; intrigued by it. I didn't know these things went on. I assume you have more on all this and can back it up.'

Alistair McIntyre came in and doused Ken a bit. 'The point is, true or not, can we risk the legals on this?'

'I can answer that,' I put in quickly, 'but do you believe in the content? That's vital.'

'I'm ambivalent,' replied Alistair. 'I'm only interested in good stimulating programs, such as your Education ones. So are our advertisers. But legal wrangles, that's another matter. We run this station for the shareholders, not our own personal beliefs or crusades.'

He looked straight at me, not exactly admonishing me but none too friendly either. Tom and Vince looked on at this exchange, anxious to see where it was going.

I was not unnerved. 'Point granted. Can I ask what your legal team have told you?'

Alistair hesitated a second or two and then answered. 'They think it is somewhat equivocal, but either way we'd be tied up in legalities and the expense for some time. On balance, do we want to tie ourselves up in this, or just move on? I understand your next offering on this is the exposure of damage cases which is now extending all this into trial by TV which seems a logical prelude to trial by court.'

'I totally see your point here Alistair,' I acknowledged, 'but did you ever consider that the Psychiatrists are in the same boat?' I paused to let it sink in 'This subject and profession are so shady, hiding behind a pseudo-science and a semblance of respectability. Essentially they are acting as the refuse bin for the unfortunate souls that can't be helped by Medicine or Psychology. These souls, who range from 'little wrong in the first place' to the absolutely psychotic, get shifted on to these institutions where they get quietened down, at best, by drugs or electrocution, or even worse, have their brains operated on.

'This is all out of sight and out of mind. They enjoy the status of Mental Health authorities only on the basis that there is no competition or real inspection. We are basically 'happy' to shove the problem over to them, just like we are happy to shove our waste products into landfills or rivers, and forget about it.'

The two Execs were listening as I was getting a toehold into a more expansive reasoning.

I continued. 'Go into one of their hospitals and look around, if they will let you. Ask for examples of cures. And here's the capper – ask them onto one of my programs to defend themselves and put their case. You call it trial by TV, well you've done that before, with politicians for instance, only this time they are trying to scare you off with suits, and the weight of their 'respected' profession.' The two of them were primed to listen.

'The point is, do they have a case? Let them present it. Give them a chance to balance the argument. If you were to do that with the medical profession, for example, there'd be no contest; they do so much good and could easily present evidence of their effectiveness.

'With this lot – no chance. They'd run scared and would be embarrassed by the evidence against. Actually I don't think they'd be embarrassed. They aren't that sensitive. It's a bluff to make you go away. They are betting you'll all get introverted and back off, not wanting the hassle, as you said. I'll bet they didn't just send a solicitor's letter but hammered it in by saying they'd take you to the cleaners and have you closed down, or other heavy stuff to that effect.'

I sat there and waited for a response. The two men shifted about a bit and looked at each other. I came in again. 'Look, yes, I am on a crusade. I am looking for a DECENT way to help people and prevent them from slipping into neurosis and worse. But quite aside from that I feel it our duty to expose the pretenders who are causing a lot of damage to the more vulnerable in society (at we tax-payers' expense I might add). A stand has to be taken. And you haven't seen the worst of it yet – the actual human casualties on display. There are court cases there too.'

'What do your legal people say about this?' asked Ken.

'I've pretty well told you that. The Psychiatrists will be asked to refute, with evidence and thus expose what hand they actually have, and we will back up our evidence, as presented in the next program, and more.

'They will bluster but in the end will not want further inspection. They'd probably rather let it slide and not have to pay both sides' expenses, nor provoke a Public Enquiry.'

Tom came in here. 'What about we invite them on to present their defence of what we have shown so far. We can shoot that down easily. Then we can do the damage cases, starring the equally formidable Julia Waterman (soon to be).

'If they have a case then it will be me that gets the gun. Did you think of that? I'll take that risk.'

I added, 'they won't show up. What they may try to do is discredit me and Julia instead and get the rags to splash it all over the reading public (which has started to happen already). That is, they'll bet on us being the David who can't really slay the Goliath and that any pot-shot by David won't hurt them at all. This is a vested interest. And we suspect there is an even bigger vested interest behind them – the pharmaceutical industry.' I smiled and added, 'but that's for another program.'

'Do you have to be a teenager to change the world these days?' asked Alistair, now with a somewhat reluctant smile on his face.

'It's not too late for you Alistair,' I joked. 'Let me just say, though this TV station is a commercial enterprise, you are in a great position to raise the moral compass of society and be a force for good, not just entertainment. I can see you are both caring people. You have to answer to this moral/ethical side of it as well as to your shareholders (providing of course that these shareholders aren't dominated by the vested interest in question).'

'He's right you know Alistair,' said Ken. 'I'm for giving it a go with the proviso we can monitor you more closely Brandon, and that our legal teams meet and agree on tactics. You know you put us in this position with your off-the-wall presentation the other day.' He added this humorously.

'Along with giving the Psychiatrists the challenge of responding to the program, this is the way to go.' Tom enthused.

Ken said to him, waving his finger at Tom, smiling. 'I think Brandon is innocent here. Don't think your covert career opportunism has passed us by.' They all laughed.

'Well,' said Alistair as he rose to his feet, signalling the meeting was being concluded. 'First let's get the legal teams together and satisfy us we are on sound enough grounds. Then we may proceed as discussed.'

We shook hands and went our separate ways. Tom, Vince and Barry discussed the legal meeting with me as we went toward the car park gate.

I decided to head toward the McDonald house on the off chance that Gavin would be there. No wasting time. I was cock-a-hoop after my meeting with the two Execs. Despite their reserve I was dealing with showbiz-infected people really. They were too tied to the entertainment business to be utterly impartial to its pull for a bit of drama. Surely it had rubbed off on them. I realised they were loosened up a bit but not exactly cavalier. Anyway I had a foot in the door.

Gavin wasn't at home, nor Julia, so I drove to the office, whereupon I was beset by the female contingent who assailed me about my lack of preparation for the wedding on the coming Saturday.

'What do you mean I'm not ready?' I protested. They were haranguing me from all sides. What about this, what about that?

'Look, my mum and Delia have it all in hand, not so?' I said casually looking at the two afore-mentioned. 'I have my speech planned, my best man organised, my bride agreeable. You have the church and reception details well in hand. We turn up at one forty-five pm, fifteen minutes before the McDonalds. We sit down at the front of the church and wave to all the guests, and wait and see if the bride is, by tradition, late. We promise to be good to each other, job done.

'Then we go to the Village Hall and have some more fun and celebration and speeches, and then....' I hesitated.

'Ah yes, I have to organise the honeymoon because no one else really knows where we're going (or when). Well, it so happens...'

Ira cut in here. 'Do you have your wedding clothes measured up and ready? Do you know where you are going to live, or shall I say, how should I put this... where this union will become a true marital affair? Do you ...'

'Wait a minute,' I butted in . 'What are you saying? Doesn't that all happen at the church? What's the service for if it isn't to join us in holy matrimony?' I was enjoying this, playing the innocent.

Ira was through being delicate. 'Let me ask you this in words we all understand – where does the holy deed of consummation take place?'

I feigned being highly embarrassed, then, 'you nosy parkers! It so happens that Julia and I have a different understanding of the word 'holy' here. We are going on a spiritual trip, beyond matters of the flesh, and it transcends such concepts as 'sex' and 'getting it off,' and all other debasing concepts.

'And none of you are invited.' They all rejected all this with much ridicule. Mum said concernedly, 'we all want to know if you are well prepared for the ceremonies, son. There's a lack of evidence, and you are never at home in normal sleeping hours, of late, to ask you about your arrangements, and Julia is all tied up with her end of it.'

'Oh ye of little faith.' Just then Sidney strode in and enquired, 'what's all this about then? Leave my grandson alone.'

I said to him, 'They think I'm too busy to be ready to be married properly and I'm not giving it enough serious attention. Can you put them straight, best man?'

'I just came in to tell you, my boy, that your suit is available for final fitting; we can go down to the tailor's this afternoon and check it out.' I was enjoying this. The women were standing there agog.

'Also, I have your plane tickets now, from the travel agents, ready to fly out immediately after the Reception. I also need you to sign the mortgage document for Number Fifteen Roseberry Ave. We can sign this on our trip down the street too.'

He turned and faced the women and we both folded our arms and smiled and observed the impact.

Gladys was the first to break silence. 'You scheming old toad. You set us all up for this with your going on about wondering if Brandon was attending to all this himself and getting us all to do something about it. All that 'innocent' acting. Julia must be in on this too.' There were six hands on hips and three mouths all going at once.

Sidney and I hunched our shoulders in innocence and then broke into guffaws and shook hands. The women filed out also in amusement now.

'Watch what they do Sidney,' I told him. 'They won't take this lying down. There'll be a sequel'.

Sidney left as Veronica came in with her usual pile of papers and notes, and executive conference began.

'Hullo Veronica. How're things? I enquired. 'Don't be surprised if your union is planning a walk-out.'

'I'm well thankyou boss. I don't really get involved in the senior ladies' conversations. I'm far too busy. Besides I'm not a fully paid-up member yet so I don't really get a vote. You know what it's like being a teenager and all.'

'You're a paid-up member all right,' I replied slowly, looking at her sideways with slightly squinted eyes and pursed lips. 'Anyway, just to keep you busy, what have you got for me. Let's reduce that pile in front of you.'

And we set about it, with me getting Veronica to come up with all the responses, as much as possible. She was a smart girl this one, too smart not to be a paid-up member of this club.

———————————

That same night Julia was at home helping Delia with the evening meal. It was to be the last get-together, probably, before the big day. I was invited too so I could have a pow-wow with Gavin.

Me, Gavin, and Dan too, were in the conservatory sharing a rare glass of best white. I was telling them of my little coup with the Office Union, with much embellishment of course.

The peals of laughter attracted the two ladies, who were at a pause in the dinner preparations.

'What's so funny,' Delia asked, as the ladies wandered in, suspecting what it was all about anyway.

Julia wasn't in on the story of the day yet. 'Yes, you three. Can't imagine what would cause you to have a fit of hysterics, unless it's the wine.'

Gavin told them, both standing there expectantly in their aprons, 'Brandon was just telling me a few anecdotes from the office. It must be fun over there, though I don't hear office tales from you Delia. I think I'll have to locate myself there so I won't miss the fun.'

Julia came up and sat beside me and leaned over and said to me, 'have you, by any chance, been having fun at the expense of the senior women in your life?'

'Julia, my love, these ladies, good-intentioned as they are, continually doubt my fitness to run my life. You know better, don't you?' I gave her a peck on the cheek.

'Maybe I do,' she agreed, 'but I think you have been winding them up in some way. On this occasion only (and only to curry favour with you until Saturday), I am on your side. After that, and with Dad in the office, you men are fair game.'

Delia and Julia started to return to the kitchen. 'I don't know how I got roped into all this modern day slavery and demeaning behaviour,' Delia 'protested' as they left.

The men returned to our conversation, with me asking Gavin could he squeeze in a meeting tomorrow with the Legals of ITV. 'I have to get this nailed down before the weekend and its subsequent extra curricula schedule.'

'What time are you looking at?' asked Gavin .

'I don't know yet, but let's say mid-afternoon-ish. I'll call Tom right now and see what can be done. He'll still be in the studio I think.

I went out and called Tom and they we agreed to confirm it in the morning. I returned to the conservatory.

I told Gavin, 'Let's say it's on for around two-thirty. It won't take long. We have confirmed the strategy already, have we not?' I suggested. 'I'll confirm the time in the morning.'

Gavin agreed. 'As long as these guys are well versed in corporate law suits and are at least half as adventuresome as us (you actually), we'll be alright.'

Dan added, 'I've heard that big institutions are quite litigious. They must all have big bucks behind them to scare away the little guys. Take that politician's suit against the Shell oil company recently. He soon got put back in his box, that is, ran out of money.'

I rubbed my hands together. 'ITV is not the largest corporation, yet, but they have us, the master strategists. The Psychiatrists'll back off. I'm hoping a Public Enquiry will come of this.'

Gavin added, 'well one step at a time. Let's see what their armoury is first.'

He continued, changing the subject. 'So you and Julia have been seeking out your palace. You did that under the radar, you two. I was fully expecting you to end up here, or at your place Brandon.

'You wouldn't expect me to short change your daughter would you Gavin? Nothing's too good for your girl, you know.' Gavin nodded agreeably.

I continued, 'we are going around to the place in the morning. I have the keys. It is pretty well ready to move into. All we have to do is buy some furniture. The kitchen and bathroom are quite modern and will do for now. We simply need some beds and wardrobes, tables, chairs and a few other things like that. We are getting all the stuff from a large furniture warehouse on the North Circular Road. They will deliver it all and set it up while we are away. We've invited all and sundry to the wedding, I hear, so we should get a good haul of domestics from that – you know, the cost of entry to the show.'

'Why didn't I think of that?' asked Gavin

'Sidney did all the organising, under the radar as you've heard.'

Dan said, shaking his head, 'you two don't miss a trick, do you? I suppose you have your 'honeymoon' all mapped out too, in similar fashion.'

'Well, that would be telling,' I replied. 'In actual fact we are going to wing it. One night we might be sleeping on the banks of the Ganges in a tent and the next at some railway station. Actually I've heard that travellers can be put up in the local temples, not palatially, but providing you have a ground sheet and a few sleeping bags you'll be alright. You get a breakfast too – not exactly bacon and eggs and toast, but... Not sure about the bathrooms. I can't imagine these holy people live without washing themselves.

Gavin and Dan smiled and looked at each other, knowingly.

I went on, 'As I told the ladies, this is a spiritual trip. We aren't just going to lay about in hotels and live as we do here. We are going to live as they do – eat, sleep, worship, meditate and travel as they do.'

As the ladies summoned them to the table, Gavin concluded, 'Well, send us a postcard, if they have such things in... wherever you are going.'

We dined in much jollity and when all was done Julia walked to the car with me. 'We ARE on for the morning aren't we, my maharajah?'

'Yep, I've got the keys. We can look at how we want to feather the nest and then go to that place we scouted and choose what we want – you know, bedrolls, prayer mats; whatever feather tickles your fancy.'

We hugged tenderly. 'It's nearly the day isn't it?' she said looking into my eyes. 'Seems almost superfluous to promise publicly what everyone knows is already promised.'

I brushed a few strands of that beautiful hair out of her eyes and kissed her on the forehead 'Not everyone knows. Besides, looks like there'll be a TV audience too.'

'Well we'll give them a show – wedding of the year!'

We untangled and I got in the car and drove off.

So much to do before the big adventure, I thought, the next morning. I rang the PI, Michael Stone.

'Hullo Michael, how's the snooping going?'

'Mr. Waterman I presume. You have given me an interesting case here I think. This 'prey' of mine indeed visits a house of ill repute in the East End. It's a sort of high class brothel. I say 'sort of' in that it's not a blatant swish joint with semi naked girls lounging about, ready to get down to it.

'It's a sort of agency. You go in there and 'order' what you want, from pictures, meet a few in the backrooms and then go out on a date. The date is actually a call-girl. She goes to the client's place, usually after a meal or something. Then the rest is done by phone from thereon after. If you want a new girl you visit again and carry on as above. I did have to go in there as a prospective client, to find out all about this place. Interesting though.'

'So what's the skinny on our predator's involvement?'

'Well I followed him there a few nights ago. He came out with a lady, all dressed in 'uniform' and he went to a place in West Kensington. She was there for an hour or so then got into a waiting cab and was off. I took pictures of all of this, by the way.

'A few nights later the same girl arrived at this place, was there for a few hours, then went off in a taxi again. I waited a while and he left five minutes later. I followed him. The interesting thing is he has a wife, so I think this address isn't his regular address. Sure enough, I found him on the electoral roll, along with a Mrs Anne Levison, of the same address which is in Hackney, North-East London.

'That's where we are at, at the moment. I'll just confirm his wife lives there too, in Hackney. I don't think this will produce much more dirt, so I'm onto his financials next.'

'OK Michael. So we know he seems to have an illicit sex life, probably to be further examined if necessary. It confirms he's a cheat. Well, press on. Call me on Friday if you would. I'm getting married on Saturday, then off to the subcontinent, to bed-in you might say.

'By the way, we'd like you to come to the wedding. You will get an official invite tomorrow morning if the Post Office works well. Bring your other half if you have one. Bring the invitation card with you in case anyone asks who you are. No need to send it back.'

'You know, I might just do that Brandon. You have piqued my curiosity.'

'See you there, Michael.' I put down the receiver slowly, thinking, then called James.

James picked up. 'James here.'

'Hullo James. I see you are not at the office. Is this good news or good news?'

'Ah, Brandon, not sure. My appeal is this afternoon. I'll call you right after it. Getting excited about the big day?'

'I'm excited by being too busy to be excited about only that. It's part of my general excitement about life.'

'That's you all right,' James replied.

'James, our sleazy friend, you know he visits a house of pleasures, extra maritally it seems. I told you there was stuff on this guy. There's more to come. I'll talk to you later then.'

Julia called and asked me to pick her up, which I did, and off we went to the big furniture place in North London. We chose (well, Julia chose) all we needed for the marital home – enough to get us started. We were actually both very spartan in our choices and I readily agreed with the style and colour choices (I wasn't fussy and Julia was tasteful). Simplistic and minimalistic was the order of the day.

We had it all arranged for one person to deal with hanging curtains and fitting furniture together. After the wedding, considering the gifts which would probably come in bountiful supply, the two mothers would complete the whole house, ready for our return.

After an hour of traversing the store we sat down in the store café and ordered cappuccinos.

'Well,' Julia pronounced, 'that's that; so easy. We can relax and return to our temple and hit the ground running, as they say. I haven't asked you about our exact itinerary,' she beamed with elbow on the table, her head forward and knuckles under her chin, expecting almost anything but nothing surprising.

'My love, it's a bit like a buffet – we get to the 'table' (Thailand first), then we choose each trip from there. I have a list of venues and we can make it up as we go. We aren't going in their main holiday season so we should be ok. We can always just live like the natives. As long as they have chapattis and poppadoms you'll be ok. We'll carry our prayer mats on our backs, and use them to sleep on if it comes to it.'

'I knew you had it all in hand, my dear. I was told by Sidney to butt out of all this. This, he said, was a spiritual journey and creature comforts didn't necessarily come into it.'

'He's a wise man, my grandpa. You'll be pleased to know that before we climb the dizzy heights to nirvana, where corporeal sensations fade into insignificance, we are going to play the game we've been itching to play since we first kissed, and to accommodate that we are staying in the Grand Hotel for two nights…. no,no…. that's Bombay. What am I thinking? I changed the first destination to Thailand, Bangkok – forgotten the palace there.'

'Is that one in Bombay grand, as the name implies, or might it be a dive?' she teased.

'Well, according to the agent it is the best they have. As the British Raj hasn't long ended I presume the finest in British culture will be still intertwined with the best of Hindu luxury to give us the best of both worlds.'
'I feel like a virgin queen already, but not for long. I have it all planned, you might be glad to know. My mum and I had a talk. So we can enjoy ourselves with gay abandon.'

'I had a talk with your mum too,' I added. I was at it again.

'I know. She told me. That must have been embarrassing.'

'No, not really, or at least not until I asked her what exactly would transport you to ecstasy. I sat and listened and took mental notes. Some of it was rather eye-opening; very graphic.' I was acting the surprised and semi-shocked tyro.

'You didn't!' she gasped in mock but convincing surprise. 'What was it that was so embarrassing then?'

'Wait and find out'.

'I'm going to ask her.'

'Why not ask your dad. He's the other experienced one in all this.

'It's all sounding too pre-planned, too mechanical,' she said disappointingly. 'I'm not sure I can go through with it, especially with pictures of my wholesome mum and dad blown to pieces.'

'Well from what I've read and heard, especially from one of those Indian philosophers, Vatsayama, your mum and dad know nothing. I've done my homework. This chap wrote a book, The Karma Sutra. It sounds more like gymnastics to me.'

'You've been reading up on all this?' she asked a bit more seriously.

'Yes. Actually it comes under the heading of Philosophy. Now I know why you studied this depraved subject. I hope you are well versed.'

'What's it got to do with Philosophy?' she asked playfully.

'Beats me. Maybe it's for us to find out. It might just be the stairway to heaven. I think we must have a good session of meditation before we indulge in wanton earthly pleasures. Then we can accomplish what we will have come to do.'

We took hands and were out of there.

Back at the office, after shooting the breeze with the Execs, I went to my office with Veronica and dealt with the traffic that seemed to be mounting.

James called, right on cue. 'Hullo James. What's the verdict – dead or alive?

James sounded quite chirpy. 'Well, I gave it my all. The Appeal chappie listened to my case, just as I'd given it to Mr. Downs. He saw my point of view but decided to go with the suggestion that I be demoted for six months and review things then.

'It's a cop-out but I think he's got more to consider than just the justice as applied to me. It's political here. I decided to go with it. I'd already decided that anyhow, especially as we are probably going to land a bomb very soon with your expose of you know who. Then I'll have another go at restitution of rights,'

'Ok. It will have to wait until after my trip to the East though. See you on Saturday.'

'Ok. By the way, how's the wife doing with you at the office?'

'She's bedded in nicely, still learning the ropes. She'll be an asset.'

'Good. She certainly comes home perky. See you Saturday.'

I then made a call to the reporter whose card I had kept – Ivis Knightly.

'Ivis, its Brandon Waterman here. Do you remember....'
'Oh yes. How are you? I'm pleased you kept my card.'

'You passed the first test that day. I've been looking for a journalist who can write straight stuff and doesn't have an editor to please.'

'Oh good. Incidentally you passed my test too. I've been looking for a subject to write about who doesn't try and spin things and who has a decent cause. Politicians like that are hard to find and celebrities are very much full of themselves mostly.'

'Well Ivis, here's another test. Come to my wedding on Saturday and write what you see and show it to me and give me an outlet or a publication that is worthy of it. Are you up for that?'

'I sure am. Where and when exactly?'

I gave her the details and rang off.

I then collected Miss Julia McDonald from the station and we went back to the McDonald house for dinner where the McDonald family provided a pre-marital slap-up.

———————————

The next day, wedding eve you might call it, I had an early call at home from Tom at ITV. 'Can you and your legal man be here at eleven?' he asked.

Gavin was pre-primed for this particular day so I could answer him quickly. 'You are on Tom. Anything I need to know before we arrive?'

'No, my man, just turn up.'

'Ok, and the same applies to you tomorrow.'

'Are you ready for it Brandon?'

'Walk in the park, or should I say walk down the aisle. Well, actually it's not me that walks down the aisle, is it? But we are all systems go; another adventure beckons. It will be more onerous for YOU doing the filming than for me inside. All I have to do is smile, say 'yes', kiss the bride and shove off to the feast. Is it all set up your end?

Tom assured him it was. 'I will do a very tasteful and flattering job of it Brandon; something to show your kids. God knows what sprogs you two will turn out.'

'First things first. See you at eleven.'

Gladys Waterman fussed around me at the breakfast table. 'I suppose this is almost the last breakfast I'll make for you son,' she said.

'Yes, first love of my life. And it's one of my favourite events of the day. Julia will have to do instead I suppose.'

Just then Sidney strolled in and sat down at the table. 'Morning Brandon my boy. Anything exciting happening in your life today?'

'Yes Grandpa, but ask me the same question tomorrow.'

'What's happening tomorrow?' he asked offhandedly.

Gladys chimed in, 'he's swapping his mum for another woman,' she said as she put a full plate of eggs and bacon in front of me.

'Oh yes,' I answered. 'I forgot for a moment. Well I guess I'll get more attention myself now.' I rang my spoon on the edge of the plate.

'Is there anything I need to attend to at the office?' I asked Sidney. 'I'm off to ITV with Gavin at eleven.'

'Better wait until this afternoon I think. Nothing that important that won't wait, I'm sure. I take it you won't be at the big debate this evening then.'

'Yep, we will. Life goes on around all this. It's only for a few hours isn't it? Also I want to suss out that new chap, the solicitor.'

'So this is your idea of a stag party?' Sidney asked.

Then, having eaten my breakfast and scoffed my tea I announced I was off to see the missus and pick up Gavin.

I picked up the team, the McDonalds, and arrived at the TV studio right on the nail. We were led by Tom to a meeting room and were introduced to two lawyers for 'the defence' plus Tom, Vince, Barry Lancolm and Ken Crofton (the latter being one of the Execs we'd met the other day).

We chatted for a minute and helped ourselves to coffee and then sat at opposite sides of a table, spread our respective papers in front of us, and got down to it.

'Let me say from the outset,' began the first, Number One lawyer. 'We have had a lot of heat from the Royal Medico-Psychological Association (the head organisation of Psychiatry) on this matter, which is really only warning us that we better back off and do no more of this, in their words, 'biased and irresponsible broadcasting.'

He was a pleasant enough chap, about forty years old, dark curly hair with a straight hairline on a furrowed brow and rimless glasses perched on his nose.

The second lawyer, Number Two, added to this: 'we recognise that these are standard scare tactics but these guys have clout, in that they have big finances, and have general Government lobby power.'

'Ok, understood,' Gavin replied quickly. 'It all boils down to whether they have a case or not. What do you think?'

Lawyer Number One answered. 'The laws of libel can be a bit complex. It IS libel- cum-defamation they are claiming. First of all the facts presented have to be true, which can get into a lot of argument. Then there is the matter of whether or not an honest opinion has been expressed. In this case that is Mr. Waterman's, and not necessarily that of the station. Thirdly is the matter in the public interest? This is our strongest suit here as this could easily be considered 'in the public interest."

Gavin responded. 'Well, being in the public interest it is incumbent on the station to present a balanced presentation of the facts, which has not necessarily been done at this point.'

I entered the fray at this point. 'Well, that is easily dealt with. The easiest way to deal with this is to offer to do a guided tour of one of their establishments, filming as we go, asking questions, observing all their treatments, having their experts present their 'defence'. Have them on the show to correct any of our facts presented. Surely if they do not wish to be defamed they should jump at the opportunity. Silence on their part would be condemnatory.'

Gavin re-iterated, 'this would be the only way they could defend their accusation of libel. It is interesting that they didn't request to come on and refute whatever offends them.'

Julia was going to have her say. 'We have these Psychiatric victim cases. You have to see these to believe them. If these are not in the public interest I don't know what is. This 'professional' organisation should produce evidence of any good results, any cured patients, if they have any. The public in general don't KNOW what goes on.'

Lawyer Number One responded. 'This is all good TV but, and you can confirm this here, Ken,' he said nodding at Ken, 'the station is not willing to risk any kind of injunction on future programming. It doesn't want to risk future revenue by being restricted in any way, not to mention the cost and time involved.'

This was quite missing the point that future revenue WOULD be missed by backing off popular/controversial programs.

'Well, fine,' Gavin put in. 'let's bring it to the point where there will be no risk. And they can only seek an injunction on THIS subject, not all your programming.

He continued more forthrightly. 'Look, they have to show what is libellous. They cannot claim this if given an opportunity to state their case. I would say that you should respond robustly and call their bluff and at least get to the stage, if it ever would, that they have had a go at rebalancing the picture and have presented a case that disproves the presentation. This won't cost you more than a letter and maybe a meeting, in the first instance.

'I can see they have rattled you here. Your top brass have to decide if they are up for being champions of the underdog, a voice for victims of injustice and maltreatment, a public forum for opinions, and stand by this. It's Brandon here that should be sued if anyone is to be sued. And he very well may be. In fact it has begun in the newspapers and BBC already. He's the originator, the accuser, the presenter of facts and any opinion on them.'

He was holding court here now. Julia was thinking that her normally unevangelical dad was in danger of becoming a second Brandon. Then she concluded that this is how he must be in court, where she'd never seen him.

The lawyers were looking at Ken and Barry, who were a bit speechless.

Gavin rammed it in. 'If I were Brandon's lawyer defending him on this libel matter I would, strictly on a legal basis, ask him if he felt strongly enough about this matter and if he did (which he does), advise him to proceed as I suggested, in the full knowledge that it is up to the defendants to show proof of their case. It's a free country and we have free speech. You didn't broadcast a rant or an inflammatory diatribe, after all.'

Ken decided to come in here. 'You are right. I will speak to Alistair, our MD. I take it you gentlemen, (talking to the two lawyers) are happy with what Gavin has said?' They gestured as if to say, 'it's up to you chaps'.

Gavin started to rise and told them all, 'I've had a number of these cases, certainly enough to know how it goes. I'll work with you all the way. He pulled out one of his cards and presented it to lawyer Number One.

We broke up and went to the car park. Tom and Vince walked with us. Tom said, 'Our Legals are under restraints, aren't they? They are in-house and really have a strict regime to follow, its plain.'

'Yep', said Gavin. 'We'll wait and see.'

I said, 'I met this chap Alistair before. He is largely a bureaucrat, not an entertainment provider, and certainly not a public information server, in a broad sense. Let's hope Ken and his henchmen can inveigh upon him.

'If they don't play ball we will change tack and up the attack and take them on in the courts ourselves. This is too big to let slide.'

Julia cosied up to me in support. Tom said, 'I see the whole picture here now. I'm going to rattle a few cages in there too and damn the consequences.' He looked at Vince and looked for agreement. 'Don't you think, Vince, we have enough kudos in this business to throw our weight around. I mean top Public Information Documentary awards in the last five years. We'd be a loss to the network.'

Vince, usually the quiet one in the background, agreed. 'I'm with you mate. We'd be snapped up somewhere, even if not in this country. More jocularly, why don't we set up our own TV station?'

'That's what we may need in the end,' I agreed, just realising how this would aid our project.

Gavin had been quiet through all of this. 'I am witnessing the birth of a modern day Renaissance.'

Lots of agreement there. We also agreed to meet again tomorrow at the Church and have a day of celebrations and no 'shop talk'.

Back to the Office we went (for lunch and pre-wedding drinks, unbeknownst to us).

I told Gavin I wanted to show him something at the Office.
'Oh yes?' he queried. 'This is mysterious.' He looked at Julia who just smiled unknowingly and shrugged her shoulders.

Julia also had HER driving test that afternoon.

When we got to the Office we walked in the front door and the place seemed empty. There was no one on Reception nor in any of the offices.

'What's this Julia?' I asked. 'Has everyone gone on a long weekend?'

They all opened the door to the main classroom and were met with a veritable cacophony of cheers. Gathered around considerably laden food tables were all the staff and all the pupils, and many parents. Everyone had a glass in hand. Ira came forward and signalled 'hush' and she said to all the crowd, 'here's to Brandon and Julia. May they have the happiest of lives together.'

Glasses were raised and more cheers rang out. Julia gave Ira a huge hug, as did I. We all mingled and ate ourselves silly.

After the celebrations I took Gavin off to show him the mystery. We walked into an office which had a sign on the door which said, 'Legal Department, Mr Gavin McDonald, JD'.

We entered and I showed Gavin to his seat behind a sizeable desk. Gavin looked at me, somewhat bemused.

'Yours, your honour. You are officially recognised as our lawyer and you should have a nice office to conduct affairs from. There's a desk over there for a secretary.' pointing to the right corner of the room.

Gavin sat down and smiled. 'You hinted at this, Brandon, a little time ago. Why didn't I connect the dots?' He stood and shook my hand. 'Thank you my boy. It will be a privilege. Now I have two offices. I think retirement is even further away now.'

Julia came in and gave her dad a hug. 'Well, welcome to the team, officially; can't have you working out of our lounge room anymore.'

'We must be off,' she said, looking at me. 'I have my test in half an hour. We'll drop you home on the way, Dad. The test is in Highgate.'

We two lovebirds left in our little Ford and dropped Gavin off and, Julia driving, hightailed it to the Test Station. There she went off with a rather serious looking old chap while I went to a coffee shop next door and spent half an hour reading through a few newspapers there. For once I was not on the front or any other pages.

Julia returned to the Test Centre after the test and went into some office to conclude the paperwork. Then she met me by arrangement in the coffee shop. I was sitting there with papers strewn around me. She hustled into a seat beside me, all fizzing with excitement. I broke out of my concentration and turned to her, smiled and gave her a big kiss and hug. 'Well done, my love. I knew you'd do it.'
'Welcome to the racing drivers club.' I said. 'Do you want a coffee and a celebratory cake?'

We had a quick celebration and then returned to the car, ripped off the L-plates, and Julia drove us to the Watermans for our wedding eve dinner there before going off to the debate.

CHAPTER TWENTY FIVE

The Sunday newspapers were full of the wedding of the year. They were all fairly consistent in their reporting of events, mainly because Tom had filmed the service and Jim Naylor had supplied the copy and distributed his version of events to the waiting gaggle of media.

One broadsheet just had to press on with the negative – 'Teenagers too Young to Marry?' One other ran the headline: 'Waterman Feathers His Nest Again'.

It has to be said that the majority of reports of a truly happy and uplifting event were pretty well reproductions of the official ones issued.

The wedding ceremony was a gloriously aesthetic event. It was laced with the religious formality and the unorthodox.

The unorthodox was in the form of me speaking to those congregated. My public speaking prowess was at its best I reckon.

It was impromptu. It made the whole gathering more inclusive. The gathering comprised not only family, and work colleagues (close friends), but anyone we had touched in our lives from James Hopkins to TV studio personnel, the odd reporter, my PI, our neighbours, the debating society, even my old Head Master. And nearly all turned up. Guess who didn't.

I thanked them all for their attendance and well wishes. I humorously described how Julia and I had met and hit it off, how we'd become kindred spirits and instantly a joint venture.

The capper was my description of Julia, delivered direct to her, holding her, face to face and for all to see. I'd described her totally clean and sunshine presence, her depth of perception of my own viewpoints and goals, her total lack of tribalism whilst being a seductive star of femininity.

I openly and unashamedly pledged, (on top of the normal wedding service pledges) to devote my life to her happiness and accomplishment, to protect her from all-comers, and all of this each day anew.

The assembled guests were in raptures and gave us a standing ovation.

Not to be outdone, Julia unexpectedly gave her side of this. She said she knew, from our first meeting that I was not an ordinary man. She then went on to quickly describe being swept off her feet, and that she too would do anything to strengthen and support my endeavours. She kissed me fervently (just short of passionately in that religious surrounding).

This brought the house (of God) down. What was the Reception going to be like?

The TV cameras were whirring outside, the news media were snapping photographs and were given Jim Naylor's report of the events inside the church (with photographs to follow later in the day).

Tom's filming of events was to be edited for ITV news only.

Throughout the Reception, which was nearly all of the church gathering, Julia and I spoke to each and every one of the guests.

The speeches and toasts were a hilarious affair. Sidney, as best man described my life and how he had predicted big things for me from an early age, and how he wondered how his grandson, too busy with his chosen path in life, was ever going to approach the rather fraught area of choosing a mate and conducting a sexual relationship, but that he need not have worried, as he accomplished this with the same amount of equanimity as everything else in his life.

I, after describing all my friends and associates as being special people, then went on to relate the many humorous anecdotes about the adventures of Julia and I, especially in relation to our spiritual plane of sexuality, which had to all extents and purposes consummated our relationship outside of wedlock. I presented our forthcoming honeymoon as an extension of this. I tried to get the guests to picture us standing on a mountainous landscape, hand in hand, the wind blowing in our hair and being transported to another world, spirits mingling in the ethos, 'forsaking' all earthly pleasures.

Julia spoke more of reality, and how she could assure them all that 'this man' was absolutely normal, and while the spiritual played a big part in it all I responded very normally to being kissed and embraced, and no doubt ...... she got a fit of the giggles, and to stave off the end of the sentence the whole gathering saved her the trouble by cheering.

The guests had a feast of all things bright and joyous and went home delighted.

Julia and I went back to the McDonalds and collected our 'things' and were driven to the airport by Gavin, along with Delia and the Waterman seniors.

Another adventure began for we magical couple. This was the first time I had taken time away from 'the business'. I was sure it would all function well in my absence.

CHAPTER TWENTY SIX

As was her custom Minister McAdam started her day with a quick flash through the assembled work on her desk and then sat back and skimmed through the few newspapers right in front of her, accompanied by her morning liquid pleasure.

She couldn't help noticing the Waterman wedding all over the first inside pages. There was Brandon, centre stage with his stunning wife and her radiant visage. He even does that with panache, she thought, with a smile on her face. Love so young.

She ignored the barbs and concentrated on the more aesthetic. It all reminded her of her own day many years ago. Some people are just envious.

She was developing an admiration for this young maverick. Is he as disruptive as they say, she wondered? If he is, isn't it perhaps a necessary disruption? She put down the papers, finished her coffee and started in on her 'in' tray. She dealt with a few items and then came to a report on the Hopkins Tribunal.

Her interest piqued. She read and discovered this James Hopkins had been demoted even after appeal. She decided to do some more snooping. She asked Alison to arrange for Hopkins to come to her office. I must hear the other side of this, to be fair. 'While you are at it Alison get Mr. Ben Downs up here at the same time.'

By the end of the day the two summoned were seated at the Minister's desk. 'Now, Mr. Hopkins, I have become very interested in this fellow Brandon Waterman. You have had quite an interaction with him I understand, to your detriment it seems.' She waved her copy of the Tribunal in the air. 'I believe you have seen this.' Her manner was reasonably polite.

'Explain to me, from your viewpoint, how we have come to this.'

James couldn't believe his luck. So he gave her chapter and verse, quite matter-of-factly, not as a hurt victim of injustice. By the time he had finished, some ten minutes later, McAdam had a completely different view. He had left out the gory details of Levison's extra-marital doings. He'd keep this up his sleeve as an ace to play when the time was needed.

Meanwhile Ben Downs was shifting about in his chair wishing he could vanish, more so when McAdam turned her attention to him. 'Mr. Downs, are you cognisant of all this?'

'Ah, um, y.yes, most of it, Minister.' He spluttered. 'I thought it best to, um, allow the Tribunal to do its job.'

'Well then,' replied McAdam, 'on what basis was the appeal decision accepted?' She wasn't accusative but it was asked as if there was a good reason for it. She was a sharp operator. She not only noted responses, but observed body language and other signs of discomfort or equivocation with the questions. Downs was unsettled and his brow was sweaty, whereas Hopkins was calm and exact with his answers to her questions.

'You have been demoted Mr. Hopkins. How does this sit with you?'

'Not well, I assure you, but I am doing my own research on what may lay behind this summary response to my attempts to improve the Education process in our schools. I think the Tribunal procedure was flawed. Now that it is over and I can do no more about it in the Department by way of procedure, I will 'take my medicine' and resurrect my reputation by effective action.'

'You may go Mr. Downs. I may need you later,' she said, looking at this unfortunate man in the straightjacket of his own nature. He left.

'I have to tell you Mr. Hopkins, I'm not entirely happy with this outcome. It does have an element of Kangaroo Court about it, if you see what I mean. Is that why you feel inclined to take it further on your own back? Mind you I don't understand what you intend to do?'

'I'd rather not say at this point Minister,' he answered. 'Nothing extreme I assure you. My friend Brandon has suffered as a result of this. As you know his sole intention is to share out his discoveries on the educative process, and this has set him back in this quest. He's played it by the book since he registered his establishment legally and doesn't deserve to be knocked for a great deal of success. Perhaps I could have played it differently, but how I don't know. Brandon is also being proactive in trying to recover his own situation, you know.'

'Alright,' she acknowledged. 'I look forward to the next chapter in this tale. Somehow I don't think I have heard the last of it. Keep me informed would you?'

Hopkins rose and replied, 'I certainly will Minister. Thankyou for your time.'

PART THREE

CHAPTER ONE

I had decided that, because Thailand contained the largest concentration of Buddhists (ninety five percent of the population), we would go there first. It seemed that though there were two or three 'versions' of Buddhism, essentially they weren't that different from each other, each retaining the basic wisdom of Buddha.

We had learned that one of the early strongholds of Buddhism was in Tibet, which was, at this time, under invasion by the Chinese. Monasteries were being closed down and followers, including the Dalai Lama, were fleeing to Northern India.

On the plane, Julia was reading from one of many books on Eastern Religions she'd borrowed from the library. She came out of her rapt attention to say to me, 'it says here that Buddhism is the belief and practice of elevating one from the state of human suffering and craving of physical acquisition and pleasure. The emphasis is on 'craving'. Are you craving physical pleasure, my love?'

I bit. 'I think you are paraphrasing, aren't you, or even making somewhat less of a noble religion that has been adopted by at least half of the human race and over a period of some few thousand years.'

'Well,' she responded, 'that half of the human race has multiplied, one might argue indiscriminately, given the existing populations of Asia. Is that not rather proof of craving or compulsive sexual practice?'

'I see,' I replied. 'Well let's just see if it catches on when we get there.' I looked at her saucily. 'What else does it say there?'

More matter-of-factly Julia continued. 'Well, Buddha, it seems, set out from a rather enclosed upper class community to see the world and decided that humanity was suffering, not just from the hardship of poverty but in his physical cravings and being stuck in the life/death cycle. His aim was to develop the means to rise above all of this transient human pursuit to a separation from suffering, which is basically Nirvana. More EXACTLY what that is I'm not sure, but he spoke of re-incarnation, which means leaving one body and coming back for another go in another body.'

She continued. 'There is a lot of emphasis on developing mental strength and fibre, which I assume translates to moral fortitude, clean living, you know, in much the same way as the Ten Commandments of Christianity advises. They do have some similar precepts, like 'do not kill or steal' and others.

I said, 'well not much wrong with that, I'd say. You reap what you sew. There are consequences for sinning, mentally. I don't like the word 'sinning'. I'd rather call it doing harm, against one's principles or agreements. At least there seems no attempt to introduce God's laws or judgement. It puts the onus on the individual to examine his behaviour and rectify it.

'The practice in the Catholic Church of confession may be a good idea but not if you can glibly just accept a priest's forgiveness, on behalf of God. Somehow that bit of it is lacking. Owning up is one thing, rectifying it is another. And you could, say, kill someone (outside of war), go and confess and be forgiven and, what, be all right then?

'From my meditation experiences I can easily conceive of separation of consciousness from the body and hence re-incarnation and the view that craving physical satisfactions leads to suffering or degradation, and that the way out of all this is a matter of mental strength, wisdom, measured decisions and all that.'

Julia took over for a moment. 'Yes, our society is steeped in a sort of 'eat drink and be merry for tomorrow we die' attitude. The demands of the body, and its upkeep, and the propagation of the race, is all consuming if there is nothing else. Basically I suppose Religion is an attempt to improve on the largely physical emphasis and graduate to a higher state, or at least enter some ethical behaviour into it all.'

I continued. 'Well put, my love. Well, at the very least we need to rid our societies of a myriad of incorrect information and practice, like Psychiatry, which only hammers the nails into the coffin, literally. We are onto this. But further, we need an improved Psychology. As I was saying about my meditation experiences, there is quite an aesthetic level to be reached, which I would assume to be part of the road to enlightenment, as the Buddhists put it. We will see if this is easily attainable by most.'

Julia added, 'I suppose I haven't taken this meditation much further than an excuse to imbibe chapattis. When we went to that temple I didn't really 'get with the program'. I will attack this seriously on our trip, promise.'

'Well, there's your answer to your question about craving. When I'm meditating I don't think of such pleasures at all, they being supplanted by higher mental activity. Don't worry it won't be a loveless relationship.'

She smiled and came straight back with, 'did it ever occur to you that sex between us might transport us to this same plateau?'

'Now there's another thought. We may get into a technology of spiritual sex, and that will bypass the need to meditate.'

We cuddled, as only we could.

The journey took ages but ended by re-entry into normal atmosphere, in fact quite a hot blast of atmosphere on alighting at Bangkok airport. Down the mobile stairs onto the tarmac and under the noisy wing saw us into the airport building which was every bit as hot as outside.

I (Sidney, really) had changed our hotel bookings slightly, to accommodate Thailand. Two nights at the Rattanakosin Hotel, the rest to be played by ear, before going on to Bombay.

We had flown into 'tomorrow' in a way – six hours ahead of London, so it was actually afternoon of the following day. This put our body clocks about half a day out of sync. However, though we'd only slept a few hours on the plane we were wide awake and quite content to 'hit the town', and flake later. We were abuzz. We dropped our luggage in our assigned room and began being tourists.

The city was a bustling affair, just like other cities, with a few local nuances, like rickshaw travel for instance and lots of bicycles, which seemed to mesh somehow rather chaotically with the vehicle traffic. It all functioned.

We noticed the immediate replacement of churches with temples. We wasted no time going into one of them, a big one. We two newlyweds were told that this was Wat Saket (Temple of the Golden Mount). It was pretty much according to our picture of such temples – lots of gold trimming to white walls and some red as well. A number of steeples, as in Europe, but different 'body shape'.

We joined a tour of the place which took us via a spiral climb to the top, some few hundred feet high, from where we had a spectacular view of this westernising city, marked by growing commercial skyscrapers.

This was all very interesting but what we really wanted to see was what went on inside the 'auditorium'.

When down below, in the worshipping area, the guide gave us a 'do and don't' advice on entering this space. For a start we had to remove our shoes which then progressed to a heightened consideration for the reverence of the place. Luckily we were well covered – no bare legs or bare shoulders. Don't point, don't talk loudly, don't touch images of Buddha or any monks themselves. Bow suitably to monks and don't stand over them if they are sitting; sit to talk to them.

I said to Julia, 'let's sit and watch what goes on. Meditate if you like. Sorry, no delicacies.'

'I feel like I am about to become holy or something,' she said.

I had been struck by the relative noise in the otherwise quietness of the space, and the rituals of it all. There were images of Buddha, both two dimensional and three dimensional. The noise came from various chantings, from perhaps a hundred people. And there were mumbled prayers. It seemed incongruous to meditate with all that going on as a group.

I couldn't get into it so I just looked around and observed the goings-on. Julia had her eyes closed but seemed to be nodding off. I nudged her to test her. She woke up with a start.

'You are dreaming your way to Nirvana,' I whispered.

'It's all done by hypnotism,' she replied.

'Let's go,' I suggested. And we left.

'In a lot of ways, it's much the same as the quietude of a cathedral, with an undertone of humming,' I remarked.

'Mmm,' she agreed. 'Can you do this on not very much sleep, or even while being hungry? she asked.

'I see where you are going with this,' I answered. So we strolled around the city to wear ourselves out whilst getting the lay of the land. We had a meal in the Thai version of a Joe's Café, which was very much workingman's but no eggs, bacon or mixed grills. We then went back to the hotel.

Back in our room we were approaching the moment of reckoning. Would it be a magical consummation or a damp squib topped off with crashing out?

We need not have wondered if indeed we did at all. We embraced and matter-of-factly undressed each other in the bathroom, with a hint of self-consciousness, and entered the prepared spa bath and took it in turns to wash each other provocatively by which time our weariness had long subsided and was replaced with much excitement, almost as if we had done this many times before. You could call it a baptism.

'My mum prepared me for this event. I mean I am fitted,' she explained.

'I know that, my love. I've been told.'

We spent many moments looking into each other's eyes whilst exploring each other's bodies. It was building to the inevitable conclusion, which, when it came, lingered quite a while and the two of us were even more enmeshed in the physical pleasure and the aesthetics between us. We sat entwined in each other's arms and legs for many minutes. No words needed to be spoken.

Slowly we came down from on high and towelled each other off which only served to re-ignite our ardour which transferred us to the cool sheets of the large bed where ecstasy beckoned again.

This time it ended with us enfolded in more comfort. Consciousness quickly slipped away.

———————————

The sunlight slipping through the wooden-slatted blinds slowly beckoned us out of our slumber.

'Good morning Mrs Waterman,' I softly intoned.

'Who is this man in my bed?' came the response. 'Am I dreaming?'

'The meditation worked then,' I said, as a realisation.

'Good morning Mr Waterman. No, I believe this is reality.'

We lay together for quite some time, dropping in and out of slumber until the day began to summon us to adventure mode.

'Do they serve breakfast in bed?' Julia asked. 'And do they serve Uncle Toby's oats and tea and toast?'

At that exact moment there was a knock at the door. I arose and slipped on my new silk dressing gown and went to the door. There on a trolley, with all the bells and whistles, was exactly what the good Julia ordered. I wheeled it in and up to the edge of the bed. 'I didn't hear what you said princess. What was it you fancied for breakfast?'

She sat up, totally as nature had made her and looked at the trolley. 'You wonderful man. Can you keep this up for a lifetime?'

'Longer,' I replied.

We ate our British petit dejeuner, dressed and sought out the local expert on Buddhist 'gurus'. He happened to be an expat who'd made his life in Thailand and, more exactly, in the tourist trade. However he did cater for the more esoteric of the non-touristy class, such as we two wisdom seekers.

This gentleman, with the unlikely double-barrelled surname of Walkendon-Smythe, Gerald Walkendon-Smythe, volunteered to hire himself out for a modest fee, to take us into the hinterland and show us around the holy sites. He had vast knowledge of the Thai culture, having immersed himself in it since university days in Wales. In fact he was a Buddhist, having denounced Christianity after a childhood of having it enforced upon him by a rather zealous family.

Gerald was slight in stature, with a thin face, dark eyebrows, and a dark goatee beard. He wore his hair straight back, tight to his head and in a ponytail. He dressed more like the locals and with the sandals and all. He may have expected to gain slant eyes and a swarthy complexion some day soon.

We met in a tea house a few miles from the hotel. We explained what we were about which was when Gerald ('call me Smithy') offered his services. He was on a not dissimilar path but rather stalled. This little expedition we agreed on was right up his alley. He'd have done it for nothing.

But today he was booked out with a few tours for normal tourists, so he arranged for us to be taken to a somewhat reclusive monastery on the outskirts of Bangkok as a more likely place to gain access to a 'guru' who might better enlighten us on the practices of the religion.

We arranged to meet early the next day at our hotel for the main expedition, but in the meantime, today, were off on our first day's adventure. In fact we decided to hire bicycles and not be guided. Armed with a good set of directions, and decked out in long shorts for me and sarong for Julia, and long shirt sleeves, wide-brimmed hats and sunnies, we set out.We were to get a better-than-tourist experience of the place. As crowded bustling inner city gradually gave way to more suburban and eventually semi-rural landscape we became less occupied with the perils of cycling in random traffic conditions and more able to look about and appreciate the rather peaceful and quite beautiful landscape.

Passers-by acknowledged us and we saw, even though largely poor, a smiley population, living in what seemed a fairly ordered and simple manner.

Temples dotted the place. We rested under a tree outside one of these. I remarked, 'this is not like the outskirts of London or Surrey or Essex is it? I am immediately struck by the lack of hectic energy we are used to.'

'It's almost as if the quietude of the inner temples is transposed to the general environment. That's possibly a good thing from their religion. By the way, do you think we've missed the chance for a cuppa?'

'I think we are close-ish to this monastery. I vote we move on and get to our destination. Can you hang on my love?'

'Of course. I'm a woman. Bearing up is what we do, isn't it.'

With that I pecked her on the cheek and got up. 'I knew you'd see it my way.'

We rode on and soon found ourselves directed along a lushly bordered dirt road which soon broke out into beautifully landscaped open area with timber buildings dotted about among a panoply of shrubs and lawns.

We made our way to what seemed the central 'Reception', from which emerged an old white-clad figure smiling in greeting, as if expecting us.

And so he was. He bowed in greeting and we guests bowed in return.

We were beckoned inside the building into modest surroundings – a series of slatted-walled rooms decked out in a semi western office set-up with a few desks and more eastern style cane chairs. The windows were without glass but covered in cane roll-up blinds. We signed a scrappy visitor's book. It was quiet; no words had been spoken at this point.

Then a young Thai woman entered and introduced herself and the Abbot, or head monk. We all bowed again. She was Achara (which means 'pretty angel') and he was called Tanawat (which means 'knowledge').

Achara said, 'Smithy send us many people. We explain Buddhism. Smithy, he say all about you. We are help you understand. Khun Tanawat show you, I explain. We serve you first tea.'

Julia smiled broadly. She was well and truly picking up the formal manners of this culture. 'Thank you so much, Khun Achara.' She'd learned the address from Smithy.

I was watching Tanawat closely while the ladies talked over tea. At first glance he looked like an old man past his best. But as he spoke to Achara in Thai, during translation, he noticed this man under the polite exterior, was as sharp as a razor. There was real life in those eyes, and when he spoke there was presence.

After tea Achara showed us around the whole establishment. There was one central temple space which was vacated at this time of eating. The other areas were a mixture of accommodation, kitchen, dining room, bathrooms, special function areas, and one enormous library space which served also as a classroom of sorts.

When we arrived at the dining room we were invited to lunch with Tanawat. The meal was rather frugal – rice and chicken and peppers.

The whole atmosphere pretty well mirrored that of Wat Saket, in Bangkok, which was subdued yet busy. Everyone was on some sort of business. No one loitered or idly chatted or lay about. There was ambience, and though austerity was the general theme it was not solemn.

We were led into the temple or worship area. Achara explained to us the basic tenets of meditation, along with the pathways to enlightenment. Tanawat conducted the indoctrination for real, through Achara. His hand motions and expressions were ingenious, especially for description of rather mental activity. He gestured whilst she explained.

We got down to it in earnest, along with at least thirty other acolytes.

I understood the procedure readily and re-iterated to Julia, in my own words, what was being told. 'The idea is not to just let the mind wander nor try not to think, if you see what I mean.'

'I see, your holiness,' she replied. 'Just be in the moment.'

This was all very much along the lines of our meeting at the Hindu temple in West London, which seemed ages ago now.

After about half an hour Tanawat interrupted the period to enquire as to our experience.

Julia had cottoned onto the idea. 'Well I was really comfortable and became hyper aware, really aware, of the now. It wasn't a matter of not being bored but just happy to be comfortable with nothing going on in my head.'

'Me too' I agreed.

We carried on for an extended period and we both experienced a repeat of the same.

'I could do this indefinitely,' Julia told Anchara.

Tanawat was impressed. He told us that our response was extremely unusual for beginners, especially among western visitors.

We drank tea again in the Reception offices and discussed the various tenets of Buddhism and exchanged experiences from our vastly different worlds. It would have been easier without the need for translation but we filled an hour of discussion in no time. The bottom line seemed to be that it is better to have a spiritual peace than to hanker after lots of possessions and pleasure-only pursuits, beyond necessary basic physical survival. This determined a better future as a society and for a desired eternity. The virtues, not really dissimilar to Christianity, were much sought after.

We were far away from the world of newspapers, television, cinemas, hurry-scurry tooth and claw existence.

It was soon time to return to the city. I thanked our two hosts and re-iterated our mission to incorporate this wisdom in our quest for a better life on this Earth.

Tanawat had told us he was impressed with our Education advances and requested a copy of our texts on the subject, to be applied to his students when studying their own scriptures. He'd noticed that some studied under sufferance and were inclined to give up or substitute their own 'understanding' to deal with the pain of learning.

We rode serenely back to our base, totally observant of our surroundings and chatting about the day's experiences. We took a number of breaks to just sit together and observe life around us.

As we gradually approached the city, with the sun going down, we began to notice the hubbub that existed when people are crowded closer together; the strain put on the population and the many less fortunate that seem to exist in any society. The West had encroached on this seemingly more backward country, to seduce them into not just the advances but the more decadent side of it all.

But the religion was definitely a big cohesive factor, though it seemed to me that for many, as in Christianity, it was a robotic exercise.

After returning our bicycles we went straight to the dining room of our hotel and after a hearty dinner, retired to our room, pleasantly weary.

We sat out on the veranda looking over the sparkling city below.

I turned to Julia and took her hand and softly asked, 'how is married life, my love?'

'It's as if we've been at it for ages – very natural. To think that a few years ago I was a somewhat drifting Philosophy student, feeling my way to who knows where. Now here I am married to a marvellous man, on a joint quest to seek the wisdom of the East in order to change the world.'

'Do you think it was your destiny?' I asked.

'Hmm, destiny? I don't think there is a destiny, that is, pre-determined; like fate. I think one is either seeking it, even if not necessarily proactively, or one is not – going along with the tide. Destiny surely implies going to a specific destination. I wasn't particularly destined back then, but I was looking. And there you were. Destiny raised its lovely head. Right then I was destined. What about you?'

I moved closer to her and put my arm around her, and thought for a moment. 'The very moment I decided to actively help my school and no longer be a bored pupil was the moment I enacted my goal, not quite so expansively at first but I was on my way. Before that I was accumulating information and observing life and becoming more and more disenchanted with the general process. I suppose I was on my path to my destiny, my goal, my calling, whatever. I had woken up.'

Julia looked at me more seriously and added, 'Do you know, I believe the vast majority of the population are NOT awake – they are sleepwalking to a not-too-satisfactory place. It's all very well for all these people here in Thailand, or probably India, China and the rest too, to be in the moment and live righteous lives, or for Christians to worship their God and beg forgiveness for their shortcomings, but it seems also an avoidance of real problems that exist worldwide. It's only part of the solution.'

We were looking up at the sky. I said, 'precisely.' I added, 'look up at all those heavenly bodies. We see them as a vast bunch of big rocks, some on fire, some not. We don't normally see them as possible civilisations. Apart from our imaginative alien stories I wonder if there are places of equal turmoil to Earth, or even places of ideal society.

'If you were from one of the latter and had ventured upon Earth, what would you see?' We had visited this concept before.

Julia sighed. 'Whoa, quite a mental institution I would think. Not to be too hard on our fellow human beings, but a collection of discordant nations, the lead nations being involved in an arms race and capable of destroying the planet, already having had a good go at it in the last forty odd years.'

I continued the narrative. 'They would see a planet of plenty but among which the majority living in poverty and ignorance. They couldn't help notice the advances in science and medicine but be dismayed at the dearth of knowledge about themselves, and like we did, would have discovered the 'knowledge' that had been dreamed up instead.

Julia's turn. 'And they would see that even among the apparently less endangered societies, like our own, quite a bit of economic duress, which is only to say that Economics and Government are rather lacking subjects. Do you happen to know how many countries are actually financially solvent? Not many I would think. Maybe Economics is just a misused tool for the avaricious or even malevolent.'

'And,' I added, 'we haven't even considered the possible fallout of our mad rush to consume, discard, burn things, with an ever-increasing population.'

Julia nudged me and pecked me on the cheek. 'We'll talk ourselves into a dismal mood soon. On the bright side, I believe the decided majority of people on this earth, though many quite under the cosh and uncivilised, are good people. Some are bad. A lot of the good guys are just ignorant. Our would-be visitors from outer galaxies would have noticed that too.'

I picked up on this upturn. 'So let's go find these extra-terrestrials and get them to be our guides.'

'Damn right,' she agreed. 'Maybe it's all down to us and a few other right-minded individuals.'

We retired to the honeymoon bath and washed the day's sweat and dirt from our bodies, totally at home in our newfound intimacy. Not a dot of our more intimate sexual pleasure had subsided. We enjoyed each other until fatigue allowed no more. And may it last forever, we both thought.

The next day we set out with Smithy, our conveniently acquired guide, and headed for the northerly expanses of our host nation.

Smithy proved to be a knowledgeable and humorous leader of the expedition. He took us through many tropical villages and towns, all laced with beautiful and not so beautiful temples, all practising variations on a theme of the Buddhist religion.

We meditated for a few hours each day and discussed the good and bad of life with many head monks and others. Smithy was not used to quite in-depth tourism but he added to his catalogue, for sure.

We three travellers argued the point deep into most nights and Smithy became the receiver rather than the provider. He had no chance with us two adventurers. Like many before him he was smitten with our precocity and depth of understanding of the world.

He hadn't heard of my reputation as he read very few publications from the old country. Later he was to read up on recent past copies he acquired from the British Embassy and keep tabs on his special friends (which we had become by this).

Smithy had half a mind to return to England and join us. By the end of our sojourn it was more than half a mind. He had lots of food for thought.

Though only a matter of a few weeks spent in Thailand we acquired a good handle on Buddhist practice and life and had observed closely normal life outside the temples and monasteries, actually staying in normal housing and eating with and talking to locals.

On our final night in Bangkok we were guests of honour at Smithy's place in the suburbs of the city. We sampled the local rice wine and moonshine. 'We have only ever had the odd glass of table wine before this. One glass of this has surpassed that for inebriative effect,' I gasped after downing the glass as if it were wine, with increased wincing.

Julia was more careful and sipped it slowly, she not caring really for the taste, let alone the effect.

'I'm used to it,' Smithy said offhandedly. 'I can't say it has much more than a soporific influence on me. We all have it in this house at dinner.' 'All' meant his western housemates and their female visitors.

'Don't you sleep well Smithy?' Julia asked.

'I sleep fine Julia,' he said, having taken her question a little more as a criticism than a joke, which opened up the subject of alcoholism, or any other dependency.

'I like the effect. It mellows me out after a hard day's work.'

So I asked him 'I can see that it would. But you could just as easily do without it, yes?' I asked this as if expecting him to agree so as not to seem critical.

Smithy came back with his rejoinder. 'I suppose you two have written a book too on the subject of dependency, along the lines of dependency on Religion.'

Smithy had become a little snide here. What nerve had been touched?

I smiled at our friend. 'No such thing. My view is that anything goes in moderation. Beyond that, it becomes negative. No criticism is meant but I'd say you have your own criticism of yourself, no?'

'I did bite a bit there, didn't I? I guess you are right. I do wonder if I drink too much, too often.'

Julia put her hand on his and said softly, 'you are a good man Smithy. It's an ethical question to ask. Do you ever get an answer?'

'I usually don't listen too well,' he laughed. 'Now that you have raised the subject' …. He paused in thought, then, 'yes, I think I do.'

I said, 'do you know, I heard a few definitions of alcoholism: one was to the effect that an alcoholic cannot face an empty glass. Another was, can't have only one drink. At first glance this seems severe, but the inference is that, like a seduction, one can't or won't discipline oneself.

'At the end of the day alcohol, opium, ether, marijuana, arsenic, coffee are all poisons. It depends how much you take for it to be a poison. A cup or two of coffee is a stimulant, ten to twenty cups is closer to a poison. A minuscule drop of arsenic is a stimulant, a bit more is a drug, and one eye-drop or less is a poison.'

Smithy was listening. He was being lectured but not lectured to.

'Either way,' I continued, 'they are not nutritious and are antipathetic to the system. You, as you have described yourself, are somewhere between a drug and a poison. And by common observation, it often ends up a slippery slope as these substances seem to have a mental effect too. They can be addictive. People get their brains scrambled.

'It's not a moral question really, that is, is it sinful or disgraceful? It's simply a matter of is it the right choice for better survival. Hence, all things in moderation I say.'

Julia added, 'I just don't like the taste of most alcoholic drinks, but I do like the odd glass of wine.'

'What do you two do for fun, then?' Smithy asked as if believing us two were too good to be true and didn't have fun.

Julia and I looked at each other knowingly and then I answered. 'We are doing it right here and now – having a meaningful conversation. We have been doing it for the last week – exploring new areas, looking for adventure, learning new things, solving the problems of our work. We don't separate much our work from other things. Our work is our game, our goal. It's fun.'

Julia added, 'We are fun together. We amuse each other. Brandon takes me out to Hampstead Heath to practise telepathy, and he takes me to the Hindu temple …' She was laughing a lot here '…. to eat chapattis and meditate.'

Smithy was leaning forward and looking seriously at me as if I was from another planet.

Julia continued. 'He once took me to a mental asylum and to a Psychiatric Convention. Do you know what? I loved it all. Better than watching TV or going to the pub. On a Saturday morning we'd go to the library. Our work is our play. Well, almost. 'When we get home nowadays, we do indulge in other normal pleasure, well at least until we learn to do it transcendentally.'

By this me and Smithy were well advanced in mirth.

We ate and chatted on happily until the evening was spent.

'I must say, you two, you are of one kind, and not normal earthlings. It has been a pleasure to meet you. You have opened up my eyes. I think I'll come to London and see you in action and survey your empire.'

Julia gave Smithy a hug. 'Thank you so much for your assistance and good company. You are welcome any time at our place. Actually WE will be welcome too; we haven't seen the finishing touches yet ourselves, nor christened the place.'

'So long Smithy,' I said giving him a hearty handshake.

Smithy had one more offering as we got to the front of the house. He went back inside and picked up the wine bottle and made a big ceremony of emptying it out on the garden outside. 'See, who needs this?' Thumbs up.

CHAPTER TWO

We serious honeymooners continued on to Bombay where we could have been forgiven for thinking the whole human race had gathered there. It was hot and teeming. London was an empty vessel compared to this place.

We were taken by Tuk Tuk, the common local taxicab, through random traffic and polluted streets. We arrived at The Grand and booked in.

When in the grand foyer, mostly in marble, I remarked, 'transports you back to the days of the British Raj, doesn't it?'

Julia, not yet impressed with anything she'd experienced, answered, 'I'll reserve judgement on that when I see the bathroom.'

She became more settled when we entered a modern lift, accompanied by a well-dressed and smiling 'bellboy'. We were ushered to our room and were relieved to find a modern bathroom and plush carpets and a whirling fan to cool the room.

We noticed a large vase of flowers on the table in front of the bed. Leaning against the vase was an envelope addressed to 'The Watermans'. Julia quickly opened it and read the beautiful handwriting of Sidney Waterman: 'Welcome to the Bombay leg of your journey my people. I hope you find the accommodation satisfactory and that your adventure has been and will continue to be fulfilling.

'The whole family sends its love and you are missed by everyone. Everything is in order here, so relax and enjoy yourselves.' It was signed 'Sidney'.

'How thoughtful of him Brandon,' she said. 'He's the man.'

We looked about and I flopped down on the bed while Julia went out onto the balcony and surveyed the steamy vista of this old city.

Back in London most things continued on in harmony. Sidney and Ira ran the 'empire' with my stamp printed all over it, so to speak.

Gavin however had his hands full dealing with the ITV Executives, Tom and Vince included. He was in the office of the lawyers. He had drafted a letter of response to the Psychiatry boys to the effect that they were invited onto the program to set the matter to rights and here was their opportunity to publicly correct any false information and that a full retraction would follow if our program were proven incorrect.

Tom and Vince were present with Lawyers Number One and Two.

Gavin told them, 'the more I think about this the more I'm convinced in law that we are on sound ground.' It was obvious to Gavin that these two had limited experience in heavy duty law suits. He was happy to lead the way and make it look like they were coming up with most of the action themselves.

Tom asked, 'would this mean we should allow a program of their own or one that debates between the protagonists?'

Gavin answered them. 'It is open-ended; up to you really. I doubt they would produce a program of their own. If they did you should see the 'screenplay' so we can warn them of our riposte or you could simply suggest the alternative of a debate. We must strongly hint there is more dirt to come if they want to challenge. This may deter them.

'The most aggressive of litigants, usually the big boys, will try and scare you off, introvert you, make you think twice. That's all that is happening here.'

Lawyer Number One said, 'well let's see what their response is to this letter. I'm beginning to smell blood myself, dare I say it.'

Lawyer Number Two said nothing, except, 'we'll inform Alistair and Ken.'

Gavin might just as well have been the station's lawyer for all these two were worth.

Gavin talked to Tom for a while. 'The two lovers are in India now, I dare say swanning around the sights, but not as typical tourists if I know them.'

Gavin went back to his new office and was met by Veronica who shoved a few newspapers under his nose. One had a big splash on Page Two making a big song and dance about the fact that ITV (because of me, it hastened to add) had been threatened with suit because of the program.

Veronica had a suggestion. 'Gavin, did you know Brandon met with a friendly journalist, Ivis Knightly? He intends to use her to get favourable press stories out. Perhaps she could be roped in to do a little investigative work on this matter. She was at the wedding you know, invited, and she had a very straight piece printed in one of the national women's magazines.

'If Brandon intended to use her she must be ok,' Gavin replied. 'I'll run it by Sidney. While they are away we could do a bit of infiltration ourselves, to gain a few points, type of thing. Call her in so we can discuss it, Veronica. Do you have her number?'

'I think Brandon put it on his desk. Leave it to me.'

Gavin did indeed talk with Sidney about this tack and agreed it would put her to the test and could do no harm; nothing like being proactive.

He had lunch with Delia and left his office at the College and went to his other office in Edgware, on the northern edge of London. Life was getting busier for this man, and for Delia too.

CHAPTER THREE

Sidney was working harder than he'd ever done in his life. At sixty three years old he was dealing with more traffic than in his army or business years. I was almost retired a few years ago, he thought to himself, and now I'm doing the job of three executives.

But this unimposing, mild mannered man was a block off the young chip, for sure. Though he was working hard he was doing it 'a la Brandon', taking it all in his stride. He went to bed each night pleasantly weary, hardly anything left outstanding, and slept like a log and awoke in the morning as fresh as a daisy and looking forward to the day ahead. It was always eventful as he (and Ira) had been 'trained' into expansion by their teenage boss. No standing still and resting on laurels.

But above all it was fun. Everything was accomplished with a light touch. It was a yardstick of who to employ – could they be managed with a light touch and with encouragement and a quiet insistence, a far cry from his army days where it was all serious and angry and where the modus operandi was that if you wanted compliance you had to yell and humiliate to 'get respect'. Punishment was the deterrent.

He could now fully appreciate why I had so quickly cottoned onto the fact that there were so few people about who were actually up to proper work and more harmonious living and that I had to expand Education into 'Psychology' (or whatever mental education was called) to make it all more worthwhile, let alone screamingly urgent.

Surrounding oneself with top grade individuals was a magnetic matter – top graders attracted top graders. It was a very quick sieving operation. Black sheep, time consumers, shirkers, pretenders, and so on, were soon shown up as such in this operation.

Sidney and Ira noticed that I had 'a few extra senses' that told me what I needed to know about someone and their potential value. Or was it just that I was super observant and saw in front of me what was simply there to see, if one was super observant one would suppose.

In any case, Sidney was doing the reverse of growing old. He even looked younger. Though his hair had thinned quite dramatically since his early days, his skin was 'younger', his colour more coloured, his movement was quicker and very upright.

Gladys had remarked about her father-in-law, that he was a new man. She in fact was catching the disease and was no longer making her life look like hard work – doing the domestic job AND a soon-to-be full time job at the college with less strain and effort than she'd been showing before.

To compare Sidney and Ira was quite a contrast. He was the quiet man who was no longer a soft touch. Ira was the rough and ready diamond who'd taken a step back from blatant confrontation.

Now here were just two examples of two good citizens living pretty normal lives, but not affecting very much, now becoming, not artificially, extraordinarily able; more of who they really were. And all they'd had was a bit of education. Not to undersell their conversion, they'd had their heads turned and led by me 'the teenage wonder boy'.

Sidney and Ira had discussed this phenomenon many times and were noticing their cohorts going through the same process.

They both agreed that part of my discovery was that innately, when people are inspired by a purpose and can produce worthwhile change about them, they automatically become more able and drop their former handicaps or excuses.

Ira and Sidney were in my office, dealing with stuff that I wasn't there to deal with, such as the PI, Michael Stone, and the reports by Ivis Knightly, our freelance journalist. There was no waiting for me to come back and issue instructions. They took on the mantle and made their decisions, ably abetted by young Veronica. After all they were the deputies. And I had left quite enough information behind before I left, so they just picked it up and ran with it. They thought like I did.

'Ira, I've found a property in Battersea for the next branch,' said Sidney.

'It's located in Northcote Rd. It's Clapham really but the more affluent tip of Battersea. There are a number of private schools in the area too. Anyone lined up for the Headmaster job?

'I'd like to persuade James Hopkins to do it but I think he's still trying to rid us of the Levison factor from within the Department of Education, so better leave him there. He told me he had a tacit green light from the Minister of Education to continue to get to the bottom of all his troubles. The Minister summoned him to an interview. How good is that?'

'I have a few interviews this morning, selected from the best of our students who have more or less interviewed themselves during their progress here,' Ira replied.

She went on. 'What about your grandson number two, Andrew?'

Sidney thought for a while and then decided, 'no, not quite ready yet. Let's give him a bit longer. I'm going to work on him at home, just as I did with Brandon – feed him stuff to consider and work out for himself.'

'By the way, just to change the subject, we don't hear or see much of your son, Cliff,' she said.

"Yes" Sidney replied, 'I'm worried about Cliff; have been for some time. Having been laid off about five years ago and having found it hard to get a job in the short term, he sort of gave up on life I think. He hasn't been in the best of health – been to lots of specialists to see what's wrong. Brandon offered him a job with us here but he hummed and hawed but never picked up on it. He has a few menial part time jobs but nothing much. I think Brandon is going to look into him a bit when he gets back.'

'Just collar him down here,' Ira more or less ordered. 'I'll give him something to do and take him under my wing. Can't have him rotting away out there when the rest of the family is flying. You two have been a bit behindhand on this matter. If he's not doing anything useful he's bound to rot away. Let's revive him.'

Sidney couldn't find fault with that. In fact he was feeling a bit guilty now that it had been pointed out to him. 'You are right. Do you know he's rather good at handyman things. We'll get him fixing things, painting, whatever. We currently get in firms to do that sort of thing. We'll even put him through the Education program, like everyone else. He needs to get with his sons and participate in their lives, not to mention his wife, and of course his father.'

They called in Veronica and between them they addressed all the things that needed to be dealt with. Ira went off to inspect the classroom and bed in a few new students, handing over these tasks to Cindy Hopkins as she did so. Then she put her attention onto the new HM job for Battersea.

Sidney went off to try and wrap up the lease on the Battersea College. There would be plenty of work there for Cliff to get on with, he thought. Then he would call Michael Stone and debrief him and plan the next move, which was likely to be getting James to start the propaganda campaign against Levison.

Veronica needed to wrap up the next College magazine for their mailing list and make appointments for newspaper people to visit and organise a press release for them. She was expanding her job nicely, this one.

CHAPTER FOUR

Me and the missus were glad to get out of Bombay. We were on our way by train to New Delhi, via Agra. You couldn't come to India without seeing the Taj Mahal after all, could you?

The train was packed out to the roof, literally. With all the windows open it was still stifling in our carriage. In some areas passengers were under the seats, in the luggage racks, and ON the roof too.

We wanted to live like the locals, and after The Grand, here we were. Well we two westerners from the comfortable suburbia of London, where the nearest thing to this was a peak hour tube ride, we'd never complain about standing room only again. This was NO ROOM only, and an invasion of the olfactory receptors. It's as well we'd not had a dose of Bombay Belly. We'd been advised anyway to empty our systems of waste products before joining this cattle truck.

Of course we were the only whites in the carriage, except for a couple of long haired hitch hikers down the other end. There were these wide brown eyes all looking us over as if they'd never seen a westerner before. Perhaps they hadn't, in cattle class.

'How far is it to Agra?' Julia asked somewhat hopefully.

I told her out of the side of my mouth, 'about eight hundred miles.'

I too was beginning to wonder if our 'close to native' travel plans were a good idea, especially as this train took an hour to get out of Bombay itself and then, when in rural India, was doing not much more than thirty mph. Even at one hundred mph it would take a whole day, so realistically we were looking at two-three days, depending on how many stops.

'Before you say it, my dear, I've done the maths and decided this won't work. Let's get off at the next big town and revise our plans a bit. We'll have experienced this aspect enough. I think, for brevity and considering the distances involved, we must be more mobile.'

'Then again,' Julia suggested, 'judging by the roads I've seen out of the window here, which take a mix of animal-drawn carts, some normal cars, and a hell of a lot of trucks, all moving slower than the train, we might well be better off where we are. We won't see any more from a vehicle. But what we do see would be better from a first class seat, for the moment, would it not?

'You've got a point. There will be plenty of opportunity to live native.'

So we enquired of the train 'guard', after scrambling through three or four like carriages and managed to upgrade ourselves to first class, which by natural progression meant it was less crowded but not a lot else; marginally more comfortable. No dining car on this one.

 I asked Julia, 'There MUST have been a really good first class in the days of the Raj, don't you think?'

'Maybe this is modern compared to those days, who knows? What is for sure is that the movement of people is limited by the infrastructure. What would it be like now if the British had never taken over the place? Look out the window and see. Early days.'

I added, 'I'm told the majority of the population live in the north, which is where we're headed. Maybe we haven't seen anything yet.'

We settled down for the long journey. We soon engaged our local passengers in somewhat difficult conversation. These people were what passed for a middle class, which had barely gotten off the ground here in the sixties.

There was one chap, in a striking turban, who stood head and shoulders above the others, literally. His name was Singh, the surname of all Sikhs. He spoke good English and was quite westernised in manner.

After we'd introduced ourselves to Anjat Singh and explained what our mission was, we seekers of the truth soon got into HIS beliefs.

'Not unlike your Christian religion we believe there is one Creator, the Immortal One, Waheguru. Like yourselves we worship this one God and through him try to live humble lives. Everyone is equal before God. There is a holy book, like your bible is holy to you. It contains God's word.'

'I see,' I acknowledged.' I notice you are wearing western clothing but have the turban, which is distinctive I presume.'

Anjat replied, 'yes, we are quite modern but our turban, apart from being a sort of uniform for men, it contains the hair, which is not often cut; it is a symbol of strength. We Sikhs broke away from Hinduism some four hundred plus years ago, mainly in disagreement with the caste system. Not only that, we have been carved into a warrior nation since our home, the Punjab, is more on the crossroads of various historic raiders from east and west. We have had to fight in our time, but we are not warlike, as have been those crossing our land over the centuries.'

He continued, 'I am going to Indore which is about half way, I suppose. I would consider it an honour to invite you to my home. You would be glad to freshen up I am sure. You can stay and continue on your ticket the next day or so. I will also take you to our temple (it's called a gurdwara, in Punjabi).'

Julia had warmed to this man. 'It is we who would be honoured, Anjat.'

The journey continued, not quite interminably. We had lots of questions to ask of each other. On arriving at our destination, a busy station for a busy city by the looks of it, we made our way through the crowd to a local 'taxi'. This was a motorised sort of golf buggy, and wound its way through the evening traffic to the home of Anjat Singh.

We had wondered what sort of a dwelling he might live in.

'Wow,' Julia exclaimed as we snaked our way around the roads, passing through densely populated areas with shacks all stacked together 'as far as the eye could see', which wasn't very far, actually, and with people and animals bustling about in the never ending business of basic survival. 'How many people live in this city, Anjat?'

'There are more people here than in your second biggest city in England – about one million or so. There are many many cities in India of this size.' He was looking at her face and reading the culture shock expressed in it.

I was taking it all in. My earlier metaphor came to mind – ant nest. I wondered how poverty on a grand scale affected the mind. In England there would be riots, but then again, in earlier centuries the slums of London and the effects of serfdom were not dissimilar to this, he supposed, but England wasn't burdened by overpopulation.

We eventually arrived at Anjat's home, in a more prosperous part of town. It was a large proper house in a street of similar dwellings.

'Welcome to my humble home, my friends.' He paid the taxi man after all the luggage had been unloaded. Most of the luggage had been his as he'd been on a business trip to Europe.

On entering, Anjat's wife, Jaya, quite a beauty (in western clothing topped with a head scarf, as was the custom), welcomed us as if we'd been expected. She had a quiet manner, but in no way lacked confidence.

'I am interested in your project,' Anjat announced to us both after a beautifully cooked traditional Indian curry, complete with Julia's favourite side dish. 'What do you expect to find in our country to add to your knowledge?'

I answered first. 'Well Christianity hasn't helped us much, apart from the obvious pleading for people to treat each other with respect and live for each other. It is a backbone to our society, as are many religions to their societies, but apart from the rather nebulous advices to find God and believe in Him it doesn't offer anything practical as a significant fix to the shortcomings of our populations.

'We more or less stumbled on this course from our experiences with Education. Education DOES fix the individual to a significant extent, if done correctly. But it only goes so far. So we are looking further. Psychology has a few answers but it seems incomplete.'

Julia continued to explain about Psychiatry and why it was so wide of the mark. She told of her abuse cases and she told them humorously about the TV program and our visit to the Mental Hospital.

Anjat continued the dialogue while Jaya brought in dessert. She was listening carefully however and asked her own questions in well above average English.

'I have to confess that although we support our Gurdwara neither of us are strict religious Sikhs. Personally I can't claim to have spoken to our God nor experienced Him speaking to me. I too am concerned about our plight as a nation, and I'm none too impressed with what I've seen overseas. We get on with our businesses and our family and manage well enough. What else can you do?'

'Yes,' I answered. 'That is precisely the right question. It's a daunting task, is it not? If you knew how to get your immediate associates and citizens to behave better and contribute more, I'm sure you'd do it.'

Jaya answered that 'Yes, we would. Starting here at home. We have three children. One is well on his way. The second eldest is a lost soul and isn't much interested in participating in life around him, but the third, the youngest, is bordering on being uncontrollable. He's eight years old. He's bright but stroppy and so disobedient.'

'There you have it,' I agreed. 'He's probably a good person really but has a loose wire somewhere, if you know that expression.' Anjat explained that one to Jaya.

Anjat asked me, 'could you fix these two younger ones with Education?'

'Maybe, as long as their English was up to it, and even then that may not be the answer. Do they do well at school? I mean do they like school and do they learn things?'

'Above average I'd say,' Jaya replied and Anjat nodded in agreement.

Julia explained, 'we do an assessment of each prospective student, mainly to see if they could WANT to learn without all the 'boredom and pain', and are they up to it? We are not on a mission at this point to salvage the bottom half of all students. We could, perhaps, but we'd take so long to get anywhere, if at all.'

'But, anyone who can be inspired and can be encouraged to persist, has a chance,' I added. 'And the change is spectacular. Learning things opens the door to a more interesting and successful life. But it doesn't solve personality problems, like mixing in groups, always upsetting others, and outright antisocial behaviour. That's what we are looking for – the character booster.'

'How do you expect to find it here in India, which seems far behind your culture in most ways?'

'Well in Thailand we found that the population was almost as stressed as yours in terms of numbers and lack of development, but the Buddhist religion seemed to be able to produce a definite cohesiveness and calmness to its citizens. They practice meditation (which we are doing every day on our travels) and we have found that it really does offer a higher plain of mental awareness and a separation from the noise of everyday life.'

'But what of the vast number of people living lives of poverty and destitution?' Anjat asked.

I responded. 'That is definitely a significant anomaly. Though we have only just begun our trip I don't expect to find any other Eastern countries who aren't similarly overpopulated. I suspect India is the extreme though. But overpopulation and poverty may not be anything to do with it. In England we don't have the population or poverty problems you have but we do have big social problems. Just as you have described with your youngsters, we have the same syndromes. We see it all the time.'

'Wow, you two are so young but you are way up there, looking for a better way,' Anjat exclaimed.

We thanked our hosts for the evening and before retiring to our bed I suggested that in the morning we'd be glad to have a go at their youngsters and see if they were able to be helped. Apparently they'd learned English from an early age and it may be passable enough to get by.

The next morning after breakfast, and with the three children introduced to we two visitors, who had been introduced as teachers, we got down to it, informally.

I had the two younger ones talk to me and Julia together about their lives, with lots of questions and lots of jokes and laughing. Then I told them about myself, and how I had discovered a new way of learning and how I'd set up a school that did the job much much better than the normal schools. I told them expansive stories of how my students became really smart and could learn more and more difficult things and were able to consider lots of exciting and interesting careers.

Then there was a break, after which we two teachers had agreed to work out how we could solve their problems with learning and school.

Julia took on the youngest boy and I took on the lost soul. On a very light basis we found out a few examples of basic missed concepts and saw to it that they really brightened up and could see how it all worked. The parents certainly could.

I finished with the example of the athlete who did lots of training, pushing himself to improve to reach his goal; and the one about the pianist who became good at piano by practice. I finished with the examples they could give in their own area, of kids who just gave up and became no one.

'You two wonderful kids are quite bright, you know,' Julia said. 'Don't waste it. Learn how to learn and then you can learn what you really want so you can do good things.'

The kids were quite excited. I gave Anjat a copy of my text on the subject and told him, 'if you really learn to use this you can transform their education. Do it on yourselves, just like we did here today. Resurrect your own learning ability and then get to work on these two. Keep it light, lots of fun, keep them at it, with lots of rewards.'

Jaya was first to respond. 'Come on husband, make your wife into a genius; I'm keen.'

'I might end up being your agent in India,' Anjat offered. 'Is this remunerative?'

Julia answered that. 'Only if it is done right and for the right reasons. We might just take you up on that.'

The two hosts, along with all the family, took us to the Gurdwara, more towards the centre of the city. It was a big imposing building, much in the mould of others we'd seen and been in. There was a small population of Sikhs in Indore, but it was a closely-knit community.

After the visit Anjat and Jaya separated themselves in earnest conversation with a few of their friends and then, smiling, came over and informed us that it had been decided that we were to be given a vehicle to take us on our way. Anjat, among other things, ran a car dealership and garage. They needed a car delivered to Delhi to their branch there, and we two travellers could be the driver.

'Wow,' I exclaimed. 'Are you sure?'

'Yes. It is in honour of your good work generally and your help with our children. Besides, you need a bit of manoeuvrability on your trip, and I need this vehicle delivered, in one piece of course. I will insure it. I had thought of accompanying you (guiding you really) but business calls and I can't take the time off.'

'You are good people,' Julia said. 'This is most appreciated.'

We then went to collect our things at the house, said our goodbyes to the children and then went to Anjat's place of business, which was a huge 'business park'; a thriving enterprise by all accounts. We collected our transport, a late VW Beetle, wished our hosts a happy life and were on our way.

'What people!' I remarked. 'If those Sikhs are anything to go by I'd say they are a more progressive race than the others around. Let's look for the turban, that particular turban, as we proceed through this very crowded country.

On the winding road to Agra we went through many 'small' towns (almost cities by English standards) and whenever we filled up for fuel, or went looking for a place to eat or sleep, we inevitably ended up meeting the stand-out Sikh, who inevitably spoke English and inevitably turned out to be the prosperous entrepreneur who inevitably directed us to a Gurdwara. These were walking the walk they talked.

After a few hot and sweaty days dodging our way along diverse 'highways' we came to Agra, a teeming mass of humanity squashed into a central hub, only broken by the grounds of the Taj Mahal, a rather magnificent but smaller than expected palace completely spoiled by the omnipresence of mosquitos in the watergardens and river behind it. Julia decided that this wasn't a place to die so we left quite shortly after arriving. It was much more comfortable walking around the crowded streets even though these were advertising their filth and poverty at every turn.

'I heard,' I announced, as we picked our way along 'pavements' and negotiated tricky street crossings, 'Old Delhi is even more of the same thing.'

'Well, pedal to the metal to Kashmir and Nepal. Maybe these places aren't so jammed up, or do we need to make it to Mt. Everest to get some real space.

'Actually I am enjoying this. We came here to discover what the products are of their religions and culture, not just to find glorious scenery and peace and quiet. It is a culture shock though, I must admit.'

'We can skip the architecture and other tourist sites and mix with the natives and talk with them, like just here,' I suggested as we approached a street café full of locals having their version of elevenses, even though it was more like 'threeses'.

We entered the shack of a shop, sat at a table and wondered if there was waiter service. No sooner had we sat when a western-dressed man approached us and in English introduced himself as Sandeep Patel, the local Police Superintendent, (off duty) wondering if we needed any help.

In a strong Indian accent he asked us, 'Are you English? I suppose you are wanting a cup of tea, yes?' He couldn't wait, it seemed, to show his knowledge of English customs.

Julia, she of the sparkling smile, responded. 'How did you know?' This was a cue for a five minute showcase of his anglification. If she had been trying to be snide it would have passed him by as it soon became obvious this man was quite literal in his interpretation of English and, as we were to discover throughout our journey, even the best spoken practitioners of the English language were far more intent on speaking than listening (except the Sikhs).

But hospitable actions were always forthcoming. One could easily assume that the respect for the English from colonial days still hung over to this day – no hard feelings after their subjugation.

As an afterthought I asked this policeman what they did here with mental cases. We thought he'd know.

'Well we get the family to take care of it; it's all in the community, not in hospitals usually. There are care centres but the family come to these as mostly outpatients. We don't have mental institutions like you do in England.'

The bottom line was that mental treatment was in its relative infancy. We had our tea and a samosa of sorts. Julia didn't ask to inspect the kitchen but did look for crawlies in the food before each mouthful. Ah well, we always had our dysentery tablets to fall back on.

We continued our journey, stopping and mingling and conversing with the locals, from the casual barefooted passers-by to the more middle class educated lot. We asked about their lives and religious practices (these quite often being as much superstition or just pure handed-down dogma than anything else), their education, their aspirations (if any).

We mostly needed interpreters and of course the most handy of these was quite often a Sikh, who in these overwhelmingly Hindu places, stuck out like a sore thumb – always the most prosperous. Maybe they were the town mayors, I often thought. Of course we now always gravitated to the Gurdwaras for accommodation.

Our little Beetle was a godsend. It was particularly suited to dirt roads and, having an air-cooled engine, never overheated.

We went in and out of Old and New Delhi in one day. This was everything our pre-stories had promised. Talk about an ant nest! More of the same really. We dropped the vehicle at the appointed destination and telegraphed Anjat Singh to notify him of the completed mission. We immediately hired another of the same for the next step of our journey which we decided to embark on immediately. If only we could wiggle our way through this free-for-all infrastructure that was 1960's Delhi!

We made our way to the nearby Punjab, the state of the Sikhs. It wasn't long before we noticed a thinning of population, quite orderly farm spreads, better roads and plenty of Gurdwaras to visit.

The Golden Temple of Amritsar was the centre of everything Sikh. Amritsar is close to the border with Pakistan, the Punjab area extending as of old into this country.

Sikhism was exemplified by the welcoming of all people everywhere across their Gurdwara portals.

The Golden Temple was indeed very golden, but not made of actual gold. It was the centre for many pilgrims, there being a long queue along a causeway across a lake square to get to the temple itself.

'Do we want to queue up, my love?' I asked Julia. 'I'd rather find a surrounding Gurdwara and settle in for the rest of the day. We still have our meditation to do as well.'

'Lead me on my guru,' she answered. 'I'm all for that.'

We did just that, got settled in, had dinner (chicken curry and chapattis), and then meditated, as decided. We had agreed to meet the Granthi after this, one Shurhab Singh, head man of the temple. We would learn more from him than spending time at the Golden Temple. Our trip had taken on the principle of avoiding the crowds and tourist spots, but talking to individuals instead.

Julia, incidentally, had cracked the meditation, big time. She had now experienced the out-of-body phenomena that she'd previously taken my word for. For her it was a sort of spectatorism of the surroundings, without her eyes; a widened space; a feeling of freedom and elation. She maintained it for quite some minutes at a time.

We were both doing it regularly; not every time, but most times. This new experience availed us of a new conversation topic, both extending our imaginations as to how far we could go with it in practical terms.

However, this night we sat with our Granthi and asked lots of questions on the subject. We were seated around a low table in a kind of reception room, with a spread of chapatti and poppadom dips.

I led off the earnest conversation. 'Sir, Julia and I have been meditating for a little while now and find it really uplifting, so much so that we often achieve being out of our bodies. Do you experience the same thing?'

Shurhab Singh responded in a quite calming and melodious voice. 'There are a number of experiences that occur in meditation. For me, always looking for Divine Truth (my main aim), I feel a sense of what is truly moral and right, not by any belief to make me feel good, but a harmony and perception of what actually is true. To just believe what is 'true' is not enough. There has to be an automatic connection with it in later action.'

'OK,' I responded. 'Do you necessarily go out of your body to do this?'

'Sometimes, but not necessarily, but one has to go out of one's mental…..
what's the word?.... mental rubbish (clutter, he meant, but couldn't quite articulate) to get there, if you see what I mean. To be honest I doubt many of our number actually get as far as you two have. They try, they feel better, maybe closer to God, but if none of those things they feel better for being in a tight group with good principles to follow.

'I'm sure you have various levels of belief in Christianity, from real believers right down to blind followers who struggle to practice what they belong to.'

There was a pause, while we refilled our cups.

Julia added her opinion. 'It seems to me that Sikhism, Buddhism, Hinduism and maybe other Eastern religions that we haven't contacted so far, have a lot in common. They are all looking for a higher plane of thinking and behaviour and use variations of meditation to get there; a voyage of self-discovery supplemented by group teachings originated by earlier founders or gurus, using that word loosely.'

'Indeed there are so many worthy similarities,' Shurhab agreed, 'and it is worth noting you don't see wars breaking out between Eastern nations on the basis of Eastern religion.' I wasn't sure of this one. I was thinking of the debacle of Partition.

'I must say you two seem to have mastered our practices exceptionally well – unusual for westerners – and have reaped the benefits. May I ask why you are doing this?'

I explained. We discussed the whole subject for at least another hour, certainly long enough to demolish the table's contents of goodies.

'Enjoy your stay here,' our host said, concluding the evening. 'Good luck on your quest. I think we should appoint you honorary Sikhs, or at least roving ambassadors.'

'We'll certainly be glad to have both accolades,' I agreed as we departed. 'Thank you for your hospitality. Our stay in India has been highlighted by Sikh hospitality.'

We repaired to our accommodation, which though spartan was clean and comfortable enough.

I lay next to Julia, cuddling her to me, but quiet and thoughtful. I said to her, 'Do you know, though this is all very interesting and there are new sights to see, I think I have extracted what is most useful for our project, and I don't expect to gain much more other than more of the same, wherever we go. There will be temples and communities practising their religions in a quest for a better life, albeit in a general environment of utter poverty and subsistence living and overpopulation.

'As far as we are concerned the best we've extracted is the practice of meditation. Is it just a matter of improving on that and marketing it?'

Julia listened. She was witnessing one of my momentous decisions; a change in course perhaps. She too had started to think on these lines I was articulating.

She cuddled herself closer to me and inevitably got me stirred up.

———————————

Early the next morning we bid farewell to our various hosts and set out to return to Delhi, to return our vehicle. We had decided to join the Ganges River at Kanpur, not far east of Delhi and then 'float' down the river to Calcutta. And then home.

Delhi was actually two cities – Old and New, the latter being the seat of government. We decided to stay the night there after returning our vehicle and set out for Kanpur by bus the next morning.

No staying 'indoors' for we two honeymooners. We tramped the streets of governmental buildings and embassies, ate in the nearest thing to a posh restaurant and spoke with both locals and resident expats wherever we went.

We marvelled at the influence of the British in all aspects of Indian life. 'I wonder what this was all like before we British came here?' Julia wondered aloud.

'Well it all ended quite badly during Partition but we left them with quite a bit of architecture, infrastructure and civilising culture, such as their parliamentary system and Civil Service. English proliferates in the institutions,' I noted.

'Yes,' Julia added, ' but, as with many parts of the Empire we tended to strip what we could from these places and left mainly because we got kicked out for not really ensuring we sought a viable handover of power and share of the wealth creation. Quite a bit of ego, eh?'

I continued. 'And only places like Australia and New Zealand stayed with us as these places were pretty well virgin territory and had no sizeable indigenous populations to kick back on us.

'What an opportunity we had to really export the best of British. Unfortunately, it was too economic and power driven. However, somewhat like the Romans, not too bad an excursion, unlike other empires before us.'

The Ganges at Kanpur was well into somewhat voluminous flow, fed from the draining glaciers and waters of the Himalayan mountains. This river is holy to Hindus, many believing it to have some sort of anointing power for the bathers though its ever-increasing filth was ignored. How spiritual is that?

Further downstream the Holy city of Varanasi, the city of hundreds of temples and numerous pilgrims emptied almost its entire gastronomical waste products into the river. The occurrence of cholera, dysentery, and other diseases was not inconsiderable. Hygiene had not been at the forefront of religious practice.

We decided that we'd seen enough of life on the holy river and decided to bus it to Calcutta.

While visiting a smallish town on the route and while the bus was stopped to refuel and the passengers were stretching their legs, we two sat at what was essentially a roadside café and drank some tea while watching an assortment of the indigenous and animals pass by.

'You would think their religions here taught deprivation. There is one thing to be humble and not get into accumulating lots of superfluous material things beyond reasonable comfort, but for the vast majority to be in utter self-denial is another,' I commented.

'Yes, and this caste system is actually a bit of a cast-aside system,' Julia responded. 'This is a downside of Hinduism, tantamount to a rigid class system – you are what you are born and what your job is. The cattle have almost as much place in society.'

'Hmm, the world is about haves and have nots,' I commented. ' Further to our conversation the other night: once the sentience and reason ebb away in Man, the closer we get to the animal kingdom, and creativity goes down the pan. There is not much Education going on here despite the thousands of temples and gurus. It's even below anarchy.'

'I feel for these people Brandon, but it is overwhelming.'

I decided to perk up. 'One thing is for sure, we can start from the top down, that is, start with those most able to respond to improvement and change AND who are most likely to lend a hand. Charity might help stem the tide a bit meanwhile.'

Continuing on our way we reached Calcutta in time to book into another oasis, otherwise known as the Sikh Gurdwara. Here, in Calcutta the ones really managing well were the Singh clan, though they were a tiny minority here.

We met the Granthi of the Gurdwara, Daler Singh (which meant heroic and fearless one) that evening at dinner – more hospitality. He was a big man by anyone's standards, and his golden turban capped off his presence, along with his affable smile. 'In the light of your experiences here in India so far, what have you discovered to help your cause, my friends?' he asked.

I discussed meditation and rules to live by and so on but I really wanted to know what Daler thought was the solution to the oppression we had observed.

'To be honest, this weighs on my heart a lot. I too see what you see and it seems not within our ability to deal with. It is definitely possible within each of our own people to uplift and put God within reach but as for India at large, I am overwhelmed. I am not going to tell you it is God's will or that He will sort it out. That's unreal. I must stay positive in what I can affect and lead the way to better lives for as many as possible.

'Perhaps more westernisation, as started by the British, will gradually bring about more economic change and thus help lift more and more out of poverty. I think what has helped our own culture most is Education and westernisation. We are economically more sound. You can't do much on overstressed bodies and empty tummies other than stay with your head barely above the water.'

Julia picked up on the underlying sadness of the man. 'You speak wisely Daler. You have the platform to encourage and reach out. How many people depend on you to lead?' This was a rhetorical question.

'I thank you, Julia. Sometimes it is a lonely journey.'

I told him of our project from earlier years (such as it was) and how it only works with a strong like-minded team around one. 'This is becoming more necessary as we grow and as we upset conventional 'wisdom'; that is, as the odds grow against us.'

I continued. 'From my meditation experiences I would say I am closer to what you would call God but I feel I am finding God within me, that is the potential for unlimited power within me, not granted by any deity. Is this not what you are seeking yourselves here?'

'You are not normal westerners, my friends. Your concepts are high and you seem to be putting them into action.' Then more lightheartedly he added, 'you must be a guru in your own right to your people.'

We both smiled at this and bowed our heads. 'This is definitely not an accomplished fact. We have an establishment that thinks IT is the only source of gurus. Don't get me started.'

We chatted more socially for a while and it ended with Daler agreeing to meet us when he next visits the UK, when the hospitality would be returned.

CHAPTER FIVE

Back in the UK, at Head Office, the executives were gathered in the canteen along with all family members of executives.

Delia commented, 'if we knew when our two lovebirds were returning from the land of the rising sun, or wherever they are, we could arrange a real good housewarming party.'

Just at that moment Veronica came in with a telegram in her hand – an overseas telegram. She handed it to Sidney, to whom it was addressed. He read it while all waited with baited breath.

'Well?' Ira couldn't wait for Sidney to tease them some more.

Sidney, with a look of disbelief on his face, read it out haltingly: 'Dear folks, we are sending this from on high, in a Nepalese monastery, high in the Himalayas, the highest Post Office in the world. Have found Nirvana and our true calling. Will see you in the afterlife, namely on the thirtieth of August, Heathrow, BOAC from Calcutta. B and J.'

'Hell,' Ira exclaimed. 'That's tomorrow! We need to arrange all this this afternoon; the party I mean!'

There was a buzz of excitement in the room.

Delia put her arm around Gladys's shoulder and announced, 'the house is totally ready. We only need the eats and drinks. All the presents are laid out there. We ladies will take care of this. You men organise the pickup from Heathrow.'

Veronica chirped in, 'I'll phone all the invitees right away. Don't worry, I know the list. I made it up after all.'

Gavin and Dan were at the airport to meet us, except they didn't pick us out from the exiting arrivals until it was too late.

Julia and I had clad ourselves in Sikh apparel, me with a stunning turban, given to me by Daler Singh, along with a false beard, and she in sari and head scarf and veil to hide her excitement.

Among a throng of arrivals we spotted Gavin and Dan and passed them by and doubled back behind them. I came up behind Gavin and tapped him on the shoulder. 'Excuse me, Sahib, I am wanting to know….'

Right then the two McDonalds cottoned on. Gavin took Julia in his arms and lifted her off the ground. Dan shook my hand vigorously.

Julia suddenly reverted to the more usual reserved mien, with veil over the face, head down and eyes up. 'Please Sahib, father, you embarrass me; this is not our way.'

She could hold it no more. She shed the veil and scarf and plunged western-style into Dan's arms. 'How do we look brother?'

'As beautiful as ever. The whole of London misses that set of teeth on full show.'

'Well,' Gavin pronounced, 'we better get you home, I mean to YOUR home.'

'Is that where we are staying?' asked Julia, playfully.

Dan replied with, 'you sure are staying there.'

I said, 'If there are no beds in the place as yet we are quite used to sleeping hard core.'

'Wait and see,' said Gavin. 'We men left it all up to the women to organise all that. For all I know there is no hot water yet. But having cleansed yourself in the River Ganges I suppose that is water off a ducks back, eh?'

'We opted to forego those ablutions.' I replied. 'You haven't seen the Ganges. We'd have had to trek to the foothills of the Himalayas to find the

Ganges suitable for bathing.'

'But I thought the bathing was for the soul,' Dan countered. 'Not so?'

'My soul doesn't need cleansing Dan,' I retorted.

We found the car park and went straight along the M4 motorway, the newish western artery of London.

Julia and I were in the back, noting the contrast of London to Bombay, Delhi and Calcutta. 'Glad to be home, my love? 'I asked her.

'You bet. Things in our society could be a lot worse.'

It was late afternoon. London was busy, for a Sunday, but no large back-ups of traffic. We quickly arrived at our nesting place which looked as we had remembered. Even our little Ford was parked outside.

In through the front door we dropped our luggage in the hall and started wandering about. The door to the front lounge room was closed. On opening it and entering we were hit with a blast of whoops and hollers and blowing of horns of all sorts.

'Oh my God!' Julia screeched. She ran straight into the arms of her mother who was beside herself with joy. Then one by one she repeated the dose with all the others gathered – everyone who mattered.

I followed, hugging mum, dad, Andrew and Sidney. The crowd of guests were overflowing into the rear garden through double doors. Outside there was a barbecue on the go and a fine spread of food laid out.

There was a raised platform with a couple of 'throne' armchairs toward which me and Julia were being funnelled. At the dais Ira gestured us to our seats, beside which was a huge bottle of champagne in a bucket of ice.

Everyone had a glass already charged and Ira poured the bubbly and called for 'order'. 'To the returning gurus! Welcome home, to YOUR home' she announced, raising her glass. Everyone shouted 'cheers', chinked glasses and drank up.

Then Ira dictated, 'you are now to bring us up to date on the state of the world and your adventures in it.' Another bout of cheering and encouragement.

I, somewhat abashed at the more than enthusiastic welcome, began to speak. 'I hereby call this meeting to order,' I said. 'Well, thank you so much, all of you. We are gobsmacked and so pleased to be back among all of you very special people. I suppose you all want to know what we got up to over there in Asia, you sticky beaks.'

Big cheers. Andrew shouted above the crowd, 'EVERY heavenly detail!' Big laughter.

Well I gave it to them in humorous detail. At the end of my relation I paused and said, looking over at Julia, 'have I left anything out, my love?'

She stood up and, not a bit embarrassed, replied, finger on cheek and frowning slightly in thought whilst looking to the sky, 'I can't imagine what else this lot would want to know.'

Dan piped up, 'did you make it to heaven?' Lots of screeches and laughter.

Julia teased them some more. 'I thought this wonderful MAN (she emphasised the word, and looked at me invitingly) covered all our meditation experiences quite well.'

The crowd egged her on. I encouraged her. 'Tell them all about it, sound effects and all.' Much hilarity. 'They need an education.'

Julia carried on the game. 'Do you know he read an erotic book called 'The Kharma Sutra' while we were on the plane. Well, we added a few more chapters of our own, let's say.' They were all in stitches.

After the hubbub died down, Julia concluded, 'despite his threats to sublimate our marriage into 'floating in the sky', I can tell you this man is perfectly normal.'

Big cheers erupted and glasses were raised once again. The two of us mingled and chatted with the guests and tucked into the food. The party went on for a few hours during which we were led on a tour of our home.

Julia was impressed with all the thought that had gone into making the house cosy and tastefully done; not a thing was omitted. All the gifts that applied had been incorporated and labelled as to their source and the few remaining others were placed in the front lounge room for us to decide on.

'We are so impressed, aren't we darling,' Julia said to me and the mainly family still remaining at ten pm.

Did you people do any work in our absence?' I asked in jest, pointing out the time and thought that must have gone into the whole thing.

'You under-estimate us, my boy,' Gladys objected lightly.

Coffee and tea was poured from new pots and into the new tea service and we all sat in the comfortable new lounge suite and on the floor, around a new coffee table, and chatted for another hour or so before seeing off our hosts-turned-guests on the front street.

We went straight upstairs and showered before then collapsing into bed, essentially half a day later than normal, honeymoon officially over.

A new day had well dawned. We young Watermans rose, brunched, and got straight down to business.

Julia got straight onto her contacts in Queen Anne Street and was brought up to date with the latest cases, of which there were a few juicy ones. She decided to hotfoot it down there and get into it all.

I was soon on the phone to Tom at ITV, James at the Education Department, and Michael Stone, my sleuth-in-chief.

Firstly I had to talk with Gavin on the legal front and was informed that the top Execs had gone cold on the idea of further shows, mainly because the Psychiatrists had backed off following the letter sent to them weeks ago offering time and response to the claims made by me on live TV. Let sleeping dogs lie, supposedly. We agreed to meet up the next day.

So, when I called Tom at ITV, although he welcomed our return he was rather apathetic about the whole matter. He'd been rather stone-walled by his seniors and had run out of energy to push the whole thing.

I'm the one breathing life and purpose into this whole thing, I thought, a little despondently.

Next I spoke to our P.I. 'How'd you enjoy the wedding Michael?' I asked.

'Great event,' he replied. 'Best wedding I've ever been to. No doubt you want updating.'

'I hope you have some good news,' I responded.

'Well, yes and no. Our target definitely has an extra-marital affair going on. I have the pictures and other corroborating evidence. His financials have been rather harder to get into. I can't find a smoking gun yet.'

He continued. 'But I haven't given up on that. He has another property in North London, under the name of a spurious company of which he is a director. This house is rented out to a family. He can't be doing all this on his salary from his day job – three houses, a mistress, a quite expensive car. I'm trying other sources to get an entry into this.'

'Ok,' I responded. 'Is this enough to use effectively against him yet?'

'Give me a day or two. We are getting there.'

'Ok, well done so far Michael. Call me when you have what you can get,' I said, and rang off. I noted that Michael had slowed down on the case without his client to urge him on.

Next was James. He'd been at the welcoming do the previous day but we hadn't really talked. He told me he was effectively being made an example of by the Department, but not by the Minister herself who had given him tacit encouragement to exonerate himself. He was moving well in the direction of my suggestion about the new boy, Jake Levison and his part in all this.

'I don't expect this will go anywhere,' James added. 'Levison will have his lies, and his bases covered, for the moment. I've decided to get on with it from where I am and see what we can do with any dope that comes up on him from your investigations.'

I uplifted him a bit with the news from the PI.

'By the way Brandon, I want to help with your costs towards all this investigation.'

'Ok, thanks James, we'll see where it goes first.' James had taken his foot off the accelerator too, I noted. Even some of our best aren't fully self-perpetuating.

I then drove to the office, not really an un-walkable distance, but I was in fast mode.

When I got there I was greeted by Veronica, who'd warned me the previous day that there was a full 'in' basket. In fact she had dealt with a fair amount of it but she'd kept that in a 'ready to go' state pending my agreement.

After dealing with the matters in hand, mostly by signing off each item she'd already efficiently resolved, Sidney and Ira came into the office. They brought me up to date.

Ira began. 'Firstly, oh lord and master, welcome back to normality, otherwise known as the real world. You will be pleased to know that the whole operation is rumbling along to its inevitable takeover of the Education mantle. We have our stalwarts in the right places, teaching resources recruited and being trained.'

'And being accommodated in economic properties, even in our new target areas,' Sidney added. 'And we are solvent. What else need you know?'

Ira came back in. 'You have stolen my thunder old man. But I'll forgive you just this once.'

'That sounds like the shortest Board meeting I've ever heard of,' I concluded from this. 'Why did I come back from travels so quickly?'

'Yes, why did you,' asked Ira. 'No faith?' I was uplifted to see my two fellow founders WERE self-motivated.

'If you really want to know, we are fast tourists and quick learners. We decided early on that we had gotten what we could from these cultures and that further dalliance would have been profligate.'

'Oh, how posh,' Ira replied. 'Care to explain?'

I did explain. 'We have our Education project, which in the short and long term gives a boost to our society. We know what subjects DON'T help, and we have discovered that meditation and some of its dictates can help individuals to improve their mental state.' I paused.

'There's a 'but',' Sidney put in.

'Yes, it hasn't worked for the masses beyond being its almost sole stable civilising force, up to a point. It needs Education too, and lots of other things, like wholesale economic acumen.

'So it's a tool, but not enough. I suspect it is much like in the Christian religion – finding God is sought after but not easily achieved by the average punter. In short I need to work harder on some additional technique of

Psychotherapy or whatever you call it. I don't like that term as it has bad associations, even if it is the right concept.

'So that's where I'm going. Meanwhile we work on the Education Department and the expansion and dissemination of our project. Broad scale Education evolution is definitely a game changer.'

'Want to hear some good news?' Ira asked, going off the subject a bit.

'I specialise in it, shoot.'

My husband, Arthur and my two younger sons want to join us here. They really see this big picture as you've described it. Arthur has had enough standing still and though Ian and Morris are young, they are enthused by their own progress and are, even in their own time, un-bugging students at their school, just for fun. I know that's depriving us of business and making their school look better than it deserves, but now they've had such success they see it as a career. Nigel is flying at the College, as you know.

'Super news Ira,' I replied. 'Maybe we should get all our graduates to do the same thing in their various schools. Another export avenue.'

'Just what I thought,' Ira added. 'We could make Nigel some sort of Field Education Representative In-charge, working here but monitoring it out there – tentacles spreading out, like geometric progressions.'

'Genius idea Ira.'

'What's the commission, boss?'

I shook my head. 'Some wise man once said that money is the root of all evil. I can't have you go that way Ira.'

'Might have known,' she added, shaking her head, and walking out with a big smile on her face.

Sidney gave me the lowdown on Corporate College and all matters financial. Then he added. 'Cliff is on board now and doing far more than I thought he would. He's loving the job and saving us a bomb. Gladys is as happy as a sandgirl.

He continued, 'You are looking good, my boy. Asia hasn't done you any harm. I see where you are going with all this. Maybe we should have a debating evening on the subject of Religion and spiritual existence. I'll be on your side. By the way I want to try out this meditation. Next time you come around to our place give me a session of it.'

'Anytime. In fact come around to our place on Saturday morning. Come around for breakfast.'

Sidney rose, then me too, and we had a man hug.

I couldn't wait for tomorrow so I arranged to meet Tom and Vince in Chiswick at three-thirty, at our favourite coffee place.

 Julia had walked right into some gifts from the Psychiatric profession. A couple of juicy malpractice cases were being taken to the courts with Gavin as the attorney.

These cases would be a gift from heaven in my attempt to continue my efforts with the studio bosses and the Psychiatric profession – landmark cases.

One concerned a gross patient violation, a lady sexually assaulted by a hospital Psychiatrist, witnessed by a patient who was himself brutally assaulted by another fellow Psychiatrist for daring to report the matter. Fortunately the latter assault was also witnessed by a cleaner who was subsequently dismissed.

'Another case involved the police trying to arrest a man who was trying to protect another victim of violence at a public meeting. The former resisted vociferously and then physically, after being truncheoned to the ground. He was taken to a Psychiatric hospital and sectioned and put into confinement and then the usual drugs. Visitations were denied, but plenty of witnesses.

Apparently there had been quite a few other cases but weren't prosecutable owing to too much 'your word against mine'. Who would believe the word of an 'unhinged' patient against that of a 'professional?'
Julia's counterparts in Queen Anne St. had assembled quite a wad of evidence. Julia phoned Gavin and agreed to meet him at home that night to hand him the cases. She also rang me before I set out to meet Tom and Vince, figuring it would strengthen my arguments. She gave me the full details.

At our meeting in Chiswick I indeed waved the cases at them and after some revitalisation of my cohorts got them to agree a meeting with Alistair McIntyre, the top director we'd met before.

'Here we go again,' Tom sighed. 'We will muster our will to yours Brandon and have another go. Bring your man Gavin along for legal support.'

'Just for more support,' I added, 'send the Psychiatrists a letter inviting them onto the next program, to defend themselves. Tell them it will be an open forum with me and Peter Hillingdon versus whoever they want to send along to defend their side. Ask for an opportunity to visit a hospital of their choice to see what they do, along with the cameras. They can see the format of the program beforehand and the film we will have of these two legal cases that will accompany it.'

'Whew, Brandon, that should put the wind up them. I can see injunctions flying here.'

'Yes, but I doubt it will come to that at first. Wait until you see these cases. We have the relatives of the victims and other witnesses ready to speak up. If the culprits don't show up we are on firm ground having invited them to 'put us down'.

'Just for good measure I am going to put an advertisement in the big dailies for people to come forward who have experienced or witnessed maltreatment and deficient results. We need lots of armoury.'

Wow!' Vince gasped. 'Will our lily-livered Execs be able to confront the storm all this will whip up?'

'Ok, it's your turn to pay Brandon,' Tom declared, getting up. 'We need to get back to the studios and get going on this. I'd like to meet them before they nick off for the day.' Tom was in the game again and Vince equally. What a first day back, I thought . This is better than floating down the Ganges and fighting off the mosquitos and flies.

––––––––––––––––––

A joyful dinner was had at the McDonalds, along with the Waterman clan. Gavin was primed to lead into the legal action and apart from a little other shop talk there was lots more banter around the Eastern trip and the new house.

Julia drove me home and parked outside our house with a perfect first-time reverse parking manoeuvre.

'What a waste of time us having had to do driving tests,' Julia remarked. 'When do our Formula One careers begin?'

'Well, my love,' I began to inform her, 'there are a few intermediate steps between parking and one hundred and fifty mph racing. But I agree, we are naturals.'

We almost skipped down our front path arm-in-arm, entered the house, and plonked ourselves down on the well-sprung sofa and reviewed the first day back together.

'Time for some meditation,' I suggested. 'Shall we?'

Julia, well beyond neophyte now, agreed. 'Why not? Do you know I think it may be possible to do the same thing on the move, you know – sort of transitional rather than transcendental, or both.'

'We can practise that on Hampstead Heath and telepath each other at the same time,' I invited.

'Brandon, we don't go on dates anymore. You don't have to dream up any more of your courting nonsense now,' she said leaning over and kissing me.

'And you don't need to try and seduce me now that we are married.'
'So we are old hands already, eh, and don't need to bother. Do you know, judging by the sounds that on occasions emanated from my parents' bedroom, young exciting love goes on beyond the honeymoon.'

'My dear,' I responded, 'I will always be under your spell, and love is perpetual between us.' I lifted her up and carried her upstairs, without any objections from her. Suffice to say, this new bed was officially christened.

———————————

Julia and I met with Ivis Knightly. She was somewhat a replica of Elizabeth Taylor, the actress, in that she was beautifully dark featured with a pretty face, but she wasn't glamorous. You would have to speak with her for a while to then see the deceptively sharp intelligence and unpretentious nature which grew on you more and more. I guessed she was in her early thirties.

Julia said to her, 'I love all these articles you have written.' Veronica had spread out three different magazines containing three different articles on me and Julia, in addition to another that covered the wedding.

'Where do you want me to go from here with all this?' she asked.

'Do you have any way into any of the nationals?'

'I've had a few things printed here and there on fairly uncontroversial and rather innocuous subjects, but my scant contacts there may adventure further.'

'What I'm looking at Ivis, is a campaign of public awareness on the subject of Mental Health; the more 'in your face' the better. I want to know how far you would go to print the truth, and if indeed you agree with what we see as the truth.'

'Well, I don't know all yet,' she confessed, 'but after having seen your TV programs I was ninety percent there, and after your wedding and meeting all your comrades here I felt I had cracked the whole one hundred. Who wouldn't have?' Julia and I looked at each other knowingly and Julia said, 'the fact that we are speaking to you and no one else is your answer to that one.'

'I have a few other possible takers,' Ivis added. 'They are not mainstream journos but they specialise in local newspapers in many parts of the country – sort of feeder lines. They are, of course, freelance. One or two have worked on nationals in the past.'

'Give us some of what they have had in print Ivis, so we can get the feel of their work, but the more the merrier.'

Julia asked her, 'how would you go about it yourself Ivis?'

Ivis hesitated for a short while, then told us, 'I've been giving this some thought. In order to get some sort of entrance into the national dailies I would position myself as a broad freelancer and submit a number of different subjects, like maverick politicians (of whom there are few), successful business people who grew small empires from nothing, effective animal welfare activists; you see what I mean?

'I don't mean frivolous things. It has to be things that capture the attention of the public. Then into that I'd throw in my coup d'etat, the Macman enterprise, a sort of serialised foray interspersed with other subjects.

'I wouldn't approach it as a sort of Macman press agent. Whilst building up credence I'd shower these publications with loads of reports and articles, giving both sides of the story, even-handedly, and not exactly expressing my opinion but putting facts to the audiences for them to make up their own minds, much the same as you did Brandon in your TV programs.'

'I like it,' Julia enthused. 'What about you Brandon?'

'Let's do it. I like your style Ivis.'

Julia thumped the desk with her hand and said to Ivis, 'come and I will educate you on the statistics of the Psychiatric regimens and the cases we have on the go. I'll tell you all we have seen and heard.'

We all rose and I welcomed Ivis anew into our fold and went off into my office to amuse Veronica as was the familiar ritual of business.

Julia and Ivis went into Gavin's office for introductions and debriefs and then they drove down to Queen Anne Street to meet with her counterparts there.

CHAPTER SIX

In our West London Chiswick College, Cindy and James Hopkins were sat around a table in the canteen cum staff room, along with myself.

'Cindy, you are a natural. I saw you dealing with that young lady out there. Brilliant. You catch on fast.'

Cindy was abuzz at this accolade. 'Thankyou sir,' she said exaggeratedly respectful. Then, after a short silence she added, 'and there's more. I have spoken obviously with Ira, Delia and Gladys, and of course Veronica and I have to warn you that I am becoming a fully-fledged member of the ladies union after finding myself being artfully, not so much coerced, but surreptitiously seduced into the somewhat compulsively attractive nature of the work here, requiring more and more time and attention. I find myself deserting my husband and children sometimes.'

I was feigning a yawn and said, 'I see where this is going.' James was smiling to himself. 'Well James, emancipated woman has arrived. Capitulate or just humour her. Tell her how much you understand.'

'Oh, I do, I do,' James said. 'I'm enjoying myself in the kitchen and at the supermarket. I know Cindy will soon learn the art of working quickly and incisively so as to be able to keep within the statutory hours of the normal workplace. The lawns and gardens I will fit in around my other helpful duties.

He went on, 'Do you know, I've realised now why womankind agreed to bow to men and become what they claim are domestic slaves. They love their role.'

'Don't go on James. I've heard it all before. They love their union. And Cindy, I am glad you are a fully paid-up member. It means you care. I will extend your contract of employment.'

Cindy shook her head. 'I was told I'd shake my head like this after a brush with officialdom.'

'Anyway,' I said, changing the subject, 'I have some good stuff for you. Michael Stone, our PI, has come up with enough dope on Levison to sink his ship. As I told you the other day, he's an adulterer, and we've found he has a few financial irregularities which explain how he lives beyond his reasonable means. All this will be of interest to the Department.'

'I am going to suggest to you, James that you tell him you have been thinking about your plight and how it came about and that you have decided that you are going to do an investigation yourself into the matter to clear your name, despite what he advised you to do. Hint that it all seems to have started around the time he joined the staff and that it should just be a matter of asking the right people about who said what to whom.

'Tell him that perhaps the error of false information may get corrected on the way and be retracted and hopefully you'll be exonerated. Tell him you have the support of the Teacher's Union in this investigation.

'If he explodes at you or reacts in any negative way, just realise he will think you are on the cusp of finding out the truth about his activities. At some point along the way he might get back into his stirrings and create a campaign against you. At the right point we can reveal our hand'

'God, you should write mystery stories Brandon,' James sighed, breathing out. 'The Teacher's Union is a good idea.'

'Go for him love,' Cindy told James. 'There's a lot at stake here beyond your job. We can't educate the world like we are. We need Department backing.'

'Right.

'Then start asking questions of your most respected friends there first,' I suggested. So the plan was hatched. How could it fail?

Michael Stone hadn't been idle. 'I think we have a smoking gun, Brandon,' he told me. 'This man has an interest in the 'Ladies of the Night' place. He takes a considerable cut from it all, along with the cream on the top, if you see what I mean, and his wife doesn't know about it.'

'Nice one Michael. Can you send me what you've got? I may not have to use it yet. What's the damage?'

'You know Brandon I so enjoyed this whole thing I almost feel guilty for charging you,' Michael answered.

'Well, examine your conscience a little more closely and consult your business principles and send me a bill for the balance. We may yet have to expand on this game.' I felt well-armed.

I was immediately into expansion mode again. I was thinking of my contacts in India and at the retreat in Thailand. They really need our methods. They really need Education, period.

I decided to invite them all to London for a complete tour of our operation, and training in the techniques, with a view to running the operation in their countries. There was Tanawat in Bangkok, Anjat and Jaya Singh in Indore and Daler Singh in Calcutta. And the cream on top – Smithy.

Then I thought about touring the English speaking world, by using my ever-increasing notoriety, to do TV programs in the many major cities, or at least on the major TV and radio networks.

I envisioned a worldwide network of Colleges which would all be stepping stones to establishments for my yet-to-be-discovered Psychotherapy. Got to think big and build up unassailable public relations, I told myself.

This brought on the subject of copyrights. I stepped into Gavin's office.

'Morning Gavin,' I chirped brightly. 'I've got another legal question for you?'

'I was warned you might increase my workload,' he responded quite affably.

'It's a simple one. Our technology of teaching needs to be patented does it not, if we want to keep it pure and unalterable or even free of being hijacked?'

'Do you know, I was thinking that myself.' Gavin added. 'Yes, in a word. It needs a name. You are obviously its author.'

'What about 'The Waterman Technique of learning' or, 'The Learning Technique' or 'How to Study'?' I suggested.

'Hmm, I like the second one best. You don't need to have your name in the title. You could possibly re-publish your materials into a proper book of the same name,' Gavin suggested.

'OK, I like it. Whatever protects us best. Can you take care of it?'

'Sure can mister. By the way what is next with our TV chaps?'

'Oh yes, I had to recharge our two boys. They became discouraged. They are setting up ANOTHER meeting with Alistair McIntyre who decided that no news from the opponents was good news. I need you to come along and help me do the final sell to these careful men.'

'Same idea as before?' Gavin asked

I explained what 'homework' I'd given Tom and Vince.

I then touched base with Ira and Sidney and lastly, Veronica.

'How're they working you Vero?' (everyone called her that now).

'Do you know boss, I've got a successful thing going here. When my boyfriend and other friends tell me they hardly see me these days I reply with that old saying, 'if you can't beat them, join them.' And do you know, when I tell them what I do they get curious and come and join me. I've been the best student recruitment agent you've ever had.'

She looked at me curiously. I picked up on it. 'I bet the Union has had something to say about that. I think I know what's coming next.'

'I can't just sit here and chat,' she said, turning back to her typing, 'I've got so much to do if I'm going to be out of here before bedtime.'

'Me too,' I agreed, leaving the point hanging. 'Wait till I promote you.' I waltzed on past. She giggled.

Gavin and I showed up at the TV studios a week later. Obviously it wasn't ITV's immediate priority. Alistair McIntyre, Ken Crofton and Barry Lancolm were all present in their meeting room.

'I think we've been over all this Mr. Waterman,' Alistair McIntyre pronounced. 'I see little point in going further, being that the Psychiatrists have gone quiet.'

'They are hoping WE'LL have backed off and gone quiet.' I pointed out. 'They didn't respond to our letter, did they?'

'No, and I think that's as far as we should go in tempting fate,' he added.

Gavin came in here. 'You are right of course, to want to protect yourselves from controversial legal matters. Have you put this matter to your shareholders? After all it is they that are the ones you are really protecting. I see the share price has taken a sharp spike in recent times. Wouldn't they want more of the same? I see your advertisers are clamouring for more peak time space to increase your revenues, with your share of the viewing public also up on anything before our programs. You COULD raise all this with the shareholders.'

McIntyre was starting to squirm a bit. 'There hasn't been a shareholder's meeting for a few months. It's not usual to discuss individual programs at such meetings. Our share price is up its true, and the viewing figures, but I don't want to tempt fate and have it crash. We are not talking about some small organisation we are up against here, rather a governmental institution. These are big boys we are dealing with. Should we get tied up in legals and all, then what will happen to the share price?'

I came in here. 'There are lots of 'what ifs', including what if ITV became the doyen of documentaries and news? What if the investors multiplied? What if the Psychiatrists don't have a case? What if their exposure leads to concrete reform in the mental health field? What if mental patients are protected by law and get decent treatment? What if they prove me wrong and I have to eat crow?

I could see I had them really listening now. 'We have a plan which I will outline just now which not only calls their bluff but makes them look ridiculous in the eyes of the law if they don't go along with it.'

I handed out copies of my plan to each. They started reading and I let them digest it. This was the plan Gavin and I had articulated earlier.

After they had read the plan I expanded. 'You need to see the videos we have of the abuse cases, plus all the other evidences. They will have a full opportunity to see the program plan before it airs. They will bluster some more and we will call their bluster. I will call their bluster. It's ME on the line here, not you.'

McIntyre asked me, 'why would you stick your neck out so far just for a TV program? I can't see it's for money?'

'The public need to know about this thing. They don't know.' I paused for effect. 'They send their loved ones in trouble to these 'experts' in good faith, thinking they know more than anyone else, and then wonder why there are no results. It gets explained to them as 'we did our best,' 'difficult case', whatever. There's nowhere else to go.

'Unless the public are disabused of this whole sham it will continue and lives are lost, people become medication addicts, and the practitioners and drug companies get richer at our expense. Alistair, it is INHUMAN,' I emphasised thumping my hand on the table.'

After a pause, for more effect I continued. 'My neck is not that valuable in the grand scheme of things, a statement made by many a soldier going to war.

I will survive. I will sleep at night. It is not a matter to be careful about. I believe it is a matter to stick your neck out about; not recklessly, but measured. I think my plan does all that. I want you to join me. There is a proposed letter to the Psychiatrists at the bottom of the plan. I will be sending that to them straight away.

I calmly rose and gathered my papers. 'Look this over gentlemen.' Gavin rose with me and we left the room leaving the others to do whatever.

Tom followed us out. 'If they don't bight on that Brandon…then on what? I'll put together the videos for them to look at and the program format. This is exciting. We will work on them. I think Barry and Ken are with us you know.'

'OK Tom, thanks. Let me know if they run with it. I suppose they may want to know what the response is to my communication with the Psychiatrists.' We shook hands and left.

In the car back to the Office I became uncharacteristically quiet.

'Penny for your thoughts,' Gavin asked as we waited silently at a traffic light.

I snapped out of it. 'I was wondering what it would take to set up a TV channel, and briefly wondered if the BBC would take us on. Then I was thinking about that glorious woman we both have a close interest in.' I was back to battery now.

Gavin told him, 'I will look into it for you, the TV channels I mean. You can take on the Julia thought. She struck gold with you Brandon you know. You are a force of nature.'

———————————

Seeing that I wasn't in the habit of stringing things out and just waiting for them to happen, many events started to come together quickly.

The exporting of our Education program came together just as I had planned, somehow magically getting our dramatis personae from Asia together at one time, giving them the training and their way forward. Smithy decided to stay on and lap up some of our stardust while the 'abbots' returned to get stuck into 'Project Asia'. Smithy was to do a full apprenticeship in the College too.

Smithy stayed at the younger Waterman's – our first guest. He was going to lap up all he could on we two prodigies and follow us around whilst taking time off too to visit his kin in Wales.

Ivis Knightly did indeed eke her way into the Dailies and put my first article into one of the Sundays.

Gavin had everything copyrighted and patented. He'd made the whole College a limited company, separate from Macman. He discovered that opening a TV channel was a non- starter for the moment, mainly because of the expense of starting up. The BBC? He didn't bother.

My communication to the Psychiatrists was met with an even stronger response than before, a response that would have most quaking in their corporate boots. But not me; been there and done that. I decided I'd do another series of TV programs just to keep the public on side and interested in us generally – nothing about Psychiatry itself except a come-on for the public to expect one with the Psychiatrists face to face. This would appear at the end of the three program series, a sort of 'watch this space' job.

Over the ensuing few months Tom and I shot three half hour programs, all under the watchful eyes of their careful Execs, who incidentally had warmed up a bit to the task. They had received no threat from the Psychiatrists. That would be my privilege.

The first program was on our tour of the East and discussed the merits of meditation. I did a live demo of how it is done using Julia as the meditator and myself as the commentator.

The second was about a possible basis for a new means of helping people come to real terms with their life traumas and deficiencies. I went into the parallel between life failures and educational failures. I did a very impinging graphic on my own idea of what one was addressing, dismantling the idea that the brain was the mind and emphasising the fact that THE PERSON is what we are dealing with.

I had a young chap, one of Peter's old subjects, just sit with me and talk about times he'd been bullied, and then times when he had successful interaction with others, back and forth, until this chap felt better about it all. I invited him to see if there were any conclusions he could draw from all this.

I then put it to the audience that there was no need for chemicals or force, and that my first idea of a therapy was far from a done deal, but simply a demonstration that, like with my students, one is simply addressing an aware person and emphasising people CAN change their minds about themselves.

The third program was a precursor to a full-on attack on Psychiatry. I excluded any counselling as I explained that the more a person loses a grip on himself and running his daily life, the gentler the approach had to be. I'd done an experiment with a chap the College actually hadn't accepted as a student as he had too many issues and was really introverted. I'd actually had this chap do a full medical to discover any physical deficiencies, such as nutrition, diabetes or any other serious illness not addressed before.

I'd arranged for this chap to take time off school, live with a young couple who lived in a semi-rural area on the outskirts of London, away from his normal life, and who took it in turns to give this chap a supervised life. There was plenty of good food and rest and walks in the local woods. He'd helped around the house, and soaked up lots of friendly communication and attention, all until he'd come upscale and demonstrated that he was up to returning to his life, with lots of advised help from his family and selected mates.

All this demonstrated that the contrast of this with the normal mental hospital was chalk and cheese. Of course people who were dangerously psychotic but appearing to be normal, and those who'd just flipped out, had to be confined and were not the subject of this study though the principle still applied – no severe or brutal treatments.

The programs were very successful for ratings and publicity and certainly warmed up the ITV Execs.

Of course I added a taster for the next program where I teased the audience with a possible debate with Psychiatrists or maybe a tour of one of these establishments, to respond to my earlier exposure.

CHAPTER SEVEN

Julia and I and Smithy were sitting in our rear terrace one Sunday morning, reading the Sunday papers, hoping to see any article from Ivis.

We found it in the Review lift-out. 'Listen to this,' Julia enthused. 'This is the heading: "Watermans head East." Then it goes on: "not happy enough with improving the education of thousands of students and tackling the shortcomings of Mental Health, these two adventurers, on their honeymoon, really went East to discover what secrets the Orient might hold in their quest for the answers to the conundrums of human advancement."

She read further with me listening intently. Ivis really did lay out matter-of-factly what we did on our tour, going into the subject of meditation and the basics of the religions we had come across, all based on a debrief I had given her, plus a few pictures provided by Julia.

'Wow, she's good this girl,' I commented. 'She's really on our side.'

Julia kept reading. I waited for her to finish. Then I said to her ' I'm planning on us going on a tour of English speaking countries once we've wrapped up the TV program on Psychiatry, which I expect to propel us further into public prominence, even abroad.'

Julia chirped in, 'Oh, instead of Waterman dates we are now doing Waterman honeymoons instead.'

'Well, if it's remotely modelled on our official honeymoon, then, yes,' I answered. 'More fun and romance and lots of career opportunity thrown in. We'll end up in L.A. and become stars in Hollywood. We could make a film on Psychiatry; I don't mean a documentary, more of a mockumentary. I'll write a screenplay. Seriously, that just came to me, which reminds me I need to finish that novel I've had on the go for years. Why not this afternoon?'

'Will I ever see you again?' she mused.

'I mean I'll actually finish it this afternoon. I'll get Veronica to find a publisher and away we go.'

'In that case I will go and visit Ivis to wrap up the articles for distribution to the Weeklies and Monthlies on the Mental Health front. You won't mind if I use the car, darling?'

'I wasn't planning on writing my book in the car now, was I?' came the response. 'Bring a take-away back with you, eh? You know, curry with chapattis and poppadoms,' I suggested, starting to remove myself toward the study.

Smithy was agog at all this.. 'Is this what you do on Sundays? Ah yes, it's not work is it? At least you are doing something normal tonight. I think I'll skip off to Wales and see my folks and some old pals. They WILL be old by now, almost.'

I took this opportunity to nail Smithy down. 'OK, you've been here Smithy for a number of weeks now. Are you ready to fire?'

'Almost. Delia and Dan are going to finish me off next week on the whole program. I've seen your TV programs, read all the articles. I know what I'm getting into here I'd say. I'll get Education into Thailand for real. I'll wind down my tourist thing as I switch over to Education. I've still got to keep afloat monetarily.'

'OK. Here's another thing.' I was thinking. 'Get a College going and a staff trained. Copy our blueprint here. You will need a deputy or two, like Ira and Sidney. Who you take on is measured by a few criteria which I will outline for you. Come to think of it I am going to put down all my steps and business philosophies into a small book – 'How to Set Up and Expand a Business.'

'And you need to find a proper Thai woman and make her a partner too. Julia is your model.'

'Wow, how many are like her?'

'My book will go into that a bit. It's all about being a proper person yourself. You are a good man Smithy. You've been under-utilising yourself. You will attract the right person when you are in the right way attractive yourself.'

'Yes, I've noticed this about you. You attract good people. And you are right, I've been coasting, living a comfortable colonial life.'

I then came straight out with it. 'Smithy I want you to be our man in South East Asia. You can exclude China at this time, and the Vietnam corner too. But there is Japan, Malaysia, Bangladesh, Pakistan, and maybe Burma. We have reps in India, as you know. They will get on with it.'

'Good God. Do you think I'm up to that?'

'You'll soon find out. First steps first. Once you get rolling you'll know better if it is real; just like we did.'

'Smithy, international executive…. never run anything much in his life, now headhunted by Mr. Big himself (and I don't mean that flippantly).' He was pondering.

'Just follow the sign posts. You have the raw materials. Incidentally you have Tanawat to help you, the chap that was here with the Indian Sikhs. And I'll give you a tip – Tanawat's assistant, Anchara. Check her out, know what I mean?

Smithy came out of what he'd been plunged into. 'I'm going to give it a go. You can count on me Brandon.'

'Excellent. I'm going to write my book. Give my regards to your folks.' I rose, as did Smithy and we shook hands firmly.

––––––––––––

Our study was the third bedroom, plenty big enough for the two of us at once, which was often the case. I got straight down to it, picking up easily from where I had left off. It was a heroic tale of mind over matter on the part of an unlikely decathlete. It had lots of setbacks and drama and injuries and personal mishaps, goodies and baddies and finally triumph on the top stage; a book for young and not so young any more.

The afternoon came and went as I immersed myself in the task, without a break. I completed it with the waft of curry reaching my nasal passages. What timing!

Fifteen minutes later I bounded down the stairs three at a time and danced into the kitchen and put my arms around my beloved and lifted her off the floor and swirled her round. Putting her down gently I held her face in my hands, gazed into her big blue eyes and kissed her gently.

'I smell the breath of an Indian,' I said, sniffing the air. 'Could this be true? I'm ravenous.'

She pointed to a seat at the kitchen table and ordered, 'Sit!'

I sat and started to chant one of our meditation lines, with my knife and fork pointed upward and head bowed down. She brought along the plate and waved it under my nose. I came out of my 'reverie' and examined the fare briefly and started to tuck in, fork in one hand, chapatti in the other. Julia joined me and I asked her about her afternoon.

'Totally successful,' she replied. 'Ivis and I bonded for real today. She's such a good sort; tailor-made for us. Good recruitment job my man. We have it all sorted, that is, what articles to go where and when. What about you?'

'Totally successful. They won't be able to put it down, the whole two hundred thousand or more of them. I got a real head of steam up there today; like pouring molasses from a barrel. And my typing speed is up to about ninety words per minute I reckon.'

'I think we have earned a glorious night of togetherness after this. Why don't we watch a movie?' Julia suggested.

'You are right, my love. Shall I go out and hire one? We have this video machine now. Why don't we break it in? What do you fancy – drama, comedy, musical?'

She was ahead of me. She got up and extracted a catalogue from the local video store and handed it to me. 'Let's see if our choices are the same.'

I read through them and their brief descriptions and after a few minutes put my finger on my choice. 'That one. 'It's a Mad, Mad, Mad World', Jimmy Durante. Isn't it just?'

She went over to a cupboard drawer and extracted a video and plonked it down in front of me. 'What! You've hypnotised me! You chose that from all of the rest?'

She sat down on my lap, kissed my forehead and told me. 'No, not at all. We are in such fine tune I just knew you'd be up for this.'

'You are amazing. I'll wash up, you make coffee, and we are off to the movies.'

This was how we lived – always in tune, ever attentive and sensitive to the other's needs, no careless communications, no arguments except fun debates on many subjects. Surreal. What might one expect from world changers? Married couples, even newly-weds don't behave like this, do they?

CHAPTER EIGHT

Julia and Gavin and I were seated in a rather austere oversized room at an enormous table, considering there were only three of us. There were a number of pictures of important-looking men (and one woman) around the walls, presumably past Presidents or Founders perhaps.

We didn't just sit waiting but got up and strolled around the room and looked out the window. This was the HQ of the Royal Medico-Psychological Association.

In came a well-tailored gent with a surprisingly genial smile. We three moved toward him. 'I am Gareth Bonnington,' he pronounced. 'Thankyou for being here. I am one of the legal team.'

'You must be Brandon Waterman,' he said to Gavin, offering his hand.

Gavin shook his hand and corrected him politely. 'Gavin McDonald actually,' he responded, enjoying the somewhat nonplussed look on Bonnington's face. Gesturing to me he corrected him. 'This is Brandon Waterman, and this is Julia Waterman, his wife, and my daughter, as it happens.'

After shaking off the embarrassed surprise Bonnington offered us a seat at the table, opposite him. 'So it is a family affair,' he said. 'I must admit I wasn't expecting you to be so youthful Mr. Waterman.'

'The story of my brief life,' I replied. 'I am the Managing Director of Macman Ltd. Julia here heads the Investigatory Department and Gavin is our Legal Director. You asked for this meeting, sir. I hope we can make our position clearer to you.' I said this with no hint of menace. 'I presume you didn't see the original TV program yourself.'

'No, I didn't, but I have surely heard of it. A few of my colleagues, who will be joining me in a moment, have certainly seen it.'

At this point the large oak door opened and another suited gentleman and a rather well-dressed middle aged woman in perfectly kempt greying hair entered the room. Bonnington stood, followed by the three guests. Introductions were made and everyone sat.

The lady, Margaret Lovett-Smith, took over the proceedings. 'I am one of the senior Psychiatrists here, and,' indicating the other gentleman, 'my colleague here is a senior Director.' His name was Charles Frenton.

Margaret Lovett-Smith began. 'As you well know by this we are more than concerned with the content of your TV program Mr Waterman. You have taken upon yourself to be the expert on our subject and somewhat ridicule it publicly, a situation we cannot take lightly.'

She had gathered all her bombast now and was talking down to me, directly. She continued. 'As expressed in our letter to you we intend to follow through with our intention to use the full arm of the law if you don't draw a line under this matter forthwith.'

She went on a bit, pretty much in total arrogance, hoping to scare the blazes out of us Macmen. When she wound down it was my turn.

'I hear you madam,' I replied confidently. 'Perhaps we are wrong in our initial portrayal of your subject, but until we find contrary evidence we feel duty-bound to report what appears to be, not even just on the surface, a matter of public concern.'

I was getting into full stride and just as the good lady was about to express her outrage I quickly went on, signalled with a quick wave of the hand. 'Now, we can go at each other and end up nowhere. We have a simple plan which will give you a complete chance to refute any claims we have made or exaggerated.

'This plan is to gather representation of successful cases, instances of complete turn-arounds and broadcast them on media, and allow your experts to appear on our films and explain your subject and correct any misrepresentation; even film inside a hospital or two and show what goes on and what you are dealing with.'

The Director chap, Charles Frenton, immediately came in on what he took to be a patronising stance I was taking. 'I think it outlandish that you have the gall to question a highly respected institution such as ours and try and drag it through the mud. We have been developing this subject for decades and you sir are hardly out of school. Are you sure you want to do this?'

I was in my element and not the least squirmy. In fact I had orchestrated the conversation to go this way, fully expecting what I had heard.

'Ok, be that as it may, we intend to bring the whole subject to light and do it more even-handedly than how it began. We would give you total preview of any intended programs so you would know what the content was to be and allow full response to any inaccuracies. You would have to take whatever action you deemed necessary to protect your interests. On our heads that would rest, of course.'

I continued after putting down politely an attempt by Frenton to butt in.

'We have documented and film evidence of abuse cases, which I'm sure you would be stunned to discover exist. Then again you may well want a right of reply to these.

Julia continued this theme. 'We intend to show you these cases before airing. We are discovering quite a number of these; more than you will feel comfortable with. We are talking about sexual and physical abuse here, beyond that of the chemical and shock factors practised in your hospitals.'

We left this hanging for a few seconds as the three opposite muttered and guffawed. Then I added, 'In fact we may be doing you a favour here and being a sort of watchdog. I don't know if you are aware of all the goings-on in some of your establishments. It must be difficult to oversee all of this. Even in the medical hospitals there are malpractices and mistakes. This would give you the opportunity to make public your own outrage and set right the violations of patients.'

'We would certainly want to see your cases as you call them,' Lovett-Smith put in. 'We would certainly investigate these ourselves. As for you pronouncing on our subject we must insist you drop this campaign.'

Bonnington, the legal man came in here. 'Should you carry on any further with this, injunctions and suits would fly you know.'

Gavin was going to have his turn and said to Bonnington 'You and I will need to meet but let me tell you that you would be on shifting sands should you not at least take up the opportunity to refute and challenge any false assertions made. We know the laws of libel. Should you want to sue in the courts you will need to present your case anyway. You would be on trial for abuse of human rights and lack of effective results.'

He continued, 'I don't think I need point out here that the abuse cases we have may go to court themselves, either under our jurisdiction or totally independently. Do you want to get into these?'

I entered the fray again, to wrap up. 'Before we get to all this unpleasant stuff, why don't you let us present your evidence to the contrary and perhaps even put us back in our box, if that's what it comes to. You seem to view yourselves as a respected and needed public service. We'll back off if we are over the top or unfair and particularly if there is an agreed way forward so that people aren't illegally sectioned, or otherwise abused in your care.'

The three had heard enough. They started to make a move to rise and end the meeting.

'Just one more thing,' I said. 'You may think we have an opportunistic axe to grind here. Look, whether your treatments are right or wrong there has to be a way to bring all illegalities to an end. Sectioning has to acquire specific guidelines that protect patient rights, informed family permission must be given before any extensive drug treatment and before ANY ECT or lobotomies are performed, and abuse of already over-the-edge patients has to cease. Proper independent inspection needs to occur as you are dealing with patients' sanity here. I know it is an onerous job – humans at their weakest and worst.

'That's all we are after here. It's not notoriety, money or anything else dishonourable. We are concerned citizens as I would think all of you are too. But at the moment it's not right.'

The three opposite all rose, saying nothing. We Macman three rose too and watched the backs of the three others start to disappear. Bonnington hesitated and simply said, 'this way people. We'll be in touch.' He ushered us out.

Out on the street Julia came up with a good idea. 'Let's have a coffee.'

'Good idea,' Gavin agreed. Into a nearby coffee house we went.

Seated and served and sipping at our cappuccinos we discussed the rather brief meeting and its fairly abrupt end. Gavin began, 'they aren't going to come on the programs or allow us access to hospitals. We will need to just follow our plan. I suggest we do a program which sets out an even-handed portrayal of their operation. We need to find patients who were treated well, who were 'set free' in a satisfactory state, or if it is possible, benefitted from the treatment.'

'We could find some Psychiatrists willing to come on the program and speak for, or at least honestly for their side, under our questioning or lead,' I said. 'Maybe these very same people could rake up the examples we want. I'm sure we can read between the lines and show the holes without going direct for the jugular. Our TV guys would appreciate this approach.'

Julia added her bit. 'The abuse cases can be the shock at the end. We actually should take a few of them to court and show what damage they are in for and then see if they will try to agree to reform, via the law of course.'

We all agreed and I immediately phoned Tom at ITV to tell him the news and arrange for the first program to be done.

––––––––––––––

The programs were two months in the making.

'We'll send this first one to the Psychiatrists; they should be somewhat mollified by this', I suggested. 'No slander, quite even handed and those two Psychiatrists somewhat fell into our plan in admitting the limitations of their subject; in fact admitting they don't cure mental illness.'

'It was good also to make it known that though invited on and having been given the opportunity to let us into their establishments, the top brass or even underling representation did not take the opportunity to state their case.'

Gavin was a little pensive for a while and then added, 'well when they get this we will have asked them for their response which could be added before airing. We can do no more. The public will now have seen the opposing view, even if made to look rather inadequate by artful questioning by Mr. W here.'

Tom said, 'and our top brass are rather comfortable with it so far.'

Julia couldn't wait to get into the act too. 'The next program is about cases isn't it – good and bad? Fortunately, their worst are so bad and their best are, to be charitable, mediocre. Besides it's my turn to star on the telly.'

'We'll give them a week to come up with a response and then we'll start scheduling the programs, say three weeks apart,' I decided.

'After we've heated up the media and stoked up public opinion sufficiently Julia and I are off on our second honeymoon, this time in the U S of A. We have already researched all the major and not-so-major TV stations, newspapers, chat shows, and radio programs. The response is positive. The more controversial the better, they tend to be saying. Hollywood here we come. Hollywood's probably the last stop on our tour, unless we want to add Canada as well.'

Tom couldn't restrain himself. 'What about a bit of glory for we makers of the programs? Aren't producers supposed to get more dosh than the stars?'

'Well we do need roadies,' I retorted. 'We are only getting expenses in all this you know. Don't worry Tom, when it comes to our blockbuster movie on the subject, you can reap your reward. Your names will be the biggest and boldest at the end of all the credits. You can pay me a commission on all future films you make in Tinsel Town. Seriously, come with us if you want, but don't spoil the honeymoon.'

'You mean fly-on-the wall stuff? Enough, I'm off.'

We broke up and went our ways, awaiting the feedback from the Psychiatrists. I had included in the mailing to them, a Bill of Reform with a video of the first program, with an invitation to meet and discuss it. More ammunition for the guns.

———————

'Ivis, you've made me a national villain. But I like it. Those who think me a villain I don't really want to know beyond the fact that they have passed the first test of being an enemy or ones to look out for.'

'Yep, you deserve it Brandon. It's all notoriety and it's all good. I have a big splash coming up in one of the Dailies which shows you as a husband, humanitarian, entrepreneur, and writer. Your book is coming out that week and what a way to advertise it.'

'You are heaven-sent Ivis. You break the mould. You should set up a new group of journalists who look for what is there and report it honestly; maybe a 'good news only' group, or, if you like, 'rogue journalists'.'

'Brandon, you have led me on this path, so I'm going to follow it. Find out what should be known that benefits broadly, and report it as widely as possible. To hell with the flack.'

'Ivis, there is a big circus coming to town. It involves the programs we are trying to air on ITV on Psychiatry. How about I give you the scoop and you put it out to the big Dailies. I want you to try and worm your way into the Psychiatric hierarchy and tell them you have wind that there are to be rather revelatory programs about to hit the screens and you would like to get their side of the story so it can be printed far and wide. Only their side, but with you questioning them as if you are ON their side.'

Ivis asked, 'how do I reveal my source of information?'

'Tell them you have been down at the law courts (I'll tell you which one) and noticed a case of Macman v The Royal Medico-Psychological Association and you want to reveal to the public why they are seeking an injunction on our programs.

'We've already done one but the second one is harder hitting. Perhaps you should see a viewing of it before you get into this.'

'Well,' she said, 'you know that Julia and I have already put our heads together on this. I have seen the cases of abuse. I know where this is going. I'll get onto it.'

'Welcome to the public enlightenment party Ivis. Don't forget to put in a bit about us wanting to reform this Mental Health fiasco. I'd be happy to leave it at that and spend my energy on what to do as an alternative. You know what we want don't you?'

'I think so,' she replied. 'No more enforced or unwilling or unconsented incarceration (sectioning) or drugs, and a ban on ECT and lobotomies.'

'Well, almost,'I replied. 'When citizens have psychotic breaks or nervous breakdowns they have to go somewhere and they would behave like caged animals without some drugs, but not the anti-depressants they dole out at the moment; something more like sleeping pills. Some (the suicidal and criminal types) would have to be isolated as they are a danger to the public.'

Ivis was thinking on this for a few seconds. 'That doesn't leave them much in the way of armoury does it? Can you imagine the reaction the Psychiatrists would have to that?'

'That's the whole idea Ivis. Reform can't be perfunctory or token. These treatments are mind-altering and exacerbate the conditions they are 'meant' to be curing. Perhaps, to give you a bit MORE ammunition here, we should visit a few institutions, further afield than around London, so you are really armed with more facts and experience than you already have.'

'I'd be in that,' Ivis agreed.

'Watch our initial programs again. You have to know the brain theory and its antithesis. Know before you go, eh? I wouldn't want you to be some kind of acolyte here. Rather, increase your independent thought and knowledge. I need more of this anyway. We are more or less closed off to the institutions around here but up north or in Scotland and Wales we might get away with it.

'I might add that the 'brothers in arms' here, the background boys, are the drug companies. What an attack on their vested interest this would be. We might end up causing the biggest unemployment statistic ever, not to mention a boon to the legal profession.

'Anyway, good job Ivis. Keep it going. We'll make this world a better place yet. By the way Julia and I are planning on doing a tour of the States very soon. It occurs to me that you might like to be our press agent on this – you know, give out releases, arrange media interviews, select out the good and the bad. What do you think? It would take a lot off my plate.'

'Wow, that would broaden my scope. Why not bring Tom along too to film it all'

'You've met Tom eh?' I had a hunch that these two would make a good item, if they hadn't already become such. 'Well, good idea. What great people you are.'

CHAPTER NINE

Diane McAdam, the Minister for Education came across James Hopkins in the lift to the upper floors. 'Hullo Minister,' James chirped breezily.

'Mr. Hopkins, such good humour this early in the morning.' She said nothing for some seconds. 'I have heard a few rumblings about you Mr. Hopkins. Why don't you accompany me to my office before you start your day in earnest. The coffee is good on my floor and you won't need to wait for the trolley to come around.'

'Certainly,' James responded. James perked up a few notches, without the coffee yet. 'Yes there have been a few fireworks lately.'

In McAdams' office, with small talk over, and coffee served, McAdam looked at James and said, 'tell me do, then.'

'You should know the whole story here Minister. Brandon Waterman realised quickly who his nemesis was in all this. As you know it started back in Finchley High. His Deputy Head there was your current Director of Standards, (or something like that). The drop in response we had to Brandon's program in the Private School sector co-incided with Jake Levison's arrival here in the Department. My 'fall from grace happened then too, co-incidentally.

'You may have gathered that Brandon is not one to take injustice sitting down, so he decided to investigate Levison.'

McAdam butted in. 'You mean he hired someone to do this?'

Yes, Audacious, don't you think?'

'I thought this only happened in the movies,' she said, smiling in admiration.

James continued. 'Consequently he has found dirt on this chap; enough to sink him. On my part I dropped more than a few hints to Levison, straight to his face, and told him I was conducting my own investigation as to who said what to whom.'

The two were somewhat conspiratorial by this. James went on. 'He blackened and urged me to relent. Why not let things take their course he told me. Well I started to ask questions somewhat noisily so that he would notice. When I saw him subsequently in the canteen he blanked me. This is working I thought.'

'The things that go on downstairs,' she said, urging him on. 'What was the result of the investigation Waterman had started?

'I don't know all the gory details but suffice to say plenty enough extra curricular goings-on to sink him, here and at home, I'm sure. Let's just say he has been living dishonestly way beyond his means as a teacher or Executive, and his wife doesn't know the half of it.'

'Why haven't you and Waterman reported this?' she asked a little more seriously.

'We are keeping this up our sleeves to use as necessary. My own investigation may just cause him to blow himself off without us using all our powder, so to speak. Do you see what I mean?' He thought about what he was saying and added, 'I'm sure you understand that the end justifies the means.'

McAdam sipped her coffee while smiling and thinking. 'You two sons of guns are doing a Hollywood style number on Levison aren't you? Do you know I interviewed him recently and, to be honest there were more than shades of the pot calling the kettle black in his very slick demeanour; just a little too good to be true.

'Let's give it a few more days and we'll see if he falls on his sword. We better be right on all this. Thank you Mr. Hopkins. If this goes the way it looks like going you will be looking to be restored to your former position.' James smiled suitably but didn't overdo it.

'What convinced you to go with Waterman, just a truanting teenager at the time after all?'

'You have to meet this man to appreciate my judgement. Some people, like Levison, can't be judged by the proverbial book cover. Others are the real deal – straight down the middle. But I let him loose on my two under-performing boys, to test out his theories. The results were astonishing. These were two good boys who were languishing in considerable mediocrity and not really planning their future, beyond a bit of sport. Cindy, my wife, and I couldn't inspire them at all.

'Brandon came in and applied his techniques to them and got them inspired and firing almost overnight. Do you know Minister, we don't teach students how to learn. That's the bottom line. Learning is a technology which the world, let alone our school system here, doesn't have. They do now.'

McAdam was really impressed with James' relation of events. 'So how did the Privates get on with all this? It seems you are guilty of testing all this out, not just on your boys but in the Private School system. How did it go?'

'Like a dream until the snake appeared on the scene,' James replied. 'Then our illustrious Department warned them off, and things went slipping from there. About a half of the gained ground back-pedalled. I can give you the ones that have stayed with us and you can have them checked out yourself. But preferably not by Levison, please.'

James couldn't believe he was really being listened to, and by the boss to boot. This lady had smelt the rat herself, he thought, even if she hadn't located the source of the odour.

'This has been the best morning coffee I've had in ages, Mr Hopkins. You know I want to meet this young friend of yours. Can you arrange it?'

'I certainly can. Not only that, I can have him demonstrate live, what he can do.'

McAdam was becoming more businesslike now. 'No, a demo won't be necessary. I saw the TV show where he turned that lass around. Impressive.' She stood and thanked James for his time.

'I'll come back to you Minister. I'm sure Brandon would like to meet you too.' He left.

CHAPTER TEN

James Hopkins met with me in Central London the same evening, near to the Education Department.

'Brandon, you lucky man, you wouldn't believe what happened today.' He told me of the meeting with the Minister. 'And she wants to meet you.'

I sat back on the park bench. 'Really?'

'Yes, Really, he enthused. 'I had already started to ask questions in the Department, as we discussed, and was taunting Levison to the point where he was ignoring me. Then along comes the boss, the top dog. She had interviewed him and was not impressed. She was suspicious. You see she'd seen your public persona on TV a number of times and it didn't gel with Levison's angle.'

'And what do you see as the outcome now?' I asked.

'Levison will end up blowing himself off as his carefully constructed cover becomes apparent. I'll be exonerated and restored to my former position and I could use that to get an Education reform and re-ignite the Private Schools. Further than that you wouldn't have to be spreading all over the country; the Department would do it. And all that investigation you've done will have been for nothing. Well it's insurance anyway. Not only that, wait and see what happens when the Minister meets you!'

I was feeling a little flippant, 'shall we toss a coin to see which way it goes, or is it in the leaves?'

'What do you think, Brandon?'

'I can see a party coming up.' I patted James on the shoulder.

James continued his good humour. 'The wife and I had discussed it all and we decided to go for the jugular. I'm going to confront Levison again and hint that I know more about him than he realises, and it's not very savoury and, then give him the choice to be exposed or go quietly. This will drive him mad.'

I sat back and smiled at him. 'James I'm going to knight you. You can be in my trench any day. The wife too. She's a blooming stalwart.'

James blew out some air and chuckled, then looked at me..

'Do you always have this effect on people young man?' I chuckled again.

––––––––––––––––––

The upshot of the momentous events of this day occurred within the next week. True to his nature Levison hissed and play-acted and threatened, but in a matter of days had handed in his notice (well no notice) and was gone.

But forever? This man had more than a hunch about who was behind his demise.

James was restored to his position and set about his mission like a man possessed. He and I were soon into restoring the private schools, with the Department's blessing. Next was the more gradual process of getting the methodology into the mainstream, starting with a few proto types, not that my old school wasn't one of these, really.

CHAPTER ELEVEN

Julia and Ivis were sent up north, way up north, to Aberdeen in North Scotland. They managed to connive a visit to a mental institution there and were shown around the place. This was very much deja vu for Julia but she forced herself to remain just curious rather than affronted.

Ivis was very much the part and conducted most of the questioning. Julia asked the questions on treatments which would elicit justifications and excuses for obvious flaws in the treatments and operations. They both played an understanding position when presented with the answers.

In lieu of a film crew Julia wore a hidden mike with a recording device in her pocket. Was that illegal? Perhaps not permissible in court.

They visited several of such institutions over a few days, in Dundee, Edinburgh and Glasgow. In the latter they were actually curtailed as soon as they got too near the bone which was them talking to the patients and some of the staff as they left the premises.

They then visited northern English towns but restricted their activities to interviewing visitors outside the grounds. Here they were actually able to film the interviews, courtesy of Tom, and collected a whole panoply of material for the programs.

Ivis was a complete convert to the project now. Her reactions to what she heard gathered more and more disgust.

She and Julia, on the last leg of their tour, headed towards Wales where they aimed to include 'care' facilities in their targets. These proved to be more impermeable than the hospital institutions but they did score at one in Brecon, in the valleys, where they filmed a visitor leaving a rather smart looking place, more like a comfortable looking hotel. This lady was distraught after her visit and had to be somewhat revived by the two conspirators. They took her to a nearby tea house and let her spill the beans, with her agreement to be filmed.

Her husband had been arrested for a violent outburst at a Job Centre. The police had taken him to a Psychiatric facility in Cardiff where he was sectioned, loaded with the usual chemicals and moved to this secure Brecon 'care home', he now having become a shell of the man he was, almost unresponsive to his wife.

This case was further investigated by Queen Anne Street and served as more grist to the mill.

'What does one do instead of this rather summary justice?' Ivis asked.

Julia's response was a précis of their alternative. 'Temporarily holding someone who is 'out of control' is one thing, but plunging them straight into this regimen is another. The laws of sectioning violate human rights in that recourse is so hard to effect and automatic treatment for being 'mentally bereft' is simply un-scientific.

'Anyone can 'lose it' temporarily under duress or provocation but that there is a road to this lady's situation is life-destroying. So what we want is independent and legal counsel before any sectioning occurs. Consent, whether by the victim or their relatives, has to come into it.

'There are definitely dangerous people – the suicidal, and the criminally insane – who should be incarcerated, but not without due process and protections. Differentiation between these and generally harmless or temporarily stressed people must be carefully made.

'Then in all cases no mind-altering drugs, and definitely the outlawing of ECT and lobotomies. If we get enough cases of abuse through the courts we can then offer legislation to protect the people from becoming victims the like of which we have seen enough of these past few weeks.'

Ivis wasn't finished. 'Ok, so someone gets hauled in by the police, they seem to have a screw or two loose so they are transferred to a Psychiatric facility and then what do you do?'

'Light methods first – proper nutrition, sleep aided by sleeping drafts, proper counselling. Call it a cooling off period. Friends and relatives should be invited to get involved and try and work out safe environments, alertness to tipping points, handling of daily stresses. We don't have more than a general grasp of this at this point.

'I suspect a lot of these people could soon return to normal life, (with a few caveats thrown in there). We don't want them becoming drug addicts, or drug dependent, which is what happens now. These drugs INDUCE psychosis, NOT CURE IT.'

Ivis took all this in and added, 'looking at this from the point of view of the Psychiatric profession I can see them regarding this as an affront to their practices and profession. We'd be almost cancelling out all the steady years of their growth and undermining their modus operandi. I doubt they'd lie down easily.'

'It's revolutionary, isn't it?' Julia declared, 'but they've been operating under a screen of public and governmental ignorance, having hoodwinked the authorities that this is all scientific and is still developing and 'what else do you do with those who bottom out'? It's much the same as dumping our rubbish in landfills or worse, out of sight, no matter what the consequences.'

'So we are waking up the authorities and general public to this phoney operation which is doing worse than the prison system in dealing with criminals and letting them loose repeatedly to offend again.'

Julia was on a roll now. 'Look, the fact that you hold up the abuses in front of their faces and you offer other alternatives and they ignore them tells you most of the story. Not even being cynical you then can come to the conclusion that this is all a gravy train and all sorts of undesirables are attracted to it under the guise of following a career and being 'respectable professionals'.'

Ivis asked, 'what about the drug companies who peddle the wherewithal? Imagine them all ceasing their operation after a few interested citizens like us question their right to be.'

'You are getting the picture Ivis. Seems daunting doesn't it? Who else is going to do it? Our friends in Queen Anne Street are the only others we know of who have sought to raise a voice but even they haven't grasped who they are up against.'

'Wow!' Ivis exclaimed. 'All right, what next?'

'For now we go back to London and get these interviews into our programs, if we get that far. According to Brandon we'll get it all aired.'

While our two investigators were close to winding up their tour of the Union, another meeting of some import was occurring in London.

I strode into the Minister's office in Whitehall, shook hands with Diane McAdam and was ushered to a nearby sofa. We sat opposite one another and made a little small talk at first, and when the tea service arrived McAdam said to me, 'I have watched your TV programs and heard all about you from both James Hopkins and your long-term 'friend', Levison. Who to believe eh?'

I put my hands up. 'It's all my fault ultimately. I provoked the beast just a little too much. And here we are. It could be said that someone had to be the fall guy. James and I had decided it wasn't going to be us.'

'Mr. Waterman, did you really hire a Private Investigator to gather some unsavoury history on Levison?'

'I sure did; as insurance really. As it happens we didn't need it; well not yet anyhow. That little exercise taught me something very valuable. I may need to use this PI again in the future.'

'What did it teach you?' she asked.

'Well, that if you don't see the logic in someone's behaviour and utterances you have to get to the truth, either by asking more questions of whomever or getting someone else to do it for you. I suppose this must be the basis of espionage.'

'Good heavens.' She leant forward and said more quietly, 'I could use you in the Cabinet Office, you know. That's a flaw in politics – too much obfuscation. Anyhow, before I do that let me tell you I have now restored James Hopkins to his former post with carte blanche to continue your program in the Private Schools. If this goes the way I think it will we'll talk about instituting it into the public system.' She was smiling at me to get my reaction.

'James is a good man,' I responded without a flicker, though a warm glow had grown within me. 'You know he came to our College in the beginning to close us down. A measure of his integrity was that he could see what was in front of him, not what was painted by some of your staff behind the scenes. This I suspect was really just via Levison.'

'Are you always this modest Mr. Waterman?' she asked.

'I needed to survive too, it's true, but I needed James to be who he is to do what he did.' I smiled broadly at her. I liked this lady.

'Very well then. What I really want to know from you, the horse's mouth, is what it is that drives you to reform my Department's raison d'etre.'

I smiled at her again and sat back to give her the performance of my life.

'I noticed teachers, students, the Head, struggling. This can't be right, I thought. I looked at my immediate environment, that is, my home, my suburb, and what I know of beyond that and from history and decided that human beings are set up for a big loss, despite all that science and engineering have brought us – bigger this, better that but not better people.

'Being better off than most, mentally, I delved into Education first and found it beneficial but wanting. So I think I have fixed it. You saw an example of that with that TV show about young Francis.'

McAdam was rapt, dare I say it. 'But you then set about a whole institution. Imagine the trouble I am going to have if I'm to institute this revolution here.'

'Yes, but it's a nice problem isn't it? It's actually just an evolution. Someone has to be the catalyst. You'll no doubt cross another Levison in the process, in which case you call on me and my private eye.' I was being a little cheeky here but I sensed an almost kindred spirit here with this lady.

'I see. How much per day do you charge for that?' She laughed. Was this actually the British Minister of Education talking here?

'Minister, if it's right it's right, and has to be followed. I'm finding this even more true when applied to my next nemesis – the industry of Psychiatry.'

'How did you get into that, for God's sake? she asked.

'How long have you got?' I immediately responded, and quickly went on. 'I'll give you the short version. You saw my expose of this subject?' She nodded 'I became interested in Psychology as a possible answer to the reasons why Education alone couldn't handle more pressing personality defects. We got so far in our College samples but we needed something more like mental treatment. In the process I stumbled on Psychiatry and found it to be a bag of nails – not just lacking in basic scientific discovery but a farce, which ninety nine percent of the population have no knowledge of.

'Per my dictum above, if it's wrong it's wrong and has to be followed up on. So here we are. You can now go through the portfolios of your entire Cabinet and see where all this leads to – Health, Defence, Foreign Affairs, Policing, Security. You name it. Maybe not Sport and Agriculture so much.'

'Are you the Christ re-risen, to save Mankind from itself?' I could see she was astonished. Its not every day she, or many, are visited by these concepts.

'I'd love to give a lecture to your Cabinet on this subject, or at least to the

Minister of Health. How do you think that would go?'

'Unreal, I'd have thought. I'm having trouble with your concepts myself. I asked for it didn't I?'

'At this point I would be happy to settle for reform of Education methods. If you are happy with what we have demonstrated so far, let's see whose corns we tread on in this quest first. I have here a copy of my publication on the subject.' I handed it to her from my coat pocket.

We rose and shook hands. 'I will be in touch with you again, Brandon Waterman,' she added with a knowing smile.

I bowed slightly. 'I look forward to that Mrs McAdam. It has been a pleasure to talk with a real person.' I turned and strode out of there. As I descended in the lift a satisfied smile took over my face.

CHAPTER TWELVE

Lovett-Smith, Frenton and legal beagle Bonnington met in the 'media' room of their headquarters. They had played the tape of the program intended and were discussing their response. Bonnington commented, 'coming from a seriously biased quarter this is not so bad. It exemplifies successes and tries to explain the difficulties of dealing with the bottom end of humanity. The Psychiatrists appearing are saying how it is from their viewpoint. To a large extent it is probably true; that is, we don't have anywhere near all the answers. It's not slanderous. And the program invites good results to come forth for the program.'

'What IS slanderous is what appeared in the initial program,' Lovett-Smith corrected. 'We can't have these upstarts or anyone else pontificating on our long-established profession. We are dealing with our science here.'

Bonnington hesitated a moment then tried to clarify his view into legalese. 'We can either have a 'trial' in the media or in court. This means we can serve an injunction now and try and stop the media trial and just have it out in the courts. Either way it will end up in the courts and hit the media. I don't think they will back off. We are not totally certain to gain an injunction but suit has to follow and then we have to prove our case in court. Of course we can try and out-finance them and protract the whole process.

'Another alternative is to take the abuse cases as hits and agree to sort them out and institute reforms proactively. We haven't seen them yet but I believe as we speak a few of these are hitting the courts, independent of the TV shows. Let's assume they are true and be on the front foot. Perhaps some reforms are necessary, dare I say it.'

Frenton looked over at Lovett-Smith and quietly added, 'Let's allow this first program which improves our profile and demand to see the abuse cases, then decide if an injunction is necessary.'

'Very well,' Lovett-Smith reluctantly agreed.

––––––––––––––––

'So far so good,' Gavin announced.

'Two weeks hence then,' Tom decided. 'Better add an intro Brandon; something like saying they wouldn't come on the program nor let us have access to their hospitals so we decided in the interests of being fair we'd bat for their side and look for some positives to balance the subject a bit.'

'Okay, let's do it.' I agreed.

The program aired and promised a sequel of results.

The Psychiatrists were extremely back-footed by the abuse cases, especially when they investigated and found them all to be true. They couldn't get an injunction to stick so had to grin and bear what was aired.

Julia made her appearance on this program and pulled no punches. The filming of the victims spoke all the words necessary.

The capper was at the end of the gruelling watch when she announced that though mistakes can occur and rogue staff can slip under the radar, what was just seen leaves no doubt that Psychiatric practices need an independent watchdog and a code of practice more akin to the Hippocratic Oath.

Two of the cases had filed for damages in the courts, just to add the necessary salt to the wound. The printed media were particularly vociferous in lambasting the institution, with headlines such as 'Psychiatry on Trial', 'Time for a Watchdog?' and, on the somewhat negative side, 'Watermans, the Self - Appointed Watchdogs of Psychiatry'.

Ivis of course was responsible for further articles in a well-known Sunday newspaper and in a prestigious monthly magazine. Naturally she expanded on the expose program using data from her own investigation in Scotland and Wales.

The aim was to get a full governmental investigation into the more than dubious practices that were commonplace in the rather behind-the-scenes

Psychiatric Institutions.

Another showing of the original program came out while all this was going on. However I had decided to dumb it down a bit and leave out the actual demonstration of an ECT session and replaced it with a simple explanation of it, using diagrams. Emphasis was placed on exactness of detail and confirmation by ex-staff nurses and patients who had participated in the treatment. Questions were raised for the viewers to decide for themselves.

Julia appeared at the end to ram it home by indicating that two abuse cases were being taken to court and she gave a full explanation of our own motives here: 'some might think we are on some kind of vendetta here or are seeking notoriety or even financial benefit. It is simply the aim of Macman to raise a very public concern here and to help Psychiatry to be brought under the law. We propose ...' and then listed the reforms necessary. 'Work is being done as we speak on alternative therapies to help the more disadvantaged and stressed members of society.'

Who could argue with that she thought? In a sensible world you'd have thought reason would prevail.

The world not being up to such, Macman put the wheels in motion for a Public Hearing. All the Psychiatrists had to do was agree to reforms and they'd not be 'hounded' any longer. This was expected to take quite a few months to instigate.

PART FOUR

CHAPTER ONE

'The land of the free!' Julia pronounced as she looked down on Boston harbour as our plane descended to land.

'And we are the brave, coming to see if the whole statement is true,' I answered. 'What are the odds on this place being the horse and not the tail. I suppose if we discovered what is the biggest drug producing company in the world we would know the answer. Or we could count the number of Psychiatrists per capita.'

'I'm also thinking of how many Colleges of Remedial Education we could set up out here.' Julia mused. 'Now there's something to get our teeth into.'

'Yes,' I agreed. 'I think there are about fifty different Departments of Education over here – one for each state. Better stick to our declared mission or we'll be splattered across the cosmos. We very well may be anyway. This country may be free but I've heard you have to be brave to stick your neck out as there are a plethora of lawyers champing at the bit to tie you up and squander your hard-earned dollars.

'We should have brought Dad in that case,' Julia added.

'Well, we may have to call on him. But for now and before we hit The Big Apple and Washington DC we'll cut our teeth here in Boston. I wonder if they saved any of that tea from years back. Surely they don't just drink coffee. Let's all get set in our 'digs' first and we'll do a bit of Boston tea partying and then we can think and plan much better.'

We landed and, to our surprise, there was a small gaggle of reporters to make us all feel welcome. The various dailies of Boston had been teed up to expect some controversy. The network of news media across the world had been working a treat. I suspected that Ivis had more than a little input into this. 'Ivis, is this your doing?' I demanded, playing with her as usual.

460

'Not guilty sir. What you've seen in the movies is true; they are like hungry cur dogs, this lot. Put on your charm and do your thing until you've wound them around your finger.'

'I'm glad she's here.' Julia beamed, wrapping her arm through mine.

'OK. Let's play,' I announced. We were ushered into what passed for a press room, after we'd been through Immigration. The TV people from CBS were there; maybe some others too.

I decided to have a bit of fun but not reveal too much before our first planned TV and radio appearances. This airport hubbub was rather impromptu and not on the main agenda.

Julia and I found ourselves seated behind a desk with microphones. The rabble quietened down as a self-appointed MC called for a bit of hush. He asked me how I'd like to do this interview.

I, on point, took control of proceedings by introducing myself and Julia. 'I am Brandon Waterman and this gal beside me is my wife Julia.' She beamed. I continued. 'We have come all the way to this famous city to sample some of the tea that we sent over here all those years ago. It must have matured nicely by this. Where can we get a decent cuppa round here,' I asked?

There was a bit of laughter already. They were warming up to the charm. 'I suppose you have a number of questions to ask us, but I warn you we don't understand Noo Yoikese or 'Alabami – only the Queen's English, so ask away. We'll give you all a chance. Just put up your hand and I'll point to you. Haven't you heard about our famous English tradition of forming orderly queues?' The yanks liked this.

I pointed to a pretty lady in the front row, the only lady in the room. 'Another British tradition,' I added. 'Ladies before gentlemen.' The lady stood and gave a mock bow.

'I thank you sir,' she said, going along with the game. 'Firstly, welcome to the United States. Your reputation somewhat precedes you. Can you tell us what you intend to put us through on your visit here?' She smiled, as did the remainder of the room. Ivis, Tom and Vince and the other boys were at the back and marvelling once again at the proceedings up front. They looked at each other knowingly.

'What is your name, madam?' I asked. She gave it. 'Norma, we are, as you see, just a few young kids on our second honeymoon, expecting you good people to put US through something here. We've heard that you devour your prey as if there is a shortage. Is this true?'

Norma was bright. 'Not I, Mr. Waterman, but these 'gentlemen' around me may very well do just that. It has been known. But, seriously, it's up to you.' The introductory mirth was over.

'Ok, forewarned,' I said. Just then a couple of plastic cups appeared with wooden sticks and sugar sachets. 'Ah, thank you, that's better,' I gasped taking a big swig. 'Now I can think straight. To answer your question, we are here to enlighten you on things you probably don't know about Mental Health. You will be shown our videos on the subject of Psychiatry and our suggested project of reform in this field.'

Norma sat. The hands went up. The most agitated of the hands was selected next. 'Of course we expected that some older professor would be the right source for this 'enlightenment' as you call it. How are you 'honeymooning kids' qualified to do this?'

Many in the room had the same question on their lips but perhaps not as snide as this one. There was a silence after the question for the brief few seconds it took me to answer. 'Age does not qualify knowledge. Experience may help, but have you ever heard of old hands who haven't gained by their experience? As you will see when we get going here there are a plethora of your professorial types in this field who prove my point.' I was gaining traction.

'To qualify to offer enlightenment you have to be able to observe and reason. You tune in to our TV and radio appearances and we will satisfy your question, I promise you. But,' pointing to the questioner, 'YOU have to be able to do those things or I will be questioning YOUR qualifications to be an impartial reporter.' That put him in his place, not that I gave him any time to do otherwise. 'Next question.'

It went on from there. The elephant in the room had been dealt with. The questioning went on for another twenty minutes, with brief answers, some of them fielded by Julia, very competently. It was all good humoured and upbeat.

I wrapped it up by standing and thanking them for their attention and saying that we had lost a night's sleep virtually and wanted to crawl into bed and steel ourselves for the next day.

We joined Ivis and Tom and the rest of the gang and went off to our quite modest hotel in central Boston. When we entered the rather small Reception area of this place we had to wait a while for the concierge to sort out the rooms. Meanwhile we grabbed a coffee (always at the ready in this coffee country) and sat on the only two large sofas there in the Reception and yawned and sipped.

'What's on the agenda for tomorrow, chaps? 'I asked. In this case 'chaps' was Ivis, the more or less self-appointed 'manager' of the group.

Ivis piped up and teasingly answered, 'well, straight into the fire. We are on Radio Boston at 11.00 a.m. Their most notorious rottweiler has you lined up for his late morning feast. His name is Kurt Lewin. So sleep well and wake up running.'

'How much more have you set up for us Ivis?' I asked.

'I'm working on their version of Panorama for Friday night, but its live, not pre-recorded. That gives you a day to do whatever you decide. On Saturday we hit New York.'

'Tom, why don't you and Vince see if you can organise some visits to some local hospitals or, failing that, see if we can meet some local Psychiatrists?' I suggested.

'Do you want to film or just visit?' Tom asked.

'Whatever you can get. We don't want to excite too much interest ahead of visiting these places. We may scare them off. I suspect a day or two's notice would be a bit short, so do what you can. Also Ivis, we should perhaps tee up a few cities in advance, especially Noo Yoik.'

Ivis looked at me as if I'd been taking her for a fool. 'What do you think I've been doing these past few weeks, boss? I came over here to become a star in my own right you know. I'll have you know I am probably more well-known than you two at the moment.'

Tom wasn't to be outdone. 'Don't steal all the thunder Ivy. I'm here to make it big in Hollywood. I too have been busy. We are a dynamic duo you know. I hope the recompense is worth it all at the end of the day. Your first revelation on the brain theory is teed up to be shown in New York.'

'So you two haven't just been…socialising… then,' I mischievously replied. Julia leant forward in her seat too and smiled at them both, as if she knew something I didn't.

At this point the concierge appeared and showed us to our rooms. It didn't escape my notice that both Ivis and Tom were ushered away separately to the 5th floor while the rest of the team remained on the 4th. 'Oh, I see we are on the 5th,' Tom said to Ivis in mock surprise. 'Well, good night everyone. See you in the morning.'

'What a pity we can't be all together on the same floor,' Vince said to me, in a certain tone.

'Enough of this,' I replied. 'We are hitting the sack. Good night.'

————————

Kurt Lewin of Radio Boston didn't know what hit him. He'd interviewed and made mince-meat of pretty much all-comers up to this. He thought he'd be in for an easy ride with me and Julia, two youngsters yet to experience what a hard time is.

As usual, when the arrogant are taken over by their egos and when professionalism takes a dip, lack of preparedness creeps in. He simply didn't do enough preparation. Lewin was typical of interviewers who specialise in making nothing of something, even if that something has plenty of substance. Their aim is to take the opposing stance, try and wrong-foot the interviewee with accusations, chopping responses to questions (accusations), and bully and harass. Little attempt is made to give an even chance for the victim to present matter-of-factly.

After a bit of this behaviour by our 'host' I decided to take the bull by the horns. Lewin had just interrupted me for the umpteenth time and I stopped him abruptly. 'Mr Lewin, I see why this is called the Kurt Lewin show. Perhaps I should be asking YOU the questions.' Lewin started to interrupt but I simply put up my hand like a traffic cop, and with silent intent and presence stopped him before he could get going. 'You can put us down if you want to but we don't intend to put up with it. You go ahead and tell all your listeners all about us and this subject matter. This 'interview' is over.'

With that we left the studio with Lewin trying to save face with more snide put-downs before going to an ad break.

Outside the studio the team all met in a bar- cum- coffee place. Ivis started the 'debrief'. 'Well, I hope they are not all like that. I'm sorry. I heard he was a hard case but not that hard. You were right to terminate him. Now we'll get more notoriety than we expected you know. I'm sure the tabloids will give it a spin in their columns. It's all good, but a fair playing field we have to have, somewhere along the line.'

She continued. 'I put out a press story about us to all the New England newspapers and TV stations. About half of the rags have printed our story up to when we arrived. One TV station wants to do a program but it won't happen before we get to New York so I've suggested they do us after that. We'd have to come back here.'

Julia said to her. 'It seems a lot more voracious over here. I watched a few similar current affairs and documentary programs on TV last night, after a few hours sleep. They aren't exactly polite. I think we will have to lay down some ground rules of our own to prevent us from becoming lambs to the slaughter.'

'Yes,' I agreed. 'Let's be sure we get the show formats in advance, do a bit of homework on the comperes, and as you say, nip any surprises in the bud. I think that chap Lewin might be the worst we can expect.

'I also have an idea here; just to make sure you aren't idle Tom, why don't you and Ivis, and, come to think of it, you too my love, go out on the streets and interview Joe public on camera, on Psychiatry and Mental Health. Ask lots of questions aimed at finding out what they know, if they've contacted Psychiatrists, do they know about the treatments, whatever you can get; just like you did in Scotland and Wales.

'In the meantime I'm going to research the hierarchy of the shrinks as they call them, and the drug companies. We might as well use our time well before we go to New York.

New York came soon enough. CBS was a huge place in one of the many skyscrapers in Manhattan. We weren't exactly ambushed but were set up in that a few of our inquisitors were leading Psychiatrists, who we weren't expecting.

The show started without the Psychiatrists. It was a general introduction to the show with me being asked about how we came to be here on a mission against Psychiatry. I answered succinctly (about five minutes) and this then led onto an excerpt from our initial TV program, including the dramatization of shock treatment. This had the live audience buzzing.

The host, Larry Green, looked at me and Julia and said, 'that's pretty harsh isn't it? How many of these events have you witnessed? Doesn't the end justify the means?'

Julia fielded this one. She was becoming less of the 'junior partner' now. 'Well, the treatment is definitely harsh. Your audience can make up its mind about that themselves. Would you care to volunteer, to test it out? Would you consent to a sizable current going through your brain?'

'No, of course not,' he replied, 'but my brain is not defective'

'Well, fine, but why not experience it then? Do you think it might do you some good or do you think it would have no effect at all?' What do you fear might happen? 'When a person has a migraine do you hit him over the head some more in the hope it might snap him out of it? I noticed you recoil when you watched that clip' The audience loved this.

'I don't know really. But the experts, a few of whom will be joining us shortly, know what they are doing, don't you agree? A defective brain needs some rectifying, not so?'

Julia was well into her stride. 'Mr. Green, when a person loses his equilibrium, when life has caused him to lose his grip and become irrational, to whatever degree, we believe he needs some respite from the pressures, some caring nursing back to normal — no harassment, no brutality, no bombardments with heavy drugs and electricity nor picking away at the brain with an ice pick or two.' There was a smattering of applause from the live audience.

'You don't have to witness first hand these treatments to see the logic of that. Incidentally you just can't penetrate these institutions to get a bird's eye view. It's a closed shop, which tells you something right there. You don't see films or programs witnessing this stuff.'

Before Larry Green could butt in and ask another question Julia cut him short. 'Excuse me Mr. Green, just let me answer your whole question. Does the end justify the means? We have seen too many cases of damaged lives, deaths and NO cures. Patients are silenced so as to become so-called 'calm' but not restored to their former normal selves. And they continue on the drugs.'

I entered the fray. 'The point is this: society has never known what to do with people who lose their sanity or rationality. Various regimes have entered the fray from the earlier days right up to our apparently respectable mental hospitals, all, I'm afraid, extreme treatments with a pseudo 'science' added.'

'You say pseudo-science Mr. Waterman. Are you two people scientists? What qualifies you to pronounce on a subject that's been developed for over a century?' The compere wasn't being snide or dismissive but asking what a lot of people might want answers to.

'We are not scientists and nor do we need to be. If we were, in any case, as scientists we would easily see the flaws in their researches and testing, as WE can. And so can you all.'

'Can you explain how you can do this when none before you have?'

I was glad of the lead-in. 'In all the writings of Psychology and Psychiatry and in talking to numerous Psychiatrists you will find NO proof that the brain is the problem and that chemicals and electricity is the remedy. This is what we mean by 'pseudo'. You have your 'experts' coming on. Try and get them to explain this to you, to prove my point.

'Look, the basic premise that mental activity, the mind, is related to the brain is a theory, a conclusion even, with all data around it made to justify the conclusion or supposition. If you were to show the earlier part of our initial program it would explain all this. It is very fanciful. The reason for us showing a brain on a table and what happens to it when fried was to illustrate the perfidy of this whole theory. The proof is in the pudding – results. A majority of Psychiatrists we have spoken to admit that Psychiatry does not cure the problem.

'And as for how long it has taken to develop, that is irrelevant. Warfare has developed for millennia and it is still destructive exponentially. This is all with the agreement of 'intelligent' world leaders and a fearful population.

It's the same drama.'

'Well what are you proposing as an alternative?' asked Green.

'For a start, to cease sectioning without proper consent, the end of ECT and prefrontal lobotomies, and the end of mistreatment of mental patients by having independent watchdogs to inspect and oversee the industry. As an immediate action to help patients recover we advocate proper rest, calm environment, good nutrition and gentle exercise. The full alternative has yet to be evolved. We are working on that too.

'The physical sciences have given us wondrous things and the future looks even more rosy with new uses for and developments of energy and matter, BUT the humanities lag badly. We aren't solving man's grossly lagging social, political or economic problems in sync with the physical sciences. Psychiatry has gone physical to solve a mental problem. Force and chemicals are being used to address the problem, if one were to be charitable in using the word 'address'.'

'What do you mean by that?' asked Green. 'Are you implying there is a conspiracy to side-track humanity and create some sort of mayhem?'

'I'm saying there is a huge vested interest at work here, not just in Psychiatry but in the Pharmaceutical industry as well. I say 'vested interest' as the main outcome here is huge profits and monopoly ahead of humanitarian benefit.' The audience were dead silent.

'That is a big statement Mr Waterman. Can you back this up further?'

'How many programs do we have? My bet is that we would probably be curtailed.'

'Why do you say that? This is an independent media organisation.'

'Well, let's test it out. We have numerous footage available to illustrate our back-up.'

'Well, we certainly can't do it all tonight. I'd like to bring in here two well-known Psychiatrists to defend the case made against modern mental treatment. We'll take a break. Back soon.'

The audience raised a busy hum while the two Psychiatrists entered the set and were seated on the other side of the u-shaped table. The phone lines to the station were going berserk.

Larry Green calmed the audience and re-opened the program. 'We have with us tonight two members of the Psychiatric profession; two practising doctors.' He introduced them and listed their qualifications, then got to it.

'Well gentlemen what do you make of the claims of our two guests here tonight? Let's start with you Professor Hinkleman.'

The Professor started off by clearing his throat and then smiled and waved his hands a bit and said, 'Well, I don't know how you got away with that program in England. It is nothing short of misrepresentation, even libellous.' He shifted in his chair a bit and was displaying being dumbfounded and shaking his head.

'Do go on,' Green invited.

'Well, for a start the film is making mockery of the science of the brain. There is every evidence, gathered over decades that the chemical balance of the brain is upset by trauma and mental breakdown. The drugs used in treatment are to rectify this imbalance and, though there are side effects, the chemicals do just that and definitely quieten down the gremlins, using that phrase loosely.

'Secondly, we do all we can to lessen seizure by administrating appropriate solutions to relax the patient before administering the shock. And brains do not fry. This is implying physical damage and some sort of sadistic streak to the practitioners involved. I'm stunned they allowed you to air this.'

'What do you say, Doctor Brandt?' Green asked of the second man

'More to the point, what education have our two guests had in our field?' He was winding up to hammer in his outrage, leaning further forward and gesticulating more and more as he went on. 'How many years, days or even hours have you spent in our consulting rooms, wards or theatres? I'm sure you can gather some anecdotal evidence of a few mishaps and go on a campaign of maltreatment and bogus science. Where are your hours in the laboratory? What time have you spent mentoring and helping the less fortunate among our citizens? You may be bright but you are only kids.' The audience murmured some agreement here.

'Well folks?' Green asked by gesturing to the rabbits in the headlights.

I was not for being in the crosshairs. 'I go back to my statement 'above'. I looked directly at Doctor Brandt and sent an arrow back, holding out my finger firmly. 'Results. One doesn't need to spend seven years in a university studying a mountain of writings by your predecessors, largely theories and opinions, nor years on the wards learning about all the myriad of supposed syndromes and their manifestations, nor practise electrocution and brain picking…' Neither the audience nor the host nor the two Psychiatrists could contain themselves.

The audience almost cheered at the starkness of my statement. Brandt talked over Green while the latter waved his arm at him to bring some sort of order.

'Let me finish, Mr. Green. I didn't interrupt our good doctors.'

'Let him finish,' said Green. They settled down.

'What one does need to be qualified in is the quality of caring and the art of observation, and dare I say it, some proper scientific thinking. Do you know what would happen if your treatments worked? They would be hallowed from the highest rooftops, as are our medical cures. But this doesn't happen here as even their own admit, as we found out, that Psychiatry doesn't cure mental illness. It is very difficult to even get in and visit your institutions or do a program. It is a closed shop. Tell me this is not so gentlemen and we would be pleased to do a program and show the public.'

Larry Green came in here and said, 'you guys did get entrance to a hospital didn't you?

'On a limited basis, yes; carefully monitored.'
'Is that the extent of your investigation – one hospital?' Hinkleman put in as if that was enough to close the subject.

I went for this. 'Of course not. On the subject of investigation it is easy to investigate something where the evidence is stark and right in front of your eyes.

'If I were to investigate, say, just by way of a simple example, a series of schools who used capital punishment (meaning physical abuse) to exert control and discipline, I don't think it would take much observation to find out if it achieved results or not. On the surface of it it might quieten it down for a bit but children don't really take kindly to being beaten, yelled at or punishment-driven by bigger people and loud authority. They would find more devious ways to rebel or simply suffer being educated in an atmosphere of fear, or become apathetic. This is somewhat of a good analogy here in that that's somewhat what happens to mental patients, and is why we are advocating a more caring and measured approach.'

The audience applauded. Larry Green asked his two experts, 'what do you say to that?'

'That is a spurious analogy,' protested Dr. Brandt. 'Here we have two youngsters, unschooled in the mental health field, on a campaign of disinformation, with outlandish claims of patient abuse, pseudo-science and generally painting a picture of malpractice across a worldwide respected institution. I think if anyone is to supply proof of case it is these two people here. I'm sure you are well meaning but sadly out of your depth.'

Larry Green looked over at me or Julia to take up the challenge. Julia took this one up very calmly. 'Dr. Brandt, this is how it goes when a nerve is struck. Let's dispense with this belittling our youth and our 'inexperience'.

You gentlemen are much older and 'more experienced' than we? Well you should know better!' She emphasised this and got a resounding murmur of 'yes' from the audience.

'Let's get down to brass tacks here. We have simply raised a point here that we feel your profession has been hiding behind this mask of respectability for a long time now and are a law unto yourselves (and it is doubtful you have the respect you think you have). You are getting away with highway robbery and criminality.'

'What do you mean by this Mrs Waterman?' asked Green after having to dampen the protests of the Psychiatrists.

'As we speak, in the U.K. there are two private suits in the courts against your field, for criminal malpractice – ECT being the culprit here. There are a stream of similar cases, ranging from sexual and physical abuse to manslaughter. We can air these if you dare. These are more than anecdotal examples of the 'results' you are producing. We have taken the trouble to travel the country to interview patients and their loved ones, in an effort to find out if our cases are 'one offs' as you suggest. We WANTED to find good results. Don't accuse us of a witch hunt or patronise us as being well meaning.'

Julia was very impressive. The audience liked her.

I followed straight on. 'I think you should explain to our audience and the public at large and to a Public Enquiry, without indulging in all the technical words of your texts, just how your theories have been proved and how you explain the failures. For instance, here's a test you can undergo right here and now. Explain how it has been proved that a brain stores memories and does our thinking for us. In other words how, if at all, was it arrived at? Did someone see this working? This could be the biggest scam ever exacted upon mankind. We might not bother with this if we had even as little as fifty percent of categorical cures and restoration of mental health. Society would be healing.'

Outrage prevailed. 'We don't have to explain this to anyone, least of all to this public forum. Are you going to allow this Mr Green?' Brandt was a dark cloud. Making nothing of we two gallantes was not working. We simply weren't intimidated.

Larry Green paused a bit, listening to something in his ear piece. 'Let's take a break.'

On return the two Psychiatrists were no longer at the table. Larry Green announced, 'our two doctors saw little point in continuing this discussion and left. Perhaps in the remaining time available tonight you would tell us a little more of your history up to now.'

I began. 'Well my first awakening to the establishment institutions was at school. I was breezing through my education, completely doing it myself and being bored out of my skull. I was giving them the history.

'In all this I learned that teachers cannot deal with big groups of students of varying IQ and backgrounds and ……..' and so on.

' My grandfather and I and one really campaigning parent set up our own college which grew like wildfire, because we got results. Students were being revived all over the place, even some hard cases.

'Basically I discovered that IQ and general ability could be increased by Education alone (and without addressing the brain, I might add). It is not fixed at birth. Then I started on this track of looking to improve the behaviour of those that we had re-educated because being brighter and able to learn now did not handle all problems …….. which took me into the field of Psychology and its offshoot Psychiatry. It soon became apparent that the latter was a festering sore which one couldn't ignore.'

Julia intervened here. 'He has left out a very important event here. I was a Philosophy student and came across this man in a library. There he was trying to make sense of this subject and I felt sorry for him' The audience oohed. 'I tore him away from his books and started on my plan to seduce him…..' Some laughter. She continued. ….'well at least away from all these books and his work. . But he WAS ignoring the female race altogether.'

'I see you succeeded,' Larry Green pointed out, the audience agreeing with some light laughter.

'It wasn't that hard,' answered Julia. 'But like everything else he has taken on he is a natural. I did have to earn some spare time though. Even when he took me on dates it was work.'
'Such as?' prompted Mr. Green.

'Well apropos our program tonight our first date was a visit to a local mental hospital. He nearly had to carry me out of there. This is where I began my education on the subject of Mental Health.

'Another time I tried to get him to...... then he took me to a Hindu temple for lessons in meditation and a sample of real chappattis. Continue Mr Waterman,' she said smiling at me.

I smiled and continued. 'As you can see it was hard on her. Anyway, after a few years we married and went on a great honeymoon.' We looked at each other and she rolled her eyes. 'We went to the East and travelled about learning about the local religions and practices........'

'Haven't you diverged a bit in targeting Psychiatry like this?' Larry Green asked.

'Yes and no. Our Education program continues full strength and our search for useful answers to non-optimum behaviour is also undimmed but we couldn't ignore this big anomaly once it hit us. So here we are.'

Larry Green asked, 'So what is your plan for the rest of your stay?'

Julia took her opportunity. 'This is our proper honeymoon of course. If we can tear ourselves away from visiting all your wonderful tourist attractions we'll do more of tonight's programs and visit a lot of Psychiatrists to see if we are seriously unhinged.'

The audience was enjoying this levity. We Watermans were showing our real character and endearing ourselves to a wide audience.

I agreed. 'Yes, between media engagements we will indeed explore what your big country has on show. We'll go to Washington, Philadelphia, Chicago, Toronto, down through the middle to Texas and Arizona and end up in Hollywood and become stars. Isn't that the height of human experience?'

Even Larry was laughing here. 'Well it's been great having you on the program. I'm sure you'll make some waves wherever you go, as you have tonight. Wait for the morning papers.'

'Thank you for the way you conducted this tonight Mr. Green,' Julia said. 'Rather different from what we experienced in Boston.'

'Yes, I heard about that,' Larry said. He was about to end the program when I interjected.

'May I conclude with just a very short game for the audience? Those at home can play too.'

'Ok, it will have to be quick,' Larry said.

I looked at the audience. 'Alright. Everyone close your eyes. I want you to get a picture of a Psychiatrist.' They all laughed. 'OK now put a white coat on him. Now a stethoscope. Have him turn green and rub his hands together.' Lots more laughter.

'Now determine where that picture is. Open your eyes. Where is it?'

I stood and pointed to a few people who had raised their hands. 'In my brain, in my head, don't know,' were the answers, as usual.

'How do you know? I wonder if it can be found or proved. Now, who made the picture?'

'Me, my brain,' were the answers.

Who is it that was making and looking at the pictures?' A bit of confusion.

476

'We leave you with that conundrum. That is the hub of this whole matter. Watch this space.' I sat down. Larry Green ended the program. Off set he asked us, 'what are you getting at here? If it's not the brain what is it?'

'The problem is,' I told him, 'you've been brainwashed. That's an unfortunate term as we are suggesting the brain doesn't get washed at all. It's simple, it's YOU, you the live entity here, the force that decides to think, feel, act or whatever. Lumps of meat don't do that. It can't be proved. It's a long-held supposition not having led to a cure for which it was supposed. The brain is a vital part of our existence but is merely the centre of our nervous system. It does some automatic functions but requires a person to run it just like a puppeteer determines what the crossbar does. And by the way, a dead body with an intact brain does not do this. More food for thought.

'Are you saying it's a spirit or a soul? It's not something tangible?' Larry asked

'Not in a physical sense. But it's sort of immaterial. You can simply talk to people empathetically and change their mood or ideas without involving doing anything to the brain apart from sound waves. Why get impatient or desperate or even sadistic and drug and physically damage people who aren't ticking over properly?'

Larry looked at me whilst mulling this over. I waited for a penny to drop. The penny was certainly in the slot. 'Plenty to get your metaphorical teeth into eh?'

'We should do another program you two.'

'Glad to but you could simply show all of our UK programs. See what rattle snakes surface then.'

We shook hands with Larry and went to join our friends .

After a good nosh, and now back at the hotel, and all abuzz from the evening's success we all decided to walk around the centre of Manhattan and look at the city. Life didn't seem to slow down at night in this town. The roads were still really busy and the pavements crawling with nightlife.

Julia decided it was time to experience some iniquity. 'Hey you guys, what about a fling in this casino here. Aren't you feeling lucky?' She dragged me and the not-so-reluctant Tom, Ivis and Vince and the gang down some stairs into a smoky den consisting of slot machines and, further on, some tables where some well-heeled patrons were throwing their excess money at impossible odds.

Most of the team were captured by the slots and had settled down with expensive drinks to see if three in a row appeared and the 'out-tray' jangled with tempting riches.

Julia and I wandered among the tables and observed the card activities. 'Never been in one of these 'joints' before, have you?' I asked.

'Nope, but let's experience it. Get out your wad and let's have a go at blackjack.' Julia was playful.

'Alright, but let me just watch these players for a while. I'm going to give myself every chance here.'

So I watched and after fifteen minutes or so said to Julia, 'I've got it cracked. It's an exercise in memory, this blackjack, with some gamble in it. I wonder what would happen if we were winning big time against the odds; would they throw us out?'

'They'd not throw a lady out would they?' Julia asked innocently

'Let's see. You be the player and I'll whisper to you what to do. If I nudge you, carry on betting. If I whisper, play anyway even if we lose, just to look as if you are on the level but don't bet big unless I nudge you hard. I'll get some chips.'

We played, carefully at first. Julia soon got the idea of when to bet and when to fold. After half an hour we were soon into the swing of things and started to break even. After another half hour we were accumulating a steady pile. The dealer was amused that this apparently naïve young thing was having obvious beginner's luck.

By this our 'entourage' had gathered around and were egging Julia on with comments such as 'cardsharp', 'thief', 'you're going to lose the lot when you get hooked', 'throw her out'.

'Shush you lot,' she demanded. 'You are interrupting my concentration.'

When I was really sure towards the end of the pack that a 'ten card' was coming up to go with her ace, with Julia acting like she was uncertain, I whispered in her ear that she should put half of her winnings on the table against the dealer, 'the banker'. The assembled crowd hushed while the dealer slowly revealed his card. We all whooped.

I said to the dealer, 'we better get home to bed and not tempt fate too far here. Thanks for the night,' I said to the dealer. We cashed in the chips and left.

'How'd you do it my darling?' she asked

'I always knew you'd bring me luck my dear. Wait until we get to Vegas. Actually I was counting cards. I read it in a story once. An autistic guy had this ability to do impossible mathematical sums in his head and remember a whole host of things at a glance. His brother made capital of this and took him into a casino in Vegas and he won so much they were kicked out.'

Ivis responded to the bait. 'Just as we thought, you are autistic then. None of what we see is real.'

'We knew it.' Tom agreed.

'Here,' I said stuffing a few $5 dollar notes in his top pocket and doing it to all the boys in the group. 'That will cover your losses at the bandits. As for you Ivis Knightly, you are the pot calling the kettle black. I saw you watching a few of the machines and working out the odds, pouncing after they'd dished out nothing for a long spell. I reckon you came out ahead, not so?'

'Have you got eyes in the back of your head? You are worse than autistic, a new condition not yet labelled.' Everyone cackled and we went back to our modest hotel, only to be waylaid by a few after-hours reporters.

'Ivis, you are our press agent, can you deal with this invasion of our privacy?' I 'ordered'.

'Thanks a lot. I'm going to reveal your crimes tonight.' Tom lingered with her and the others went upstairs.

The next day brought a storm of notoriety in the papers, most of it favourable, surprisingly. Ivis handled all-comers with press releases about our history, aims, and reform suggestions for the Mental Health industry.

Julia and I went off to interview and film rather unsuspecting Psychiatrists who hadn't seen the program or been forewarned. The crew did the filming. We also filmed outside a few mental hospitals, after being refused entry of course.

This sort of program went on through Washington, Baltimore, Chicago, Toronto, Denver, St. Louis, New Orleans, Dallas and Phoenix. Our notoriety was preceding us and we were becoming more like rock bands on tour, except without the usual groupies.

Los Angeles beckoned. By this the Psychiatric profession, or more exactly their bigwigs, were starting to scream louder and were organising a counter offensive.

This counter offensive was none more evident than in California, in which 'shrinks' were a dime a dozen, we discovered. In fact it seemed that

Americans were not backward in coming forward in communicating to a Psychiatrist – complaints from feeling the stresses of life generally (hopefully an expert shoulder to cry on), through to more serious 'diseases' of breakdown. These of course were enumerated in their world-wide bible, the DSM – the Diagnostic and Statistical Manual of mental disorders. At the bottom of the heap were the outright insane (those that had fallen into the deep end and couldn't differentiate wrong from right, even if very clever in seeming to).

In the Los Angeles vicinity, say a radius of fifty or so miles, the team started our activities by contacting and interviewing many Psychiatric Practitioners and their patients too and started doing interviews of random people in the streets as to their use of and take on the variety of practitioners.

We were listening to Tom talking to Ivis about this at dinner one night, after a long day on the streets. 'Do you know Ivis I'll bet Sales, Advertising and Public Relations companies make up the majority of businesses in this neck of the woods. Look in the streets at the plethora of signs; look at the TV programs – at least fifty percent ads. You could be excused for becoming a consumer, or trying out this and that, especially to solve one's smallest complaint. And the language is hard-sell.'

'And,' added Ivis, 'I don't think it would be like this in a less affluent society. The techniques are not subtle. It's a brainwashing operation – soap powder, magical elixirs, lawyers, real estate, cars, and, dare I say it, Doctors of Psychiatry; they are all at it. There's no holding back. It's as if everyone needs a shrink almost as much as they need soap powder.'

Tom agreed. 'Yep, you can hang out a shingle here, on almost anything and go for it. It's like a big extension of our Yellow pages, but gone mad.'

'But what does it say about this population if they buy all the snake oil they are offered?' Ivis commented. 'You don't see Doctors, or Psychologists, or even Lawyers advertising overtly like this in Britain.

'You and I would probably become very cynical about all that is offered and let it all sail by us. I would say we are not so gullible at home; which means for all this to persist like this, assuming a fair amount of it IS snake oil, there is a fair amount of gullibility going on here, which itself attracts shysters. Some of the people I have spoken to in the last weeks give me the impression this place has been psycho-analysed up the ying-yang and are looking for all the labels that are available to explain any slightest difficulty or behavioural quirk.'

'Good grist to the mill, eh?' They both agreed.

I said to Julia later, 'those two are beyond the point of no return. It could have been we two 'veterans' having that conversation.

'Yep,' Julia replied. 'They have weathered the opening chapters and now have the T-shirts.'

CHAPTER TWO

'Here we go again,' Julia remarked to me, having just been served, at our Glendale hotel, a writ from local solicitors Parker and Selwood Associates. She stood there with one hand on her hip leaning to the side on one leg and the papers in the other. 'I wondered when they'd get around to this. I wonder how much daddy knows about American Law.'

'I don't think he knows the nuances but a suit is a suit isn't it? What does it say exactly?'

She started to look at the first paragraph of the document in her hand. 'Lots of legalese, bla bla bla....'

She was reading on. 'It's a threat, not a suit at this stage but we are to desist, of course.'

'Well all right, we'll just pack up and go home shall we? Talking of home let's call our family, the enlarged one I mean. You go first as I know you want to speak to your mum and dad and brother. You can debrief Gavin on the court cases while you are at it and then let me speak to him. Come to think of it why don't we set up a conference call for around five p.m. their time. We can speak to all the gang at once.'

There was lots of shrieking and laughing as news of our TV and radio appearances was relayed, embellished my-style. Then we got the news of the court cases which were midstream and progressing with much publicity. Gavin gave his thoughts on the American legal threat and decided to set us up with one of his own company overseas associates here in San Francisco.

Sidney piped up and told them Ira was bored out of her skull, what with record applicants, new teachers and buildings and publicity to take care of. Ira told us when we return they want to be given some challenges. Veronica, we were told, was looking for a second job to stretch her a bit more. Gladys and Delia wondered why they were there at all.

Julia was smiling broadly. I concluded with, 'I see the Women's Union is in full flow. I suggest you all work part time and take half wages. We'll save a bomb. I have a few ideas on how to keep you more entertained though.'

Before ringing off Gavin said, 'One little setback people – the Public Hearing isn't a foregone conclusion. It all has to go via the government and in this bureaucratic machine it gets lost in rules and obstacles. Though we have an MP pushing this, the pernickety rules of evidence and presentation have to be complied with and then it all needs to go through the entire Civil Service it seems in order to come into reality. It only needs an officious or outright antagonistic official to grind it to a halt.

'But don't worry Brandon I'll get it through whatever it takes. Don't interrupt your successful tour for this.'

Nevertheless I came down a notch or two at this news. 'You're right Gavin. We'll press on. It looks like we have another Department of Education scenario, or should I say another Levison?' We wound up.

'They are dynamite,' I said.

'Back to our program. All right, let's get Ivis, Tom and Vince, to sort things out with the TV stations. They can tell them how things went in the UK. Meanwhile my dear let's go out and enjoy Hollywood for a bit.'

'You mean be tourists, or interview the stars and their shrinks, or what, a real date-like afternoon?'

'I want to show this town what real beauty is. With you on my arm heads will turn, producers will be scurrying out of the Hollywoodwork and autograph hunters will bar our way at every turn. Then the paparazzi will fill their pages with your image. With that warning, let's try to be tourists.'

'Of course you didn't mention that they would be clamouring to know who is this lucky man at my side and all attention would divert to him and I'd be left there like a wallflower. Devious, anyhow, I'm going to dress down and wear a scarf. See what happens then, you hanger-on.'

We started by tourist bus, up and down famous streets like, Rodeo, Santa Monica, Sunset, Melrose and then alighted somewhere near the Hollywood Hills. We were determined to walk a good portion of the length of Hollywood Boulevard and see how long it took us to find the recently opened Walk of Fame.

We soaked up the sunshine, the bright atmosphere, the space and yes, the stars. As we went east to west we branched off to Rodeo Drive and spent the afternoon looking at shop windows and sitting in pavement eateries where coffee was poured nonstop. Of course, we couldn't resist talking to people, nearly all of whom were willing to engage in conversation, especially with Brits. No conservatism here. Loads of loud voices and laughter. Friendly as hell.

At one place such was the interest in we visitors that a crowd gathered to join in and listen as I held court. Some had seen me in the papers or on TV. I asked, 'how many of you good people here have a Psychiatrist?'

Quite a few did. One of the gathering said, 'shrinks here are like doctors of medicine. You use them when things go wrong. Don't you do that in England?'

I decided to amuse them. 'Well you see these chaps haven't made it to England. We are all hard cases over there. They can't figure us out. In any case, mentally, things don't go wrong.' Much friendly derision. 'Didn't you ever wonder how we conquered the world and ruled an empire?' Ridiculing groans.

I continued as the crowd grew. 'Anyway, what goes wrong over here?' I waved my hands indicating the surroundings. 'Look around us here, nothing but success and affluence, no? I have yet to see a hovel or a homeless person. If there are any they surely couldn't afford a shrink.'

There were lots of jocular interjections. Then I asked, 'why do you call them shrinks? Isn't that disrespectful?'

That was a good question for the locals. 'We just love being told how and why we are all so insecure. And we don't bottle it up,' said one.

Another added, 'there are so many of them and they sound so plausible maybe, but they are disrespected because they are on a bandwagon. A lot of them need shrinks themselves. Tells you a lot don't it.'

'I'll tell you what,' I said. 'If we were to set up an opposition practice which banned any diagnoses of mental illness and certainly no pills would you support us?' Various answers came out of this lot, amounting to 'don't know'.

Julia came in here. 'I think you good people have more than enough going for you without the shrinks making up a list of imaginary 'diseases'. Did you know there are scores and scores of theses phoney diseases and added to by the day? I apparently suffer about half of them, one of them being 'fear of shrink syndrome.' Right now you are suffering from 'inferiority of Brits syndrome.' '

She got an ovation of sorts. 'When you listen to someone of authority telling you something you can't just believe them because they have letters behind their name and should know what they are talking about. We have done a big look into this subject and we think it's a sham, a big clever confidence trick. I think that's why they are disrespected and parodied. You guys have some idea of this really.'

'What's the alternative then?' one asked.

'Well, to be honest, apart from doing nothing, which is actually better, there isn't much as it's not been evolved yet,' I told them, ' but as a holding action start weening them off mind-altering drugs, make the hospitals a safe place. No harsh treatments, good nutrition. Give them a break from the environment and problems that got them there. TLC. And for you normal guys who think something is wrong with you, let's throw away the DSM. Let's have a Patients Charter which protects their rights. Sooner or later a mental therapy will be evolved which will render Psychiatry obsolete.'

Julia finished it off. 'Ladies and gents, it's a sunny afternoon and there's plenty to be thankful for and lots to do. Dwell not on the negative. For all our wisdom and for our 'show' that will be fifty dollars each thank you.' This tickled them and was very pertinent.

We got up and shook the hands of everyone there (or was it the other way round?). Hand in hand we continued on our way passing some famous landmarks. We were particularly taken with one of the big motion picture lots (Paramount was it?). We went in and were awestruck with the size and the bustle of the place. We even saw a few recognisable stars there. One, Clark Holden, was holding court at a coffee bar. He appeared a little reluctant, but, ever the pro.

We tourists stood nearby observing the goings on, sipping on our cappuccinos. Suddenly the star paused and looked over at us and called, 'don't I know you two? Weren't you on TV last night? How ya doin?'

We approached and Clark Holden got up and introduced himself. 'I can't remember your names,' he said, prompting us to introduce ourselves, which we did. 'Come and join me. Me and some of the film crew are just taking a break from the studio.'

'Thankyou sir,' I said. 'We are having a break from filming ourselves – being tourists. Do we stand out as such that much?

Humorously he agreed. 'Well no,...no I'm a liar, you do a bit but no problem. Welcome to the heart of Hollywood, home of movie stars, big dreams and lots of shrinks.'

Julia said, 'you really did watch our program, didn't you? What did you make of it.?'

'I think you are onto something. It's gone too far. Do you know I didn't know they did those things in mental hospitals. I know a number of hard cases in our business who need some shrink attention. Hey, I just realised, that's why they are called shrinks. They shrink peoples' heads.'

'Do you know what,' I suddenly realised, 'I hadn't put that together myself.

I wonder who coined that phrase. Whoever he or she is, or was, may have done mankind a favour in the long run. It's certainly not complimentary.'

'Bit like calling a doctor a quack, eh?' said Holden .

'Well, let's go one step further and call them quack shrinks. That'll do the job,' I cracked. We were in.

'Can I buy you another coffee? What'll you have?'

'Well, we are coffee'd up ,' Julia answered, 'but I'd kill a soda water. You too darling?' looking at me.

I nodded. 'Thank you.'

'I love your English accents. It's so hard to do on screen while you are trying to remember your lines. Do you people come from London? There are a few accents there. Did you see 'My Fair Lady'? There was the accent from the streets and the accents of the gentry. It's on down the road at the moment.'

'We didn't see it. I don't think it's in London yet. Do you know Jules, why don't we go and see it tonight?' I suddenly suggested.

'Beats interviewing shrinks,' Julia replied.

Holden said to her, looking her up and down, 'a beautiful lady like you should be seen out and about. Let Hollywood gaze upon you.' The others around the tables clapped.

This didn't phase Julia one little bit. She and I looked at one another knowingly, recalling our conversation earlier. 'Why thankyou good sir, you old flirt.'

This hit the right note. He smiled broadly. 'Fancy a screen test Julia? You've got presence. And as for you Brandon I can see you playing the part of some famous person, say Winston Churchill, standing on a platform and waving your arms about as you mesmerise and galvanise the crowd with your oratory.' He then went into a dramatization of Churchill's famous speech – 'we shall fight them on the beaches, we shall fight them on the landing grounds, we shall never give in.' Everyone acted out the imaginary crowd cheering.

'Better get rid of that accent Clark,' Julia said.

I asked Clark, 'Do you have a shrink yourself?'

'As a matter of fact I do. I'd like you two to meet him; not in his surgery; perhaps on neutral ground. I would say he is one of the more individual thinkers among that lot. He doesn't go for the brain frying or worse. In fact I don't think he goes for the drugs either though I'm not sure of that. You can analyse HIM.'

'Brandon, let's do it. It's all fuel for the fire,' Julia enthused.

'You're on. We could do it on film. We have our own film crew here with us. Do you think he'd go for that? He sounds more like a Psychologist to me, anyway.'

'What's the difference? It's all about the mind isn't it?'

'Mind, brain, head. You know they don't even know. But a Psychiatrist treats the brain under the pretence he's fixing the mind, which must be in the brain. Confusing isn't it?'

'What do YOU think?' asked Clark. A number of the film crew started to wander off during this discussion.

'To treat a person you deal with THE PERSON. The rest you don't need. It's all too complex to the point they've buried themselves in volumes of books that give diagrams of the brain and they've got one big volume that lists scores and scores of human manifestations and have called them diseases. Complex. To us it's simple.

'So what do you do? My guy lets me talk and asks me leading questions to get me talking. I'm just unloading what's on my mind.'
'Do you feel better for it?' I asked

'Yeh, I do; at least temporarily.'

'Well so that is at least a good part of what to do, to answer your question. Beyond proper communication the full answer simply hasn't been discovered yet as few people have even tried. Freud reckoned that it had something to do with earlier life and then got into sex somehow. Nothing to do with brains though. People feel better when they get things off their chest but WHAT to get off their chest is hit and miss. We are all too fond of trying to figure out what's wrong; we are answer hungry, to the point we can buy any nonsense even if its sounds sort of reasonable. We can put a tag on it. I don't think we need a tag, like, 'he was mistreated as a child so that's why he's introverted', but he continues to be introverted.'

'Wow, you really are serious about all this aren't you? I'll set up a meeting with William Grant, my shrink. How do I contact you? '

I gave him our hotel and number and reminded him to ask this William Grant if we could film our meeting. We shook hands and strolled off, me saying, 'we're off to see My Fair Lady. Where is it again?'

'Literally just around that first corner.' He said, and waved.

———————————

'What a wonderful movie,' Julia exclaimed when we were out on the street (where we were living) again. 'Those composers and writers know how to put stuff together, and the actors …. something else!'

'Brilliant,' I agreed. 'We should see more of these musicals.'

We wandered hand in hand around the streets, looking in shop windows and generally taking in the culture. It seemed the entertainment business was the hub of life in L.A. It didn't hurt that the sun shone every day either.

There was life. I wondered how much actual reality accompanied what we saw. But this place could easily represent the apex of humankind. 'Well,' I said, 'we've seen a lot of affluence today, tempered with a certain amount of insecurity. I wonder if they have slums in L.A. It can't be this good all over, surely. Let's ask someone.'

It was about eight p.m. so we thought we'd have a complete touring day. We had been directed to the Central City East. We decided to get a cab. We asked the cab driver to cruise around it for a bit and, happy to let the meter run, he gave us a running commentary on the area as he slowly drove from block to block, stopping occasionally to expand the narrative.

'Is it safe to walk these streets?' I asked.

'By day maybe, man, but best not at night. These people are desperate. Most of them are relatively harmless but there are thieves and rowdies on Skid Row, some more desperate than others.'

'Is this place actually called Skid Row?' Julia asked. 'I thought it was just a metaphorical name, you know, a descriptive term.'

'Yeah, that's what it's called. These guys skid off the road and end up in the ditch. This is it. Don't you have places like this in England?'

'Yes we do, well, not quite like this. This is rather hard core.' We had seen block after block of ramshackle temporary shelters made from all sorts of waste materials, and 'tents'. We saw a good mixture of races scurrying among these shelters and the myriad of waste around them. It was noisy still. This was a ghetto and it had plenty of blasters to go with it.

'How far does all this spread?' I asked.

'Well, maan, this is a square mile and it goes on beyond to a lesser degree into surrounding areas.'

We cruised around a few of these areas and then made our way back to our hotel, paid the cabbie and retired to our safe area of repose. In the elevator

Julia remarked, 'Not all so glamorous then. I believe New York is pretty well padded with these places too. What's our equivalent?'

'Funny, its mostly black or Asian areas, like Brixton, Peckham , parts of East London. There are homeless people sleeping in odd places and scrounging by day. We'd call our Council Estates depressed areas too. Well, I guess there are a number of white areas too. I know we have our underclass so to speak, but it's not so in-your-face as we saw tonight. We must go back there in the daytime and speak to people.'

For now we took a long bath, singing the more well-known songs from the movie and then crashed.

———————————

'What's on the agenda today?' Julia asked Ivis at breakfast. 'Who can we shrink today?'

'There's a topical radio station to start with, and tonight you are on a 'late show' where you make your main L.A. debut,' she answered.

'I am going to contact the lawyer Gavin has given us, in San Francisco. 'I announced. 'Better to be well armed before we get shot at. You other guys can be tourists and go out and interview some more of the masses. There's plenty of variety in this town. We also have to arrange a filmed meeting with a movie star we met yesterday, or should I say, his shrink.'

Clark Holden did ring that morning. He'd contacted his shrink, William Grant, and arranged it for the next day, film crew and all. The venue WAS at his clinic. I'd never understood why these offices were called clinics or surgeries; sounds more professional or medicinal than it is in truth. I was speaking to Clark. 'Get your man to tune into our radio program at midday today (2NL) and on the late show tonight on TV. Can't think of the station for now. This will give him a flavour of where we are 'coming from', as you say over here. I'm starting to get the lingo now, hey Clark, even if not the accent.'

'Way to go Bro, but keep your accent. The broads love the limey stuff.'

CHAPTER THREE

Tom and Ivis were indeed becoming an item, in between her managerial tasks and his filming jaunts. In the lounge area of the hotel I was watching them, much amused.

'Are you self-perpetuating here Ivis?' Tom asked 'Or is it that Brandon has got you trying to keep up with him.'

'I'll have you know, Mr. Movie Producer, that it is he who is trying to keep up with ME. What about you; are you keeping up?' She looked over at me.

'I'm keeping up with you, fair lady,' he retorted, giving her a pinch on his favoured bottom.

'Concentrate Thomas; we have work to do. I'm off to the radio station with Julia and Brandon. You get out on the streets and do some award-winning reporting.'

'I thought so,' said Tom.

'Thought what?' Ivis asked. He wafted out grinning and waving.

Ivis was a quite petit, but well-formed member of her sex. She was bright, and fooled many an on-comer with her rather demure exterior but quick wit.

Tom was a perfect foil for her, being gentle in nature and endlessly attentive and sensitive to her sometimes self-effacing doubts. She was a little bit 'later on the streets' shall we say, but learning fast.

'We should have a tape to give to all these radio programs,' Julia decided after our rather repetitive and somewhat banal radio interview. 'I think some of our earlier radio shows in New York and middle-America have aired here before us, anyway. Maybe tonight we should dress up as shrinks and bring in some props and re-enact the 'brain program'.'

'Well, Ivis has done some homework, as we decided, and this woman tonight has been known to be quite snide. You know how we love 'snide' don't you' I replied?. 'Considering our legal warning we'll leave out the live brain bit I think. Maybe they'll show an excerpt anyway. I'll get Ivis to suggest they do. Meanwhile I still haven't got hold of that lawyer in Frisco.'

The TV date came around quite quickly that day. We tourists had done what we had suggested and gone back to Skid Row and done a lot of walking and talking. We cut it fine to get to the TV station on time.

We were greeted by Gloria Sanchez, the show's star compere. She was all effusion and welcoming. As her surname implied she was partly of Latin American extraction, but nevertheless typical Californian. She obviously spent a lot of time in the beauty parlours and fashion shops to look that well made-up and coutured.

There was a 'green room' which was rather more like a swish lounge bar, with more than a full range of liquid stimulants.

'You folks don't drink?' Gloria asked. 'You'd be the first, you know. Why not have some coffee then?'

She was trying just a little bit too hard to be a friendly benign host. 'We'll give it all a miss thanks. Maybe just mineral water,' Julia replied. 'What have you got lined up for us Gloria?'

'Well, just a few questions about your background to start with. We are going to include a few excerpts from your British TV show and then some chit chat about this and some audience participation.' Gloria was all smiles and off-handedness, as if it were all water off a duck's back. 'We will have a few expert comments from local Psychiatrists too, to balance it all up.'

The latter had not been revealed to Ivis so warning bells were ringing already.

'So we are somewhat on trial here?' I asked somewhat innocently, giving the impression I was anxious.

'No, no, nothing like that.' she said laughingly waving her hand quickly across her face dismissively. A staff person came and took her off at this point.

'OK girl, its game on. We've had it too easy up until now. I think they might want some ammunition here. We'll give them our best shot if you see what I mean?' I was treating it all as sport.

The program started with a friendly but thickly veiled sarcasm. 'Welcome our Mental Health gurus all the way from the UK. They have been touring America and putting us right on the subject of Mental Health. Give them a big welcome,' and then announced us as we came on and then sat.

A few harmless questions at first then the excerpts of my appearance on Tom's show including the shock treatment bit.

'You've come to the right place folks,' Gloria said. 'We welcome actors all the time here in Hollywood. You must have gone over real big back there in the UK with that little drama. I believe you are being sued for that thing we just saw, is that right?'

The audience were not really getting the undercurrent yet. They just thought it was funny, not ridiculing.

I was in there like Flynn. 'Gloria, I hope you got our British humour there. I'll pass on the acting invitation. Anyhow the star of that little clip was 'the patient'. But on your research, it is incomplete. I'm glad we are here to correct you. The Psychiatric lot over there threatened all sorts of things, from castration to beheading.' I was loosening up the audience here.

'But you know, they couldn't make it stick. The 'mud' was sticking to them. We offered them a chance to rebut, we invited them onto our programs to put us right, but they stayed silent. We met with the head honchos and offered to help them clean up the abuse that was taking place in their establishments, but they refused even after finding out the abuse was actually happening. There are abuse cases of some magnitude in the courts right now, and enough cases lined up to scotch the idea that this abuse is just anecdotal.'

'Do you think this abuse goes on in the U.S?' Here was a loaded question.

'What do YOU think Gloria?' I asked, keeping her on her toes.

She took a few seconds to regain her big front and then sent it back. 'I was hoping you would tell US Mr. Waterman.'

'This is a very good question. How about we ask this audience what they know? That will tell us something.' I got up quickly and faced the audience, before Gloria could do anything. 'Show of hands – do you know this goes on in your wonderful country?'

There was a murmurous buzz and a few hands popped up, probably less than a quarter. 'I see the majority are in the dark, or very shy,' I commented whilst doing a quick appraisal of the response.

I sat again and immediately faced Gloria. 'Par for the course Gloria. These things go on behind closed doors and brick walls and no one questions it seriously. No one questions the results.'

Gloria was losing a bit of her carefully constructed face. 'Surely it must be effective Mr. Waterman or they wouldn't be allowed to do it.'

Julia came in here. 'You'd think so wouldn't you? It's a bit like the vast amounts of rubbish we throw out, not knowing what else to do with it. Once it's gone from sight it's gone, thank heavens. What they do with it we're not sure, or really care. We know they dump it out of sight, and then what? But in the case of our mentally damaged, or even not-so-damaged, we don't have any other answers. As long as the victims are kept quiet we assume it's done – out of sight, c'est la vie.'

'You intimated there Mrs Waterman, that some people get this treatment who AREN'T mentally ill.'

'This is so. You know you have to visit these places. You have to tromp the streets and speak to patients and ex-patients. You won't get a rating of success for the perpetrators.'
Gloria was about to butt in but Julia cut it off. 'In fact you may be hard pressed to find an 'ex-patient.' She let that hang.

'What are you saying?' asked Gloria, creasing her face a little.

'When you leave these institutions you AREN'T FIXED. You are quiet and stay that way as long as you keep taking the supplementary drugs. We numb our 'out-of-line' citizens to keep them quiet. That's the most common result, if they don't die in the process. Add to that the side effects of the drugs and you have effectively a revolving door of mental disorder.'

'And you two have taken it upon yourselves to dig up all this dirt and reveal all?'

'What would YOU do if you suspected the above was happening, or one of your loved ones ended up in a mental hospital?'

She ducked this one but I persisted. 'It's uncomfortable Gloria. What would you DO?'

'OK. Then let me ask you this: how far do you take all this? Is there going to be all-out war with the authorities?' She asked all these questions with a disbelieving frown and incredulity.

I came back at her quickly. 'It's a war of sorts. We think there are enough sane and reasonable people in high office who can see what's going on, despite all the attempts of this vested interest to degrade our case, threaten mayhem and ruin, and protest to the same high authorities. We want reform and it's going to take a lot of public information and education and law suits unfortunately.

'There is a multi-billion industry going on here. A microcosm of this would be your street drug trafficker. What we have is a big corporate drug manufacturing and trafficking operation here under the guise of being knowledgeable and respectable.'

Gloria chose to duck this one. She was losing the battle.'Well, going back to the patients, what do you do with these people instead?'

We repeated our plan of reform, and then added, 'mind you some people are actually too far gone for a simple fix, that is, the dangerously psychotic and criminally inclined. They have to be contained, but NOT inhumanly treated.' Gloria was looking at them unbelievingly.

I continued. 'Here's another factor here Gloria: there are some psychotic people out there who appear normal. They don't walk around raving and threatening but on the quiet are undermining good people and projects and under a guise of respectability and believability are disturbing those around them. The confusion they create helps mask their actions. Your good audience may be able to think of such examples' I invited the audience to look at this.

'These ones get away with murder, literally. A lot of the poor specimens you see in institutions are a product of such people – the victims. These victims get picked up by police for being obviously temporarily out of control, stirred into anti-social behaviour or being noisy and no one sees the stirrers behind them. They are then quietened down with 'the treatment'.

'What do you plan to do with THAT lot, if that's true? You'll have your hands full, not so?'

'One thing at a time Gloria,' I replied.' Let's put some protection in place and outlaw harsh therapies first. We'll get to the other.'

'Well we'll take a break here. After the break we have a few inquisitors for you. They will tackle you no doubt from all sides.'

And they did. This was an organised put-down, except it didn't have their desired effect, as has been the case every time this sort of under-estimation of our campaigning strength has been shown up.

There were three practising Psychiatrists, all of whom prescribed drugs and one of whom operated out of a mental hospital and delivered ECT. I insisted they drop the premise of we two being out of our depth and look at the results we had turned up so far. I invited the Psychiatrists to demonstrate THEIR successes by allowing access and filming of their facilities. I pointed out that it would be a good thing if I was proved wrong; it would be an opportunity for them to showcase their methods and their overall beneficial effect, as the hierarchy in the U.K. had been invited to do (but didn't).

Julia added, 'you might be interested to know that the same violations of patient rights and outright abuse has been documented here in the U.S.A. Perhaps you would like these to be broadcast.'

The audience were siding with us by this as the shrinks protested disproportionately.

Gloria got lost in all this as the shrinks couldn't just listen but indulged in over-talking too much which was left to us to control, which we did masterfully.

The audience questioning was rather benign and didn't last long. The 'panel' were thanked by a now less personable Gloria and the shrinks continued to try and harangue the two main guests even off air.

Another successful public showing. A good portion of California would have seen this.

One of the TV panel, the ECT practitioner, threatened legal action.

'Get on the bandwagon then. The threat is already extant. We welcome it. A public court hearing is what we want. Do you want to invite us into your place and show your side? This is a great opportunity for us.'

They skulked off instead. Gloria re-appeared 'backstage'. 'Now what have you done?' she asked in an almost friendly manner. She was looking at the three 'gentlemen' disappearing in a flurry of gesticulations and animated disapproval.

'They aren't used to being stood up to.' Julia answered.

'Well, I have to say you acquitted yourselves very well tonight. I expected it to be somewhat of a blood bath. Where does the 'circus' progress from here?' Still the denigration.

'San Francisco is next. We're going to do a program with Scientists and Psychiatrists on the 'brain theory'. Do you want to compere the show Gloria?'

'Not after tonight. I normally do only lightweight shows you know. Enjoy the rest of your trip.' She was coming rather upscale by this. That last comment was actually sincere.

We walked out of there, with Ivis and Tom in tow. Tom suggested, 'shall we hit the casinos then? Teach us how to get rich Brandon.'

'We topped out in New York,' I told him. 'What else can you suggest?'

'What about a seedy strip club? If we are going to study mankind, body AND soul, we surely must hit the skin.' Tom was largely baiting Ivis, but all she did was wave him on with a 'go for it' gesture.

Julia added, 'we saw enough degradation on Skid Row today. This town dishes up the best in creativity and human nature but it's definitely got its human 'waste'. They have this attitude, I think, 'let it all hang out'. What would you call it? Liberal?'

I said, 'You two should go and see 'My Fair Lady'. That will uplift you in a more healthy manner than a strip club.'

'Very funny. Shall we Ivy?' asked Tom enthusiastically.

'Yes please. What's the saying? 'All work and no play makes Tom......' .'

We parted ways after a quick coffee. 'Be fresh tomorrow; we have the shrink do with Clark Holden,' was my parting comment.

On the way back to the hotel I was a little pensive. Julia enquired, 'what's on your mind lover?'

'You know, we've spread the word rather successfully. We've peaked I think with the media stuff. We need to get that Public Hearing to actually happen. It's one thing to have a bit of outrage going on but the shrinks are weathering the storm I think.

Julia said, 'You know it may just be as simple as taking the body to court for abusive treatments and crimes against humanity. We're not that far off having enough ammunition for that. Better media attention too I'd reckon.'

I put my arm around her and said, 'you're not just a pretty face you know.'

CHAPTER FOUR

An important emergency meeting was being held at this time in a plush boardroom in Indiana. The discussion was about the adverse media being generated by the Waterman bandwagon.

'The Psychiatric profession have been inundated with complaints about treatments and care in their clinics and hospitals, according to their National Association (the APA). They are a bit behindhand, in my opinion, in combatting this so-called 'threat'. Surely it is simply a matter of going on the offensive and conducting a counter campaign and making nothing of whatever is coming out of this interest.' This was the Chairman of the group speaking.

Another of the gathering added, 'the trouble is our Psychiatric friends have been a little careless in their practices and have created enough perceived abuse of patients to not have clean hands. I think we may need to bypass them or orchestrate the counter-offensive for them. This can't be allowed to fester.'

The Chairman pooh-poohed this somewhat but agreed it was best to lend a hand.' We must be seen by shareholders to be doing something about this even if it turns out to be a flash in the pan. These people have small resources I would imagine and wouldn't be willing to be bankrupted by our muscle. What do you propose gentlemen?'

A third, then a fourth grey suit got up and outlined a large media campaign which advertised far and wide the efficacy of their drugs and the science behind them, along with law suits that would tie their adversary up in legalities for ages.

'Who would listen to a few maverick dissenters over an overwhelming public service ministering to the mentally needy on the peripheries of our society? Besides which we have enough officials in our pocket to obviate any serious access to whatever justice is sought.'

They outlined a division of labour and the other pharmaceutical companies to be raked in to help squash this flea.

The Watermans were meant to run scared from this fuselage of the big guns, and anyone else who threatened their share prices.

'The Watermans', in the meantime were meeting with William Grant at his clinic in Hollywood. This Psychologist/Psychiatrist, licensed by having a medical degree minimally, was basically a professional who was qualified to listen to and diagnose, to varying degrees, someone's mental malaise and engage in Psychotherapy of chemical or non-chemical nature. He could then refer certain cases to a hospital for more concentrated treatment under closer supervision.

Grant was a personable fellow. When introduced by Clark to the two guests and the film crew it was obvious he was inclined to quite a bit of glad-handing, which would have gone down well with his Hollywood clientele no doubt. He was in his late thirties, well built, athletic looking; who knows, maybe an actor himself.

I was talking to Julia as we all sat rather informally in his rather plush 'waiting room'. 'I have been forewarned to expect a handsome woman this morning. I am not disappointed I must say,' as he looked Julia up and down rather pointedly.

Julia flashed her teeth and sparkling eyes. 'Well thankyou good sir.' She was neither gushing nor dismissive to this flirty man.

Clark Holden asked about coffee which was had while Tom and Vince set up. After this we got on with the business of the day.

'Do you have a preconceived view of a practitioner such as me?' William asked.

'Somewhat I suppose.' I replied. 'Steeped no doubt in psychological dogma, labeller of mental diseases, dispenser of anti-psychotic drugs all in a cold clinical atmosphere. I'm already letting go of the latter,' I said looking around at the surroundings. 'Disabuse me of the rest if you will.'

'I've heard of your project from Clark here. He was impressed with your dismantling of the brain theory. Tell me more about this.'

I did and concluded with, 'you see, if it's not physical, there's no need for chemicals and the road that that leads to.'

William surprised me. 'I agree with you.' He left that hanging for a few moments. 'As Clark can verify I have never even thought of prescribing drugs for him or any other of my patients (though licensed), beyond a few quite extreme cases who only get the mildest of anti-depressants.'

'Do you diagnose anything from their conversations with you?' Julia asked.

'No, not really. I'm a shoulder to cry on, type of thing. People get wound up by life, and their family and friends don't really listen to them or they trot out the most amazing mumbo-jumbo that my field is fond of propagating. They come in here and are somewhat already psycho-analysed on arrival.

'I rejected the DSM at an early stage in my training. In fact I am as much a dietician and health advisor a lot of the time. A lot of so-called mental complaints get down to lifestyle things – alcohol, sugary/fatty diets, gambling and lack of exercise. These days street drugs are playing more and more a role in mental conditions. Who wants to add more to the list?'

I was pleasantly surprised by this. 'Are you a one-off here William?'

'I probably am.' He smiled. 'I try and spread the gospel; but not too far mind you. I don't mind having a monopoly on this treatment. It's good for business.'

I said to him, 'we have come to the same conclusion, that being able to listen and direct peoples' attention is very effective. We use it in our Educational techniques but after we have boosted someone's self-worth and IQ just so far we run into a dead end somewhere along the line, such as someone having unaccountable mood swings or a propensity to self-doubt; things like that. No use in telling them to be just positive. That is limited.'

'Yes, you are right,' came William's response. 'It is somewhat a holding action we do, to prevent a ship from sinking altogether. Sorry Clark, I don't mean you particularly,' he said touching him on the arm in the seat next to him.

Julia asked, 'what do you do with the hard cases then?'

'I don't ship them off to the spin bins, if that's what you mean, Julia. I give them a number of books to read by what I call helpful authors, or my own booklet on healthy life style, and beyond that I just tell them I can't help them any further, but not to go down the normal Psychiatric route.'

I asked, 'Are you ambivalent to the practices in vogue in other clinics and in your hospitals?'

'I must say I have been closing my eyes to this. Your program on TV the other night, with the demonstration of shock treatment, jarred me a bit. I have preferred to shut that out though I must say, of late, I have had a few victims of this treatment come in here to be treated and so have only recently had it poked under my nose. '

'Did you see that charade of a discussion with the Psychiatrists?' Julia asked.

'Yep, I did. Not my brotherhood you know.'

'Well, the cat is well out of the bag, William,' Julia said. 'We are going for these chaps in a big way. We have a considerable batch of abuse cases now; not just from mishandlings by staff but from misdiagnosis and harsh brutal treatments. It's a sham. It says a lot of yourself that you rejected that road and stayed off it.'

I leant forward and asked him pointedly, 'what are you prepared to do about this William?'

'You guys get straight to the point don't you?' He shifted about in his chair a bit then responded, 'can I see the armoury you have – your cases and the far reaches of your exposures?'

'You certainly can. I'll set it up with Tom, and our film crew here. Julia is the gopher on these abuse cases. She's the collector of outrages.'

Clark came in here. 'You know William, I'm not sure I need you anymore. I think my 'insecurities' or whatever you want to call them are so trifling laid up against the more mortally wounded of our society, I think I'll just get a life and be more positive. '

'I'll miss your fee,' he joked, 'but way to go man.'

I gave William another concept to grapple with. 'We need a qualified person here in the States to take hold of this matter and advance it to its logical conclusion.'

'And what is that?' he asked, 'the eradication of Psychiatry?'

'First things first – the reform of its practices and bringing Psychiatry under the law.'

'Just how much have you become a marked man Brandon?'

'It's an occupational hazard. But what do you expect if you go out of your way to stir up the hornet's nest and ruffle the feathers of those who have much to hide? It does wonders for your integrity.'

William was impressed with his two guests, I could see. We shook hands, he bowed before Julia but not flirty this time. Tom gave him contact details.

After they all left William sat in his comfortable chair and no doubt wondered what had just happened to him, and began to visualise the future on this new tack.

After a few more days of filming and interviewing and attempting to get into local mental hospitals, we left for Frisco. We had arranged to return to L.A. to see William again.

San Francisco was well oiled to experience the 'Brain Theory' program. The cynical expected the 'neophytes' to be chewed up by the Scientists. Those on the fence were simply dying to see the results secretly hoping the 'underdogs' were going to be the Davids slaying the Goliaths. The advertisers were hoping for much better sales figures.

Batting the scientific facts around didn't require me to be a Scientist. My reason alone would win the day. I did this program on my own.

I rebuffed all attempts for me to show an alternative technology and simply kept re-iterating the fact that Man was getting nowhere with force and that the Scientists had to come up with proof that their theory worked. No proof was cited. I got the audience on side with humour and stark facts about results and consequences. I hammered home the vested interest aspect of all this and at the end of the day the Scientists and Psychologists ended up with some egg on their face.

The ensuing media coverage was sensational. I was all over it. Everyone wanted a piece of me. All good.

Back in L.A. William Grant stood up in his living room and gave me a round of applause. If he needed any more closing this did it for him. He'd been taken with both of we English people – our sheer perception and outright audacity and courage in devoting ourselves to a humanitarian cause.

CHAPTER FIVE

Julia and I were looking out over sunny San Francisco Bay from the offices of Percy Rosenthal, Attorney at Law, on the 18th floor of a perfectly rectangular skyscraper in Oakland. The only thing separating us from the outside was a glass wall, seemingly fragile enough to cause one to ponder the worst.

'Are these buildings as fragile as they seem Percy?' Julia asked.

'Not had one fall down yet, but then again they are not that old either,' he replied.

She didn't miss the slight glint in his eyes. 'That's comforting. What about the glass? Does it shatter easily?'

'You know I've not seen anyone try to jump out or throw stones at it. We like to live dangerously. I guess you like solid walls and proper windows Julia, and a sane society around you.'

'Hm. Ok, I'll take my chances. Great view anyway. How do you get any work done with a view like that?'

'Take it for granted I guess. Anyhow, do you want us to proceed with the plan?'

I answered this while Julia remained captivated by the panorama. 'You know a Congressman or two, yes? Well that's the way to go?'

'I think so. Send me all you've got. I want to absorb your history (brief as it is, timewise anyway) and get into your shoes, as it were. How do you finance these escapades?'

'Well, we get a bit from TV appearances, some is from our Education operation. We need to get back to the UK and do a proper fund-raising exercise as I have a feeling we'll need more than we bargained for, especially over here where you lawyer chaps alone seem to have created the affluence we see around us.'

'Yes,' he said. 'This is becoming more and more a litigious society. Not the same over there?'

'Not really. We are a more law-abiding lot Percy, and very tolerant. Maybe we are just poorer and can't afford lawyer fees.'

Percy was a smiler. 'You wait. Just like Hollywood arrived over there so will the best of our other ways arrive too. The Psychiatrists arrived didn't they?'

Percy was Jewish, a dead ringer for Phil Silvers the comedy actor, and not far off that in nature as well. I like a good sense of humour and a more insouciant attitude. Percy had this in spades. Another convert to our cause?

'Percy, what do we do about this threat to sue?' I gave him the papers.

'Leave that to me. I'll call Gavin and get all the gen on your operation. I'll start with the usual defence, which is attack.'

'OK then. Percy, secondly, we have a new agent here. You'll laugh at this one. Officially he's a Psychiatrist. Takes one to know one, eh? He ministers to the Hollywood elite and helps them remain on an even keel. They seem to be a neurotic lot them actors et al. Anyway he can see that his profession is perpetuating the societal problem. When we get back to L.A. we'll close him up (sign him) and introduce you to him. He's the way into these Congressmen. Right now I better get my dear wife out of this vertigoist building before she decides to jump from the roof to end it all.'

'Great you came by folks. This is the best project I've had in years.'

'Yes, you'll be world renown after this. We collect a modest ten percent on increased profit on the back of our cases. That answers how we will pay you.'

'Who's Jewish around here?' We parted in this spirit.

'Going down in the lift Julia remarked that she was feeling better by the floor. 'I actually haven't been in a high building before and looked out — except in New York. That one was rather enclosed.'

'It's as well I didn't take you up the Empire State Building. You can see the whole planet from there I believe. Fancy being an astronaut?'

At terra firma I put my arm around my woman and suggested that while we were in this neck of the woods we might take a walk over the Golden Gate Bridge. Let me treat your vertigo. It's all in your head you know'

'Technically incorrect,' she said. 'I want you to prove to me that it's in my head.'

'Wish I'd never started this argument,' came my response. 'Actually it very well might be, you know. How do you think you get that dizzy feeling from vertigo if it's not in your head.'

'OK then. Take me to the Bridge but buy me a decent meal before we do. I'm starving.'

'Did you know that one of the best foods for vertigo is chappattis? I think I saw an Indian on the next corner there, do you see?'

'Take me to it. But no meditating. Actually that is what we should do on the Bridge. We've never done it in the wide open spaces before.'

'Chappattis and meditation it is.'

She raised herself on her toes and pecked me on the cheek.

CHAPTER SIX

Tom and Vince, and to a lesser degree Ivis, couldn't believe what they were hearing. I had actually suggested that we all take a week off and hire a large vehicle and drive to Las Vegas and through Death Valley on the way back.

'If you'll pardon my cynicism, and my sense of humour, that leads to a dead end.' Tom was all for it though. 'We can make a film about Brandon getting rich in Vegas and dying in Death Valley.'

'Firstly we'll wrap up William Grant and then its reward time for all your efforts.' I announced.

We visited William and were surprised to learn he'd been following us on TV and had not backed out at all; in fact he'd driven right in. He'd listened to all our videos and interviews. He got our whole history and worth.

'You know, I don't really help my patients that much when push comes to shove. It's as I said, a crutch for them to use in their crazy world. I want to join your quest for a decent therapy that actually eradicates life's traumas, in much the same way as your Education methods do for learning disability. Not only that, I am in a good position, as one of the profession, to help fix this hocus pocus from the inside.'

'Do you have any contact with Congressmen or Senators in this town?' I asked.

'Well only through a few of the more stellar names in the entertainment business – the stars. I know a few. Clark may be able to help with this too.'

We got a plan rolling. I put William in touch with Percy Rosenthal. William arranged to visit Percy in the next few days. This man was proactive.

'We'll get in touch from Vegas in a few days then,' I said. Julia went up to him and gave him a big hug. 'You have a good man there Julia,' William said. 'I'll do my bit to back him up.'

The team were itching to hit Vegas. We were outside all packed and waiting. We had a sort of minibus. One of the TV crew did the driving and we headed east towards the Mojave Desert, the gateway to Nevada.

Once a cameraman always a cameraman it seemed. Tom couldn't resist making a travelogue of the trip, as if to prove to the folks back home that this actually happened.

Vegas was an eye-opener for us. We'd seen a few programs on it but driving into the city and down the main thoroughfare was unrealistic and beyond – huge signs and hotels, water fountains, longer cars, big names advertised for entertainment, and so it went on, all in the middle of a desert.

'We must get settled in our crumby motel and then walk the length of this joint and take it all in, ending up in the casinos of course. Brandon, you've got to break the bank here in this place. Make yet another name for yourself.' This was Tom speaking.

'I think you'd get sussed as a ringer before you break the bank. This place looks like it is a bottomless pit anyway.'

We walked the walk, and now eight p.m., we then ambled into a casino and were confronted by a huge bank of fruit machines. There were row upon row of customers piling in the coins and pulling the handles. It soon became apparent that these were mainly regulars who seemed to be paying homage to their gods, with ' paying' being the operative word. As for dress, there were no restraints on gaudy and flashy. The crew were looking positively plain.

'We won't beat these Tom. The odds have to be stacked in favour of the house, unless you just happen to chance on a machine that happens to be feeling generous, which probably isn't that often. Come and let's have a look at the blackjack tables. That's where some money is to be made.' I was egging my compatriot on.

'First of all, do you know the rules?

'Sort of,' Tom answered, 'You have to get as close to twenty-one without busting, right?'

'That's pretty well it. You have sixteen cards that count as ten – tens, jacks, queens and kings. An ace is worth either one or eleven. Do the maths. There's a five and under, which is five cards adding up to twenty one or less. But if the banker there, the dealer, has the same as you, you lose.'

'Now, without revealing my secret I'm going to nudge you with my knee when I want you to bet high. I'll tap you on the shoulder when you should bet low, or fold. Just watch these players for a while. In fact Julia and I will play and you can watch.'

'I'm going to have a go too,' Ivis almost ordered. 'If he loses I'll rescue the situation. I think I know what you're up to Mr. Waterman.'

'How do you know when to bet? Are you clairvoyant?'

'Have you heard of that very scientific datum, the law of averages? Well I reckon that sooner or later you are going to win.'

'That's after having gone bankrupt in the meantime.' Tom grumbled.

'Well, there's another law which Julia knows. It's called beginners luck, where you are so naïve about it all that the law of averages comes into play early. It's mystical.'

'You still have something up your sleeve, don't you Brandon,' Tom said looking into his eyes as if looking for the answer.

'Perhaps. It's a bit hard to explain. It's all to do with the spirit world, by which I mean if you meditate long enough you get to be so outside the situation you can see both sides at once. We haven't got time to get you to that stage so go with the flow Tom.'

Julia stabbed me in the ribs as a sign for me to stop pulling Tom's leg and get on with it.

The gang watched me and Julia for a few rotations of the deck and then chose an empty table and Ivis and Tom sat down. Julia stood behind Ivis and me behind Tom.

The two players got the hang of it quickly and then started betting in earnest. I suddenly gave Tom a hefty nudge and he put down two hundred dollars in chips, with his heart in his mouth. He had broken even at this point, thinking this was rather boring. Then up turned an ace to go with his ten and the chips began to come his way significantly.

'Had enough Tom?'

'No, let's see how good you are.' Ivis was doing well too under Julia's counting. 'Looks like you too Ivy.'

Vince and the other two crew gathered around, and egged Tom on when he upped the ante and shouted 'beginner's luck', and other derision when he won.

It was an hour and a half later and both players had a healthy pile in front of them. At the right time I nudged Tom so hard he nearly fell off his chair. 'Be a devil Tom, put the whole lot on this next card.' I was enjoying this.

There was a metaphoric drum roll and up came the card. 'Bingo!' shouted Tom, with his arms in the air. The others were up as well. Then, not to be outdone Ivis received a big nudge too and on the very next three cards got a five and under. More whoops and hollers.

The dealer couldn't believe that these two beginners had fleeced the table at the same time.

'Time for a celebratory lemonade,' Ivis shrieked.

'Go and cash in your chips you two. Don't forget to give Julia and I our twenty-five percent.'

The mood was ecstatic. Tom said to me, 'you know I could be cynical about the first win in New York but today, its real. I'm going to start meditating and give up work and become a professional blackjack player, or even a poker cardsharp.'

'Julia told him, 'keep the day job Tom. You'll soon be barred from all casinos in the world as news spreads of your cheating the system. Then what?'

'It'll be fun. Brandon did you really know an ace was coming up or were you gambling with my money.'

'Law of averages Tom. But you missed the star of the show. Julia bet on three more cards after that and won. Now that is not the law of averages. If you want to know how we did it you have to go through a rigorous process and then join the 'magic circle'.'

'Ok Brandon, let me see the official rules of the game. Don't bother – you were cheating. But because I won I'll take this no further.' He dealt a few hundred dollar bills to all the crew. 'Come on Ivy, your turn to dish out the dosh.'

We rolled out of the casino and went further down the main drag and went into a fancy looking restaurant and had barbequed ribs and corn-on-the-cob, which ate into our winnings, unfairly we thought.

We then completed the first lap of the 'High Street' and on the way back we started to notice other things, mostly in side streets, like Realtors, Massage Parlours, Poodle Parlours, and, would you believe it, Psychiatric Clinics. Most of these places were closed at this hour, the massage places being the obvious exception.

Ivis remarked. 'I guess the word 'massage' covers a multitude of sins.'

'You don't need to spend your winnings on this, Ivy,' Julia suggested. 'Tom will do it for nothing.'

Tom started to massage her 'obviously tight' neck. 'See, nothing seedy about my massages.'

We spent a few days in Vegas, soaking up the atmosphere, the ladies pampering themselves with hairstyling, nail embellishments, and facials, the men checking out car sales showrooms, pool rooms, and the like.I even indulged myself in interviewing a couple of Psychiatrists. These people seemed to specialise in 'ministering' to the addicted gamblers of the city, who were in plentiful supply. I soon found out that this was just cheap psychotherapy, the consumers of which carried on with their addiction but happy to know they had a label for it at least, and had 'faced up' to their lack of self-worth.

Talking of spending money, the crew almost managed to get through the profits made in the casino, so it was agreed that we'd push on back to L.A. via Death Valley.

At this aptly named place we experienced some extremes of space and heat, new phenomena to us in both regards. We spent a whole day on the ' rim' of the valley, at various look-out points. We stayed a night and high-tailed it back to the melting pot of the Pacific.

William Grant was no dilettante. He'd gotten hold of Frank Menzies, a Californian Congressman and pitched his project and was gladdened by an enthusiastic response. With my 'coaching' I brought William up to scratch with the whole scene. He was given a few local abuse cases to feed to the Congressman, from the girls' interviewing and research. Any case would be aimed at the Governor of California. Each state had its own ruling body which covered everything which wasn't legitimately federal, like defence, national security, immigration.

Psychiatric licensing was a state function.

More cases were needed and more investigations. Julia found a kindred spirit group which operated like her friends in Queen Anne Street. She got this group more fired up to recruit and expand more armies across the state. She put them in touch with William Grant, who in turn had formed his own 'Reform of Psychiatry' group, made up of Psychologists and

Psychiatrists who thought alike; not all faithful acolytes to their profession. The TV crew had flown home soon after our jaunt in Nevada, leaving me, Julia and Ivis to put the wheels of reform into motion.

'Well William, we have lift-off in the U.S. of A. You are indeed the man.'

We were at his own home in a very comfortable suburb of L.A. 'You have a great program, a support group, a good lawyer, and large amount of integrity. What else do you need?'

'Notoriety, on a par with you two.'

'Well, Ivis is going to hunt out a good journo for you and the most upbeat of media. She's more than half way there. The host on our TV program in Noo Yoik, Larry Green, he's a good guy. Don't think about the creep in Boston, Kurt…. what's his name… I've forgotten. You'll know him. Toronto was a good visit too. Good press and very fair coverage on TV. Create havoc among your own profession. Add to your group of more ethical practitioners.'

'We're always on the blower and on the end of an airline too, if you need it,' Julia added. 'Don't let ANYONE push you in. You'll get pressure and ridicule but just push back harder. If you need counselling find a good Psychiatrist.'

'I'll call you Julia. What now for you two?'

'Well I think we'll go up to Seattle and Vancouver after all. We have open-ended invitations in these places. They are so close together we may be able to hit them in one. I think we should pay a visit to New Zealand and Australia on our way home, (sort of). Then back to the U.K. and really deal a blow to the shrinks back there; that is, see our reforms enacted.'

'Then you retire?' William asked half-heartedly.

'We then have Europe to play with. This whole nonsense all kicked off for real in Germany and Austria you know – Wundt, Jung, Freud et al. That area certainly kicked up a lot of mayhem in the last century or so. The subject is well entrenched right throughout Europe, including Russia. That will be a challenge. But once you've dealt with America William, come over and help us.'

'All in good time folks. Well I wish you well and you can consider me a partner in crime.'

Clark Holden had arrived as we were winding up. I said to him, 'don't take this lightly, Clark, but you did your country and mankind a favour that day we met. Join the club.'

We all shook hands and the remaining trio went back to our hotel, collected our things and caught a bus to the airport.

CHAPTER SEVEN

Seattle was enough to cover the two cities. We did the job there and flew off to Aukland. Ivis had set up the media there. The TV would no doubt follow. Sydney was the stage in Australia. Our British TV shows, in summary form, went down a storm in the Antipodes. The Waterman brand had landed. We made a few contacts in Sydney that might take up the mantle, just like in L.A.

We were on our flight back home. 'Well that's about the English speaking world my love,' Julia concluded. 'I suppose we could go to South Africa, strictly speaking a bi-lingual country, but our project in the U.K. beckons. We have sewn some seeds. When we get the U.K. and America wrapped up maybe all the rest will fall like cards'

'It's hard to believe our evolution would be all wrapped up in a matter of a few years. That would be naïve of us. Our biggest battles are ahead.' I was looking into the distance and recalling the time span of change that normally prevails on this planet. This subject is much bigger than women's rights or slavery, to name a few examples, I thought.

'Then again, that's not necessarily the way it has to be. But our bigger obstacles are ahead – to reform Psychiatry and proliferate Education. And we haven't even touched on the thorny subjects of Politics and big Finance and International Armaments yet, and who's really behind all these things. Do you believe in the accidental theory of history, my love?'

'What, as opposed to the conspiratorial theory?' she asked.

'Maybe. I haven't given it much thought up to now, but more recently I have become aware that far from all bad conditions just happen. Psychiatric monopoly didn't just happen accidentally. It was dreamed up and caused by someone(s) and perpetuated. We come along and draw attention to its obvious flaws and we are told to butt out and if we don't we'll be shot. They aren't about to turn around and say 'we made a mistake, we thought we were doing the right thing. Sorry'. Criminals don't do that. They know what they are doing. And they 'know' they are right.

'Of course you could say they are so far gone they can't really know what they are doing. But they plot and plan and take action and react to opposition. And they put up smoke screens and lie and hide their real intentions and attempt to avoid discovery. What is actually pushing them under it all is I suspect not known to them.'

'So there are basically good and basically bad,' Julia suggested.

I thought for a long moment. 'Or there are only good and to varying degrees they GO bad. To get to criminal or psychotic (homicidal or suicidal, or as in the case of Hitler and Stalin, genocidal) an awful lot has to go wrong. They become badly wired up.'

Julia decided, 'well it doesn't matter which when we are up against it. It's reason against unreason. For our planetary society to be so conflicting for so long, even in times of relative peace, there are good guys and bad guys. To find out who is winning we only need to examine the conditions that we see around us. When Man has won you see a resurgence and when he's lost or is losing…..it is evident, even under the veneer.'

'Yes. Jules, we need some more really high-powered reasoning people with us. I fear the forces of unreason are larger in number and in more high places than we know of, for such a shambles to exist. We were talking about who is causing things beyond the accidental. It's got to be from the top, unless, according to the conspiratorial theory, it's from behind the scenes, which would be the REAL top. That's an interesting question isn't it?'

We were flying near Singapore, close to Indonesia. Looking out of the window to the north, with the skies as clear as a bell, I remarked, 'just out there we have the mainland of Asia, and Vietnam in particular. They are engaged in a major war, basically to stop the spread of communism from the north to the south and thence into Laos and Cambodia. Mighty force, billions of dollars of munitions and weaponry and largescale slaughter. A similar war occurred further north ten or so years ago – Korea. About ten years before that the Japanese tried to conquer a large part of South East Asia out there.

'The Indians and Pakistanis, a little ahead, are sabre rattling as we speak. If you were to count it up, since the world wars it still goes on. There's trouble in the Congo, Israel and the Arabs.... And not to mention the Cold War which very recently brought us to the brink of nuclear war and sits there as a threat – the so-called solution with the continued nuclear testing, to the detriment of the environment.'

'Of course these big boys all sit around important tables and say to each other ' if we develop more and more advanced destructive power the masses will laud us for our wisdom and foresight. Let's get the Brits and the French at it too and anyone else sensible enough to be able to develop this stuff. We'll help them. But it's an exclusive club and we'll decide who joins. All the others can play war games if they like but they'll have to use just reasonable force which we'll make for them and sell them. Think of the profits – planes, tanks, guns, you name it, but not the really dangerous stuff.'

'Sounds logical to me.' Julia offered flippantly.

'OK, work to be done. It looks so calm and beautiful out there, doesn't it? First things first; let's really nail down what we've started. It may be that bringing a lot of relief to society with our current projects may end up tipping the balance between turmoil and peace; like diffusing a ticking bomb.'

Julia leant over and nestled on my shoulder. We slept a bit and sat it out until Heathrow. Home again. Mission accomplished, somewhat.

CHAPTER EIGHT

'How was the second honeymoon?' Delia asked after we'd got to the carpark at terminal Three.

'We're going to introduce this sort of honeymoon to all travel agents. Lazy sight-seeing and endless swimming pools and casinos may become yesterday's custom.' Julia was in full flow about how I had won her over to this random touring and impromptu activity. All the details would be revealed at our re-union with both families and close friends who were all gathering at our place.

'The fact is,' I told the assembled group at home, 'we are going to accelerate things and work faster. We've discovered that beside real Education the dearth of man's solutions to his underlying problems is pandemic. The USA, the leader of our civilisation, is not leading. So, good people, we will not really make a big enough dent in Education by setting up alternative schools alone. We have to get it into the existing institutions as well, and not just in the U.K. We have sewn seeds in Thailand and India. Now we're going to tackle the rest too.

'And we need to gather a considerable army of sound individuals/allies and reform Education and Psychiatric practices quickly, worldwide. These two prongs of attack will swing the balance back in our favour.'

I noticed the gathering looking a little serious. 'Look, you good people, I don't mean to in any way demean what you are doing. Don't change anything except for looking further ahead. The big picture can get lost in the day to day activity. We've seen it from outside the box as it were. It is a game. There are lots of floundering people out there and the vast majority are good people. Let's reach them with our Education. Let's start by making the UK a beacon of hope and evolution.

'Macman will get on with the Psychiatric prong of the program. We are happy to be back among you wonderful people.'

Ira gave a big whoop. Sidney gave it a 'way to go'. Everyone clapped.

Tom and Vince were there, and Ivis. They related the story of our trip with lots of embroidery on the matter of me and Julia cheating in the casinos of New York and Vegas. 'We saw Julia pocket thousands of dollars from this illicit activity, and Brandon just stood in the background, encouraging it all when we should have been out filming.'

Dan added, 'What hypocrites! This doesn't look good to us. My sister was an innocent before meeting this man here. What else did they get up to Tom?'

I held out my arms, calling for hush. 'You can't live in a puritanical bubble you know. You've got to experience the opposite ways too. So I led the team to see what iniquity exists in this world. We even went to Skid Row in L.A. It's an actual district where life really is on the skids. Now my wisdom has been recognised; those naïve people there have had their eyes opened, thanks to us.'

There was much mocking. Then I added, 'well we had to pay our way somehow, and it was fun.'

Next, down to business, serious but not serious – two different definitions.

CHAPTER NINE

Two weeks later, the judge of Macman v Royal Medico-Psychological Association was about to pronounce on the case before him. 'This is a disturbing case,' he pronounced quietly but with some warning. 'While our institutions clearly work under some provocation, dealing with patients at their extremes, it is also true that in this case we have seen staff behaviour at its extremes too. It is the judgement of this court that the hospital and its practitioners have been negligent in diagnosis and process, inflicting unnecessary damage to the patient involved.

'I am given to understand that the hospital has already taken summary action on the staff and the two Psychiatrists involved by dismissing them and barring the two from practising further. This is commendable action but does not ameliorate the damage done. This court hereby awards to the plaintiff the sum of ten thousand pounds in damages, to be paid to the court within fourteen days.'

Gavin was a happy man. I was not in the court, but Julia was. She was cock-a-hoop. 'There's the first one. They got off lightly there. We must strike again quickly and have enough cases lined up to make this more of a common occurrence.'

'We have these lined up my dear. There's another next week and a further two in the following month. Then we get our MP to push for that Public Hearing to actually happen and gather more failed cases so we are way beyond the mere incidental.'

Ivis was really the Press Officer for Macman while still maintaining her independence as a journalist, all on the basis that I didn't favour anyone else but her to be in charge. She received a 'commission' for her work in this way. Regarding the court case, she wrote and issued the press release and sent it to all the dailies and local newspapers, particularly to Jim Naylor at the Hampstead Gazette.

She even spread her contacts as far afield as Edinburgh, Aberdeen, Newcastle, Manchester, Southampton, Bristol and Cardiff, to name a few of the largest centres. In fact whenever there was a release it went to all local newspapers and magazines in the country. She was the ideal person for all this. She had a cause to write for, and she helped keep Tom on the case too. He was not quite so self-perpetuating.

They were indeed 'an item' and their relationship was moving to that critical point of decision time. It was doing Tom some good. He'd been very casual about relationships up to then, not liking big commitment. Ivis was expertly 'training' him in this and a lot of me was rubbing off on him too.

He was gaining more 'balls' when it came to effective communication with his upper echelons in the TV world.

———————

Gavin strolled into my office with an official looking paper in his hand. I was wrapping up a phone call. 'OK James we'll meet next week. See you later.' I put the phone down and sighed pleasurably and leaned back and put my hands behind my head. 'Morning Mr. McDonald. You look a little serious. Is it that paper you have in your hand?'

Gavin handed me the letter. I read it and pushed it away slowly. 'Hmm. What do you make of that Gavin?'

'Seems we don't have enough armoury yet, but, judging by the barriers we've had in getting this through the procedure so far, I'd say they are expecting us to present something like a popular revolution before this would go anywhere. I asked a few of the officials, off the record, what other unstated objections they have to this Hearing and was met with equivocal replies, meaning perhaps there is more to this than meets the eye.'

'Yes, that would be par for the course,' I replied. I was thoughtful for a while then slapped my hands down on the desk and stood up. 'OK, if its revolution or at least revulsion they want, let's give it to them. I guess it's got to be so voluminously fallacious that even THEY can't deny it…. unless 'they' are actually in the pockets of the culprits. Oh to be a fly on the wall. Roll on the other pending cases, demonstrations and media pressure and maybe a bigger army of more gutsy MP's to push from the inside. We just up the ante, so to speak.'

'I'll see if I can get a bit more feedback from the Legal fraternity too,' Gavin added.

'Yes,' I agreed. 'I would get Michael Stone, our effective PI to look into this too but I'm not sure this is his area of expertise. But you know, perhaps we can get a list of the likely lobbyists involved here and get him to research them for conflicts of interest, criminal activity, or even conspiracy to thwart the process of justice. I'll sound him out.'

Gavin left the room and had clearly seen that I was 'down' for a few seconds and then straight back up again.

————————————

At Finchley Head Office a precedent was set for our wholly holy group – a visit was requested by Her Majesty's Revenue Collector (the British tax collector).

Sidney told his staff that this was a normal activity but privately to Ira he added, 'what a co-incidence; and it's not Macman they want to see, it's the College.'

'Are we squeaky clean?' asked Ira.

'You bet. Not a figure out of place, not a tax payment late, ledgers all in order, yearly audits done. So this's not quite normal. We have a rat behind this. I sort of expected this before now, but funny it coincides with the court case against you know who.'

'We'll drug them with lots of tea. It will be a holiday for them and I will be as nice as pie,' Ira promised.

'What a PR machine you are Ira.'

Well the Taxman came and went and could be no more complimentary.

'See. It's all in the tea leaves,' Ira boasted.

I asked her, 'did you get any skinny on who and why?'

Sidney told him, 'Nope. These were just lackeys. No purpose in 'shooting the messenger'.'

'Hmm. Not enough dope in the tea leaves then. Good work though. We should have put them onto Jake Levison, talking of whom, I wonder if he had anything to do with this. Maybe we have another nemesis. Never mind. It's done. Onwards and upwards.

'Sidney came in. 'There is also employment law and teacher qualification to consider. I'll look up on this and see if we are at all vulnerable lest we invite other visitors.'

Julia and her henchmen in Queen Anne Street continued to gather additional cases to add to their court appearances. 'The Psychiatrists have taken a few hits but surely won't put up with a storm of them,' she said while she and I 'lazed' at home one Saturday morning.

I added, 'And to make these cases more notorious Tom and Vince are doing another program on these cases, basically to raise a public call for this Government Hearing . Our local MP, Mr Adrian Heaton, is aboard on this and is raising the matter in parliament, to effect a sort of Bill of Rights for mental patients, the Patients' Charter. He's willing to appear on the program to add more political clout to the subject.

'Meanwhile Ivis is taking the stories to the further reaches of the Kingdom and printing our Patients Charter which outlaws ECT and lobotomies and psychotropic drugs and institutes protections to the subject of consent, and treatment in wards. And I am nearly finished my proposals for an interim alternative. Both of these publications are going to be distributed forthwith to all MP's, doctors, local government offices, newspapers, magazines. Complimentary copies will of course go to the Royal Medico-Psychological Association and the British Medical Association.'

'This all sounds easy my love but I'm sure you are taking into account a likely backlash from the prospective losers here.'

'Of course. Can you imagine that a small group of spirited citizens like us can cause such evolution in an entrenched institution without there being an almighty struggle?'

'Yes, I can see the boardrooms of Glaxo Smith Kline and I G Farben plus however many more drug companies there are, having strategy meetings and organising parliamentary lobbies, media counter offensives, even investigations and dirty tricks. They control more opinion leaders and people in high office than we do. I propose we expand our staff and have our own version of their strategies. We need more people out getting cases, contacting MP's and potential allies. Our organisation, though effective, is scant. We need demonstrations and people to man them. We need people to give out leaflets and to raise the funds necessary to run all this stuff.'

'My love, you've got the right estimations of effort here. Why don't you appoint Ivis your assistant on a full time basis? She can get people to help her with the press stuff.'

'Already IP, darling; even the good people at Queen Anne Street are upping their efforts in all this.'

'What a woman you are. I'm going down to the library to see what other dilettante students I can find to join our cause. Alas I expect you were definitely a one-off my dear.'

We two not-now-so-newly-weds finished scanning the papers, finished off the teapot, cleaned up and of course took the rest of the day off (like hell, 'off' having a different meaning to us – sort of 'more leisurely work' perhaps).

We first of all went to visit my folks. Cliff was in his shed attending to some machinery he needed at the College. Gladys was cleaning the house and cooking. Sidney we learned was at the College. Andrew was out romancing a pretty young thing from the College.

After an hour we went to Julia's to find Delia at the kitchen table writing a program for one of the students. Gavin was in his office poring over a legal text. Dan was out at the library.

All was a typical weekend scene for these new stalwarts of the cause.

'Gavin, I set you up a proper office, why aren't you using it?' I asked as I strolled into the room and as Julia wrapped herself around her father.

'Just for this very express experience,' came the reply, as they hugged.

'What's that thick tome you have your nose into?' Julia asked.

'It's one of a whole encyclopaedia of law books; the official record of all cases ever, with precedents, and judgements and all sorts. It seems not even our educational skills allow one to understand this, including me. I am using it to disprove what I just said so that Brandon can be one hundred percent validated and so that lawyers and judges aren't allowed to be on a pedestal. But if I can't sleep at night I read this. That does the trick, just as Brandon suggests.'

'You're still awake so you must be winning. So what have you discovered that applies to what's at hand?' I asked.

'Well, basically it confirms we are on sound ground and have taken all the right steps so far, but in particular we can have that chap Littleton released under certain caveats (you know, the one that ran out of the building when they tried to give him shock treatment). I thought sectioning was non-optional but they didn't follow all the rules of sectioning, not that they aren't rather spurious anyway. We managed to get a separate opinion as to his state of mind, which went our way, which tells you it's a bit of a lottery, eh?'

'Daddy you do know it's the weekend don't you?'

'Not since we became proper citizens. 'Week' has become a misleading term, or at least redundant. Looks like you two don't agree. What are you up to?'

'We are supervising our staff, our senior junior staff, checking on their welfare, and trying to organise a cheap afternoon tea, as a break in our already overfilled 'in' baskets.'

'See, he has an answer for everything,' Julia added, taking the opportunity.

'Probably just as well. That's why he's paid the big bucks, eh Brandon.'

'Too right. We'll have no arguments about that reasoning.'

We did have a brief afternoon tea and then went off to Queen Anne Street. I had never been there before and was soon suitably impressed with Beverly Simpson, the leader of the group. Though her name was not particularly Scottish she spoke with a fairly broad Scottish accent out of a fairly hefty but not really fat body, set off with a cheeky mischievous smile.

As this was Julia's domain I just listened as Julia spoke with Beverly. They were going over all the cases. The more they spoke the more I was impressed. Another coup, I thought.

'We need more offices like this and in other cities,' Julia was saying. 'Imagine the effect we could have if just this small band, producing such sterling results, were replicated in many areas.'

'Funny you should say that,' Beverly replied. 'I have sourced one or two people from up north (Manchester and Newcastle). I'll suss them out down here first and fire them out with some finance to set up where they come from. And I have a maybe prospect for Birmingham'.

'Wow, you are one powerhouse, Beverly.'

'Trying to keep up with you Mr. Waterman, from all I've heard.' Her cheeky smile broadened.

'In that case you'll end up on TV. What do you think about that?'

'You can't have all the glory you know.'

Julia rubbed her hands together, then stopped abruptly. 'Wait a minute I've been on TV a bit, but when do I get to be a star?'

'You speak too soon my dear. You are doing all the next programs if the Psyches haven't given up by then, and it's very imminent. So better keep using the same tooth paste that's served you so well up to now.'

'I think you'll end up wishing you hadn't said that, Brandon, especially when we both get into the act. You'll be yesterday's man.' Beverly was inaugurating herself into that club.

Julia sashayed past me and flicked her middle finger at my chest as the two ladies left me to chew on that.

I looked around the office for a bit, pausing to examine a few issues on the notice board. I was suddenly startled by a loud splintering sound and a crash just behind me. I spun around to find a broken window, glass everywhere and a brick on the floor. I quickly went to the window and saw a figure speeding off into the distance on a pushbike.

As I started to pick up the larger of the glass pieces the two ladies rushed back into the office. 'What's this?' Beverly cried.

'It's called progress, action, response,' I explained.

'Well I don't like it. If you hadn't been here I'd have been spooked a bit....well, for a bit, then really angry.'

I was on the case. 'I'm going out to find a timber yard and board this up. Better still let's find an emergency glazer and get it fixed properly. I'll do that while one of you phones the police. Then we can clean up this mess. Tell the police just so it's on record. They probably won't do anything about it. Think no more about it now. Get on with what you planned. There'll be more opposition and reaction than this before long. Hope they don't go to the College too, or even to our place or Mum and Dad's.'

I wasn't being nonchalant nor fearful but rather calm and resolute, as if I expected such things. 'Someone wants us to back off. What's our response to that?'

They knew the answer to that and they got on with calls and cleaning up. Another staff lady appeared and was surprised but soon calmed down and helped in the clean-up.

Julia and I soon got Beverly's attention onto the work at hand and they got on with it productively until the window man arrived two hours later. After he was done we wrapped up and called it a day.

'I want to take you two ladies on a date,' I announced. Julia sighed in mock exaggeration. 'Have you ever been to the theatre ladies?'

'Come to think of it, no,' Beverly said.

'Me neither,' Julia agreed, starting to warm up.

'Well we are so close to theatre land why don't we do something completely different? I've never been either. I think we deserve a comedy, don't you?'

We all immediately grabbed our coats and hats and that then took care of the night.

CHAPTER TEN

'All the privates are back on board now,' James announced to Cindy. They were standing in the garden admiring James's landscaping. 'And we are a step closer to having our learning technology adopted by the Department. Diane McAdam has been as good as her word.'

'How did you manage that?' Cindy asked whilst wrapping her arms around him and looking up into his triumphant looking eyes.

'Firstly, I took the boss and a few other interested parties down to Finchley Central School where all this began. Brandon had primed it all by getting the Head, without the old snake there, to get aboard with the program. He isn't a bad chap you know. I'm sure he would have let Brandon have his head when he had been a student there, if Levison hadn't been there. He couldn't help but notice the raised standards at the school with so many students getting the treatment, albeit on the side.

'We now have the majority of the teachers there getting trained at the College, as a prototype, directly resulting from our visit. Our Department chappies were very impressed, particularly the Minister for Education. How many of that breed would have bothered to inspect themselves?'

Cindy gave him a kiss and then unhanded him. 'Levison is dead now; exposed for all to see.'

'Yes, and I've made sure all the affected staff in our offices have been disinfected with the truth, particularly Ben Downs. I don't see any dissidents there now.'

'Great, James, and you've been re-instated and I can buy a new coat with the restored proceeds. We've benefitted hugely from our association with the Watermans, haven't we? To think you went to his College initially to close it down.

'And our own boys are really picking up on their studies and are looking at careers after it all. Education breeds ambition, eh? Maybe we can steer them towards the College, either as apprentice lawyers under Gavin or teachers under me. They think Brandon is the greatest thing since sliced bread.'

'It's not my normal type of work but, you know Brandon, it might be more interesting,' said Michael Stone as he considered what had been put to him. 'So you want to dig up who's been whispering what in high places? I've been itching to use these new bugging devices. Or do you want me to use an army of flies who'll report back? Or, more likely I'll get my secretary in on the job — she can seduce these flaky establishment types using her unconcealed assets to good effect.'

'You have quite a mammary, I mean armoury there Michael. I'll leave it up to you. Perhaps we can use the insouciant media to help ruffle the holier-than-thou feathers of the great and the good.'

Michael came out of his flippancy and decided. 'Yep, let's do it. You are spurring me on to bigger things Brandon. Put your feet up and watch this space.'

The program rolled out — bigger and bigger demonstrations culminated in one big rally outside the offices of the Royal Medico-Psychological Association preceded by a march from Trafalgar Square. More and more regional offices were established, and a whole fund-raising blitz resulted in more than enough to pay for these offices and the cases they generated, mostly from influential richer relatives of victims and free-thinking business entrepreneurs, all given a complete education on the subject of Mental Health.

Each regional office acquired volunteers to distribute leaflets in shopping areas all of which generated more recruits to the fray.

Oddly enough media coverage subsided, except for Tom's ever-inventive ways of keeping the subject going on ITV. 'I can't figure it out,' Ivis told him. 'Once it was oh so easy to get into these papers. It's like it has become yesterday's news.'

'I don't think it's that Ivy,' Tom said. 'We are getting reaction from the TV audiences and the viewing figures are still up. Something else is going on here.'

That something else was being revealed to me as I sat in Michael's office. 'I have discovered that there are certain large investors in Glaxo Smith Kline, Bayer, Bristol Meyers and others who are Board members, as also are Government officials, mainly Civil Servants and two MP's. And here's an interesting one – two big daily newspaper editors are also on Boards.'

'For a start that explains the newspaper changes, even without proof,' I replied. 'Do you have any info on their lobbying activities?'

'That's been harder to get to. I suspect it's mostly done by phone. There is a public record of shareholder meetings of these big companies. I've tried a few but nothing telling so far. It should start to show up as the big guys are experiencing share price downturns. That should generate more flap and noise.'

As all this was occurring opposition forces were putting their limitless resources into battle.

PART FIVE

CHAPTER ONE

A year later I was in my office and Veronica put a call through to me from Percy Rosenthal from his lofty perch over San Francisco Bay.

'Hi Brandon, Percy here. I have William Grant here with me. He has psychoanalysed you from a distance and says you are suffering from megalomania and workaholic syndromes. He looked these up in his book of tricks. Easy one that one eh? I spent five years at Law School to get started in my profession and all he has to do is look it up in a book. So that makes me a Psychiatrist too, and I'm suffering from a persecution complex as a result of your doings.'

'Good morning to you two indefatigable soldiers over there in the U.S of A. Yes, Percy, William is a fake. But that's the whole point isn't it? And you, being Jewish, are only dramatizing your forefathers' experiences. I've been told by my doctor that hard work does not kill. Anyway, if you aren't in the firing line you aren't alive.'

William piped up at this invitation. 'You are so predictable Brandon. How did I know you'd say that?'

'Quit moaning you lot. What's the skinny?'

William answered this one. 'Well we've a U.S. Senator and a Congressman aboard on this train and they are starting to stir up a storm in Washington. I knew the Senator locally but the Congressman is from Maryland and saw the TV shows and he was trying to contact you when you were here but missed you somehow. The initial Congressman we thought we had, bombed out. Anyway I was on TV here in L.A. the other night and this Congressman picked up on it. So he's come over to meet with the Senator here and myself. Now we are really up and running.'

'Great William. What else?'

'Well I had written, as you know, to all my fellow shrinks here in California and invited them to join the club.'

'What further response?'

'Not bad. I'd say fifteen percent of them in all have responded favourably, ten percent railed and more or less called me a fake (pot and kettle, eh?). I'm inviting all the positives to a conference here next month with you as the guest of honour.'

'I'd be delighted. I'll polish up on my American jokes and top it up with some proper English ones. Yes, I'll come by all means. Any news on you cloning yourself?'

'Oh, yes, five of my associates in this area are coming to the conference and are aboard already. I have a fifty mile spread here now. I even have one in Frisco here.'

Wow, you're the man, William. Well that's you, so what is Percy moaning about?

Percy entered the fray. 'I'm glad you asked. I'm thinking of employing another staff here to help with the invoicing.'

'Percy, I thought I made it clear that this is an altruistic operation here. I'll save you the bother, don't worry about the invoicing. Or isn't it in your blood?' I could imagine him sitting at his big untidy desk and smiling broadly.

'Look we have a few injunctions flying here and a number of other threats which I won't worry you about just yet. It's all under control. Their over-the-top indignation means they are justified or guilty as sin. I prefer the latter. Anyway when you come over I'll redirect all the flak to you, the true source of all this.'

'Do what you will. It all means progress. And you can pay yourself from the expenses won in court. The more cases, the more expenses. I'll take ten percent.By the way William, how are you financing your activities?'

'Just as you described – membership donations. We're planning an army of demonstrators to block the streets. They all donate time and money.'

'I like it. Well give me the details of the conference and I'll schedule it in. I'll bring Julia and a couple of abuse victims. Perhaps they can speak at the do.

'On our end we have action as well. We have six MP's (our version of your Senators and Congressmen) working with us. We have one particular case in the court at the moment which is very likely a catalyst for our Patient's Charter being instituted into the Mental Health system. We were shooting for a closure of one particular hospital but I don't think that is likely. It's all under one system here. Maybe over there it works differently. You may be able to have particular hospitals or hospital groups investigated and then closed down. That's worth a spin when you get to it.

'But if you haven't yet done it, push the Charter. We're not going to get Psychiatry closed down until after it is reformed. That will be the acid test of the whole thing. Will it die a natural death without its destructive practices or will they connive something else? In other words what are their true intentions? Do we believe that they embarked on a genuine, if misguided attempt to help mankind or are they of more sadistic nature. Is indulging in more surreptitious mind control of some sort a kind of sophisticated western version of the Russian gulag setup? There dissidents and undesirables are picked up and summarily shipped off to Siberia never to be heard of again. Or is it just a big cash cow and will they let that go? Or both?

'I'm talking about the head guys here, the perpetrators. Anyhow who is the horse and who is the cart? Methinks the shrinks are the horse.'

'Compulsive listening Brandon,' William replied after a significan't pause. 'Well, yes, we'll push the Charter. I think you are right about our institutions here. They are in groups, like private companies. What do you have going nationwide over there?'

'Well we have branches of independent anti-Psychiatry groups here, all now spreading the Charter and discovering abuse cases to bring to court and to the notice of officials. We are now in Scotland, Newcastle, Manchester, Liverpool,, Birmingham, Cardiff….. you don't do Geography over there do you, you insular lot. I can see you scratching your heads wondering why I'm dealing with Manchester, New Hampshire and Birmingham, Alabama.'

'We are both Manchester United fans,' Percy retorted. 'I'll bet YOU don't know what THAT is.'

'OK chaps, you can end on a victory. It's good to speak and 'shoot the shit' as you would say. We'll talk closer to the time. Go and watch the Forty-Niners – the kick off is tonight, Seahawks is the opposition. Bye.'

Percy was offended. 'He just snatched victory out of the jaws of defeat.'

'Apparently he is famous for having the last word, except when he is patronising the opposite sex. What a guy. He'll be going to China next. He's already been to India, at least educationally. It seems the shrinks haven't got much of a foothold there. Why don't we do just as he suggested William and go and get a burger and fries at Candlestick Park? How'd he know they were on tonight?'

I sat and turned over the conversation. The Americans had done so much in such a short space of time. I then thought about the more onerous task of finding such people in Europe, with the language difficulty. I'll just have to find an even more rare breed who speak English, I mused, or is it that such stars would speak English anyway. Was China out of the question? Australia, Canada and New Zealand first I think. Then again a lot of this started in Austria and Germany. Hmm. Closer to home and more populated. Where to start?

I called Ivis. 'Hullo young lady,' I effused.

'Hullo yourself, you old fart.' She could play this game too. 'To what do I owe this call, boss?'

'To being so able. I was wondering if you had any journalistic connections in Europe, in particular Austria, Germany and France. Maybe Italy too.'

'I don't but I may know a man who does. A sort of old flame, who became just a flickering over a paltry matter. But we still communicate at times.'

'What's his English like, and where is he based?'

He was in Belgium but in Paris now I think. I can get him 'on the wires'. What's the plan? Remember I'm part of the club now.'

'This is the thing; I want to expand into Europe and I want to get our story into Europe and our videos too. I'd have to get the videos subtitled if that could be done. But I need some entry point. You know the sort of person we need. Just think of yourself and multiply it.'

'Ok, I'll see what I can come up with. We could do a tour, just like in America. Tom would love that now he's reached the climax of your TV programs.'

'Let's see if your old flame can come up with anything first, but that's a good idea.'

'Ok. I've always wanted to do The Louvre and Eiffel Tower, and the Vienna opera houses, and in Italy, see The Colosseum and…'

'That's enough. You'd only have time for the odd raid on the casinos. We had a good time in California didn't we?'

'Life is always fun with you Brandon. I'll come back to you.'

Tom came round to the College one Friday afternoon. He bowled into the building and was accosted by Veronica, whom he grabbed and swirled around Reception. 'Take me to your master,' he demanded.

'You are here Mr TV. I am my own master, or should I say mistress.'

'Alright. Start by offering me coffee and I'll not bother you anymore and saunter off and find an underling to deal with me.' At this point Julia wandered by and gave Tom a big hug. 'Are you harassing this lady here Tom?'

'I thought I was being polite. I am off to save her the trouble of interrupting Mr Waterman and interrupt him myself.' He waved as he went off down the corridor. The girls just stood there with their backs to him, shaking their heads.

Tom found me and knocked. I was on the phone but gestured him to a seat while I wrapped up the call.

'What day is it Tom? Oh yes, it's Friday and the rest of the world is knocking off for the week. How's tricks?'

'I've come to complain. I have become practically redundant since we wrapped up the programs. Haven't you got anything else for us Brandon?'

'You put all your eggs in one basket Tom and now you're paying the price. But, fear not. I have sketched out a program which puts the lid on the last series and opens up another. I have written a booklet on our latest 'Psychiatric' techniques. I want you to disseminate this on TV. Your bosses will have no problem with this. And, if that's not enough, I am maybe arranging a tour of the European casinos, just like before.'

'Now I'm not complaining.' Tom said rubbing his hands together.

'I really came round to hear all this from the horse's mouth. You know I have contacts within your Organisation and a little bird (broad) whispered in my ear.'

'Yep, security is not tight around here. Can't get the staff. Let's get my bird and we'll go out for some dinner, if we don't get knocked over by the rush hour. I think Ivis is around somewhere too Tom. She may like to join us.

Any objections?'

'Let's do it.' We went off to a new Indian restaurant we'd found in Golders Green, a nearby suburb. Tom and Ivis had to get used to the ever increasing phenomena of strangers gawking at the magical couple and the odd ones accosting us for a bit of notoriety and even to give abuse on odd occasions. No problem for us – all water off a duck's back.

Once ensconced at our table Tom asked, 'what's in the booklet Brandon?'

I produced a copy from my inside pocket. 'Here, it's the first ever copy. I've even signed it for you. But don't hang it on a wall; read it. Basically I start off with some general advice on how to create and maintain harmony – things like don't go to bed on an upset, don't try and handle situations of tension when you are tired, eat healthily, exercise, take a walk if you are simmering, lots of stuff on owning up, listening carefully and lots of other goodies.

'Then it goes into how all this applies to a person under stress, or in situations that might lead to visiting Doctors or Psychologists – stuff like gentle handling, lighter actions, doing physical work, calming down the environment. Lots of stuff.'

'Are you any nearer to a Psychological technique for the masses to resolve common human affairs?'

'Well a holding action anyway, at first. It's modelled on the Educational techniques in that in order to get to the bottom of problem behaviour one has to look at the failures, small ones first. Sometimes people just need revisiting their pleasurable times. I'll give you a demo if you like.'

'I'm not up to it,' he said. 'Not while I'm hungry'

'There you go Tom, you're getting the idea. You ARE up to it.'

We ate and had a joyous time. This lot had had many joyous times together on our travels to recall and banter about.

After the meal I pointed out to Tom, 'Just as an exercise Tom, just go back to when we came into the restaurant and remember your mood then. I'm not indicating you had some bad mood but, do that.' I waited a few seconds and then told him 'now compare then with how you feel now.'

'Well I feel quite high just now. I see what you are getting at: a bit of food and lots of reliving of pleasurable times. Wow.'

Ivis was doing the exercise too. So was Julia. They were far from being down before but were perhaps a little jaded and conservative and now they were really out there.

'What about you Brandon?' asked Ivis.

'Do you know it works on me too. Who would have thought? I feel just like I do after a meditating session.'

'He's not such a hard case after all.' Julia concluded, holding his hand. 'Why don't you all come round to our place and we'll show you how to meditate. That's in the book too. Maybe we could watch a movie as well. I'm video-in-charge.'

We did just that before the new week began again in the morning.

CHAPTER TWO

Four months went by in which at least a normal year's worth of progress was made – a successful tour of Europe, albeit compacted, as was Europe itself. The major cities felt the impact of our campaign – Hamburg, Frankfurt, Stuttgart, Munich, Vienna, Brussels, Paris and Milan.

Julia played a leading part in the TV shows, getting a summary of our British shows onto most networks. The Patient's Charter had a good airing, especially in the big newspapers.

Though our theme was Psychiatry, Education extracted quite a bit of interest as well, to the point that I had interviews with Education authorities in both France and Germany and made allies with quite a few 'mavericks' in the field who were invited to the College to inspect and get trained up to spread the subject in these places.

I even addressed a meeting of world health bodies in Geneva (slightly off our route). This too was televised.

To cap it all, Michael Stone dug up just enough dirt on the conflicts of interest and he and I devised a letter to each of them, making it known that their actions were indeed reprehensible and all the facts would be presented to the media that wasn't 'their own'. To cap it off I arranged a meeting with the Minister of Justice to present our case and, short of a big media storm, co-opted a review of our Hearing application.

The Minister of Justice was urged to meet up with Diane McAdam. This would surely help the process.

Back at the College a whole staff meeting was being held. I suitably praised Ivis for her superb work in arranging the tour around Europe, and Julia got a standing ovation for her TV interviews which had done most to garner both controversy and genuine interest.

Sidney and Ira were honoured for their unstinting work in taking the whole running of the College and its expansion off my plate in the interim.

No one was left out. The whole college staff were there as well as Tom, Ivis and Vince, James Hopkins and even Jim Naylor from the local paper and Michael Stone the PI. We even had a conference call going with Percy and William in the USA who were listening in, busting to join in.

I specifically acknowledged the relative local newcomers, namely my own family, and Cindy.

I spoke into the phone: 'hey yanks, are you listening to all this? There's more. Your turn will come.'

It was at this point in the celebrations that I dropped my bombshell. 'You may not know that a few months ago I met with Sir Henry Carlisle, the Minister for Justice.' I was quite serious at this point and paused for effect. 'We were hoping he'd be able to move our Hearing application on. Well, I heard this morning, now brace yourselves for this, it has finally come down to this: owing to our outlandish activities and public outcries the Government has decided that in the interest of all parties …' I couldn't hold it any longer .. 'the Hearing will go ahead on the 14th of September!'

The room was in uproar. Everyone hugged everyone else. I was shaking all hands and was surrounded. This went on for some five or ten minutes. 'Let's celebrate! I shouted.

As we were about to tuck into tea and goodies and listen in to the Americans, Sidney rose, clanged a spoon on a cup loudly, and called for attention.

He got their attention and said softly, 'everyone has been acknowledged except one.' He looked at me. I was holding a saucer with the cup to my mouth. I had no idea.

'Nine years ago, there was a schoolboy. He had a dream.' He paused for effect. That was enough; the room erupted with shrieks and hollers and banging of tables. I didn't know where to put myself, so I grinned and hung my head slightly.

'Here we are today with all this. And we've only just got started,' Sidney added by raising his voice on the last sentence. Pandemonium reigned again.

After the acclamation calmed down a bit and with calls for a speech, I held out my hands to 'gain the floor'.

'To quote a wise man, nine years ago,' I paused as everyone laughed. 'Nine years ago there WAS (as if agreeing) a schoolboy and he DID conceive a dream. But not completely by himself. He had a mentor who listened and encouraged him. Then he met an indomitable woman who carried him through his first fall and joined the dream. Then to put the cappers on it a beautiful kindred spirit entered his life not so far along the road (literally). I refer to the three most influential bastions of my life without whom all this would probably not have happened and to whom I will always be eternally grateful.' More raucous behaviour.

'I thank you all again for your work and your unstinting loyalty, a substance money can't buy,' then more lightly, holding up my hands and nodding my head to silence any imagined agreement, 'as you might all have proved yourselves.' There was lots of chortling at this.

'But I don't want to acknowledge you too much in case you think this is the end and you slow down. Without much of a rise in pay I intend to work you harder. We are a winning team. Really, what else would you rather be doing?' Big cheers.

I raised my voice a bit now. 'Oh, we have left out our American team, still on the phone I hope. Just listen to this, Percy and William. Beat that then.'

Percy came on. 'Our team isn't here. It's a bit more widespread in this big land. In fact they are all out working their socks off. You guys will use anything as an excuse to drink tea, won't you?' More banging and cheering.

I explained, 'Percy, no chemist has yet been able to diagnose the magic constituent of tea. The magical tipple was once rum you know. We sobered up and took up tea. Whatever it is in tea it has spawned a superior gene.'

More clamour.

Percy came in again. 'OK, modesty isn't one of the things spawned. Anyway we'll update you. I hand you over to our MC, Professor William Grant.' He got the same noises. The office was buzzing.

William added his data with mock modesty. 'We've only got eight offices now set up here; only eight.' The audience oohed and aahed loudly. 'And that's only on the west coast,' he added to mock 'nooo's'.

And so it went on. William Grant was a phenomenon and becoming more in demand it seemed than the President of the country. Psychiatry was up in arms, even if not yet on the run.

He then added, 'and might I add to the legend of Brandon Waterman, without whom I'd still be sitting in my comfortable premises listening to the neuroses of the spoiled and the rich. You have woken me up, and the country too. You may very well be Man of the Decade.' What a noise.

'Thanks for that William. What you've done is awesome.' He turned to the group and, whipping them up, 'What is it?'

'AWESOME!'

'Do you feel acknowledged guys?' 'Sure do. Power to you Brandon. Goodbye chappies.'

'BYE', ended the call.

Brandon asked the group, 'was that a successful trip or not? Onward and upward!'

We then partook of our magical drug and side plates and chatted among ourselves. Ira and Julia caught me in a female sandwich with smackers on each cheek, then a full hug from each separately.

Sidney joined in with a man hug. 'Yes, we are winning.' We original two eventually walked slowly out of the room, arms draped around each other, while the others partied on.

THE END (for now)

Printed in Great Britain
by Amazon

58563360R00304